The
Arabian
Nights in
Transnational
Perspective

Series in Fairy-Tale Studies

General Editor

DONALD HAASE, Wayne State University

A complete listing of the books in this series can be found online at wsupress.wayne.edu

The Arabian Nights in Transnational Perspective

Edited by Ulrich Marzolph

 WAYNE STATE UNIVERSITY PRESS   DETROIT

11   10   09   08   07   5   4   3   2   1

Library of Congress Cataloging-in-Publication Data
The Arabian Nights in transnational perspective / edited by Ulrich Marzolph.
    p. cm.—(Series in fairy-tale studies)
Includes bibliographical references and index.
ISBN-13: 978-0-8143-3287-0 (pbk. : alk. paper)
ISBN-10: 0-8143-3287-0 (pbk. : alk. paper)
1. Arabian nights. I. Marzolph, Ulrich.
PJ7737.A733 2007
398.22—dc22   2006102232

Earlier versions of the essays by Cristina Bacchilega and Noelani Arista, Sabir Badalkhan,
Hande A. Birkalan-Gedik, Francesca Maria Corrao, Thomas Geider, Donald Haase,
Ulrich Marzolph, Margaret A. Mills, and Marilena Papachristophorou
were previously published in *Fabula*, 45.3–4 (2004).

Earlier versions of the essays by Aboubakr Chraïbi, Hasan El-Shamy, Susanne Enderwitz,
Geert Jan van Gelder, Heinz Grotzfeld, Lee Haring, Robert Irwin, Sylvette Larzul,
Sadhana Naithani, and Joseph Sadan were previously published in *Marvels & Tales*, 18.2 (2004).

∞ The paper used in this publication meets the minimum requirements
of the American National Standard for Information Sciences—
Permanence of Paper for Printed Library Materials, ANSI Z39.48–1984.

Published with the assistance of a fund established by Thelma Gray James of Wayne State University
for the publication of folklore and English studies.

Contents

Contents

III. Framing as Form and Meaning

IV. Translation, Adaptation, and Reception

V. The *Arabian Nights* in International Oral Tradition

Preface

Ulrich Marzolph

In 2004, three hundred years had passed since the introduction of the most influential work of Oriental fiction to a Western audience. Published in 1704 for the first time in a European language, Antoine Galland's *Les Mille et une Nuits* presented the adapted French translation of a work that through the centuries of its previous and posterior existence can best be characterized as humanity's most ingenious device to integrate heterogeneous narrative material into a cohesive whole, as a collection possessing the potential to combine tales and stories from the most diverse origins, sources, and genres, as an *omnium gatherum* and a true shape-shifter in terms of narrative content. While arching back to ancient Indian tradition, the collection probably originated at some unknown period in Sassanian Iran under the title of *Hazâr afsân[e]* (A Thousand Tales); it was translated into Arabic as *Alf layla* (A Thousand Nights—the thousand and first night only to be added later), and in English tradition gained popular renown as *The Arabian Nights' Entertainments* or simply the *Arabian Nights*. In presenting his translation in 1704, Galland achieved more, in fact much more, than to make a work of literature known to an audience different from the one for which that work had originally been created and by which it had been read and listened to. His translation initiated a wave of translations and adaptations into all major European (and, subsequently, many other) languages that itself resulted in a vogue of fiction in the "Oriental style" and inspired an endless number of imitations and re-creations not only in literature but also in the arts, music, dance, and architecture. Even a simple collection of short autobiographical statements about the influence of the *Nights* on their work by writers and creative artists from the past three hundred years would fill many pages. At the same time, scholarly knowledge about the origin and development of the *Nights* is still far from being exhaustive, as important contributions—such as Muhsin Mahdi's (1984–94) edition of the Arabic manuscript that served as the basis of Galland's translation—have only been presented to the scholarly community in recent decades, and numerous questions concerning the collection's history, growth, and character remain to be studied in detail.

In view of the tremendous impact the *Arabian Nights* have exercised on Western creative imagination and following a joint proposal by the French and German national commissions, the general assembly of UNESCO voted to include the *Arabian Nights* in its list of commemorative events for the period 2004–5. Besides the preparation of an *Arabian Nights Encyclopedia* (Marzolph and van Leeuwen), various international meetings had been convened in order to celebrate the occasion and to document the state of scholarship on the *Arabian Nights*. Major symposia focusing on the *Nights* were held in Rabat, Morocco, in October/November 2002 (Joly and Kilito), in Osaka, Japan, in December 2002 (Yamanaka and Nishio), in Paris, France, in May 2004 (Chraïbi), and at Harvard University in April 2005; and a large exhibition was organized by the National Museum of Ethnography in Osaka, Japan, in the fall of 2004. It was in this framework that, following an invitation by the baroque Herzog August Library at Wolfenbüttel, Germany, the symposium "The *Arabian Nights:* Past and Present" took place in September 2004. This meeting presented the work of nineteen international scholars on points ranging from the history of manuscripts of the *Arabian Nights* through positioning the *Nights* in modern and postmodern discourse to various aspects of the international reception of its tales in written and oral tradition. The present volume contains the meeting's proceedings, some of them revised, as originally published before the meeting in 2004 in special volumes of the journals *Marvels & Tales* (18.2) and *Fabula* (45.3–4). The essays in the present volume have been rearranged in five sections. The first section contains essays on Galland's translation and its "Continuation" by Jacques Cazotte. The second section, titled "Texts and Contexts of the *Arabian Nights*," treats various aspects of the *Nights*, including manuscript tradition, the transformations of a specific narrative pattern occurring in the *Nights* and other works of medieval Arabic literature, the topic of siblings in the *Nights*, and the manner political thought is mirrored in its tales. The two essays of the third section deal with framing in relation to the classical Indian collection *Panchatantra* and as a general cultural technique, with particular attention to storytelling in the oral tradition of the Indian Ocean islands off the African coast. The concluding, and largest, sections focus on various aspects of the transnational reception of the *Nights*.

While the essays of the fourth section predominantly discuss written or learned tradition in Hawaii, Swahili-speaking East Africa, Turkey, Iran, German cinema, and modern Arabic literature, the fifth section encompasses essays on the reception and role of the *Nights* in the oral tradition of areas as wide apart as Sicily, Greece, Afghanistan, and Balochistan.

Introducing the first section, Aboubakr Chraïbi deals with the tale of "Ali Baba." In order to write "Ali Baba," a tale of thirty-six published pages, Antoine Galland amplified the text he had noted down in his diary that comprised only six pages. In doing so, Galland also omitted certain details, such as the presence of food in the cave. These details enable present-day researchers to find out whether the versions of the tale of "Ali Baba" recorded in the Maghreb and other Arab regions are dependent on Galland's text or whether they are independent.

Sylvette Larzul considers hitherto neglected aspects of the tales told to Galland by the Syrian narrator Hannâ Diyâb. Whereas the earlier volumes of Galland's French translation are based on Arabic manuscripts, the later volumes include a variety of tales originating from the oral performance of Hannâ. This second part of Galland's work leaves more room for creation than the first one and emphasizes exoticism to a larger extent. Apart from being constantly concerned with the representation of cultural specificities, the author multiplies the exotic leitmotifs and thus depicts a universe composed of khans, sofas, and veils. Galland's penchant for luxury also reigns freely in those tales, with his artistry giving rise to a magnificent Orient overflowing with gold and gems.

Joseph Sadan deals with Jacques Cazotte and his novel *Xaïloun*. Jacques Cazotte was a distinguished eighteenth-century French writer who, about three years before the guillotine put an end to his life (1792), published the *Continuation* of the *Mille et une Nuits*. A number of the stories transmitted to him by his "informant," Denis Chavis, are contained in an Arabic manuscript dated 1772 that is preserved in the Bibliothèque Nationale in Paris. The origin of Cazotte's novel *Histoire de Xaïloun*, included in the *Continuation*, until now was unknown. The comparison between the short Arabic story *Hamîda the Kaslân*, recently discovered in another Arabic manuscript, and Cazotte's long novel demonstrates the writer's creativity.

In the second section, Heinz Grotzfeld's contribution deals with the compilation and transmission of the *Arabian Nights*. According to him, the number *alf* (1,000) in the collection's Arabic title has been a permanent challenge for copyists and compilers committed to the transmission of texts of the *Nights*. "Complete" sets of the work seem to have survived in their entirety only a short time. Consequently, copyists must have felt invited to (re)create a complete *Nights*. Grotzfeld presents the different solutions applied by copyists and compilers in order to achieve their ambitious goals, the honest and deceitful methods and the tricks displayed in the Arabic texts as well as in the European translations of the *Nights*.

In his essay "Slave-Girl Lost and Regained: Transformations of a Story" Geert Jan van Gelder discusses a story found in many forms in Arabic literature, with the following basic structure: A man owns a slave-girl; they love each other; he becomes destitute and is forced to sell her; the new owner, aware of their attachment, magnanimously returns her to her previous owner. The *Thousand and One Nights* contains two such stories as well as some others with closely related motifs. Many more versions, some of them virtually identical to those of the *Nights,* are found in works belonging to Arabic "polite" or "elite" literary culture from the ninth century onward. An appendix offers summaries of several versions.

Hasan El-Shamy discusses patterns of interaction between siblings in the male-oriented *Nights*, conforming to his theory labeled "The Brother-Sister Syndrome." He sees the core of this dyadic relationship in a stable pattern of sentiments (learned feelings) involving the entire family: Brother-sister mutual love; sister-sister rivalry; brother-brother rivalry; child-parent(s) hostility; husband-wife hostility (or lack of love and affection); brother-sister's husband hostility; sister-brother's wife rivalry; brother-sister's child affection; and a brother-brother's son hostility.

Robert Irwin points out that there is more political thought in the *Nights* than would appear at first sight. Political concerns are to the fore in the story collection's exordium. Some of the stories can be seen as belonging to the "mirrors-for-princes" genre and, if much of their content seems banal, this was usually true of the nonfictional essays in the genre. It is also true that philosophers sometimes used fables as vehicles for their thoughts on politics. Although criticism of tyranny and the positing of alternative societies are quite rare in Islamic literature, examples of both can be found in the *Nights*.

The two essays of the third section deal with framing, probably the most remarkable narrative technique of the *Nights*. Both the *Arabian Nights* and the Indian *Panchatantra* contain a large number of stories under one umbrella or frame story, and the umbrella story of each work has remained more stable through the ages than the set of stories contained within. Sadhana Naithani devotes her comparative study to the two umbrella stories, both of which have an identity independent of the stories they shelter. Naithani proceeds from the observation that the structures of the two frame stories are strikingly similar, though composed of completely different elements.

Lee Haring starts his reflections on framing in narrative by pointing out that the device of framing, in narratives, is but a formal stylization of people's annoying habit of interrupting their discourses and switching messages. Narrative artists everywhere use the device for which the *Thousand and One Nights* is famous, though the device is most favored in stratified societies. Modes of criticism and commentary also function as frames, for interpretive purposes. The varieties of framing—frame stories, opening and closing formulas, the "runs" of Irish storytellers, interruptions by the performer, channel-switching—call for various modes of criticism. Haring's examples come from Madagascar, Mauritius, Réunion, and the Comoros and Seychelles.

The fourth section is introduced by Cristina Bacchilega's and Noelani Arista's study of the *Arabian Nights* in the nineteenth-century Hawaiian newspaper *Kuokoa*. Translations of the *Arabian Nights* into non-Western languages have received little attention. A Hawaiian-language translation of selections of the *Arabian Nights*, published in the 1870s, was part of the Hawaiian-language newspapers' large-scale production of foreign texts in translation and of printed Hawaiian narratives that had been circulating orally. Sharing an interest in the politics of translation, Bacchilega, a fairytale scholar with an interest in gender, and Noelani, a Hawaiian historian and practicing translator, examine *He Kaao Arabia* as a foreign *kaao* (fiction or tale of wonder) within the dynamics of Western and Hawaiian "storytelling" played out in the newspaper *Ka Nupepa Kuokoa*.

Thomas Geider deals with the occurrence of the *Thousand and One Nights* in East Africa and offers a survey of available data relating to the Swahili-speaking coasts of Kenya and Tanzania. Issues discussed include versions of tales from the *Nights* documented between 1860 and 1890 that can be related to printed Arabic sources, the canonical edition of *Alfu Lela Ulela* (1929) translated as part of the colonial endeavor and aiming to mediate world literature in the perspective of the British Empire, and a new project of translating the *Nights* into the Swahili language initiated in 1996.

Hande A. Birkalan-Gedik discusses the reception of the *Thousand and One Nights* in Turkish tradition. Turkish versions of the *Arabian Nights* have enjoyed a great popularity. On the one hand, there are translations designed for a popular adult audience. On the other, the *Arabian Nights* have been perceived as an appropriate source for the entertainment of children. Birkalan-Gedik's contribution aims to analyze various issues concerning the Turkish translations. Some of the questions are: What were the political and cultural reasons for translating the *Arabian Nights* into Turkish? What were the criteria for editing and revising the material for children's literature? In pursuing these questions, she ventures into the relationship between literature and cultural politics.

My own essay is concerned with the links between the *Arabian Nights* and Iranian culture. While the links are to some extent quite obvious and have been extensively discussed in previous research, some implications are less visible. In surveying these links, I discuss five major areas, including the Iranian prototype of the *Nights*, tales of alleged Persian origin, Persian characters within the tales, Persian translations of the *Arabian Nights*, and the position of the *Arabian Nights* in modern Iran.

Donald Haase focuses on two cultural developments in Germany and their intersection in the period from 1880 to 1935. One of these developments is the robust reception of the *Arabian Nights* in print. The other is the emergence of visual culture in the form of motion pictures. Haase shows how the literary reception of the *Arabian Nights* as a visual experience can help explain why filmmakers like Ernst Lubitsch (*Sumurun*, 1920), Fritz Lang (*Der müde Tod*, 1921), and Paul Leni (*Das Wachsfigurenkabinett*, 1924) adapted the content and narrative structure of the *Arabian Nights* in their cinematic work.

Susanne Enderwitz starts her essay by pointing out the transnational character of the *Nights* as resulting from a cultural and ethnic melting process in which Indian and Persian—besides Greek, Egyptian, and Turkish—elements were blended together. Shahrazâd herself is such an amalgam, as she speaks the Arabic language, bears a Persian name, and displays an Indian narrative mode. Today, in Europe and America as well as in the Near East, writers still use the characters of Shahrazâd's tales and her narrative mode for their own writing. Against this backdrop, Enderwitz sets out to explore Shahrazâd's multilayered roles as a heroine, narrator, and woman.

In the first contribution to the fifth section, Francesca Maria Corrao discusses Sicilian stories of Eastern origins and aims to show analogies and differences. While little evidence is left of Arab rule in Sicily, Sicilian oral tradition has preserved stories inspired by the *Thousand and One Nights*. In the nineteenth century, ethnologist Giuseppe Pitrè gathered a considerable collection of stories from Sicilian oral tradition in which numerous motifs also occurring in the *Nights* can be recognized.

Marilena Papachristophorou presents a comparative study of Greek oral tradition related to tales from the *Arabian Nights*. She introduces her essay with a survey of the most important Greek translations of the *Nights*, from the second half of the eighteenth century to the 1920s. The following comparison shows several degrees of exchange between the two narrative corpora. At the same time, various plots and themes in Greek popular tradition have often evolved in unexpected ways, probably because of a distinct cultural background and different ways of transmission. The presentation focuses on the motif of the "Swan Maidens" and related tales as an interesting example of the interaction between the *Nights* and Greek oral tradition.

Margaret A. Mills discusses an oral performance of the tale of Judar recorded by her in Afghanistan, 1975. Considerable scholarship has developed tracing possible oral sources for important examples of early written literature, as well as the observable features of oral narrative style and the processes of oral performance and transmission in various traditions and settings. The specific changes in a written narrative, when it turns, or returns, to oral performance and transmission, have not received as much attention. Mills's comparison of a story from *Alf layla* in its nineteenth-century literary Persian translation with an oral performance recorded in prewar Afghanistan identifies elements of the then-current oral folktale style in Dari (Afghan Persian), both in plot structure and gross content, and in surface stylistics, that the teller(s) introduced into the performance.

Sabir Badalkhan analyzes three versions of the tale of "Aladdin and the Magic Lamp" documented from Balochi oral tradition. The versions, collected from Makran in Pakistani Balochistan in 1996, 1997, and 2003 from two illiterate nonprofessional storytellers, are compared with the tale as it appears in the *Nights* in order to show how a highly popular tale with a strong written tradition is transformed in oral tradition, and how oral storytellers feel free to creatively modify such a famous tale.

It is with great pleasure and sincere gratitude that the editor once more acknowledges the kind invitation to host the original conference at the Herzog August Library at Wolfenbüttel, as extended by the energetic and extremely efficient head of the library's research department Friedrich Niewöhner, who died unexpectedly in November 2005. He will be greatly missed. Don Haase and Rolf Wilhelm Brednich kindly published the essays before the conference in special volumes of the journals *Marvels & Tales* and *Fabula* as a most welcome contribution toward enabling all participants to read the full text of one another's contribution before or during the conference and thus committing ourselves to a lively and challenging intellectual debate. My special thanks also go to all of the contributors for their patience and endurance during the editorial period. While at the time of the original publication the actual symposium at which the essays would be discussed was still in the future, all of the authors have striven to present original and concise studies originating from their fields of expertise. For the present publication, most of the papers have undergone a certain revision, some of them to a considerable extent. Finally, I am grateful to Don Haase as the editor of the series in fairy-tale studies at Wayne State University Press for agreeing to publish the complete proceedings, and to Heiko Hartmann of Walter de Gruyter, Berlin, for consenting to have the essays originally published in *Fabula* included in this publication.

Because the work is a shape-shifter, it is virtually impossible to grasp the phenomenon of the *Arabian Nights* in simple and unambiguous statements, much less in one clear thesis. Diverse as the subject of research is, so are the topics of research, offering new approaches as well as more detailed insights into previously explored arenas. This multitude of approaches is probably the most vigorous aspect of the fascination that the *Arabian Nights* continues to exert until the present day. Even though each of the studies presented here might appear to be no more than a single drop when viewed against the "ocean of stories" of the *Nights*, it is hoped that they will contribute to a deeper and more adequate international appreciation of the collection, numerous facets of whose composite character, despite its long history in the West, in many respects still remain unknown.

WORKS CITED

Chraïbi, Aboubakr, ed. *Les Mille et une Nuits en partage.* Paris: Sindbad, 2004.

Joly, Jean-Luc, and Abdelfattah Kilito, eds. *Les Mille et une Nuits: Du texte au mythe.* Rabat: Faculté des Lettres et des Sciences Humaines, 2005.

Mahdi, Muhsin: *The Thousand and One Nights (Alf Layla wa-Layla): From the Earliest Known Sources.* Part 1: Arabic Text. 1984. Part 2: Critical Apparatus. Description of Manuscripts. 1984. Part 3: Introduction and Indexes. Leiden: Brill, 1994.

Marzolph, Ulrich, and Richard van Leeuwen, with the collaboration of Hassan Wassouf. *The Arabian Nights Encyclopedia.* 2 vols. Santa Barbara, Denver, and Oxford: ABC-CLIO, 2004.

Yamanaka, Yuriko, and Tetsuo Nishio, eds. *The Arabian Nights and Orientalism: Perspectives from East and West.* New York: I. B. Tauris, 2006.

Galland's Translation and Its "Continuation"

I

Galland's "Ali Baba" and Other Arabic Versions

Aboubakr Chraïbi

The text of reference in which the tale of Ali Baba appears for the first time goes back, theoretically, to the ninth century. It was around this period that a Persian book called *Hazâr afsân[e]* (*A Thousand Tales*) was translated into Arabic, taking the new name of *Alf layla wa-layla* (*The Thousand and One Nights*). Since this mythical period, the *Thousand and One Nights* (henceforth: *Nights*) have continuously changed.

The manner in which its various contributors perceived the famous collection of tales over the centuries is undoubtedly the prime cause for its numerous metamorphoses. The *Nights* of the ninth century are not identical to those of the fifteenth century, and those of the fifteenth century are quite different from those of the eighteenth century. Similarly, the French translation by Antoine Galland, published 1704–17, differs from its Arabic source text, and the translation by Joseph Charles Mardrus, published 1899–1904, differs both from the Arabic text and from Galland's translation. In modern literary criticism, the *Nights* were never considered as a specific book compiled by an individual author. On the contrary, they were regarded as a work in progress that acquired its content and character in the process of an open development in which different authors could contribute and introduce their own variations. The result, in today's terminology, is a complex "literary creation." It is precisely in this category of "literary creation" that we have to understand Galland's work in respect to the *Nights*. This evaluation applies both to the collection as we know it today in general and more particularly to the tale of "Ali Baba and the

Forty Thieves," a tale that was, from a certain point of view, created by Galland.

As is well known, there is no reliable Arabic text of "Ali Baba" prior to the eighteenth century. No Arabic text older than Galland's French version exists. The handwritten version preserved at the Bodleian Library in Oxford and published by Duncan B. Macdonald ("Ali Baba") dates from the nineteenth century. As the wording shows, this manuscript constitutes an Arabic translation prepared from Galland's text, a fact Macdonald himself recognized a few years later ("Further Notes"). The safest information at hand about the ultimate origin of "Ali Baba" is contained in Galland's *Journal*, which is preserved at the Bibliothèque Nationale in Paris (see Galland, *Journal* May 27, 1709; Macdonald, "Further Notes" 41–47). Here, Galland gives the summary of a story titled *Les finesses de Morgiane ou Les quarante voleurs exterminés par l'adresse d'une esclave* (*Morgiane's Tricks or The Forty Robbers Exterminated by the Skill of a Female Slave*). The story was narrated to Galland on the same day as the tale of *The Ten Viziers*. Both these tales, and several others, were told by Hannâ, a Maronite monk originating from Aleppo in Syria, with whom Galland had become acquainted through his friend, the traveler Paul Lucas. The text Galland presents in his diary is rather short, hardly comprising six pages. Ali Baba is here called Hogia Baba. The descriptive passages later elaborated are here very condensed and barely visible, and the text focuses on the articulations of the intrigue. Some years later, Galland reworked the original notes and created a beautiful story, now comprising more than thirty-six pages, that he included in—and, in fact, introduced into—his edition of *Les Mille et une Nuits* together with other tales that Hannâ had supplied. Subsequently, this story became part of the standard repertoire of the European notion of the *Thousand and One Nights*, although its author clearly is Galland himself. Yet the story originates from the narrative tradition of Syria, Hannâ's native country, and contains specific native components.

In this essay, I propose to analyze the tale of "Ali Baba" from various angles. I will start by studying its variations in sources originating from or close to Arab narrative tradition. Following this, I will evaluate Galland's composition and its inherent meaning, as compared to various other traditions, by giving a detailed attention to the source text, that is, the six pages that Galland jotted down in his diary.

In terms of content structure, the story of "Ali Baba" may be analyzed and shown to contain the following elements:

1. There are two brothers: Ali Baba is a woodcutter who is poor and good; Cassim is a merchant who is rich and malicious.

2. Hidden in a tree, Ali Baba overhears forty thieves tell their secret.

3. The secret is a magic formula ("Open Sesame"/"Close Sesame") that makes it possible to enter and leave a certain cave containing their treasures.

4. Thanks to the secret formula, Ali Baba enters the cave, takes some gold, and walks away.

5. Intending to count the money, Ali Baba's wife requests a scale from Cassim's wife.

6. Cassim's wife coats the bottom of the scale with grease in order to find out what substance they will measure.

7. As a gold coin remains stuck in the scale, Cassim discovers that Ali Baba has become rich and convinces him to tell his secret.

8. Cassim then enters the cave to take some gold. When he is inside, he forgets the formula and remains locked up until the arrival of the robbers who cut him to pieces.

9. Alerted by Cassim's wife, Ali Baba goes to the cave where he recovers his brother's corpse.

10. In order to calm Cassim's wife, whose tears threaten to cause attention, Ali Baba promises to marry her.

11. The slave-girl Morgiane buys drugs while pretending that her master Cassim is inflicted by a severe disease. After a while, she pretends that he has died.

12. Morgiane calls on a cobbler whose eyes she bandages while leading him to her home. The cobbler is to stitch together the pieces of Cassim's body; they want to bury him whole.

13. After the burial, Ali Baba lives in Cassim's house and marries Cassim's wife; his son takes over the merchant's shop.

14. The robbers try to find out who is responsible for the disappearance of the corpse.

15. They find the cobbler who leads them to Ali Baba's house.

16. The robbers mark the house, but clever Morgiane puts the same mark on all the other houses in the street.

17. The captain of the robbers introduces his men to Ali Baba's house. The robbers are hidden in large leather vessels supposed to contain oil. Morgiane discovers the scheme and kills the robbers.

18. The captain of the robbers visits Ali Baba disguised as a merchant. Without him noticing, Morgiane recognizes him and, pretending to dance with a dagger, stabs him to death.

19. Morgiane marries Ali Baba's son, and all of them enjoy the treasure together (see Galland, *Journal* May 27, 1709; Macdonald, "Further Notes" 41–47; Galland, *Les Mille et une Nuits* 241–76).

The tale inserted into the *Mille et une Nuits* by Galland is an embellished development of the summary contained in his diary. Curiously, certain elements of the summary, instead of being developed and amplified, were deleted. This elimination applies in particular to two passages mentioning food. When Ali Baba enters the cave for the first time, before enumerating the various treasures, the summary mentions "la table mise et beaucoup de provisions, de vivres, des amas de riches choses, etc., et surtout de l'argent, de l'or, par tas, etc." ("A table set with numerous provisions, food, large amounts of sumptuous dishes etc., and, above all, heaps of silver and gold etc.") (Galland, *Journal* 141; Macdonald, "Further Notes" 42). Instead, the published text of the *Nights* has him find "de grandes provisions de bouche, des ballots de riches marchandises en piles, des étoffes de soie et de brocart, des tapis de grands prix, et surtout de l'or et de l'argent monnayé par tas, et dans des sacs de grandes bourses de cuir les unes sur les autres" ("great provisions of food, bales of rich merchandise in piles, cloth of silk and brocade, and, above all, gold and silver coins in heaps and in large leather bags, piled one upon the other") (Galland, *Mille et une Nuits* 243). While the description of the treasures was amplified, the set table and the prepared dishes have disappeared. Evidently, Galland preferred to remove the elements relating to the cave as a dining (or storage) room and retain only the treasure. Contrary to the published version, in Hannâ's rendering a person entering the cave would initially have been confronted with a table set with food and dishes ready to be consumed.

Even though it might be regarded as a minor and, hence, negligible motif, the "table mise" in the diary's version is neither invented by Galland nor mentioned by accident as a "blind motif." In Hannâ's original Arab version, the "table mise" served a specific function. Some paragraphs later, when the robbers return, surprise Cassim, and kill him, the summary says that the robbers "sortent après avoir mangé" ("leave after having eaten") (Galland, *Journal* May 27, 1709; Macdonald, "Further Notes" 43). This opportunity to eat and refresh inside the cave was removed in Galland's published version.

Now, if the original version of the cave included a dining room, in which way is this fact important? It is important because the dining room represents an element that is both ignored by the public (that, from Galland's version, could not know of it) and that is quite ancient. Narrators who rely only on the long version published by Galland, the version that most readers know, would not mention a "table mise" nor any of the robbers' food. Consequently, if a narrator in an Arabic or any other version speaks about the "table mise" and food, this version does not originate from Galland, but must go back to the sources that inspired Hannâ. The underlying image presented in those sources shows the robbers taking their meal regularly inside the cave, and so the cave more or less serves as their house. Let us first consider a Syrian tale that employs the same plot as "Ali Baba," which, in terms of folk narrative scholarship, draws from a combination of international tale-types. The tale-types of Aarne and Thompson (henceforth AT), AT 676: *Open Sesame*, and AT 954: *The Forty Thieves*, do not, however, help in studying the early versions of "Ali Baba," as they are most probably inspired by the text of the *Nights*. The Syrian version has been published by Ahmad Bassâm Sâ'î under the title "al-Hattâb wa-l-'afârît" ("The Woodcutter and the Jinnis," 86–88; for another version see Djafaar 15–24). This version is composed of the following elements:

1. A woodcutter sells wood to make a living for his family.

2. A tree speaks to the woodcutter and indicates to him a cave full of treasures belonging to jinnis; it also teaches him the secret formula to move the rock in order to enter the cave: "Silsila, by the capacity of God, open!"

3. The woodcutter waits until the jinnis have left, then enters, takes some gold, and walks away.

4. Back home, the woodcutter wakes up his rich brother and takes him along to the cave.

5. They visit the cave several times until the woodcutter is satisfied with the gold he has taken.

6. The rich brother is greedy and continues to visit the cave every day.

7. The jinnis realize that the amount of gold is diminishing.

8. In order to catch the person stealing their gold, the jinnis deposit some delicious meat in the cave.

9. The rich brother arrives in the cave, finds the meat and eats it, and then fills his bags with gold and jewels; when he wants to leave, he does not remember the magic formula.

10. When he is surprised by the jinnis, they decide to bind him inside the cave while attaching a large rock above his head.

11. The rich brother's wife worries about his absence and alerts the wood-cutter, who rescues his brother and brings him back home.

12. Returning to the cave, the jinnis do not find their prisoner. In order to locate his whereabouts, one of them disguises himself as a doctor while the others hide inside some trunks. They all go to town.

13. The jinni disguised as a doctor seeks a patient who has been crushed by a stone.

14. He finds the rich brother's house and enters it together with the other jinnis hidden inside the trunks. The rich brother's wife understands who they are, burns them with pokers, and obliges them, by alerting the people, to run away.

15. Thanks to his wife's clever trick, the rich merchant is saved.

This version contains two interesting elements. On the one hand, the newly introduced "jinni of the tree" motif also appears in other tales, such as AT 563: *The Table, the Ass, and the Stick*, or AT 1168B: *The Tree-Demon Pays the Man to Save the Tree*. On the other, the presence of the "delicious meat" the jinnis leave in the cave to catch the greedy brother constitutes the equivalent of the food mentioned in Galland's summary. Although this element in the Syrian version is employed in a different manner and, hence, may be understood as somewhat "faded," it documents that this version does not originate from Galland's *Nights* but from Syrian folklore. Similar traces of food, which in the two versions discussed so far appear in a rather vague form, play a more marked and clearer role in a Kabyle tale (Frobenius 2: 143–48, no. 13):

1. There are two brothers: one is poor and has only daughters; the other is rich and has only sons.

2. The poor one goes to cut wood in the forest.

3. Hidden behind a tree, he overhears the magic formula a band of ogres uses to enter their treasure trove.

4. By means of the magic formula "Open Rock!" he enters the ogres' cave.

5. Inside the cave, the table is set with seven large dishes of couscous; besides, he finds an enormous heap of gold.

6. The poor man enters the cave but does not touch the food. He only takes some gold and then walks away.

7. Wishing to measure the money, the poor man requests a scale from his brother.

8. The rich man coats the scale with glue in order to know what his brother will measure.

9. As a gold coin remains stuck in the scale, the rich brother discovers that the poor man possesses gold. He threatens him and manages to get his brother to inform him where he found the gold.

10. The rich brother enters the cave to take the treasure; he is attracted by the dishes of couscous, which he eats entirely and is thereby delayed a long time inside the cave.

11. The rich brother is surprised by the ogres. The ogres kill him, leave his corpse in the cave, and go away.

12. Learning that his brother has not returned, the poor man enters the cave and transports his brother's corpse back to the house, leaving a trail of blood on the way.

13. Alerted by the disappearance of the corpse, the ogres follow the trail and arrive at the poor man's house.

14. The poor man invites them to eat. He seats them in a part of the house covered with bales of straw, puts fire to it, and burns the seven ogres.

Here, then, we encounter again the "table mise" that Galland referred to in his diary but that he chose not to reproduce in the published version of the *Nights*. In the Kabyle version, the table of delicious food serves as a kind of test, or in other words, as an element used to find out the moral qualification of the respective characters. The character able to control his carnal desire does not touch the food or only eats a little, such as in the Algerian version published by Christiane Achour and Zineb Benali (65–71). This character succeeds and is deemed worthy to take the gold, because he acts in a moderate and adequate manner. On the contrary, the character who greedily takes all the food is disqualified, because his behavior does not suit the situation he is in. Accordingly, the way different characters act in relation to the food presented is highly significant as it is used to demonstrate their qualities and defects. As if to further stress this point, in a sub-Saharan version collected from the Yoruba (Basset 217–20), gold is not mentioned at all, only food. In addition, the story of "Ali Baba" here appears as an animal tale:

1. In times of famine, the lizard goes to the countryside and finds a stone filled with yams.

2. The lizard overhears the secret of the master of the field when he enters the stone.

3. The secret is the magic formula "Open Rock!" and "Close Rock!"

4. On the following day, by means of the formula, the lizard opens the stone, takes the yams, and carries them home where he eats them. He continues to do so every day.

5. Promising to keep the secret, the tortoise learns the secret from the lizard.

6. The lizard leads the tortoise to the stone, takes what he needs and goes away. The tortoise refuses to leave and continues to pile up yams.

7. When the tortoise wants to leave, she has forgotten the formula and is caught by the master of the field.

8. Being hit by the farmer, the tortoise denounces the lizard.

9. When the farmer arrives in the lizard's house, the lizard pretends to die of hunger.

10. The farmer kills the tortoise, and the lizard is saved.

Besides the acquisition of gold and other treasures, food plays an important role in many versions of "Ali Baba," including that by Galland. As if mirroring the tale's beginning, where the "table mise" is used as a test to select the worthy character and disqualify the undeserving one, at the tale's end, we also sometimes encounter the mention of food serving a specific function. In the Kabyle tale, the hero employs the ruse to invite the ogres to a meal and subsequently burns them. In both Hannâ's and Galland's versions, a meal also serves as a setting to eliminate the chief of the robbers. More strikingly still, the way the chief of the robbers acts concerning the food offered to him eventually causes his failure and death. When he asks for a special food prepared without salt, he arouses Morgiane's suspicion, for salt symbolizes hospitality and friendship, and a guest refusing to share salt with his host behaves in a hostile manner.

Galland's version of "Ali Baba" remains the tale's richest and most complex realization to date. The tale's attraction to a large extent relies on its dual composition, as the roles of the characters are duplicated. The tale successively treats two exemplary characters. In its first part, the hero is the good and morally sound Ali Baba; in the second part, the heroine is the intelligent and, in fact, clever slave-girl Morgiane. Two evil characters oppose these positive ones. In the tale's beginning, the hero's brother Cassim is malicious and envies his brother's success; in the second part, it is the robbers who investigate their case, in the first place actually seeking to protect their own treasure but eventually aiming to practice their murderous profession. This distribution of roles is representative of the two narrations combined, resulting in two different sequences to follow.

Ali Baba is opposed to Cassim in the same manner as the envied is opposed to the envier in a tale included in the earliest preserved manuscript of the *Nights* dating from the fifteenth century (Chauvin 14, no. 158). This tale is quite similar to that of Abû Niyya and Abû Niyyatayn (Chauvin 11, no. 8) as well as to that of Muhsin and Mûsâ (Chauvin 13, no. 9). The correspondences show that the tale AT 676: *Open Sesame*, constituting the first part of the tale of "Ali Baba," belongs to an ancient tradition. This tradition is well established in Arabic narrative tradition and is related to AT 613: *Truth and Falsehood.*

In this context, it is interesting to note that in Japanese tradition peculiar forms of this kind of story exist. Such versions treat a contest in which one must catch a pellet of food that falls down. If one calls the pellet—as if using a magic formula—it leads to an underground cave in which other creatures live that endow the Good with riches, while envious characters go there to their disadvantage. This structure could help explain the formula "Open Sesame," as if it were an offering of food (Kunio 123–24, 126–27; see other versions 133, 137, and 138).

The second sequence opposes the clever and intelligent slave-girl Morgiane to the robbers. In a reversal of roles, it is actually Morgiane who plays the part of a robber who has decided to keep the spoils, and the robbers play the part of a detective trying to trace and regain stolen possessions. This opposition between the crafty Morgiane and the previous owners of the treasure is quite similar to the one between the crafty robber and

Pharaoh Rhampsinitus—the second sequence adopts elements from AT 950: *Rhampsinitus.*

The two sequences—on the one hand similar to "The Envier and The Envied," on the other sharing elements with *Rhampsinitus*—are connected under a common theme: "Profiting from a certain secret, one brother becomes rich, and the other is killed." It is here argued that this connection and the transformation it necessitates were motivated by the teller's intention to raise the moral standard of an originally not very moralistic story of robbery and murder. Accordingly, in "Ali Baba," the motif of the hero as robber was moralized, since the hero's amoral behavior is now justified by the fact that he steals from ogres or other robbers. More significant, the motif of the hero who decapitates his own brother so as not to be recognized (in the tale of Rhampsinitus) was also moralized, since the brother in "Ali Baba" is a malicious man who is killed because of his greed by the owners of the treasure. Amid the numerous versions of the tale of Rhampsinitus there actually is an Arabic version in which the hero kills his uncle. Even though this deed originally constitutes a grave breach of social behavior, it is alleviated by the uncle being portrayed as a malicious character (Reesink 57–73). In another version of the tale of Rhampsinitus, the entry to the treasure trove is achieved by way of a magic formula, as in "Ali Baba" (Aceval 99). If we add to these correspondences the motif of "marking of the doors" (element 16 of "Ali Baba"), frequently encountered in versions of the tale of Rhampsinitus (Laoust 98–104, particularly 103), it becomes almost certain that the second part of "Ali Baba" originates from the narrative tradition of the crafty robber.

But then, if the heroes duplicate themselves and if, by the effect of the association of two initially independent traditions, the two brothers live in two different houses—toward which house should the investigation move? How to stay in contact with the equivalent of the mother in tears claiming the body of her son (in the tale of Rhampsinitus)—that is, in "Ali Baba," the wife of Cassim, whereas the hero is elsewhere? At this point, the meaning of Ali Baba's marriage with Cassim's wife and his change of place to his brother's house become clear. The marriage, considered as a curiosity by Tzvetan Todorov (36), clearly serves as a kind of rhetorical device. By having only one family and house the tale can pass from one narrative tradition (as in "Truth and Falsehood") to the other ("Rhampsinitus") in the most natural way and, by fusing the two sequences, can concentrate the drama in one geographical space.

All the characters—Ali Baba, his first and his second wife, their son, and Morgiane—from now on live in the house of a rich person, with walls, a garden, adjacent buildings, and numerous servants. The robbers, even as they locate this house, cannot penetrate easily and have to use a stratagem. This ruse is actually an old motif that is, once again, already documented in Pharaonic literature, where it is known as "The Capture of Joppa" (Lefebvre 125). The stratagem employed is often connected with the confrontation of two armies or the conquest of a city. It demonstrates that the story's ethics are undecided. Its use is not motivated by the ratio of force in this confrontation, as the robbers are obviously stronger than the inhabitants of the house. The story's ethics rather deal with the will on both sides to maintain the secrecy that served to imagine this trick as well as the means of neutralizing it. Neither Ali Baba nor the robbers want other people to know what they do, because neither Ali Baba nor the robbers are in a morally acceptable situation. They are placed at the margins of society, and it is precisely this fact of living at the margins, in secrecy, that guarantees them, as the text says, to be "happy and content" (Macdonald, "Further Notes" 47). However, contrary to the robbers who are bad marginal characters, Ali Baba is a good marginal character. In this manner, the story pictures a vision of the individualistic and optimistic world because it is voluntarily detached from the regular standards of human society.

Other elements in "Ali Baba" remain to be treated. The motif of the man who recognizes the house he has been to with his eyes bandaged exists in another tale from the *Thousand and One Nights*, where it is associated with a different narrative (Chauvin 102–3, no. 176). The motif of the cobbler who sews a corpse apparently is only known from the tale of Ali Baba (El-Shamy, *Folk Traditions* K 414). In conclusion, it appears sound to state that the majority of components in the tale of Ali Baba are old and generally relate to Pharaonic Egypt ("Truth and Falsehood," "Rhampsinitus," "The Capture of Joppa").

The scarcity in oral tradition of versions that in detail and specifics would equal Galland's version seems to indicate that "Ali Baba" underwent, in its scenario, a special treatment. This is not surprising. None of the stories Hannâ narrated to Galland exactly belong to popular tradition. The same day Hannâ narrated "Ali Baba," he also told Galland a tale of the *Ten Viziers*, following the well-known literary version in a book circulating at the time (Galland, *Journal* May 17, 1709). Hannâ also told Galland the story of the Ebony Horse (May 13, 1709; Chauvin 221–27, no. 130).

The *Ten Viziers* as well as the story of the Ebony Horse belong to a more elaborate literature, a genre that might reasonably be regarded as standing in between learned and popular literature. One might also consider the role of Hannâ, himself a learned man, involved in the transmission of "elaborated and chosen" stories he transmits. Due to the ingenious way in which "Ali Baba" employs motifs originating from various traditions that usually are not connected to one another, it has to be regarded as a specific work and probably as a new creation. Moreover, the ingenious combination of motifs has turned the tale into a particularly successful one. Thanks to its publication by Galland, the tale of Ali Baba, besides generating innumerable retellings, has given rise to treatments in opera, film, and numerous artistic works. In addition, the topic of food has assisted the gradual construction of a myth around the name of Ali Baba, a name given today to various institutions—particularly restaurants—inside and outside the Arab world. In this way, the present image of Ali Baba in popular tradition constitutes a great homage, even though it is perhaps a little nostalgic, that living reality now pays to fiction.

WORKS CITED

Aarne, Antti, and Stith Thompson. *The Types of the Folktale: A Classification and Bibliography.* 2nd rev. ed. Helsinki: Academia Scientiarum Fennica, 1961.

Aceval, Nora. *L'Algérie des contes et légendes, hauts plateaux de Tiaret.* Paris: Maisonneuve et Larose, 2003.

Achour, Christiane, and Zineb Benali. *Contes Algériens.* Paris: L'Harmattan, 1989.

Basset, René. *Contes populaires d'Afrique.* 1908. Paris: Maisonneuve et Larose, 1969.

Chauvin, Victor. *Bibliographie des ouvrages arabes ou relatifs aux Arabes publiés dans l'Europe chrétienne de 1810 à 1885.* Vol. 5. Liège: Vaillant-Carmanne, and Leipzig: Harrassowitz, 1901.

Djafaar, Abd al-Razzak. *Contes populaires de Syrie.* Trans. Hafci Benhafci. Paris: Publisud, 1991.

El-Shamy, Hasan M. *Folk Traditions of the Arab World: A Guide to Motif Classification.* 2 vols. Bloomington: Indiana UP, 1995.

———. "Oral Traditional Tales and the Thousand Nights and a Night: The Demographic Factor." *The Telling of Stories: Approaches to a Traditional Craft.* Ed. Morten Nøjgaard et al. Odense: Odense UP, 1990. 63-117.

———. *Types of the Folktale in the Arab World: A Demographically Oriented Tale-Type Index.* Bloomington: Indiana UP, 2004.

Frobenius, Leo. *Contes Kabyles.* Trans. Mokran Fetta. 4 vols. 1921. Paris: Edisud, 1996.

Galland, Antoine. *Journal.* 1709. Paris: Bibliothèque Nationale de France, ms. fr. 19277.

———. *Les Mille et une Nuits.* Vol. 3. Paris: Garnier-Flammarion, 1965.

Kunio, Yanagita. *Contes du Japon d'autrefois.* Trans. Geneviève Sieffert. 1930. Paris: Publications Orientalistes de France, 1983.

Laoust, Émile. *Contes berbères du Maroc.* Paris: Institut des Hautes Études Marocaines, 1949.

Lefebvre, Gustave. *Romans et contes égyptiens de l'époque pharaonique.* Paris: Adrien-Maisonneuve, 1949.

Macdonald, Duncan Black. "'Ali Baba and the Forty Thieves' in Arabic from a Bodleian Ms." *Journal of the Royal Asiatic Society* (1910): 327–86.

———. "Further Notes on 'Ali Baba and The Forty Thieves.'" *Journal of the Royal Asiatic Society* (1913): 41–53.

Ranke, Kurt. "Ali Baba und die vierzig Räuber." *Enzyklopädie des Märchens.* Vol. 1. Berlin: Walter de Gruyter, 1977. 302–11.

Reesink, Pieter. *Contes et récits maghrébins.* Sherbrooke: Naaman, 1977.

Sâ'î, Ahmad Bassâm. *al-Hikâyât al-sha'biyya fî 'l-Lâdhiqiyya.* Damascus: Wizârat ath-Thaqâfa wa 'l-Irshâd al-Qawmî, 1974.

Todorov, Tzvetan: *Poétique de la prose.* Paris: Éditions du Seuil, 1971.

2

Further Considerations on Galland's *Mille et une Nuits:* A Study of the Tales Told by Hannâ

Sylvette Larzul

Published between 1704 and 1717, the first European translation of the collection of stories commonly known in English as the *Arabian Nights* is the work of the French orientalist scholar Antoine Galland (1646–1715). His twelve-volume collection bears the generic title *Les Mille et une Nuit[s],*[1] *contes arabes traduits en françois* (*The Thousand and One Nights, Arabic tales translated into French*). This title veils both the sources exploited and the strategy practiced in rewriting. The collection's initial eight volumes and the beginning of volume nine are based on Arabic manuscripts of *Alf layla wa-layla* (literally: A Thousand Nights and a Night) and other sources. In accordance with the practice current in the seventeenth century, they contain an adapted translation of the Arabic source material. The collection's final volumes are based on the oral tales procured from the narrator Hannâ, and it was Galland who inserted them into the corpus of his *Mille et une Nuits.* These tales—particularly the stories of Aladdin and Ali Baba—in the following came to be regarded as prototypes of the stories in the *Nights.* At the same time, except for the tale of the Ebony Horse, these tales do not form part of the Arabic redaction of the *Nights* known in scholarship as Zotenberg's Egyptian Recension (ZER). Drawn primarily from oral sources, the set of tales deriving from Hannâ's performance leaves more room for creation than do those tales translated from a written source text. In my earlier work on Galland's version, I studied the first part of his collection and, by comparing the translation with the source text, was able to show that Galland had adapted the original Arabic text without essentially distorting it (Larzul, *Les traductions*). In the present contribution, while taking into account the conclusions from my previous study, I propose to examine the collection's second part, the one based on Hannâ's tales. In introducing this matter, it is useful to briefly recall Galland's sources.

A Work of Creation

In the initial eight volumes of his collection, published between 1704 and 1709, Galland exhausted nearly all the material from the Arabic manuscripts of *Alf layla* in his possession. The "Histoire du dormeur éveillé" ("Story of the Awakened Sleeper")—accomplished by the end of 1708 (Omont, December 20, 1708) and published in volume nine in 1712—is already taken from an Arabic manuscript not belonging to the tradition of *Alf layla*. When his written source material was exhausted, Galland in vain tried to obtain more tales from the Levant. Then, in 1709, he had the fortune to become acquainted with Hannâ, a Christian (Maronite) Syrian from Aleppo, in the home of his friend, the traveler Paul Lucas. From him he was able to collect a total of thirteen Arabic tales from oral storytelling.[2] Between May 6 and June 3, 1709, he took down the summaries of twelve tales in his *Journal*. Already on May 5, 1709, the "Histoire d'Aladdin" ("Story of Aladdin")—with its title alone being mentioned in the *Journal*—had become a part of his collection. As mentioned in a later notice, Hannâ provided him with a copy of the tale in Arabic (Omont, November 3, 1710). At one point, Galland also received a written version of the "Aventures du calife Haroun al-Rachid" ("Story of the Adventures of the Caliph Hârûn al-Râshîd" [Omont, January 10, 1711]), though the exact status of the final tale contained within this frame story, the "Histoire de Cogia Hassan Alhabbal" ("Story of Khawâja Hasan el-Habbâl") is not clear. Galland might even have received a written copy of the "Histoire d'Ali Baba" ("Story of Ali Baba"), mentioned as "Hogia Baba" in his summary. Unfortunately, none of the written texts prepared by Hannâ have survived to the present day,[3] and so the only available source for these tales remain Galland's summaries (Abdel-Halim, *Antoine Galland* 428–70). In his *Journal*, Galland never referred to Hannâ's narratives as tales of the *Mille et une Nuits*. Nevertheless, as of November 1710, eighteen months after having heard them, he used these tales when he began to write new tales that he linked to the previous ones by having Shahrazâd tell them. Galland's decision to continue the publication of the *Mille et une Nuits* by resorting to material extraneous to the original collection may seem rather surprising. After all, it came from a demanding scholar and translator who had been scrupulous enough to point out certain liberties he had taken in regard to the original tales, such as the fact that he had deleted the division into nights or eliminated the description of the seven dresses of the vizier's daughter in the "Histoire de Nourredin Ali" (Galland 1: 320). It also appears rather peculiar that Galland allowed himself a practice he otherwise firmly condemned, that is, to introduce tales that did not belong to the original *Alf layla*. After all, he had been deeply affected by the fact that, in volume eight of his work, two tales translated from the Turkish by the orientalist scholar François Pétis de la Croix had been inserted, and he had asked his publisher to add a prefatory note to volume nine: "Les deux contes par où finit le huitième tome ne sont pas de l'ouvrage des *Mille et une Nuits*: ils y ont été insérés et imprimés à l'insu du traducteur. . . . On aura soin, dans la seconde édition, de retrancher ces deux contes comme étrangers" ("The two tales with which volume eight finishes are not from the work *A Thousand and One Nights:* they have been inserted and printed without the translator's knowledge. . . . We will ensure to eliminate them in the second edition as tales foreign [to the collection]" [Galland 2: 423]). Finally, it is striking to see that Galland resumed work on the *Mille et une Nuits* in November 1710, just a few months after the publication of Pétis de la Croix's *Mille et un Jours* had begun, around May 1710. This coincidence suggests a relation between the two activities. Considering Pétis de la Croix as a competitor, Galland might have decided to emulate him and satisfy his own readers, who were asking for the continuation of the *Mille et une Nuits*. In order to do so, he drew upon Hannâ's tales even though a Turkish manuscript of *Alf layla wa-layla*, including several tales he did not translate from the Arabic, existed at the Royal Library (Zotenberg 21–25).[4]

Galland, however, only exploited half of the stories furnished by his Syrian informant. He began to write his version of these tales told by Hannâ in November 1710 and finished in June 1713. Volume eleven of the *Mille et une Nuits*, which includes the "Histoire d'Aladdin"—begun in November 1710—was published in 1712, at the same time as volume ten, which had been completed on January 10, 1711. Besides the end of the "Histoire d'Aladdin," the latter includes "Les aventures du calife Haroun al-Rachid," which contains three enframed stories: The "Histoire de l'aveugle Baba-Abdalla" ("Story of the Blind Man Baba Abdullah"), the "Histoire de Sidi Nouman" ("Story of Sîdî Nu'mân"), and the "Histoire de Cogia Hassan Alhabbal." According to Galland's summary, the last was originally a separate tale that was added to the preceding pair on his own initiative. Both volume eleven (written between August 1711 and May 1712) and volume twelve (composed between June 1712 and June 1713) were first published posthumously in 1717, two years after Galland's death. Volume eleven includes: The "Histoire d'Ali Baba," the "Histoire d'Ali Cogia marchand de Bagdad" ("Story of Alî Khawâja and the Merchant of Baghdad"), and the "Histoire du cheval enchanté" ("Story of the Ebony Horse"); the last tale is included in ZER. As for volume twelve, it includes the "Histoire du prince Ahmed et de la fée Pari Banou" ("Story of Prince Ahmed and the Fairy Perî Bânû") and the "Histoire des deux sœurs jalouses de leur cadette" ("Story of the Two Sisters Who Envied Their Younger Sister"). As for the conclusion of the frame story, it is in accordance with what Galland wrote in 1702 in a letter to Gisbert Cuper about "the purpose of this great work" ("le dessin de ce grand ouvrage"): "De nuit en nuit la nouvelle sultane le [Schahriar] mesne jusques à mille et une et l'oblige, en la laissant vivre, de se défaire de la prévention où il étoit généralement contre toutes les femmes" ("From night to night, the new sultana leads him to a thousand and one and obliges him, by keeping her alive, to cure himself of his general prejudice against all the women") (Abdel-Halim, *Antoine Galland* 287).

In rewriting Hannâ's tales, Galland also made use of complementary sources to create his work. Thus, the evocation of the Indian temples (Galland 3: 333–34) in the "Histoire du prince Ahmed" is an exact copy of the description the Persian historian 'Abd ar-Razzâq gave in a work Galland translated under the title of *Histoire de Schah Rokh, des autres fils et descendants de Tamerlan* (Abdel-Halim, *Antoine Galland* 235, 280–82). The description of the Sodge valley included in this tale (Galland 3: 340) derives from Barthélemi d'Herbelot's *Bibliothèque orientale* (1697), a work encompassing the knowledge available about the Orient at the end of the seventeenth century that Galland had cooperated in compiling and that was published by him after d'Herbelot's death (Laurens 17–18). In addition, Galland not only profited from his own erudition but also from the experience he had gained traveling in the Levant and, in particular, residing for periods in Constantinople. There is a striking resemblance between the passages in his diary that cover the period 1672–73 of his first stay in Constantinople and his version of Hannâ's tales. Besides some terms such as *chiaoux* (a category of civil officer [Galland 3: 134, 136, 151; Schefer 1: 92, 96, 98, 100]) or *bezestein* (covered market where precious goods are sold [Galland 3: 336; Schefer 1: 24, 32]), both texts contain similar motifs, such as the famous *concert de trompettes, de timbales, de tambours, de fifres et de hautbois* (concert of trumpets, kettle-drums, tambourines, fifes, and oboes [Galland 3: 133, 314, 318; Schefer 1: 100, 117, 133, 140]). Moreover, the magnificence of the processions in the "Histoire d'Aladdin" is reminiscent of the pomp displayed by the sultan on his way to the mosque. The long and detailed descriptions evoking the outings of the "Grand Seigneur" in Galland's diary (Schefer 1: 94–103, 122–43, 2: 107–9) document how much these manifestations of regal splendor had impressed Galland. These examples document Galland's creative rewriting in both the oral tales and those produced in writing. As a matter of fact, Galland's work is buttressed by his intimate knowledge of the Orient and by the impressions that shaped his vision of the Oriental world during his sojourns in Constantinople. On the whole, his attitude resembles that of other authors of the classical period, who also chose their subject matter from a traditional stock and subsequently reshaped and reworked it in their own manner.

In the following, I propose to address the question of whether Galland's writing and goals undergo any changes as he moves from adaptation to creation. In a previous essay, I have argued that while Galland's translation was in accordance with French classical aesthetics, he also intended to introduce his readers to the Arab-Islamic civilization (Larzul, "*Les Mille et une Nuits*"). Accordingly, even the minimal loss of original text was a matter of concern for him. His work is presented then as an adaptation in which material details are all but evanescent and sociocultural features come to the fore. Furthermore, Galland yields to the temptation of sublimating the Orient as evidenced by his frequent allusions to *or* (gold) and *pierreries* (precious stones) as well as by his taste for certain exotic elements such as the patio *fontaine* (fountain) and the *sofa*. Such practices do not abound in the first part of the work, though, for that part was intended, on the whole, to be close to the original text.

As to the process of their rewriting, Hannâ's tales do have some points in common with the stories drawn from the manuscripts. The summaries recorded in Galland's diary show that the plot of the rewritten tales generally follows the outline provided by his informant. In this way, Galland more or less faithfully continues the practice observed in the collection's first part, apart from narrative digression. The writing also proves Galland's command of narrative techniques. He cherished the art of prolepsis in order to arouse the readers' interest, he made a point of providing reasons that would prompt the actions of the characters, and his elegant prose revealed his consummate artistry of discourse.

Besides analyzing Galland's transmission of the plot, it is important to know whether he maintained the same writing strategy when he got further involved in creating. In the *Avertissement* (Foreword)—which appeared in 1704 on the first pages of volume one of the *Mille et une Nuits*—Galland insisted on the moral scope of the tales presented: "Pour peu même que ceux qui liront ces Contes soient disposés à profiter des exemples de vertus et de vices qu'ils y trouveront, ils en pourront tirer un avantage qu'on ne tire point de la lecture des autres Contes ("If those who will read these Tales show the faintest degree of disposition to learn from the examples of virtues and vices they will find, they will be able to draw an advantage that cannot be drawn from other tales").

The tales in *Alf layla wa-layla* are not, however, moral tales in the stricter sense, and their adaptation by Galland was not orientated in that direction. Basically, Galland limited himself to qualifying the characters morally. He would speak of a *bon vieillard* (good old man), a *père barbare* (barbarous father), or a *détestable vieille* (detestable old woman). The same technique is taken up in the second part, in which Galland additionally made a point of drawing a "moral" lesson from the tales. Thus, at the end of the "Histoire d'Aladdin," he did his utmost to provide the readers with some instructive teachings, even though he did not quite succeed. Similarly, in the "Histoire du cheval enchanté" the moral is presented in the form of a maxim, a common practice among fairy-tale writers like Charles Perrault and Mme d'Aulnoy: "Sultan de Cachemire, quand tu voudras épouser des princesses qui imploreront ta protection, apprends auparavant à avoir leur consentement" ("Sultan of Cashmire, when you wish to espouse princesses who implore your protection, learn first to obtain their consent" [Galland 3: 326; Beaumont 4: 237]). The "Histoire de l'aveugle Baba-Abdalla," built on the opposition between a good dervish and greedy Baba-Abdalla, is an even better example of Galland's effort to endow his tales with a moral tinge. Even so, Galland's vague desire to add a moral tone to Hannâ's tales does not seem to have turned into a systematic and accomplished process.

Exotic Leitmotifs

Even if Galland's work does not conform to his conventional declaration as to the moral scope of the tales, the project's didactic aim as described in the *Avertissement* in 1704 appears to be achieved: "Sans avoir essuyé la fatigue d'aller chercher ces peuples dans leurs pays, le lecteur aura ici le plaisir de les voir agir et de les entendre parler. On a pris soin de conserver leurs caractères, de ne pas s'éloigner de leurs expressions et de leurs sentiments, et l'on ne s'est écarté du texte que quand la bienséance n'a pas permis de s'y attacher" ("Without getting involved in tiring procedures to go and meet these people in their own countries, here the reader will enjoy seeing them take action and hearing them talk. We have made a point of preserving their characters and of providing a close reflection of their expressions and feelings; the text has only been altered when propriety did not allow us to be faithful to the original words").

In fact, sociocultural specifics are well rendered in the first part of the *Mille et une Nuits*. Galland's point of view apparently had not changed in 1710, when he began to work on Hannâ's tales, as can be deduced from his remarks about the first passages of Pétis de la Croix's *Mille et un Jours*: "Je lus chez le président d'Oléde environ la moitié du premier volume des *Mille et un jour*, composé à l'imitation des *Mille et une nuit*, sous le nom de M. Pétis. . . . J'y trouvai un nombre d'endroits susceptibles de critique de la part de ceux qui ont un peu de connoissance du Levant" ("I read at the President of Oléde's house about half of the first volume of the *Thousand and One Days*, composed after the fashion of the *Thousand and One Nights*, under the name of Pétis. . . . I found in this work many things that deserve criticism from those who have some knowledge of the Levant" [Omont, June 16, 1710]).

In his version of Hannâ's tales, Galland made it a point to create an Oriental atmosphere through the evocation of habits and customs as well as an abundant use of ritual phrases. Thus, the characters go to their *prière du midi* (midday prayer [Galland 3: 284]) or *prière de l'après-dinée* (afternoon prayer [3: 181]), and *se prosternent le front sur le tapis* (they prostrate themselves, heads bowed to the carpet [3: 104, 123, 288, 367]), by way of reverent salute. Their speech is loaded with phrases related to God, such as "Que Dieu vous conserve" ("May God protect you"), "Dieu prolonge vos jours" ("May God prolong yours days"), "Dieu veuille" ("God willing"). Their words often reflect their acceptance of divine decisions: "C'est la volonté de Dieu, nous devons nous y soumettre" ("It is God's will, we must accept it" [3: 408]) or "Il n'a pas plu à Dieu de me l'accorder" ("God did not consent to grant me this" [3: 197]). Furthermore, Galland did not hesitate to explain the meaning of words that in his opinion would be unknown to the reader, such as *goule* (ghoul [3: 199]) or *Nevroux* (the Persian New Year's Day [3: 291]). Similarly, he provided information about funeral rites (3: 251, 253), the levirate (3: 251, 254), and the holy towns of Islam (3: 278–79).

The rules of French classical aesthetics, which apply to the processes of both creation and translation, do not permit precise descriptions. Accordingly, it was quite difficult for Galland to convey an authentic image of the material world of Islam. However conventional the Arabic texts were written, they were often loaded with details, and Galland could not emulate these evocations of the universe of palaces, their dwellers, and the multifarious dishes they enjoyed. Hence, his portraits of young women—which did not correspond to Arabic canons in general—always evoke the qualities of the characters by using abstract epithets.[5] This is the case when he describes princess Nourounnihar in the "Histoire du prince Ahmed": "Avec une beauté singulière et avec toutes les perfections du corps qui pouvaient la rendre accomplie, cette princesse avait aussi infiniment d'esprit, et sa vertu sans reproche la distinguait entre toutes les princesses de son temps" ("To the possession of uncommon beauty, and every personal grace and accomplishment, this princess added an excellent understanding, and her unsullied virtue distinguished her among all the princesses of her time" [Galland 3: 327; Beaumont 4: 238]).

Similarly, readers will try in vain to find a precise description of architectural or culinary details. By introducing leitmotifs, Galland, however, graced his tales with a certain exotic flavor. This technique is in line with his practice already applied in the collection's first part, but now Galland employs it much more widely. Limited in number but systematically recurrent, these leitmotifs, by recalling specific connotations, convey a specific image of the Orient. Above all, three elements contribute to the creation of the external scenery: the *mosquée* (mosque), the *khan* (caravansary), and the *bain public* (public bath). In the "Histoire d'Aladdin," the text reads: "Il lui fit voir aussi les mosquées les plus belles et les plus grandes, et le conduisit dans les khans où logeaient les marchands étrangers, et dans tous les endroits du palais du sultan où il était libre d'entrer" ("He took him also to the grandest and most celebrated mosques, to the khans where the foreign merchants lodged, and through every part of the sultan's palace which he had liberty to enter" [Galland 3:

73; Beaumont 3: 302]). As for the interior decor, the *sofa* is an essential item appearing in almost every tale, from China to Africa, all the way through India, Persia, and Baghdad. It is a piece of furniture present in all houses, luxurious and modest alike, as in the home of Aladdin's mother or Ali Baba's. In the "Histoire d'Aladdin," there are no less than thirteen instances, as if the verb "s'asseoir" (to sit down) was linked to a single complement of place, the sofa. The evocation of the interior atmosphere is further enriched by the term *eunuques* (eunuchs). In Galland's universe, the presence of young women in an aristocratic milieu systematically gave rise to the appearance of *eunuques*, who were in charge of their surveillance. As to their use, these terms are frequently used on purpose and often stand isolated, although Galland also knew how to assemble them to create a splendid imagery, such as the harem that prince Firouz Schah discovers in the "Histoire du cheval enchanté": "Il vit que ceux qui dormaient étaient des eunuques noirs, chacun avec le sabre nu près de soi; et cela lui fit connaître que c'était la garde de l'appartement d'une reine ou d'une princesse, et il se trouva que c'était celui d'une princesse. . . . Il vit plusieurs lits, un seul sur le sofa, et les autres en bas. Des femmes de la princesse étaient couchées dans ceux-ci pour lui tenir compagnie et l'assister dans ses besoins, et la princesse dans le premier" ("He . . . perceived that those who where sleeping were some black eunuchs, each lying with a drawn saber by him; from which he concluded, that they were guarding the apartment of a queen or princess: of this he was soon convinced. . . . His attention was wholly engrossed by observing several beds, only one of which was raised on a sofa, the others being below it. The princess's female attendants were lying on the lower ones, and the princess herself was in the bed that was elevated" [Galland 3: 299; Beaumont 4: 211–12]).

In the "Histoire d'Aladdin," the use of another requisite, the *voile* (veil) is also emphasized by a series of repetitions, as one reads: "Elle ôta son voile en entrant et j'eus le bonheur de voir cette aimable princesse avec la plus grande satisfaction du monde ("She did, in fact, take off her veil as she went in; and I had the happiness, and the supreme satisfaction, of seeing this charming princess" [Galland 3: 95; Beaumont 4: 14]); "Quand elle eut quitté son voile et qu'elle se fut assise sur le sofa avec lui: 'Mon fils,' dit-elle" ("When she had put off her veil, and seated herself on the sofa by his side, 'My son,' said she" [Galland 3: 107; Beaumont 4: 26]).

Finally, special attention is given to the particular character of *derviche* (dervish). In the "Histoire de Baba Abdalla," the systematic repetition of the word *derviche* serves as a reference to one of the two main characters. In the summary of the "Histoire du prince Ahmed et de la fée Pari-Banou," Prince Houssain's decision to become a dervish is not mentioned and it rather appears to be a later addition, devoid of any narrative function. In the "Histoire des deux sœurs jalouses de leur cadette," Galland creates a detailed portrait of this emblematic character by using the information he had carefully recorded in his diary. Making an exceptional deviation from his usual practice, he decided in this story to describe ugliness in detailed terms:

> Il aperçut sur le bord du chemin un vieillard hideux à voir, lequel était assis sous un arbre à quelque distance d'une chaumière qui lui servait de retraite contre les injures du temps. Les sourcils blancs comme de la neige, de même que les cheveux, la moustache et la barbe, lui venaient jusqu'au bout du nez; la moustache lui couvrait la bouche, et la barbe avec les cheveux lui tombaient presque jusqu'aux pieds. Il avait les ongles des mains et des pieds d'une longueur excessive, avec une espèce de chapeau plat et fort large qui lui couvrait la tête en forme de parasol, et, pour tout habit, une natte dans laquelle il était enveloppé. Ce bon vieillard était un derviche qui s'était retiré du monde. (Galland 3: 402–3)

> He perceived a most hideous old man by the side of the road: he was seated at the foot of a tree, at some distance from a cottage, which served him as a retreat against the inclemency of the weather. His eyebrows were like snow— as was also his hair, his mustache, and his beard—and they reached to the end of his nose: his mustache quite covered his mouth, while his beard reached almost to his feet. The nails of his hands and feet were of an excessive length: and he wore on his head a kind of flat hat, very large, serving as an umbrella. The remainder of his dress was comprised in a single mat, wrapped entirely round him. This good old man was a dervish, who had long retired from the world. (Beaumont 4: 309)

Ingredients such as these were taken from genuine Arabic tales and were here employed to represent the Orient. In addition, Galland borrowed words from seventeenth-century decorative arts. Thus, in the "Histoire du prince Ahmed," the shops in the kingdom of Bisnagar displayed some of the Oriental objects that were highly prized at the court of Louis XIV: "La multitude des boutiques remplies d'une même sorte de marchandises, comme des toiles les plus fines de différents endroits des Indes, des toiles peintes des couleurs les plus vives qui représentaient au naturel des personnages, des paysages, des arbres, des fleurs, des étoffes de soie et de brocart, tant de la Perse et de la Chine et d'autres lieux, de porcelaines du Japon et de la Chine, de tapis de pied de toutes les grandeurs, le surprirent si extraordinairement qu'il ne savait s'il devait s'en rapporter à ses propres yeux" ("The multitude of shops, each filled with one kind of merchandise—such as the finest linens from different parts of India; linens painted, in the most brilliant colors, with figures, landscapes, trees, and flowers, all resembling nature; silk stuffs and brocades from Persia, China, and other places; porcelain from Japan and China; floor carpets of every size—so much surprised him, that he could scarcely withdraw his eyes from them" [Galland 3: 330; Beaumont 4: 240]).

In this manner, Galland, in the second part of his work, does not cease in his effort to diffuse knowledge about the Orient. The recurrent use of elements related to Oriental customs, habits, and religion serves to create a particular atmosphere. Since in his evocation of the material world he cannot reproduce the highly connoted models of the original Arabic tales, Galland instead takes recourse to specific leitmotifs. His exoticism results in the use of a limited number of elements that are systematically chosen and are frequently used to convey what ends up to be a highly reduced notion of "Oriental" culture: *sofa, tapis, khan, eunuques, derviche* . . . This representation—simplistic as it is—leads to stereotyping.

A Marvelous Universe

Faint as the exoticism of the scenery in the *Mille et une Nuits* may seem to modern readers, the decor is nonetheless remarkable, for Galland strives energetically to enhance it and create a marvelous oriental universe. From the beginning, the author intensifies the luxury depicted in the original tales, as when he inserts additions of *or* (gold) and *pierreries* (precious stones). In the rewriting of Hannâ's tales, this technique is used with increasing tendency and reaches its peak in the tales that are set in a royal environment. To that end, Galland intensifies the use of writing techniques that had already appeared in the first part, such as the application of positive adjectives to all kinds of elements within the universe described. Hence, the epithet *magnifique* (magnificent) is used to qualify a palace, a chamber, or a dish equally and is interchangeable with *très beau* (very beautiful), *excellent*, or *superbe*: "très beaux jardins" (very beautiful gardens), "excellents mets" (excellent dishes), "superbes festins" (lavish feasts) follow one another in the text. Superlatives are equally well represented, as "les diamants les plus gros et les plus brillants" (the biggest and most dazzling diamonds) are followed by "l'étoffe la plus riche de toutes les Indes" (the finest fabric in all the Indies). The adverb *si* (so)—recurrently used by

Galland—further contributes to the creation of his marvelous environment, as in the following extract from the "Histoire d'Aladdin": "On ne saurait exprimer la surprise et l'étonnement du sultan lorsqu'il vit rassemblées dans ce vase tant de pierreries si considérables, si précieuses, si parfaites, si éclatantes, et d'une grosseur dont il n'en avait point encore vu de pareilles" ("One could not describe how surprised and amazed the sultan was when he saw so many precious stones assembled in that vase, for they were so impressive, so magnificent, so perfect, so bright, and so big in size that they did not resemble any of the gems he had seen before" [Galland 3: 106]).

The creation of Galland's wonderful Orient also relies on an embellishment of the decor through the addition of *or* and *pierreries* used to decorate houses, plates, pieces of furniture, clothes, gifts, the goods on display at the shops, and numerous other items. The description of the slaves who are asked to take the jewels to the sultan in the "Histoire d'Aladdin" is a good example of the degree of saturation Galland's text can reach: "L'habillement de chaque esclave était si riche en étoffes et en pierreries que les meilleurs connaisseurs ne crurent pas se tromper en faisant monter chaque habit à plus d'un million. . . . Le bel air, la taille uniforme et avantageuse de chaque esclave, leur marche grave à une distance égale les uns des autres, avec l'éclat des pierreries d'une grosseur excessive enchâssées autour de leurs ceintures d'or massif dans une belle symétrie, et les enseignes aussi de pierreries attachés à leurs bonnets qui étaient d'un goût tout particulier, mirent toute cette foule de spectateurs dans une admiration si grande qu'ils ne pouvaient se lasser de les regarder" ("The dress of the slaves was of rich stuff, and so studded with precious stones that the best judges thought they did not deceive themselves in reckoning each of them at more than a million. . . . The graceful manner, elegant form, and great resemblance of each slave to the others, with their steady pace, at equal distances from each other, and the dazzling jewels which were set in their girdles of massive gold, added to the branches of precious stones, attached to their head-dresses, which were all of a particular fashion, produced, in the multitude of spectators, so excessive a degree of admiration, that they could not avert their eyes so long as they could distinguish the procession" [Galland 3: 122; Beaumont 4: 42]).

In long cumulative passages, Galland sometimes allows himself to specify the elements generically known as *pierreries*. His description of fairy Pari-Banou's palace illustrates this point: "La fée Pari-Banou le mena d'appartement en appartement, où il vit le diamant, le rubis, l'émeraude et toutes sortes de pierreries fines, employées avec les perles, l'agate, le jaspe, le porphyre, et toutes sortes de marbres les plus précieux, sans parler des ameublements qui étaient d'une richesse inestimable" ("Pari-Banou led him through the different apartments, where he beheld diamonds, rubies, emeralds, and all sorts of precious stones, mixed with pearls, agate, jasper, porphyry, and every variety of the most valuable marble, besides furniture of inestimable value" [Galland 3: 351; Beaumont 4: 262]).

The splendid scenery characterizing many tales is the setting for sumptuous celebrations, hereby reinforcing the image of a wonderful Orient. In the second part of the *Mille et une Nuits*, the display of luxury is even more impressive than in the first one. The passage evoking the reception organized by the fairy Pari-Banou in honor of Prince Ahmed is a perfect illustration of the writer's accomplished artistry, which has evolved from the original adaptation into a completely emancipated style:

> La salle où la fée fit entrer le prince Ahmed, et où la table était servie, était la dernière pièce du palais qui restait à faire voir au prince; elle n'était pas inférieure à aucune de toutes celles qu'il venait de voir. En entrant, il admira l'illumination d'une infinité de bougies parfumées d'ambre, dont la multitude, loin de faire de la confusion, était dans une symétrie bien entendue, qui faisait plaisir à voir. Il admira de même un grand buffet chargé de vaisselle d'or, que l'art rendait plus précieuse que la matière, et plusieurs choeurs de femmes, toutes d'une beauté ravissante et richement habillées, qui commencèrent un concert de voix et de toutes sortes d'instruments les plus harmonieux qu'il eût jamais entendus. Ils se mirent à table; et, comme Pari-Banou prit un grand soin de servir au prince des mets les plus délicats, qu'elle lui nommait à mesure en l'invitant à en goûter; et comme le prince n'en avait jamais entendu parler, et qu'il les trouvait exquis, il en faisait l'éloge, en s'écriant que la bonne chère qu'elle lui faisait surpassait toutes celles que l'on faisait parmi les hommes. Il se récria de même sur l'excellence du vin qui lui fut servi, dont ils ne commencèrent à boire, la fée et lui, qu'au dessert, qui n'était que de fruits, que de gâteaux et d'autres choses propres à le faire trouver meilleur. Après le dessert enfin, la fée Pari-Banou et le prince Ahmed s'éloignèrent de la table, qui fut emportée sur-le-champ, et s'assirent sur le sofa à leur commodité, le dos appuyé de coussins d'étoffe de soie à grands fleurons de différentes couleurs, ouvrage à l'aiguille d'une grande délicatesse. (Galland 3: 351–52)

The hall into which the fairy and Prince Ahmed went, and where the table was set out, was the last apartment that remained for him to see; and he found it not in the least inferior to the others he had beheld. On entering, he was much struck with an infinite number of lights, all perfumed with amber, and notwithstanding their multitude, arranged with so much symmetry that it was a pleasure to look at them. He admired also the large sideboard, covered with golden vases, the workmanship of which rendered them still more valuable; and several choirs of females, all superbly dressed, and of ravishing beauty, who began a concert of vocal and instrumental music, the most harmonious ever heard. They sat down to table, and Pari-Banou was very attentive in helping Prince Ahmed to the greatest delicacies, which she named to him as she invited him to taste them; and as they were entirely new to the prince, and he found them exquisite, he praised them as they deserved, declaring that the feast surpassed all he had ever partaken of among mortals. He spoke in the same terms of the excellence of the wines, which both he and the fairy began to drink when the dessert was served, which consisted of fruits, sweetmeats, and other things proper to give a better flavor to the wine. When the dessert was finished, Pari-Banou and Prince Ahmed quitted the table, which was instantly removed, and seated themselves at their ease on a sofa, furnished with cushions of a rich silk stuff, delicately embroidered with large flowers, in various colors. (Beaumont 4: 262–63)

A comparison of this scene with similar previous ones based on manuscripts clearly shows the evolution of Galland's style in the last stories,[6] since the author did not intend a close imitation of the Arabic texts but created oriental tales in his own manner (Larzul, *Les Mille et une Nuits*).

In conclusion, the detailed analysis of elements of language and style reveals that the insertion of the tales told by Hannâ in Galland's *Mille et une Nuits* clearly marks the transition from adaptation to creation. Nonetheless, both parts of the work are linked by a distinct continuity. This continuity consists in the overall conservation of the original tale's plot, the absence of a systematic moralization of the tales, and an effort to diffuse knowledge about the Orient. Through the evocation of customs and religion, Galland attempted to depict an Oriental atmosphere as seen from inside. Since the rules of literary creativity did not allow him to furnish a detailed representation of the material world, he was often forced to resort to abstract terms. Literary tendencies that were rather modestly present in the first part became fully developed in the second part with the use of exotic leitmotifs and lavish allusions to luxury. These are the choices upon which Galland relied to recreate the Orient of the *Mille et une Nuits*, which he shaped into an enchanting world that will endure for centuries in the realm of literature.

NOTES

1. According to seventeenth-century usage, "nuit" agrees with "une."
2. Taking into account the framed stories included in "Les aventures du calife Haroun-al-Rachid" ("The Adventures of Caliph Hârûn al-Rashîd").

3. Arabic manuscripts of the stories of Aladdin and Ali Baba were later discovered in France (Zotenberg) and England (Macdonald). It has been demonstrated, most recently by Muhsin Mahdi (3:51–86), that these manuscripts are forgeries derived from Galland's text.

4. Galland certainly knew about the existence of the Turkish manuscript of *Alf layla wa-layla* (ancien fonds no. 356) that had entered the Royal Library in 1668. Besides the primitive stories—translated by Galland—it includes some fables, the long story of 'Umar ibn Nu'mân and eight other shorter tales. Why did Galland not use at least these eight stories to supplement his French version? Did he know that they do not correspond to the stories that generally appear in the Arabic manuscripts? Was he reluctant to translate from a language that was not the original one? Or did he simply prefer Hannâ's tales? It is difficult to answer these questions with certainty because Galland does not mention anything in relation to this manuscript, neither in his *Journal* nor in his *Correspondance* (see Abdel-Halim, *Correspondance*).

5. The one exception to this rule is the portrait of princess Badroulboudour in the "Histoire d'Aladdin" (Galland 3: 94).

6. See, for instance, Galland 1: 119 and 377.

WORKS CITED

Abdel-Halim, Mohamed. *Antoine Galland: Sa vie et son oeuvre.* Paris: Nizet, 1964.

———, ed. *Correspondance d'Antoine Galland.* Édition critique et commentée. Thèse complémentaire pour le doctorat d'Etat. Paris: Sorbonne, 1964.

Beaumont, G. S., trans. *The Arabian Nights' Entertainments, or, The Thousand and One Nights: From the French of M. Galland.* 4 vols. London: E. Wilson, 1808.

Galland, Antoine, *Les Mille et une Nuits.* 3 vols. Paris: Garnier-Flammarion, 1965.

Larzul, Sylvette. "*Les Mille et une Nuits* d'Antoine Galland: Traduction, adaptation, création." *Les Mille et une Nuits en partage.* Ed. Aboubakr Chraïbi. Paris: Sindbad, 2004. 251–66.

———. *Les Traductions françaises des Mille et une Nuits: Étude des versions Galland, Trébutien et Mardrus.* Paris: L'Harmattan, 1996.

Laurens, Henri. *La Bibliothèque orientale de Barthélemi d'Herbelot: Aux sources de l'orientalisme.* Paris: Maisonneuve et Larose, 1978.

Macdonald, Duncan B. "'Ali Baba and the Forty Thieves' in Arabic from a Bodleian Ms." *Journal of the Royal Asiatic Society* (1910): 327–86.

Mahdi, Muhsin. *The Thousand and One Nights (Alf Layla wa-Layla): From the Earliest Known Sources.* Vol. 3. Leiden: Brill, 1994.

Omont, Henri, ed. "Journal parisien d'Antoine Galland (1708–15)." *Mémoires de la Société de l'Histoire de Paris et de l'Île-de-France* 46 (1919): 25–156.

Schefer, Charles, ed. *Journal d'Antoine Galland pendant son séjour à Constantinople, 1672–1673.* 2 vols. Paris: E. Leroux, 1881.

Zotenberg, Hermann. *Histoire d'Alâ al-Dîn, ou La lampe merveilleuse: Texte arabe, publié avec une notice sur quelques manuscrits des Mille et une Nuits.* Paris: Imprimerie Nationale, 1888.

3

Jacques Cazotte, His Hero Xaïloun, and Hamîda the Kaslân: A Unique Feature of Cazotte's "Continuation" of the *Arabian Nights* and a Newly Discovered Arabic Source That Inspired His Novel on Xaïloun

Joseph Sadan

The French writer Jacques Cazotte (1719–1792) deserves to be ranked among the more distinguished figures of French literature and, according to some critics, even among those occupying the front ranks. He is remembered mainly for his novel *Le diable amoureux* (*The Devil in Love*), published in 1772, a work known as a "Spanish novella" because of its special blend of fantasy and romance. Among the scholars quoted in this essay who have written about Cazotte and his *roman fantastique*, Edward Pease Shaw and Georges Décote—the most important scholar specializing in Cazotte—deserve particular mention. These two have described in detail his life, the intellectual and spiritual contexts of his tempestuous historical period, and his numerous literary works.

Cazotte is connected to the *Arabian Nights* through his work called *Suite des Mille et une Nuits* (*Continuation of the Thousand and One Nights*), which claimed to be a continuation of the famous Oriental collection of stories. The earlier editions of this work were also called *Continuation des Mille et une Nuits*, and both titles are given at the beginning of identical volumes, sometimes even on opposite title pages, as if one of them is the work's title and the other its explanation. Printed in the congenial small format of many contemporary editions of stories and legends, the work was first published—as volumes 38–41 of the famous series *Cabinet des fées*—in four volumes in Paris and Geneva in 1788–89.[1] This was the eve of the French Revolution and was just a short time before the guillotine put an end to the author's life on September 25, 1792, in the square known as the Place du Carrousel. In some library catalogues, we find the work listed under the heading of "traduction des *Mille et une Nuits*," as if it were a translation of the *Arabian Nights*. Whether or not it may be regarded as such depends on the interpretation of the term "continuation/suite" in the work's title. In this regard, two trends can be distinguished: (1) In some parts of the work, Cazotte and his "informant," Dom Denis Chavis, have pretended to rediscover materials that might have belonged to the *Arabian Nights*—similar to those tales published, a few years later, by Joseph von Hammer-Purgstall and his translator Guillaume Stanislas Trébutien. (2) The other parts contain stories not known to be included in any of the different manuscripts or redactions of the *Arabian Nights*. In these parts, Cazotte and Chavis have rather compiled stories from various manuscripts in the Royal Library that contained suitable material (Décote, *Correspondance* 100–101, 103, 107, 142–43: a letter dating from 1790 [Richer, *Passion* 1789]). A similar phenomenon is known from anthologies by various other authors, published both previously and later, such as *Les Mille et un Jours* (*The Thousand and One Days*, 1710–12) by François Pétis de la Croix (1653–1713); *Les Mille et un Quarts d'heure* (*The Thousand and One Quarters of an Hour*, 1712) and other works by Thomas-Simon Gueullette (1683–1766); or *Rosenöl* (*Oil of Roses*, 1813) by Hammer-Purgstall (1774–1856), collected from a variety of written sources that are not the *Arabian Nights*.[2]

Both trends existed in those days. Even if we prefer to interpret the work as being characterized by the former trend, the latter practice remains in the background and enriches our understanding of the contemporary attitude toward a creative translation of fiction, even allowing for the freedom of inventing or adding new passages (Shaw 80–81, especially n. 277). These aspects of creative writing in the period under consideration are also illustrated by Cazotte's question (Décote, *Correspondance* 127), whether his stories are inferior to those rendered by the famous scholar and writer Antoine Galland (1646–1715), the first French translator of the *Arabian Nights*.[3] For the present contribution, I have used a later edition of Cazotte's tales, published under the interesting title *Les veillées du sultan Schahriar avec la sultane Schéhérazade* (*The Nocturnal Conversa-*

tions of sultan Schahriar with his wife Schéhérazade, 1793). This edition faithfully reproduces the text of the first edition.

Cazotte's *Continuation des Mille et une Nuits* has not received the same amount of scholarly attention as have his novels, particularly *Le diable amoureux*. While the four-volume anthology has interested some scholars concerned with bibliographical aspects and/or the scope of Cazotte's literary works (Shaw 79–90; Décote, *L'itinéraire*), there are few indeed who have cared to evaluate any part of the author's work in depth, such as examining the moving legends contained in the *Continuation* in an attempt to identify a certain mystical-esoteric spirit, Martinism, or Cazotte's moral intentions.[4] Whatever else these legends might be, they surely mirror the refusal of the author-translator to depend solely on Arabic sources—known to Cazotte only through his "informant" Chavis. Instead, they demonstrate Cazotte's preference for working independently and creatively, as his slightly mocking attitude toward Chavis—both because of the latter's great fondness for cash and because of his naïve belief that he is the one who ought to be acknowledged as the true narrator and translator—shows. In contrast to his "informant," Cazotte strongly believed that the odd materials Chavis presented to him in his outlandish mixture of French and Italian were merely a foundation for his own truly creative literary work. Consequently, he regarded his work as much more than just a translation.[5]

Cazotte's attitude was perfectly normal within his contemporary context, since it had long been an accepted method for European writers to invent purportedly "Oriental" stories entirely lacking a textual basis in any Oriental literature. An interesting remark by Gueullette, author of *Les Mille et un Quarts d'heure*, a title that alludes to both the translation of *Les Mille et une Nuits* by Galland and the *Mille et un Jours* by Pétis de la Croix, comments on this custom.[6] Using humor and sarcasm in order to justify the way in which he expresses himself as an author supposedly creating pseudo-Oriental fiction, Gueullette wrote: "Messieurs Galland, & Pétis de la Croix, ou au moins ceux qui leur ont prêté leur plume pour rédiger & écrire les Contes Arabes, Persans & Turcs, paroissent avoir épuisé la matière, & il semble qu'il n'y ait plus qu'à glaner après eux" ("The gentlemen Galland and Pétis de la Croix, or at least those who have lent them their pen in order to edit and write the Arabic, Persian and Turkish tales, appear to have exhausted their matter, and it seems as if there is nothing to collect after them" [245]; see also Sadan 176). It should come as no surprise then, that Cazotte—although to a lesser degree than Gueullette, who, after all, used stories told to him by a "native informant"—would be aware that the creation of purportedly Oriental fiction did not exceed the bounds of accepted literary technique in his time.

The topic of the present essay is Cazotte's novel *Histoire de Xaïloun, ou l'Imbécile*.[7] This novel is an excellent sample of creative writing that is almost entirely liberated from any purported Arabic "source." I call it a novel, as it may easily comprise some eighty to ninety pages in length, depending on the format of the edition. As mentioned, such stories were often presented to the reader in volumes of quite small dimensions, so that in a modern layout the same text would probably take up fewer printed pages.

The materials Cazotte's "informant" Chavis provided were compiled in dubious French mixed with Italian. They have not survived to this day, and only a partial collection of Chavis's Arabic stories is still extant (Paris, Bibliothèque Nationale ms. arabe 3637, dated 1772).[8] Since most experts on Cazotte are not well versed in Arabic literature and the characteristics of Arabic manuscripts, other possible sources have been neglected. Moreover, the process by which the Arabic materials passed from the "informant's" versions into Cazotte's elaborated form still needs to be scrutinized. As an exemplary case, I will try to show in the following what happened to Chavis's novel *Xaïloun, ou l'Imbécile* during its development from the Arabic source to Cazotte's text. *Xaïloun*'s Arabic source text has not been discussed in previous research and is here presented for the first time.

As a general assessment, the novel about the character Xaïloun has truly suffered from unfortunate circumstances. First, it was not well received by either scholars or critics. In fact, Shaw, who knew that Cazotte intended to write a sequel to the novel, so much detested *Xaïloun* as to express his satisfaction that Cazotte's tragic fate had prevented him from doing so (87).[9] Second, scholars until now have not been able to locate any Arabic version of the novel—unlike some of the other stories of Cazotte's *Continuation* whose Arabic versions have been preserved (in the Paris manuscript arabe 3637, previously mentioned).

While perusing the manuscripts at the Bibliothèque Nationale in Paris I came upon a short story in a manuscript that presumably existed—or was written—in eighteenth-century France at a time when Cazotte was still alive. This story may well have reached Cazotte, perhaps through his "informant" Chavis. The manuscript in question bears the shelf mark arabe 3651 (fols. 215a–217a).[10] I suggest here that the story contained in this manuscript could have given Cazotte the impetus to compose his novel *Xaïloun*; at the same time, it certainly did not constitute the novel's only foundation. Quite to the contrary, the novel must be considered an original work of the author's fiction. Still, the story solves a number of problems connected with Cazotte's much longer novel. The manuscript's short text is here quoted as *Hikâyat Hamîda* (or *Humayda*) *al-Kaslân*, a title that could be translated as "The Story of Lazy Hamîda." In order to stress the similarity in sound between the protagonist's characteristic in the Arabic tale and the protagonist's name in Cazotte's novel, it may be better rendered as "The Story of Hamîda the Kaslân."

In folkloric terms, the story constitutes a case of Aarne and Thompson (henceforth AT) AT 1351: *Who Will Speak First?* It tells of a wager between an absurdly lazy husband and his wife. When the two have eaten their fill, both of them are too lazy to fetch some water to quench their thirst. In order to solve their dispute, they make a wager to keep silent, and the first one to break the silence and speak will have to fetch the water. Now a series of strange events begins. At first, a beggar enters their home. As the beggar's pleas are met with silence, he takes from the house whatever strikes his fancy. When the beggar leaves, the man follows him to see where he goes, so that he will be able to find him and regain his property after the wager will have ended. Then a friend, a barber by profession, feels offended by the man's silence and shaves half the man's beard and half his head. Another person takes his clothes, and after some other unfortunate events, Hamîda is finally caught in a fisherman's net. Those who see him think him to be some kind of demon or aquatic creature and that eating this creature's flesh will bring them good luck. Only when the knives are drawn to cut him to pieces does Hamîda's wife step in and explain that the creature is her husband, a human being, and not a monster. Hamîda then also speaks up and tells his wife that, since she has opened her mouth first, she has to go and fetch water.

In the end, the caliph Hârûn al-Rashîd learns about their story and summons the lazy couple. This ending is vaguely reminiscent of an encounter between the caliph and a lazy man that is contained in both the regular printed versions of the *Arabian Nights* and a fourteenth-century collection of Arabic tales known as *al-Hikâyât al-'ajîba* (*Wonderful Stories*; see Wehr). This older story may have constituted a precedent for Hârûn al-Rashîd's interest in lazy people, and storytellers were then able to utilize this trope down to the relatively late period to which "The Story of Lazy Hamîda" probably belongs.[11]

Cazotte rendered the Arabic word *kaslân* (lazy person) in a slightly contorted phonetic transcription as Xaïloun, which must have sounded similar to him, and then treated the word as a personal name. Even though the protagonists' names are similar in the two tales concerned, the content of Cazotte's novel *Xaïloun, ou l'Imbécile* is quite different from that of the Arabic story. In Cazotte's novel, only Xaïloun is indolent, besides not being very bright. His wife, on the contrary, is quite astute and does her best to make her husband go out and work.

Despite Xaïloun's mental debility, the author appears to sympathize with the character. Xaïloun's wife finds a way, albeit somewhat painful, to educate her husband. She beats him with a branch she broke off a bush and, when the need arises, with a harder stick as well. Xaïloun is repeatedly made to go out to work, but each time he is unable to persevere. Whenever he begins to work somewhere, he is at first happy with his job. Eventually, since bad luck continues to haunt him, he finds he is always given unpleasant tasks to perform. When working in a bakery, he first enjoys the taste of freshly baked bread but then suffers from the heat of the oven and begins to feel imprisoned. When working in a restaurant, he enjoys the smell of food and eating the leftovers, but when he is given the job of cleaning the pots, he finds the work dirty and hard. When working in the orchards, he enjoys eating fresh fruit; then suddenly the owner without previous notice decides to harness him to a plow to replace an ox that had died.

Xaïloun's misadventures also include spending a night in a cemetery. There he escapes from some gravediggers who mistake him for an animal that was overturning graves looking for dead bodies to devour. He has to run again when walking through a neighborhood whose inhabitants try to catch and beat him because they think he is a demon. One of the story's happier moments occurs when Xaïloun finds the entrance to an underground treasure trove. Even though he mistakes the golden coins for dried carrot slices, he does as his wife tells him, and together they carry the treasure back home.

Later, the couple experiences some adventures in Hârûn al-Rashîd's palace. At first the caliph tries to make Xaïloun believe that he is in heaven. Hârûn gives him a sedative, and when the victim has fallen asleep, enhances him with cosmetics and clothes him appropriately. Moreover, he puts him into a fantastic surrounding with a large number of mirrors. When Xaïloun wakes up, he believes that the palace and garden, in which a musical reception is being held in the guest's honor, is in fact heaven. Meanwhile, those present only want to have their fun with their simple and naïve guest—some humorously and others cynically.[12] Later, some servants in the middle of the night, and without the caliph's permission, try to convince the guest that he is in fact in hell and not in heaven.

Finally the caliph summons Xaïloun's wife. He is so impressed by her sagacity that he sends the couple home. Now the story reaches its climax. The originally poor and mentally deficient Xaïloun becomes the most popular man in Baghdad—with the help of his wife, and by relying on both the treasure he found and the caliph's gifts. He becomes so famous that all the city's nobles and other important people want to be invited to his house. Even so, his wife hires guards who accompany her husband everywhere and keep him from saying or doing anything stupid.

Cazotte's novel is full of elements that both Oriental readers and orientalist scholars might find indicative of a lack of sensitivity for primary sources or for knowledge gained from them. This evaluation applies in particular to the atmosphere in Baghdad and the customs of the Arab Orient. In my opinion, these elements of ignorance constitute a sound proof that Cazotte developed and made up the materials by himself. Consequently, his story is to be regarded as by and large a European composition. Some examples of these elements, divided into three groups, can be mentioned quickly.

The first group consists of elements of everyday life, topography, and so on. Certainly Cazotte was interested in "classical" Baghdad, but he mentions the Tigris (Dijla in Arabic; Cazotte's transliteration is different) only rarely; the Euphrates (al-Furât) is mentioned much more frequently. Xaïloun's she-donkey, for example, goes through the streets of Baghdad to the Euphrates in order to quench its thirst—although it is only on a map that the Euphrates would look close to the streets of Baghdad in those days. At the same time, no beast in reality would go to drink at the Euphrates when it had the Tigris at hand, flowing right through the city. As for the customs Cazotte describes, he claims, for example, to know of a custom of laying babies on fresh clay and covering them with the same material. Xaïloun tries to make a living from selling such clay, which he carries around on his she-donkey's back. I have it on the authority of people quite familiar with Iraq that according to popular custom at most a small amount of clay was placed on babies' mosquito bites or skin rashes as a kind of ointment.

A second group of elements estranged from their original meaning consists of customs in the domain of religion, cult, and spiritual values. Thus, the formulas uttered at the funeral of an important Muslim sage have no connection with any actual custom. Here Cazotte modified or perhaps made up the words, probably because his intention was to present the reader with an interrelated series of comic scenes in which the funeral formula also played a role—striking, of course, a jarring and humorous note. A more significant example demonstrating that *Xaïloun* does not reflect the faith of Islam is Cazotte's particular idea that a mosque is a place where one prays to Muhammad, and believers should not seek God there. Cazotte's hero looks for God in places where perhaps He will hear him and help him to change. Change is the great aspiration of Xaïloun the simpleton, who is aware of his condition and trusts that God will be able to improve it. God, however, is not necessarily to be found in the official place of prayer and may, as a sublime being, be approached on a spiritual plane. This is a beautiful literary idea, and it demonstrates the author's sympathy toward the handicapped. However, the concept of God displayed in the novel reflects French attitudes and the author's own spiritual or mystical observations rather than the world of Islam he supposedly describes. According to this concept, the simpleton Xaïloun prefers to address the caliph as if he were something like God in order to find out whether the apparently omnipotent sovereign would be able to fulfill his prayers.[13] In this manner, the novel reflects the unique personality of Cazotte, his own spirituality, religious hopes, and doubts, despite the fact that it is supposedly set in the ambiance of medieval Baghdad.

A third group of examples may be drawn from descriptions that in reality fit France and especially Paris much more than Baghdad. All the descriptions of courtly hospitality at the palace of Hârûn al-Rashîd illustrate the writer's knowledge of court life at Versailles. The ladies of the court, the lantern parties, the balcony from which the sovereign observes the garden party, and the orchestra from behind a balustrade, all have a distinctly French flavor.

Given these elements of indifference toward an authentic Oriental context, one may well ask: What, if anything, ties Cazotte's lengthy, involved and complicated French novel about Xaïloun to the short Arabic story about Hamîda the Kaslân? I believe the arguments are quite clear: first, the similarity in the names Kaslân and Xaïloun indicates that Cazotte probably knew the story of Lazy Hamîda; second, in both stories, although in somewhat different contexts, the wife saves her idle husband from being slaughtered with a knife or from being hanged; third, both heroes foolishly get caught in a fisherman's net; fourth, both are perceived by the public to be demons or monsters and have to cope with troubles and dangers as a result; fifth, in both the French novel and the Arabic story the couples (Xaïloun/Kaslân and his wife) are summoned to the caliph's palace at the climax of the narrative plot. In my opinion, the Arabic story constituted no more than the spark that kindled Cazotte's authentic literary talents. Accordingly, *Xaïloun* should be regarded as Cazotte's original creation that was inspired by the Arabic story of Lazy Hamîda.

In terms of literary criticism, several characteristics distinguish *Xaïloun* as a novel that, to a certain extent, is still of interest to readers at the beginning of the twenty-first century. The author's sympathy with a handicapped person demonstrates his humanist spirit. In addition, from the point of view of gender politics, Cazotte demonstrates a positive attitude toward Xaïloun's wife. She is portrayed as an intelligent woman, and the author lets her educate her husband until he ascends to the peak of Baghdad society. Moreover, Cazotte demonstrates writing skills far beyond the requirements of mere translation and follows the path of creative writing pointed out by Gueullette. Elements such as these, from the point of view of literary tools and perceptions, mark *Xaïloun, ou l'Imbécile* as a modern novel.

Appendix: *The Story of Lazy Hamîda*
Translated from the Paris Manuscript

Many tales have we heard from the storytellers, but only God knows what happened and only He possesses manifest and occult wisdom. His majesty fills the universe and He is the Sublime and the Merciful.

The storytellers relate that in the days of yore there lived in Baghdad a lazy weaver who was married to a lazy wife. One day the woman had a desire for a spicy rice dish with meat. Her husband said to her: "I am going out to buy rice and meat, so that you can cook this dish." The woman replied: "I will not cook for you! Bring the rice and the meat to the restaurant of the steak-man who will prepare the dish properly." So the husband bought rice and meat, brought them to the steak-man, and went back home. He waited there for quite some time, until he calculated that the rice and meat were certainly ready. He thus hurried over to the steak-man and came back home with the meal in his hands. At home, Hamîda the Kaslân took the vessel in which he brought back the dish from the steak-man's restaurant, filled a bowl with the dish, and served it to his wife.

"Eat!" Hamîda said to her. "But I am thirsty," said the wife, "Go and get me some water to drink!" Hamîda the Kaslân replied: "I am thirsty, too; why don't you go and get us some water to drink!"—"You are the one who should get up and bring us water," answered the wife. Hamîda said: "You're the one who should get up!" She said: "Be quiet! From now on, both of us will be silent, and the first one to break the silence will fetch water for both of us."—"I agree," the husband replied. She said: "So be it!" And he added: "Indeed so!"

The storytellers went on to describe: They both became silent and did not touch the rice and meat dish. They sat in front of their meal and looked at each other. As they sat there, a poor man came, one of those beggars who go around asking for charity,[14] and stood by the house entrance begging aloud: "Oh generous inhabitants of this house! Give me a donation, in the name of God!" No answer came from the house. Not the slightest whisper was heard. The poor man entered and saw the two sitting in front of the rice and meat dish without touching it. The poor beggar thought: "Perhaps they have been struck with the madness of silence, or they have eaten something which made them lose their sanity." The poor man said to them: "Don't bother!" and immediately reached out to the rice and meat dish with his hand, served himself some bread as well, and began eating heartily until he was contented. The rest of the food he left inside the vessel in which it had been brought from the steak-man's restaurant. He took the vessel and went his way.

Hamîda the Kaslân did indeed see the poor man, noticed quite clearly what he was up to, and even reached with his hand for a nearby rod in order to beat the beggar. But the poor man saw Lazy Hamîda's movements and removed himself quickly from there. The lazy man went out after the beggar in order at least to find out into what streets he went and where he lived. The lazy man's wife also came out and followed her husband. Thus the two of them walked a long way without uttering a word.

Suddenly one of Lazy Hamîda's friends accosted him on the road and greeted him: "Hello there!" But the lazy man did not reply. The friend said: "You scoundrel! Have you suddenly become deaf?" To this the lazy man also did not reply. His angry friend attacked him and took off his clothes. He took the jacket the lazy man was wearing and the rest of his clothes and left him naked as on the day of his birth. None of the bystanders tried to intervene or to retrieve Hamîda's clothes.

Another friend of the lazy man happened to come by, a barber by profession. The barber, very good at his craft and possessing a shrewd and clownish character, asked him: "Hamîda, who took your clothes?" but the lazy man did not answer. His friend the barber then threatened: "By God, if you do not answer me I shall shave off your beard." But the lazy man persisted in his silence. The barber then took out his razor and shaved off half the lazy man's beard. Still the lazy man remained silent. The barber went on to shave off half his friend's head and his brows. In such a ridiculous state he left him and went away.

Suddenly a third friend appeared, a painter by profession, and asked the lazy man: "My dear Hamîda, what happened to you? What is this strange state that you are in?" Hamîda persisted in his silence and said nothing in response. The painter threatened: "If you do not answer I shall paint the remaining half of your beard and add all kinds of decorations." But the lazy man did not open his mouth. So his friend painted the remaining half of his beard and decorated his body with dots and paint spots in all colors—red, yellow, blue, green, and black. When he finished decorating he went away.

Lazy Hamîda continued wandering and eventually arrived at the bank of the Tigris. He thought he would wash off the paint in the water of the river. All this time his wife continued to follow her husband. A certain man, an acquaintance of Hamîda's, was standing on the riverbank and noticed the spotted lazy man. The acquaintance said to him: "Hamîda, how (strange) you look!" and pushed the lazy man into the river. Hamîda floundered in the water and tried to extricate himself from the river by swimming, but no one came to his aid. At that very moment a Tigris fisherman arrived and spread his net in the hope of catching some fish, but the net caught Lazy Hamîda, who had grasped it in order not to be carried away by gusts of wind and the river current. When the fisherman pulled his net in, it felt heavy, and so he quickly called others to help him to pull it out. The people looked and saw the figure of a kind of big fish holding on to the net. They pulled the net and took the lazy man out of it to the riverbank.

Those who were gathered there saw the colorfully decorated and spotted Hamîda and cried out: "This is the Old Man of the Sea!" The fisherman tied Hamîda tightly with rope and carried him through the city streets, shouting: "The flesh of this creature heals backaches, helps those who suffer from pains in their tailbone, and is good for pregnancy and bearing children!" One of the passers-by asked him: "How much does (the weight of) one *ratl* of the Old Man of the Sea's flesh cost?"[15]—"Go to Hell!" answered the fisherman: "What *ratl*? Can you not see that even a tiny piece of this creature's flesh is worth a silver *dirham*?" All the while Hamîda's wife was standing there, watching in silence. A second passerby intervened and said: "Here, take two *dirhams*." A third passerby offered: "Take ten *dirhams*."

The storytellers went on to describe: Those who were gathered there offered many *dirhams* and asked: "Slaughter the creature, and let us immediately divide its flesh, before a large crowd gathers here, for then you will not be able to hand out anything because of the crowding." But when the fisherman approached the creature in order to slaughter it, he noticed that it was staring at him and trying to tell him something with its eyes. The fisherman was frightened and thought that he was in the presence of a demon. "Go away!" he shouted to the gathered crowd. The man then tied the lazy man's feet in rope, took out a sharp knife and was about to slaughter him.

Only then did the lazy man's wife begin to scream and cry out: "This is my husband! This is my husband!" The wife then also turned to her husband and said: "You stupid fool! Why don't you open your mouth and tell them?"—"You spoke first," said the husband. "And now get up and get us some water to drink!" Then the wife told those gathered there everything that had happened between her and her husband. They all laughed and mocked the couple. This extraordinary story reached the caliph, who ordered that these two lazy people be summoned to him. When they arrived he demanded of them: "Tell me exactly what happened." So they told him the tale. The caliph burst out laughing and told the lazy man: "Ask me for anything you want." The man answered: "I ask the gracious caliph to give an order that the royal herald proclaim about me in the city streets thus: 'Inhabitants of Baghdad listen! Come and see the laziest of men!'" The caliph then issued a royal proclamation on this matter. The herald placed Hamîda on a horse, led him through the city streets and announced in a loud voice: "This is the laziest of men!" And the horse trotted and passed round the streets of Baghdad with its rider.

This is the story of the lazy man and his wife, thus it reached our ears, and we have passed it on in its entirety. Praise be to God for all His deeds.

NOTES

1. I would like to thank the British Library for providing me with photocopies of the stories I needed from Cazotte's *Les veillées*.
2. For the influence of Gueullette and other authors on Cazotte see Shaw 28; Dufrenoy 1: 54 ff. and 2: 344–45; Trintzius 134; and Décote, *L'itinéraire*.
3. Décote (*L'itinéraire* 353–81 and 544–49) dedicates an entire chapter to Cazotte's Oriental stories.

4. The term "Martinism" here refers to the doctrines of *cohen-élus* and the movement inspired by Martines de Pasqually (d. 1774) and later by Louis-Claude de Saint-Martin (d. 1803), which was close to the ideas of the early Freemasons. See Shaw 82–83 and 87; Trintzius pass. and 132, where the author speaks about the *Arabian Nights*, mysticism, and a certain "madness" that made Cazotte create these stories; see also Richer, *Aspects* 55–82; Décote, *L'itinéraire*, especially 365, 377; and Taittinger 112–17.

5. Shaw (79–80) also hints at the relationship and dispute between the "informant" and the writer, the latter of whom preferred his techniques of adaptation and creation to mere literal translation; see also Rieger 45; Décote, *Correspondance* 100; and Décote, *L'itinéraire* 355–56. Richer (*Passion* 53–56) defines Chavis as Lebanese or Syrian of origin and as a member of the Christian Melkite church (since he belonged to the St. Basil congregation). The very fact that the manuscript arabe 1445 (*Catéchisme des Druzes*) of the Bibliothèque Nationale in Paris is defined in a relatively recent catalogue (Vajda and Sauvan 305) as having been written either by (as the colophon claims) or for a certain "Shawush" (as read by the authors of the catalogue who did not recognize or identify Chavis) in Acre probably indicates that Chavis had relations with this town or region, in which a certain number of Melkites lived. Here, I would like to thank the librarians of the Bibliothèque Nationale in Paris who drew my attention to the incomplete reference in the catalogue.

6. As to the general background and a list of anthologies whose titles begin with *Mille et un/une*, see Dufrenoy.

7. This is the novel's title as given in the 1793 *Veillées du sultan* edition, at 1: 286. In Décote, *L'itinéraire* 356, the title is given as *L'Imbécile ou l'histoire de Xaïloun*.

8. See Slane 621. According to my examination, the ms. arabe 3637 could have been written by a non-Arab hand or by someone who did not know how to hold and use an oriental pen. I have also examined the ms. arabe 3613 (*Alf layla*—the *Arabian Nights* in Arabic; see Slane 619) on which one of the librarians wrote with a pencil—probably a century ago—that it belonged to Chavis. If one also takes into account the manuscript arabe 1445 (mentioned above), it turns out that the respective handwritings differ to the extent that they are certainly not written by the same hand. Maybe the first is a sample of Chavis's handwriting and the others samples of handwritings of scribes he employed?

9. For further criticism see Chauvin 5: 137 and 6: 89; at 7: 156, Chauvin criticizes the "endless repetition" in this story; the Bastien edition (see Cazotte, *Le fou de Baghdad*) totally omits this novel. See also Décote, *L'itinéraire* 545, n. 16; Décote, *Correspondance* 128, n. 8; Milner 1: 155.

10. I have adapted the title from the end of the story; it is lacking at the beginning. Slane (623) mentions the tale as *Histoire d'un homme paresseux et de sa femme* (*Story of a Poor Man and his Wife*). Vajda (567) invents the title *Qissat al-hâ'ik* (*The Story of the Weaver*), as the story actually qualifies the protagonist as a weaver. Weavers, by the way, in classical Arabic literature belong to the stock characters of jocular prose, being represented as the ultimate incorporation of stupidity. The title mentioned in the manuscript is *Hikâyat al-Kaslân* (*The Story of the Lazy Man*); the name Hamîda appears in the story itself. A collection of tales older than the eighteenth

century (fol. la, colophon: 1696), the stamps (*estampilles*) indicate that our manuscript was probably not at the Bibiothèque Nationale (Bibl. du Roi) when Chavis was visiting the library (Décote, Corresp., 100; see 101, 107, 128n8: how Cazotte disdained his literal "translation"); but was the Hamîda story in Chavis's own manuscripts (ibid. 109 and n6) exactly the same version?

11. Cazotte himself described an encounter between the caliph Hârûn al-Rashîd and a crazy old man from Baghdad (Cazotte, *Fou*) many years before he made the acquaintance of his "informant" and created his novel on the simpleton Xaïloun (Trintzius 133). Both the *Arabian Nights* (*Alf layla* [Bulaq edition] 1: 473 ff.) and Wehr's *al-Hikâyât al-'ajîba* contain the story of the absurdly lazy man named Abû Muhammad the Kaslân who was invited to the palace by the caliph Hârûn al-Rashîd in order to tell his story (see Miquel 143 ff.; Marzolph). The purpose of this invitation and the story's plot have little to do with the lazy man's idleness, and only one anecdote about his laziness when he was a young man is reported. In the Mardrus translation of the *Arabian Nights* (2: 252–59), this Kaslân is called "Abou Môhammad les-Os-Mous" (Abû Muhammad Soft-Bones).

12. According to Chauvin (7: 157), this episode is adapted from the *Arabian Nights* story of "The Sleeper Awakened" (Chauvin 5: 272).

13. Cazotte vaguely knew that the term caliph in some way refers to God. He even labels the caliph Hârûn al-Rashîd as "le vicaire de Dieu sur la terre" ("God's representative on earth" [Décote, *L'itinéraire* 379]; for this formula, see Goldziher as well as Crone and Hinds). In an Arabic tale included in a late Ottoman manuscript, a simpleton sees the sultan and concludes that he is in the presence of God (*Hikâyât*, Cambridge, University Library, ms. Add. 3484, fols. 10b–11a).

14. The Arabic term employed here is *ju'aydî*, denoting a pauper. The Wortley-Montague manuscript of the *Arabian Nights* (*Alf layla*, Oxford, Bodleian Library Or. 552), a relatively recent text compiled in the second half of the eighteenth century, contains a series of *ju'aydî*-tales in which the word refers to idlers who make a living by begging, searching through rubbish and getting themselves into adventures in which they employ their cleverness and cunning.

15. The supposed virtues of the flesh of the Old Man of the Sea would seem to indicate that this creature is not very similar to his namesake, the dangerous straplegged monster making its appearance in Sindbad the Sailor's fifth voyage as related in the *Arabian Nights* (*Alf layla* [Bulaq edition] 2: 27; for Indian and other sources of this legend, see Chauvin 7: 23–24). In fact, the ideas connected here to this creature recall the Sea Man, also called Old Man of the Sea, found in the zoographic encyclopedia compiled by al-Damîrî (1: 40) and other medieval Arabic authors. These authors mention a humanoid creature living in the sea that has a white beard and brings luck to all those who see it.

WORKS CITED

Aarne, Antti, and Stith Thompson. *The Types of the Folktale: A Classification and Bibliography.* 2nd rev. ed. Helsinki: Academia Scientiarum Fennica, 1961.
Alf layla wa-layla. Cairo: Bulaq P, 1836–37.

Alf layla wa-layla. Oxford: Bodleian Library, ms. Or. 552 (Worltey-Montague).

Alf layla wa-layla. Paris: Bibliothèque Nationale de France, ms. arabe 3613 (believed to be the copy of Denis Chavis).

Catéchisme des Druzes (Su'âl wa-jawâb). Paris: Bibliothèque Nationale de France. Ms. arabe 1445.

Cazotte, Jacques. *Continuation/Suite des Mille et une Nuits, contes arabes, traduits littéralement par Dom Chavis . . . et rédigés par Monsieur Cazotte (Le Cabinet des fées,* vols. 38–41). Paris and Geneva: Bard, Manget, 1788–89.

———. *Le fou de Bagdad, ou les géans: Œuvres badines et morales, historiques et philosophiques.* Vol. 3. Paris: J.-F. Bastien, 1817. 483–89.

———. *Les veillées du sultan Schahriar avec la sultane Schéhérazade.* Geneva, 1793.

Chauvin, Victor. *Bibliographie des ouvrages arabes ou relatifs aux arabes, publiés dans l'Europe chrétienne de 1810 à 1885.* 12 vols. Liège: Vaillant-Carmanne, and Leipzig: Harrassowitz, 1892–1922.

Crone, Patricia, and Martin Hinds. *God's Caliph: Religious Authority in the First Centuries of Islam.* Cambridge: U of Cambridge P, 1986.

al-Damîrî, Kamâl al-Dîn. *Hayât al-hayawân al-kubrâ.* Cairo: al-Matba'a al-Khayriyya, 1891–92.

Décote, Georges. *Correspondance de Jacques Cazotte: Édition critique.* Paris: Klincksieck, 1982.

———. *L'itinéraire de Jacques Cazotte: De la fiction littéraire au mysticisme politique.* Geneva: Droz, 1984.

Dufrenoy, Marie-Louise. *L'Orient romanesque en France.* Montreal: Beauchemin, 1946–47.

Goldziher, Ignace. "Du sens propre des expressions Ombre de Dieu, Khalîf de Dieu." *Revue de l'Histoire des Religions* 25 (1897): 331–38.

Gueullette, Thomas-Simon. *Les Mille et un Quarts d'heure (Le Cabinet des fées,* vols. 21–22). Geneva and Paris: Barde, Manget, 1786.

Hadîth [Hamîda] al-kaslân. Paris, Bibliothèque Nationale de France, ms. arabe 3651, fols. 215a–217a.

Hammer-Purgstall, Joseph Freiherr von. *Rosenöl, oder Sagen und Kunden des Morgenlandes.* Stuttgart: J. G. Cotta, 1813.

———. *Der Tausend und einen Nacht noch nicht übersetzte Mährchen, Erzählungen und Anekdoten.* 3 vols. Stuttgart: J. G. Cotta, 1823–24.

Hikâyât. Cambridge, University Library, ms. Add. 3484.

Hikâyât. Paris, Bibliothèque Nationale de France, ms. arabe 3637.

Mardrus, Joseph Charles Victor. *Les Mille et une Nuits.* Paris: R. Laffont, 1980.

Marzolph, Ulrich. "Narrative Strategies in Popular Literature: Ideology and Ethics in Tales from the *Arabian Nights* and Other Collections." *Middle Eastern Literatures* 7 (2004): 171–82.

Milner, Max. *Le Diable dans la littérature française: De Cazotte à Baudelaire, 1772–1861.* 2 vols. Paris: J. Corti, 1960.

Miquel, André. *Sept contes des Mille et une Nuits, ou Il n'y a pas de contes innocents.* Paris: Sindbad, 1981.

Pétis de la Croix, François. *Les Mille et un Jours.* Ed. P. Sebag. Paris: C. Bourgois, 1980.

Richer, Jean. *Aspects ésotériques de l'oeuvre littéraire.* Paris: Dervy, 1980.

———. *La Passion de Jacques Cazotte.* Paris: G. Trédaniel, 1988.

Rieger, Dietmar. *Jacques Cazotte: Ein Beitrag zur erzählenden Literatur des 18. Jahrhunderts.* Heidelberg: C. Winter, 1969.

Sadan, Joseph. "L'Orient pittoresque et Aladin retrouvé." *Emergence des francophonies.* Ed. David Mendelson. Limoges: Presses Universitaires, 2001. 169–84.

———. *Et il y eut d'autres nuits.* Paris: Médicis-Entrelacs, 2004.

Shaw, Edward Pease. *Jacques Cazotte (1719–1792).* Cambridge: Harvard UP, 1942.

Slane, William MacGuckin de. *Catalogue des manuscrits arabes. Bibliothèque Nationale (de France), Département des manuscrits.* Paris: Bibliothèque Nationale, 1883–95.

Taittinger, Claude. *Monsieur Cazotte monte à l'échafaud.* Paris: Perrin, 1988.

Trébutien, Guillaume Stanislas, trans. *Contes inédits des Mille et une Nuits, ouvrage faisant suite aux différentes éditions des Mille et une Nuits, extraits de l'original arabe par de Hammer,* traduits en Français. Paris: Dondey-Dupré, 1828.

Trintzius, René. *Matérialisme et spiritualisme: Jacques Cazotte ou le XVIIIe siècle inconnu.* Paris: Athéna, 1944.

Vajda, Georges. *Index général des manuscrits arabes musulmans de la Bibliothèque Nationale de Paris.* Paris: Centre National de la Recherche Scientifique, 1953.

———, and Yvette Sauvan. *Bibliothèque Nationale (de France). Département des manuscrits. Catalogue des manuscrits arabes.* Vol. 2.3: *Manuscrits musulmans.* Paris: Bibliothèque Nationale, 1985.

Wehr, Hans, ed. *Kitâb al-hikâyât al-'ajîba wa-'l-akhbâr al-gharîba: Das Buch der wunderbaren Erzählungen und seltsamen Geschichten.* Wiesbaden: Steiner, 1956.

Texts and Contexts of the *Arabian Nights*

4

Creativity, Random Selection, and *pia fraus:* Observations on Compilation and Transmission of the *Arabian Nights*

Heinz Grotzfeld

The earliest proof of the very existence of the work titled *Alf layla* is the paper fragment published by Nabia Abbott. The last decisive act in the textual history of the work now commonly known as the *Thousand and One Nights* (henceforth: *Nights*) took place with the printed editions Bulaq 1835 and Calcutta 1839–42, which, by their wide distribution, put an end to the development of the work's Arabic text. In between these two points, there is a period of a thousand years during which the work has changed continually. Except for the fragment mentioned above, dating from the middle of the ninth century, no texts or fragments of texts of *Alf layla* have survived from before the second half of the fifteenth century. Nevertheless, the few times the work is mentioned in Arabic literature allow us to assume that the development of the manuscripts of *Alf layla wa-layla* and their embedded stories prior to the fifteenth century did not differ decisively from the development we can observe in the extant manuscripts dating from the end of the fifteenth century up to the 1830s. The work's continual change is already mirrored by significant variants in the two earliest references. In a note by the tenth-century historian al-Masʿûdî (the extant version of his *Murûj al-dhahab* was written in 943 and revised in 947; see Pellat), Dînâzâd is the slave-girl (*jâriya*) or—according to other manuscripts of Masʿûdî—Shahrazâd's nurse (*dâya*);[1] in the passage included in the *Fihrist* (Catalogue) of Ibn al-Nadîm, dating from 987, Dînâzâd is the king's stewardess (*qahramâna*). In the extant texts of *Alf layla*, she is, as everybody knows, Shahrazâd's sister.

Ibn al-Nadîm's note is particularly valuable. He mentions that he has seen the book in its entirety several times.[2] Moreover, he adds that it contains a thousand nights but less than two hundred stories. In the first place, this remark proves the existence of complete sets of *Alf layla* in Ibn al-Nadîm's time. From the fact that he explicitly states "in its entirety" (*bi-tamâmihi*), we may even infer that complete sets were rather an exception, and that incomplete sets and fragmentary copies were far more common. The title and the first text page of the fragment published by Abbot prove that such fragmentary manuscripts of the *Nights* already existed in the ninth century.

Ibn al-Nadîm's remark that the book "contains less than two hundred stories, for the narration of a story often lasted through several nights," has to be evaluated against the background of the book's Persian title *Hazâr afsân[e]*, "A Thousand Stories." This title gave rise to a misunderstanding that prompted peculiar developments, already in the tenth century. Originally, the term *hazâr*, "a thousand," within the title only indicated a large number. When it was taken literally, it became obvious that "a thousand" did not correspond to the actual number of stories. The exaggerated expectation of readers seeking exactly the number of stories mentioned in the book's title, no doubt, has stimulated the Arabic author al-Jahshiyârî (d. 942) to start his ambitious project of compiling a book truly containing a thousand full-length stories "each part independent in itself and unconnected with another." According to Ibn al-Nadîm's account, al-Jahshiyârî eventually brought together 480 nights, "for each night a complete story consisting of fifty folios, more or less." From these notes we may deduce that story cycles or frame stories—like that of "The Merchant and the Jinni" at the beginning of the later standard texts of the *Nights*—were typical of the book *Alf layla*, and that the portions told by Shahrazâd during the consecutive single nights did not really "fill" the nights. Most likely, these portions did not differ much from what can be observed in the first nights of the extant texts, namely, some 35–40 lines.

Ibn al-Nadîm's account of al-Jahshiyârî's project does not mention whether al-Jahshiyârî's Nights were embedded in the frame tale of *Alf layla* (the stories being told by Shahrazâd) or whether the single elements (or chapters) of his collection were simply denoted as "nights." The latter assumption is, in my opinion, more likely. Nevertheless, though more or less disconnected from *Alf layla*, al-Jahshiyârî's collection, or rather what was left of it some centuries later, appears to have contributed to the repertoire of *Alf layla*.

I think we can assume that al-Jahshiyârî was not an isolated case. Complete sets of *Alf layla* could not be found easily, while at the same time there was a demand for them. This situation must have stimulated other individuals to compose or assemble complete sets out of the materials at hand, which consisted of fragments of a set of the *Nights* and other, often independent stories. Complete sets, however, never survived for a long time. In Egypt, complete sets of the recension directly preceding the one known as Zotenberg's Egyptian Recension (henceforth ZER) must have been extremely scarce in the last quarter of the eighteenth century. In consequence, there was a need to compose a new recension—ZER. This new recension, of which complete copies could be easily purchased in Cairo at the beginning of the nineteenth century, became scarce in the late 1820s (Lane, *Manners* 420), hereby again prompting a new recension—the Reinhardt manuscript in Strasbourg (see Chraïbi). In the course of some forty to fifty years, a new recension disintegrated and was replaced by a new composition prepared both from parts of the preceding recensions and additional materials that were not included previously in a recension of the *Nights*. In this manner, the development of manuscript tradition prevented the formation of a canonical repertoire of *Alf layla*. This assumption makes it understandable why the manuscripts of the *Nights* dating from the fifteenth and sixteenth centuries differ from one another not only as to wording but also as to both repertoire and order of embedded stories. Most of these manuscripts are fragments of different recensions; others constitute new recensions in which it is possible to distinguish echoes of two or three different preceding recensions.

For the compiler, fragmentary manuscripts of the *Nights* had the advantage that they easily lent themselves to his purpose. They were already divided into nights and they contained the relevant formulas and often a few resuming words that connected the narration to that of the preceding night. New materials required a preparatory processing. They had to be divided, preferably so that the narration was interrupted just before a culminating point. But even interruptions at less prominent points were acceptable, provided the king could be imagined to be curious about the continuation. Night formulas had to be inserted, and a transition had to be formulated for Shahrazâd, so she could continue on the very level where she had interrupted her narration.

The dividing of stories incorporated into the repertoire of the *Nights* deserves our special attention, for just as Edward W. Lane disliked the narration's "tedious interruptions," so did his forerunners already in the tenth century. Originally, the structure of the single nights was merely a literary convention. The interruption of the story was justified because "morning overtook Shahrazâd and she lapsed into silence"; Shahrazâd need not tell her story for hours on end and actually "fill" the night. Only al-Jahshiyârî's stories, covering an entire night from beginning to end, transgressed this literary convention.

Against this backdrop, it is interesting to see that in the extant manuscripts of *Alf layla*, the portions narrated by Shahrazâd do not vary significantly. In the cycle of "The Trader and the Jinni," which has to be considered a very old if not a genuine element (perhaps even the only genuine one extant) of the repertoire of the *Nights*, their length varies between some 35 to 45 lines in Muhsin Mahdi's edition (1984), corresponding to about the same amount of lines in the Galland manuscript. In the tale of the two viziers "Nûr al-Dîn 'Alî and His Son Badr al-dîn Hasan" (nights 72–101) and again in the Hunchback cycle (nights 102–70), both of which have been incorporated into the repertoire of the *Nights* comparatively late, probably during the first half of the fifteenth century, their length (including some verses) rarely exceeds 35 lines, with the exception of the first nights of the first mentioned tale.[3] I do not think that we have to interpret this as a proof that the original literary convention was still fully accepted. I rather understand the convergent lengths of the story portions as the continuation of an older standard. The portions told by Shahrazâd had always been around 40 lines; they had never been long enough to last through an entire night. Obviously, such a standard length was quite convenient for compilers aiming to compose a new complete collection of the *Nights,* because it allowed an economic dealing with the materials at their hands. It would be unjustified to label this procedure of filling the single nights with only 30 to 40 lines of text a fraud. Rather, I see a *pia fraus,* or deceptive suggestion, in the fact that, by this literary convention, readers are expected to believe that the small portions of text told by Shahrazâd fill the rest of the night until the break of day.

At the same time, some true attempts of cheating can be observed in the transmission of the text. In three manuscripts presenting "The Story of 'Umar ibn al-Nu'mân" as a part of the repertoire of the *Nights*, the numbering of the nights is discontinuous, whereas the text continues without a break. The Tübingen manuscript (MA VI 32; N'a in Mahdi) contains this story in nights 283–464, 475, and 529–41; the Manchester manuscript (John Ryland's Library, Arabic 646; N in Mahdi) in nights 280–470 and 530–41; the Maillet manuscript (Paris, Bibliothèque Nationale de France, arabe 3612; F in Mahdi), which is essentially a transcription of texts belonging to at least three different recensions—with their original night numbers—without any serious attempt to integrate these texts into a new recension, contains the story in question in nights 277–310 and 411–65,[4] followed by a text block of twenty folios without night breaks and completed by fourteen nights without numbers.

Such leaps in the numbering of the nights are not confined to the transmission of the text of the story of 'Umar ibn al-Nu'mân. In a Paris manuscript (Bibliothèque Nationale de France, arabe 3619), constituting the only extant sixth and final volume of a recension different from ZER and its precursors, night 909 is immediately followed by night 1000. This recension contains an elaborate conclusion of the frame story, quite different from that of ZER; it is prepared by the last story told by Shahrazâd, here the tale of "Baybars and the Sixteen Constables." There is an insignificant lacuna in the text but overall no real gap, so the leap from 909 to 1000 has no other purpose than deluding the reader into thinking that this copy of the *Nights* really contains one thousand and one nights.

Skipping one numbered night is a phenomenon that occurs quite often and may be regarded as excusable; in most cases, it is probably unintentional. But skipping nights in the numbering by four, five, or more, a phenomenon that occurs from time to time, is certainly intentional and can be compared to the above-mentioned leaps in numbering.

It is very unlikely that sets comprising stories with such a discontinuous numbering of nights were transcribed in order to sell them to the copyist's regular customers, or that they were commissioned.[5] Like other products of inferior quality, called *bâzârî* ("pertaining to the market") in colloquial Arabic, they were tailored to a market of less demanding customers not expected to raise any complaints about the shortcomings of a certain manuscript. The leaps therefore constitute a precious proof that there was a steady demand for complete sets of *Alf layla*.

As to the insertion of night formulas, we can distinguish two types of compilers or copyists: those who obviously regard these formulas as an unpleasant duty and those for whom they are a means of inflating the text. Both types of compilers start with a relatively long formula, by telling that morning overcame Shahrazâd, and so forth, that in the following night—which was the night number so-and-so—the king and Shahrazâd went to bed, and such, and that finally Dînâzâd asked her sister to continue the story she had interrupted (or to tell the story promised) in the preceding night. The former group of compilers does not repeat the formula every night in its full length. Very often, the formula is shortened, most frequently the part at the beginning of the new night. This is the case, for example, in the Galland manuscript. In general, this manuscript contains an elaborate formula at the transition from one story or story cycle to the next one, that is, between a night in which Shahrazâd completes a story (probably promising to tell a new one in the following night, if the king lets her live on) and the following one, in which she starts to tell her new story. In the other nights, the formula is often reduced to a minimum. The latter group of compilers repeats the formula meticulously in its full length every night. In the Strasbourg manuscript (see Chraïbi), in which the story portions of the nights vary between two and a half and three and a half pages (rarely four pages), the night formulas comprise half a page, so that 15 percent and more of that particular manuscript is filled by nothing else than night formulas.

In catalogues of Arabic manuscripts, one usually encounters manuscripts classified as parts or fragments of *Alf layla wa-layla*. Mostly, this classification is justified. Manuscripts in which the stories are divided into numbered nights are no doubt parts of a recension of the *Nights*, even if their numbering, such as that of the Tübingen manuscript of " 'Umar ibn al-Nu'mân," does not harmonize with the numbering found in the familiar recensions. Besides the manuscripts with numbered nights, manuscripts in which the stories are divided into unnumbered nights, such as the manuscript Gotha (MS A 2637, 1), undoubtedly constitute fragments of recensions of the *Nights*.

In theory, one should also expect to find texts in the very process of being prepared for inclusion within a recension of the *Nights*. I know of only one such manuscript where we have reason to assume that it reflects this kind of preparatory process. In the Tübingen manuscript of "Sûl and Shumûl" (in which the first quarter of the story is missing), the first third of the extant text is divided into (unnumbered) nights and night formulas have been inserted, while the rest of the story remains unchanged. This state of the manuscript may be explained by the fact that somebody started to prepare the story for inclusion within a recension of the *Nights* but failed to complete it. In the present condition, the story was not (yet) suitable for incorporation into the *Nights*, and, in fact, no recension of the *Nights* including the story is known. Probably, the incomplete editorial adaptation is no more than a false label. It pretends that the story was already a part of *Alf layla* so as to benefit from the collection's popularity.

There are numerous manuscripts containing single stories that are also contained in recensions of *Alf layla* and for that reason are classified as *Alf layla* texts. This evaluation applies to tales like those of Tawaddud, the City of Brass, or the Ebony Horse. The stories in these single manuscripts, however, do not have night breaks, nor is there any evidence that such breaks were either intended or eliminated. In some manuscripts, such as two fragments of the *Nights* preserved in Berlin (Ahlwardt nos. 9103 and 9104), the night formulas and Shahrazâd's words recapitulating the passage in which she has interrupted her story in the preceding night have been crossed out. It seems to me that these are exceptions; the "editing" probably took place very late, when the printed editions of *Alf layla* provided (what was thought to be) the complete authentic text of *Alf layla*, so there was no longer any demand for manuscripts of the work, particularly when these were incomplete. Editing these texts—which constitute fragments of a recension other than ZER—and turning them into a "new" work was certainly a means for improving their market value.

Manuscripts of stories lacking the formal elements of night breaks and night formulas presumably do not derive from a corpus of the *Nights* but are part of an independent transmission. This assumption can easily be confirmed, as a closer inspection of the relevant texts in general shows a series of details in which the version of such stories differs from those in the *Nights*. I would like to emphasize that quite often—as David Pinault has shown—the "independent" versions are better, or less deteriorated, than those in the *Nights*. This is not surprising, because in many cases, the "independent" manuscripts are a hundred or more years older than the manuscript of the *Nights* in which the corresponding versions have been incorporated. The compilers, by enlarging the corpus of the *Nights*, have preserved many a story that would have otherwise been lost. While this fact deserves to be appreciated, one should not disregard the fact that they have chosen what was nearest at hand.

Scholars dealing with the *Nights*, particularly those who do not know Arabic, often ignore these facts, but even scholars of Arabic tend to neglect them. Most researchers regard ZER—accessible through Burton's or Littmann's translation—as somehow canonical. On the one hand, when a specific research problem deals only with the components of a given repertoire of the *Nights*, the textual condition of the version included in the *Nights* is not necessarily relevant, and "independent" parallels that might have preserved better versions can be neglected. On the other hand, if research focuses on the narration, one should always consider the fact that the compilers were not philologists by modern standards. They would not collect a number of manuscripts of a given story with the intention of choosing the best version, nor did they intend to produce a critical edition. Instead, they simply included the particular textual version of a story they had encountered by chance.

On the whole, the various repertoires of the *Nights* give the impression that the later a compilation was produced, the more it appears to be patched together at random rather than to result from deliberate organization. Some sequences of stories have no doubt been arranged intentionally, such as those relating to subject, structure, and protagonists or their names. Only rarely, however, can these attempts at organizing the material be attributed to the compilers. In most cases there is evidence, or at least reason, to assume that such sequences were already encountered in the materials the compilers had at their disposal. These materials normally comprised fragments of older recensions of the *Nights* or collections of stories already arranged by subject. In some cases, the compilers appear to have enlarged sequences of stories already existing by adding a similar story when assembling their new repertoire.[6] In other cases, the actual creation of such a sequence might result from their effort, such as by adding "The Story of the Saʿîdî and His Frankish Wife" after "Miryam the Belt-Maker." In a similar manner, in subsequent manuscript transmission, the compilers have expanded sequences of anecdotes by adding other anecdotes, such as in the repertoire of Bulaq I/Calcutta II as compared to that of von Hammer's manuscript (copied thirty years earlier).[7]

Traces of creativity are more frequent in the older repertoires, of which we know only fragments—especially in the story cycles at the beginning of *Alf layla*. The narrative cycle of "The Porter and the Three Ladies of Baghdad" appears to be an elaborated version of a much shorter cycle that has been enlarged by frivolous scenes, long verse passages, and the introduction of the three calendars as well as the caliph. Unfortunately, the oldest extant version of this cycle is already partly deteriorated. The Hunchback cycle, meanwhile, still displays in its present version the features characteristic of a perfectly planned composition. In order to continuously raise the tension, the compiler has rearranged the stories he has chosen to incorporate into the planned story cycle and partly rewritten the text.[8]

The discovery of the *Nights* by the Europeans implied a new quality of creativity as well as a new quality of *pia fraus*. Antoine Galland, who introduced the *Nights* to Europe, never had a complete text at his disposal. All his efforts to procure the text of a complete manuscript of the *Nights* failed; but before he could have realized that it would be extremely difficult, if not impossible, to find a complete text, he had already inserted the stories of "Sindbad the Sailor" into the repertoire of his *Mille et une Nuits* (nights 69–80). He had translated this story cycle from an independent manuscript long before he learned that it was apparently part of a larger collection titled "Les Mille et une Nuits." This information, as everybody knows, was the reason why he procured the manuscript of that collection. It appears that once he had understood the structure of *Alf layla* and had realized that there was no strong relation between the stories told by Shahrazâd on the one hand and the frame story on the other, he could feel entitled to his interpolation. With regard to both its external form and the subject of the embedded tales, the Sindbad cycle is not at all out of place here. Similar to the *Nights* in general, it also possesses a frame story uniting a series of stories related to one another by the identity of the protagonist; and as for the embedded tales, they also conform to the general pattern of tales of adventure or the so-called *faraj ba'd al-shidda* ("relief-after-hardship") stories. In this regard, the way Galland "constructed" (Mahdi 3: 27) his *Nuits* by inserting the Sindbad stories and adding the tales told by Hannâ, deserves to be called a creative act.

Galland's creative act is not, however, free from mystification. Galland never disclosed his sources but rather attempted to obscure them. For this, he may be excused, perhaps even for inserting night breaks and night numbers into the stories he included in his volumes 3 and 4 that originate from sources extraneous to the *Nights*. He cannot, however, be excused for the misinformation in the *Avertissements* at the beginning of volumes 3 and 9, in which he asserts that the stories contained in those volumes are part of the *Nights*. French scholars have always hesitated to criticize Galland for having created a recension of his own. Quite to the contrary, French Arabists later "legalized" after the fact what they called the "Galland recension." ZER manuscripts were already at their disposal in Paris around 1810. By analyzing them—or by studying Hammer's articles—they must have realized the discrepancy between the repertoire of Galland's *Nuits* and that of ZER. Even so, they published their own "continuations" by simply adding stories they had translated from ZER manuscripts to Galland's *Nuits*, as if it was the core. In this manner, they made their readers believe that the "complete" *Alf layla wa-layla* also includes those stories that are only encountered in the repertoire of Galland's *Nuits*.

The only contemporary scholar who criticized Galland for his interpolation was Joseph von Hammer (1: xliii), who reproached Galland for having confused the order of the *Nights* arbitrarily.

In the final analysis, the *pia fraus* of Galland's "construction" is as serious as the two mystifications achieved in Europe early in the nineteenth century, namely, the construction of Maximilian Habicht's "Tunisian manuscript" from which the Breslau edition has been prepared and Michel Sabbagh's recension of the *Nights* (Paris, Bibliothèque Nationale de France, arabe 4678–79). Judged by the intention of their authors, these two mystifications are far from being "innocent." The authors are, however, to be excused to the extent that they acted in the same way as Galland and as many others before them had.

The true nature of Habicht's manuscript was unraveled a century ago by Duncan B. Macdonald ("Maximilian Habicht"), who showed that its alleged "Tunisian" provenance was a fake. Habicht himself had compiled it. In consequence, Habicht has been vehemently blamed for his apparent forgery, and after the publication of Macdonald's article the Breslau edition has been discarded almost totally for serious research on the *Nights*. At the same time, this particular manuscript and edition contain far more "authentic" materials from the *Nights* than several other editions, including Galland's *Mille et une Nuits*.

The recension of the *Nights* preserved in the Sabbagh manuscript has only quite recently been unveiled as a conscious forgery (Mahdi 3: 61ff.). The colophon at the end of volume 2 of this manuscript states it to be copied in AH 1115 (1703 CE) by a certain Ahmad ibn Muhammad at-Tarâdî in Baghdad. This date has never been accepted at face value by subsequent scholarship, since the manuscript, in the well-known hand of Sabbagh, is written on European paper. However, rather than doubting its origin, the manuscript was considered a true transcript of the manuscript purportedly compiled in Baghdad. In reality, the manuscript was compiled by Michel Sabbagh himself from texts available in Paris libraries in the beginning of the nineteenth century. That Sabbagh could carry out such a forgery "under the nose of his masters," Silvestre de Sacy and Caussin de Perceval, may be somewhat puzzling. After having reconsidered Caussin's strange behavior toward Hammer—he published parts of Hammer's translation under his own name and, in referring to Hammer's findings, he mentioned him only as "M. de ***" (cf. Hammer 1: x–xi)—two explanations offer themselves. Probably Caussin encouraged Sabbagh to his forgery or he commissioned the manuscript (which he later purchased from Sabbagh).

Sabbagh's forgery has left no trace in the further transmission of the *Nights*. This cannot be said of Habicht's forgery.[9] Parts of the printed text of the Breslau edition were integrated into the second Calcutta edition, and these additions, alongside with other additions taken from Calcutta I, eventually contributed to—if they did not produce—the erroneous opinion that the text of Calcutta II constitutes the authentic text of the *Nights*.

Macdonald, who recognized the origin of these additions, attributed the additions to the "editors" of the Macan manuscript that served as the basis of the edition Calcutta II. Mahdi, however, suggested harmonizing those facts with the information gathered by him concerning the Macan manuscript and the British scholars in India responsible for printing the text of this manuscript. According to his hypothesis, the manuscript was commissioned in the middle of the 1820s by the British general consul in Egypt, Salt, who must have provided the copyists with copies of the Calcutta I and Breslau editions. The copyist then expanded a standard copy of ZER with passages from these editions, by either following his own taste or Salt's instructions. After Salt's death in 1827, the manuscript was sold in London. Macan purchased it there and took it with him to India, where he sold it to the future publishers. This hypothesis explains a lot, but it does not explain several important details. Why is the wording in (most of) volume 2 and in volumes 3 and 4 of Calcutta II almost identical with that of Bulaq I? Why is the night numbering in night 261 of Calcutta II skipped, exactly as in Bulaq I, while in volume 1 of Calcutta II the night numbering in some places is not congruent with that of Bulaq I? Considering these arguments, we have reason to assume that the final accord in the tradition of texts of the *Nights* is the result of a definite plagiarism. The last volumes of the Calcutta II edition are nothing but a reprint of the Bulaq I edition.

NOTES

1. It is obvious that the two variants derive from one and the same *rasm;* most likely they came into being during the transmission of the Mas'ûdî text and remained confined to it; they need not reflect variants in the circulating text of the *Nights*.

2. Even when using its Persian title, Ibn al-Nadîm is referring to its Arabic version, since his *Fihrist*, as stated in the preface, is "the catalogue of the books of all peoples, Arabs and foreign, existing in the language and the script of the Arabs."

3. Night 72 contains 118 lines plus 9 verses, night 73 contains 75 lines plus 10 verses, and night 74 contains 43 lines plus 20 verses.

4. The numbering of the second part is somewhat chaotic: 411–13, 404–13, 414–34, 433–65.

5. The above-mentioned Tübingen fragment of the *Nights* constitutes an exception in this respect. Its numerous miniatures and its quality in general suggest the commission by a wealthy customer (who perhaps ordered the manuscript as a gift for a high-ranking person). This manuscript was obviously appreciated rather for its miniatures than for the text.

6. Some scholars (e.g., Gerhardt, 410–11) believe that the initial series of five enframing stories (nights 1–170 in the Leiden edition, nights 1–33 in the Bulaq edition) originally consisted of "Merchant and Jinni," "Fisherman and Jinni" and the "Porter Cycle" only and that the expansion—by adding "The Three Apples" and the "Hunchback Cycle"—took place relatively late. But since manuscript texts of the "Fisherman" independent of *Alf layla* exist (e.g., Ahlwardt no. 9087 in Berlin), we have reasons to suppose that this story has been inserted secondarily into an existing series, most likely comprising "Merchant," "Porter," and "Hunchback," the latter in a shape less sophisticated than in our extant texts (cf. Grotzfeld, 103–5).

7. The stories in nights 344–46, night 351, and nights 383–84 are not in Hammer's text.

8. The order of the stories of the Barber's six brothers, as compared with what must have been its model, a text very close to "The Story of the Six Men" (in Wehr, 45–76, German translation by Sophia Grotzfeld in Marzolph, 67–106), has been rearranged in such a way that the disability and/or mutilation of the protagonists increases from one story to the next; the narration has been transposed from the first person sg. to the third person sg. (in the manuscript edited by Mahdi, there are still some cases of inconsistency).

9. On the one hand, the Breslau edition made available the Arabic text of the Galland manuscript (even if in an unsatisfactory form, by modern standards); on the other, it presented materials, such as the conclusion, from recensions that may be labeled "authentic" with the same right as the Galland manuscript and its relatives or the ZER manuscripts.

WORKS CITED

Abbott, Nabia. "A Ninth-Century Fragment of the 'Thousand Nights': New Light on the Early History of the Arabian Nights." *Journal of Near Eastern Studies* 8 (1949): 129–64.

Ahlwardt, Wilhelm. *Die Handschriften-Verzeichnisse der Königlichen Bibliothek zu Berlin*. Vol. 20: *Verzeichnis der Arabischen Handschriften*. Vol. 8. Berlin: A. Asher, 1896.

Burton, Richard F. *Arabian Nights with Introduction and Explanatory Notes*. Benares [i.e., London]: Kamashastra Soc., 1885.

Chraïbi, Aboubakr. *Contes nouveaux des 1001 Nuits: Étude du manuscrit Reinhardt*. Paris: Maisonneuve, 1996.

Gerhardt, Mia. *The Art of Story-Telling: A Literary Study of the Thousand and One Nights*. Leiden: Brill, 1963.

Grotzfeld, Heinz, and Sophia Grotzfeld. *Die Erzählungen aus "Tausendundeiner Nacht."* Darmstadt: Wissenschaftliche Buchgesellschaft, 1984.

Habicht, Maximilian (and H. L. Fleischer). *Tausend und Eine Nacht. Arabisch: Nach einer Handschrift aus Tunis.* 12 vols. Breslau: J. Max, 1825–43.

Hammer, Joseph von. *Der Tausend und Einen Nacht noch nicht übersezte Mährchen, Erzählungen und Anekdoten, zum erstenmale aus dem Arabischen ins Französische übersezt von Joseph von Hammer, und aus dem Französischen in's Deutsche von Aug. E. Zinserling, Professor.* 3 vols. Stuttgart and Tübingen: J. G. Cotta, 1823–24.

Lane, Edward W. *Manners and Customs of the Modern Egyptians.* London: Dent, 1954.

———. *The Thousand and One Nights, Commonly Called, in England, The Arabian Nights' Entertainments; A New Translation from the Arabic, with Copious Notes.* 3 vols. London: Charles Knight, 1839–41.

Littmann, Enno. *Die Erzählungen aus den Tausendundein Nächten.* 6 vols. Leipzig: Insel, 1921–28.

Macdonald, Duncan Black. "Maximilian Habicht and His Recension of the Thousand and One Nights." *Journal of the Royal Asiatic Society* (1909): 685–704.

———. "A Preliminary Classification of Some Mss of the Arabian Nights." *A Volume of Oriental Studies, Presented to E. G. Browne.* Ed. T. W. Arnold and R. A. Nicholson. Cambridge: Cambridge UP, 1922. 125–44.

Mahdi, Muhsin. *The Thousand and One Nights (Alf Layla wa-Layla): From the Earliest Known Sources.* 3 vols. Leiden: Brill, 1984–94.

Marzolph, Ulrich, ed. *Das Buch der wundersamen Geschichten: Erzählungen aus der Welt von 1001 Nacht.* Munich: C. H. Beck, 1999.

Pellat, Charles. "al-Masʿûdî." *Encyclopaedia of Islam.* 2nd ed. Vol. 6. Leiden: Brill, 1991. 785b.

Pinault, David. *Story-Telling Techniques in the Arabian Nights.* Leiden: Brill, 1992.

Wehr, Hans, ed. *Das Buch der wunderbaren Erzählungen und seltsamen Geschichten.* Wiesbaden: Franz Steiner, 1956.

5

Slave-Girl Lost and Regained: Transformations of a Story

Geert Jan van Gelder

An Arabic story found in many forms has the following basic structure:

1. *A man owns a slave-girl.* Usually, the man is young and wealthy, and the girl both beautiful and accomplished, especially in singing and playing. It is understood that the girl is the man's concubine (as is normal according to traditional Islamic law).

2. *The man and the slave-girl love each other.* This is not always stated explicitly, but must then be inferred from the rest of the story.

3. *The man becomes destitute.* Often this is the man's fault, by spending all his money on his girl. In one version (see nos. 14–15 in the appendix), it is not his fault but caused by the discontinuation of a regular stipend.

4. *The man sells the girl.* Either may take the initiative. There is a touch of paradox here, for one would expect true lovers to prefer suffering extreme poverty to being separated. Some versions explain it as an act of unselfishness on the part of the man or the girl.

5. *The slave-girl's new owner becomes aware of their attachment.*

6. *He generously returns the slave-girl to her lover.* He does not ask for his money back and often gives some extras.

The sequence 1–6 can be further reduced to the following very elementary plot summary:

Union/Possession (1 + 2)

Separation/Loss (3 + 4)

Reunion/Repossession (5 + 6)

This is a basic structure of the "Relief after Distress" genre; it is not surprising that al-Tanûkhî (d. 994), author of a collection of stories on this theme, offers many versions. The linking of (re)union with (re)possession and of separation with loss is of course a result of the traditional Muslim system of concubinage. It does not necessarily imply that from a narrative point of view the girl is inferior to the man. On the contrary, morally, intellectually, and artistically, she is usually the superior partner.

Some versions are expanded by complications coming between 4 and 5 or 5 and 6. Exceptionally (see no. 17 in the appendix), a reduced structure is found: a man sells a slave-girl and only afterward falls in love with her. This may be represented as (1-4-5-6-2).

All versions are essentially realistic, without demons, magic, or other supernatural elements. The realism is often enhanced by means of details from everyday life, by real place names and names of real-life protagonists, or by providing a chain of authorities for the story. Several clusters of closely related versions can be discerned.

The *Thousand and One Nights* contains two stories of this type (as well as some stories with closely related motifs). Far more versions, some of them virtually identical to those of the *Nights*, are found in works belonging to "polite" or "elite" literary culture, from the ninth century onward. It is likely that the type was around already in the time of al-Madâ'inî (d. ca. 850; see no. 8 in the appendix). The oldest source used here is *al-Muhabbar* by Muhammad Ibn Habîb (d. 860; see no. 2).

From a narrative point of view the stories are often rather uninteresting since they lack a human opponent, Fate being the principal adversary. To make up for this, some elaborations enhance the role of Fate, either by introducing the usual unlikely coincidences or by introducing real adversaries, such as is found in the story of *al-Hikâyât al-'ajîba* (no. 19).

An inventory of plot summaries of the versions I have found, with some comments and references, is attached here as a lengthy appendix. The authors' sources, often given in the form of a chain of authorities, are omitted. It is impossible to establish a precise chronological order, and the order in the following presentation is to some extent arbitrary. Mention of historical persons in the story is of course no guarantee for its veracity, and the story may have been invented much later. However, if such persons are relatively obscure, rather than famous, there is a good chance that the story is not much later than the time frame of the person mentioned.

I shall not attempt to construct a stemma or draw up a genealogy of the many versions. In some cases, the parentage is all too obvious from passages being reproduced verbatim, but in other cases the relationship proves more tenuous. Since all the narrative elements—lovers, penury, separation, beneficence, reunion—are common in everyday life, it is by no means impossible for very similar stories to be invented independently or even to occur more than once in reality. Nevertheless, it is clear that there are several clusters of versions, each with their own characteristic elements such as names, verses, and specific motifs. Broadly speaking, the story grows in length and in implausibility through the centuries. In the background there is usually a moral point, the emphasis shifting from text to text. Either the virtue of generosity is being shown, or the folly of excessive love, which can lead to destitution and, worse still, separation. In al-Tanûkhî's *Faraj,* moreover, the general message is that one should never despair: even to those who do not really deserve it, a happy ending is often granted. This makes the tale ideal for popular storytelling. Especially in some of the shorter versions, the poetry quoted may have been the main focus of interest, a point made by Joseph Sadan: it is "[t]he main element in this kind of plot, even more important, for certain readers, than all the other actions of the protagonists" (18). Here is the poetry as found in no. 1, where it forms the major part (46 out of 79 words) of the story; with some variations, it is also found in many other versions (nos. 2, 3, 5–10):

(The girl:)
Enjoy the money you have laid your hands on!
In my hands nothing remains but grieving.
For I am in pain, sad because I am parted from you,
confiding my grief to my long-pondering heart.

(The man:)
If Fate had not taken you away from me
nothing but death would have parted us. So forgive me!
Farewell! We shall not visit each other
nor be united—except if Ibn Maʿmar wills.

In this poetic exchange, the girl's bitterness is obvious, as is her sincerity. It is true that, slightly disingenuously, she publicizes what she describes as her private intimations, but this is normal in lyrical poetry. The man's reply is not quite convincing, in making destitution ("Fate") override death. The final clause, however, effects the reversal of their fortunes and ensures the benefactor's lasting fame by immortalizing him in a rhyme-word.

Sadan deals with transformations of stories from elite *adab* ("polite literature") to popular *hikâyât* ("stories") and briefly but with rich information discusses the present theme (which he calls "the Bartered Slave Girl") (17-19). He connects it, on the one hand, with the theme of the erudite slave-girl, most famously represented by Tawaddud in the *Thousand and One Nights*, and on the other hand with the more general theme of the generous man who returns a sold property. The story of Tawaddud, another accomplished slave-girl offered for sale by her indigent master and regained in the end, has already received much attention (see Wesselski; Gerresch; Parker). Greek antecedents have been surmised not only for Tawaddud, but indeed in general for the tale of loving couples being separated and united after some tribulations (Daiber 59); but surely for such a universal theme there need not have been a Greek model.

The stories may be divided, on the basis of their narrative similarity rather than their genealogy, into two groups, one in which the main theme is the generosity of some unselfish buyer and one in which the love and the adventures of the original owner and his concubine are central. In the stories of the first group the generous man is often named, which implies that the altruism is not absolute: in exchange for the girl and the money the benefactor receives undying fame on earth, as well as, no doubt, God's favor—surely not a bad bargain. Most frequently he is a leader of the clan of Taym ibn Murra (a subdivision of Quraysh, the Prophet Mohammed's tribe) and a prominent figure in the late seventh century, 'Umar ibn 'Ubayd Allâh ibn Ma'mar (nos. 1, 2, 8, and probably no. 7, which mentions "Ibn Ma'mar"). 'Umar's father 'Ubayd Allâh is also mentioned (nos. 5, 6, and appearing as 'Abd Allâh ibn Ma'mar in no. 10), and is in fact often listed among people noted for their generosity, so some confusion is understandable. In two stories, obviously related (nos. 3 and 4), the generous man is said to be their contemporary 'Abd Allâh ibn Ja'far, nephew of the caliph 'Alî, who is similarly listed as a great benefactor. In one of these stories his deed is explicitly said to surpass Ibn Ma'mar's, and the wording (in a verse in which Ibn Ja'far's deed is said to fly up to heaven and Ibn Ma'mar's act down to hell) suggests that the story is a tendentious variation or invention of 'Alid provenance, indicating rivalry with another clan within Quraysh. A non-Arab famous for his generosity, Abbasid caliph Hârûn al-Rashîd's Barmakid vizier Ja'far ibn Yahyâ, is the protagonist of one story (no. 10). Although buttressed with an impressive chain of authorities, the story, which only appears in a late source, seems to have no basis in reality, especially in the light of Ja'far's fictional career, well known from the *Thousand and One Nights*. One wonders if there was some confusion in the oral or written transmission between the names of (Ibn) Ma'mar and Ja'far, the latter, more renowned name replacing the relatively obscure one; once the vizier is named, the other persons mentioned in the story (the caliph Hârûn and Ibrâhîm al-Mawsilî, his musician) would follow naturally. Finally, in this group, there is one story in which no name is given but only a vague designation: a member of the clan of Hâshim (no. 12). The same Hâshimite (if he is the same) reappears in closely related versions that I have put in the second group (nos. 12-13). 'Abd Allâh ibn Ja'far belonged to the clan of Hâshim, and one could imagine that his story (nos. 3 and 4) served as the basis for the elaboration. Obviously, his name could no longer be used, because he lived long before Baghdad was founded, but the designation "Hâshimî," in this favorable light, is conveniently suitable to enhance the reputations of the Alids and the Abbasids alike.

In the second group, the benefactor is rarely mentioned by name. In a relatively early story (no. 11), he is a member of the Khurâsânî family or "dynasty" of the Tâhirids who were famous as generals and governors in the ninth century. One benefactor is named, a certain Abû Bakr ibn Abû Hâmid, the treasurer (nos. 14–16). This cluster seems to fall near the borderline between the two groups, but even though the lovers are not named, their feelings seem to be more important to the narrator than the treasurer's noble deed. The lovers are sometimes named, as they are in the first group (see nos. 2–4), but often they remain anonymous. This is common in short anecdotes, of course, but somewhat unusual in longer stories (such as nos. 12–13) and is possible only in narratives involving few persons so that no pronominal confusion can arise. In the oldest story of this group, no. 11, in which the benefactor is "one of the Tâhirids," the lovers are historical persons: the poet Mahmûd al-Warrâq (d. ca. 845) and Sakan the singing-girl. Among the lovers in this group who are either historical or potentially so are the famous al-Hasan ibn Sahl (no. 17), and more obscure persons such as 'Abd al-Wâhid ibn Fulân (no. 16) and Muhammad ibn 'Ubayd Allâh al-Zâhid (no. 18).

Obviously, the lovers named in the popular collections are fictional: Talha and Tuhfa in *al-Hikâyât al-'ajîba* and 'Alî Shâr and Zumurrud in the *Thousand and One Nights*. If in the second group the lovers and their feelings are central, one could further differentiate between the lovers themselves. The man is socially far superior to the girl. In ordinary Islamic discourse and in many stories in Arabic literature, social superiority implies moral superiority, as is apparent from the very language (and Arabic is obviously not alone in this), in which words for genealogical excellence and nobility are largely identical with those for moral excellence, and where a key word for virtue, *murû'a*, is derived from the word for "man" (as is the Latin term *virtus*). The slave-girl is a woman; worse, she has no pedigree that counts; worse still, she is a slave. As chattel, she should not be an actor in the narrative at all. Indeed, in many stories belonging to the first group she functions as a piece of property, valuable perhaps but not essentially differing from an inanimate possession. In many versions she is a singing-girl, for well-trained skillful singing-girls were extremely valuable, like an expensive instrument. However, there is more to it than mere pecuniary value. Music is perhaps the most powerful force to evoke emotions and ecstasy, as is attested in many stories in Arabic, and music and love are closely linked (note that the man is himself a singer in nos. 12–13, and a poet in no. 11). A singing-girl is therefore a focus of emotion, love, and sexual attraction, since it is understood in the stories that singing-girls are also beautiful and charming. Even in a story belonging to the first group, about generous people (the generous 'Ubayd Allâh ibn Ma'mar in this case), the girl is far more than a chattel. In al-Marzubânî's version (no. 6), she is called al-Kâmila, "the Perfect One," and more than merely a pretty musician, she is skilled in singing, playing the lute, recitation of the Qur'an, and in the arts of poetry, writing, cookery, and making perfume, thus anticipating the even more accomplished but rather less real Tawaddud. It is she, al-Kâmila, who suggests resolving the financial mess for which her owner is responsible by suggesting she herself be sold. Although unwise, since it breaks the laws of romance, the suggestion should be interpreted as an unselfish gesture and a not unreasonable attempt to solve their problems; in other versions the girl would rather die than be separated from her owner, or she only consents after strongly resisting the suggestion. In any case, the girl is obviously superior to her nameless owner, intellectually, artistically, morally, and in terms of narrative structure. It is this paradox that is elaborated in numerous later versions and forms the main attraction of the story.

Appendix: Plot Summaries and Notes

1. al-Isfahânî, *Aghânî* 15: 389. Also in al-Hamdûnî, *Tadhkira* 2: 347–48; and al-Ibshîhî, *Mustatraf* 1: 166, in chapters on generosity in both sources.

A man, in love with his slave-girl, is forced to sell her. She is bought by 'Umar ibn 'Ubayd Allâh ibn Ma'mar. She and her lover each recite two lines of poetry expressing their grief. 'Umar restores the girl to him and leaves him the money.

This is the shortest version of all. 'Umar ibn 'Ubayd Allâh, who died, sixty years old, in 701 in Dumayr (Syria), was the son of 'Ubayd Allâh ibn Ma'mar (see below). He was governor of Basra; he is also said to have been a singer and lute player (Ibn Qutayba 576). He is listed among the generous men of early Islam (see no. 2). There seems to be a confusion between 'Umar and his father, who is mentioned in other versions and who was noted for his generosity.

2. Ibn Habîb, *Muhabbar* 151–52, in a chapter on generous people in Islamic times.

Abû Huzâba al-Taymî has a slave-girl named Basbâsa, with whom he is in love. He is forced to sell her. 'Umar ibn 'Ubayd Allâh ibn Ma'mar al-Taymî buys her for a large sum. When the girl is led away, her lover clings to her dress and utters four lines of verse. Ibn Ma'mar gives her back and does not want the money back.

For Abû Huzâba al-Walîd ibn Hunayfa al-Tamîmî (thus), see al-Isfahânî, *Aghânî* 22: 260; al-Kalbî 2: 586; al-Safadî 27: 456–59.

3. al-Tanûkhî, *Faraj* 4: 343–44.

'Abd Allâh ibn Ja'far ibn Abî Tâlib buys a Meccan slave-girl. Hearing that a boy of her family is in love with her, and she with him, he unites the lovers. Soon after that, he buys from the clan of Talha for 'Abd al-Salâm ibn Abî Sulaymân a girl called Rawâh, with whom he is in love. Gratefully, 'Abd al-Salâm makes an epigram in which he declares Ibn Ja'far's gift to be superior to that of Ibn Ma'mar, just as heaven is superior to hell.

This is a deviation from the basic structure, since the boy does not own the girl. But the story is related to the following one. 'Abd Allâh ibn Ja'far (d. 699) is mentioned, with 'Ubayd Allâh ibn Ma'mar al-Taymî, among the eleven generous men of their time, the former in the Hijaz, the latter in Basra (Ibn 'Abd Rabbih 1: 293–94); but elsewhere it is not 'Ubayd Allâh but his son 'Umar who is thus listed: Ibn Habîb 151–52; al-Safadî 17: 108; Ibn Shâkir 2: 170–71.

4. Ibn ʿAbd Rabbih, *ʿIqd* 1: 297 = (pseudo-)Ibn Qayyim al-Jawziyya, *Akhbâr* 24–25; German translation by Bellmann 65–66. With some more details and dialogue also in Ibn ʿAsâkir, *Tahdhîb* 7: 338–39.

ʿAbd al-Rahmân ibn Abî ʿAmmâr, a scholar from the Hijaz, sees a girl at a slave dealer's place and falls in love. ʿAbd Allâh ibn Jaʿfar hears about it. On pilgrimage in Mecca, he buys the girl for 40,000 (dirhams, rather than Bellmann's fantastic "40,000 dinars"). Ibn Abî ʿAmmâr visits him. Ibn Jaʿfar asks him if he is still in love, and when the answer is Yes, the girl is brought in, to Ibn Abî ʿAmmâr's surprise. Ibn Jaʿfar says he has bought the girl for him; he has not touched her.

He also gives him 100,000 dirhams.

The story is obviously related to the preceding one about Ibn Jaʿfar (no. 4), although the other names are different.

5. Ibn ʿAbd Rabbih, *ʿIqd* 1: 300-301 (in a chapter on generous people).

A man from Basra has trained a slave-girl. When he is struck by poverty, the girl suggests that he sells her to ʿUbayd Allâh ibn Maʿmar al-Qurashî al-Taymî. She is sold for ten purses (i.e., 100,000 dirhams). The man recites three verses by way of farewell. ʿUbayd Allâh restores the girl to him, letting him keep the money. ʿUbayd Allâh ibn Maʿmar was killed, forty years old, near Istakhr during the caliphate of ʿUthmân. He was "very generous and valiant" (Ibn Qutayba 289) and counted, with ʿAbd Allâh ibn Jaʿfar, among eleven famously generous men of their time (Ibn ʿAbd Rabbih 1: 293). But see above, no. 1, where his son ʿUmar is mentioned instead.

6. al-Marzubânî, *Nûr al-qabas* 197–98.

ʿUbayd Allâh ibn Maʿmar al-Taymî buys for 20,000 dinars a slave-girl called "the Perfect One" (al-Kâmila), as she is skilled in singing, playing music, reciting the Qurʾan, poetry, writing, cookery, and making perfume. She used to belong to a young man who had trained her for himself. He loved her passionately and spent so much on her that he became impoverished. The girl suggested that he should get rich by selling her. After the sale, both are distraught; they recite some verses. ʿUbayd Allâh takes pity on them, gives the girl back, and does not want the money back.

It is not clear why ʿUbayd Allâh is given a section in al-Marzubânî's work on grammarians and philologists. Here, the man's poverty is directly linked to his love for the girl, which makes the story more self-contained and thus more "literary." It is one of several versions in which the girl takes the initiative in suggesting the sale.

7. al-Tanûkhî, *Mustajâd* 114–15.

A wealthy young man who possesses a skillful singing-girl becomes poor. They talk together; the man suggests selling her to a benevolent new owner. The girl protests: she would rather die with him than be sold to another. But her owner offers her for sale; a friend suggests approaching Ibn Ma'mar, *amîr* in Iraq. The latter asks her price. She is offered for 100,000 dirhams, though 100,000 dinars had been spent on her (an unlikely large sum). In the end she is sold for 100,000 dirhams, ten suits (?) of clothes, ten horses, and ten slaves. When the girl is led away, she and her previous owner recite verses. Ibn Ma'mar gives back the girl without asking restitution of the price.

It is not said explicitly that the two love each other. No cause of the poverty is given. The man is the one to suggest the sale.

8. al-Tanûkhî, *Faraj* 4: 328-30. The same, with slight changes in the wording, in al-Tanûkhî, *Nishwâr* 5: 168–69; Ibn al-Jawzî, *Dhamm* 467; al-Sarrâj, *Masâri'* 2: 184–85; Ibn Hijja, *Thamarât* 260–61. The story is said to be similar to one in a lost work by al-Madâ'inî (d. ca. 850).

A wealthy man from Basra buys and trains a slave-girl. He falls in love with her and spends so much on her that he becomes poor. Two versions are offered: in one, the man suggests selling her, if she agrees; the girl would rather die with him than be sold to another. In the other version, the initiative comes from the girl. A friend recommends 'Umar ibn 'Ubayd Allâh al-Taymî, governor of Basra. (The following as in no. 7).

9. *Alf layla wa-layla:* see Littmann 3: 432–33 = Burton 4: 35–36 = Lane 2: 518–19 (not in Subayh edition of *Alf layla*): Story of 'Abd Allâh (thus) ibn Ma'mar and the Man of Basra with his Slave-girl; see Elisséeff no. 53; Chauvin 5: 106, no. 36.

A man from Basra buys a slave-girl and has her trained and educated. He loves her passionately and spends all his wealth on her. The girl tells him: Sell me! He consents and offers her to the governor of Basra, 'Abd Allâh ibn Ma'mar al-Taymî, who buys her for 500 dinars. The girl and the man recite the customary lines of verse. The governor gives her back, saying that "the separation of lovers brings grief to both." They live happily ever after until death parts them.

10. al-Tanûkhî, *Faraj* 4: 331–38 = Ibn al-Jawzî, *Dhamm* 466–67.

Caliph Hârûn al-Rashîd goes on pilgrimage with his vizier Ja'far ibn Yahyâ and the narrator, the musician Ibrâhîm al-Mawsilî. In Medina, Ja'far asks Ibrâhîm to buy him a singing-girl. Ibrâhîm finds one belonging to an apparently rich man, who offers her for 40,000 dinars. This is agreed, on condition that the buyer is allowed to see her first. Ja'far, in disguise, sees the girl, hears her perform, and is pleased with her. The girl asks her owner what is happening. He explains that poverty forces him to sell her. The girl says that if she were him, she would not sell him for all the world. The man is touched, gives her her freedom, and marries her, giving his house as dowry. The sale is off, and Ibrâhîm is about to have the money taken away, but Ja'far leaves the happy couple the money.

Obviously related to the other versions, although here the girl is never actually lost. See especially the following version of Ibn al-Mu'tazz (no. 11); and see Bray, "Verbs and Voices" 171–77.

11. Ibn al-Mu'tazz, *Tabaqât* 366.

The poet Mahmûd al-Warrâq possesses a beautiful and accomplished singing-girl called Sakan, who is also a poet. Struck by poverty, he suggests selling her if she agrees. The girl agrees. After lively bidding, one of the Tâhirids offers to buy her for 100,000 dirhams. A tearful parting between Sakan and Mahmûd is about to take place. The girl asks, Would you really prefer the money to me? He asks, Would you really live in poverty? Yes, says the girl. Mahmûd then grants her her freedom and gives his house as a bridal gift. The Tâhirid hears this and gives the money to Mahmûd anyhow.

As Bray observes ("Verbs and Voices" 175-76), one should compare the short tale in al-Isfahânî, *Aghânî* 17: 54. Mahmûd al-Warrâq (d. ca. 845) was a poet from Baghdad; he also worked as a slave trader. For Sakan, see al-Isbahânî, *Imâ'* 79–80; al-Suyûtî 29; al-Safadî 16: 394–99. The story resembles that of Ibn al-Jawzî (no. 10).

12. al-Tanûkhî, *Faraj* 4: 316–27; German translation by Hottinger (al-Tanûkhî, *Ende gut* 345–58). With minor deviations in al-Ghuzûlî, *Matâli'* 1: 187–93, presented as the first in a series of seven "nightly tales," thus anticipating its inclusion in the *Thousand and One Nights* (below, no. 13). The same story in al-Tanûkhî, *Nishwâr* 5: 274–83; and al-Sarrâj, *Masâri'* 2: 229–33, apart from some slight variations, but omitting one very long passage. This omission, obviously an oversight by some copyist, makes the story wholly unintelligible. The editor of *Nishwâr* has completed the story using *Faraj*. With more changes in wording, but without the lacuna of al-Sarrâj, also in al-Antâkî, *Tazyîn* 1: 343–46.

A man in Baghdad loves and is loved by a slave-girl, whom he buys and on whom he spends much, squandering the wealth inherited from his father. The girl suggests that he should sell her so that both can live in luxury. A rich man of Hâshim from Basra buys her for 1,500 dinars. Immediately afterward the former owner repents. [He continues the story in the first person.] His money is stolen; desperate, he throws himself into the river Tigris but is rescued by bystanders. He decides to seek employment in Wasit and arranges passage on a boat, dressed as a sailor. The boat happens to belong to the Hâshimite who bought his slave-girl; she is aboard the ship, too. He faints when he hears her sing, but later signals his presence to her by secretly changing the tuning of her lute, which she recognizes. She tells her master, who is touched. He has not yet had sexual intercourse with the girl; he promises to free her and marry her to her former owner once they are in Basra, on condition that he is allowed to hear her sing whenever he wishes. Everyone is pleased.

However, accidentally left behind on shore, the man loses contact with his beloved. He is employed in Basra as the accountant of a grocer, whose daughter he marries. His situation is greatly improved, yet he is always sad. After another two years, at an outing on the occasion of Palm Sunday to watch the Christians celebrate in Ubulla, near Basra, he spots the Hâshimite's boat again. They are glad to see him; they thought he had drowned. The girl has been inconsolably sad and has led a life of abstinence. The lovers are now reunited and married, handsomely supported by the Hâshimite. The grocer's daughter is divorced and her dowry is returned. It is hinted that the marriage has never been consummated (Bray 12–15, especially 13).

This version has been included in the *Thousand and One Nights* (see no. 13). Gerhardt (134) mentions the rarity of references to suicide. Hamori (67) calls the episode of the grocer (and the hero's marriage and subsequence divorce of his daughter) "a curious example of Tanûkhî's (or some predecessor's) adaptation of folkloric material. . . . This [the divorce] is very likely a realistic touch. It is also a point though where the price is paid for turning romance into anecdote, where the magical fluidity of society in the romance is relinquished." One wonders if the character of the Hâshimite is a remnant of the Hâshimite 'Abd Allâh Ibn Ja'far who figures in older versions.

13. *Alf layla wa-layla*: Littmann 5: 764–75; Burton 8: 104–12; Lane 3: 524–30; *Alf layla* (Subayh) 4: 129–34.

The story is set "in times of old." It closely follows no. 12, also in wording, although there are many small differences. Numerous details are identical. Several specific place names have been replaced by expressions such as "a village," presumably because they would be unfamiliar to an Egyptian or Syrian audience. The Christian feast is replaced by a general outing without reference to religion.

See Chauvin 5: 152–35; Gerhardt 133–34; Hamori 65–67; Sadan 18–19.

14. al-Tanûkhî, *Faraj* 4: 345–49.

A young man from Khurâsân, who studies with the narrator under Abû Ishâq al-Marwazî buys a slave-girl with whom he falls in love and who stays with him for some years. One year, the annual stipend sent by his father does not arrive because of the latter's illness. The young man cannot settle his debts until he has sold his slave-girl for 1,000 dirhams. In the night after the sale, the man knocks on the narrator's door. He says he wants to buy his girl back, putting himself in debt again and hoping his father's money will arrive after all. In the morning the two find out that she is now living in the house of Abû Bakr ibn Abî Hâmid, the treasurer. A letter is written by their teacher, which they take to the treasurer. They tell him the story. He is not aware of the girl's presence in his house; she has been bought by a woman of his household. The girl is brought and is asked if she wants to be returned. She answers tactfully: No one could be preferred to her new master, but she owes her education to her old master. The treasurer is pleased and gives her back, refusing the money and adding some valuable presents that had been promised to the girl. He also promises to give a monthly stipend of flour and two dinars, so that the man is able to pay his debtors and continue his studies. This was in fact paid as long as Abû Bakr ibn Abî Hâmid lived.

See the next two closely related versions, nos. 15 and 16.

15. al-Tanûkhî, *Nishwâr* 7: 270–72 = Ibn al-Jawzî, *Muntazam* (Hyderabad) 6: 251–52; (Beirut) 13: 319–20.

Abû Hâmid al-Marwarrûdhî notices that one of his pupils has been absent for several days. He is told that the pupil had bought a slave-girl, but that his stipend has been cut off. He had to settle debts and was forced to sell the girl. Immediately afterward he repented and longed for her, to the point of being unable to study. The girl had been bought by Ibn Abî Hâmid, the treasurer. The teacher approaches him, hoping to make him revoke the sale. The treasurer is not yet aware of the matter, since it was his wife who bought the girl. The girl is brought in. The treasurer can see from the boy's change of color that his story is true. She is returned to him, and the price, 3,000 dirhams, is not accepted. Clothes and jewels are also given. The treasurer asks the girl: Which one of us do you love best, me or your former master? The girl answers: You have been good to me and made me rich. But as for my master, if I owned him just as he owned me,

I would not have sold him for enormous riches. Everyone is pleased with this reply.

In Ibn al-Jawzî's *Muntazam*, the story is found in the biographical note on Ibn Abî Hâmid (Abû Bakr Ahmad ibn Muhammad ibn Mûsâ, d. 933). Here he seems to be confused with Abû Hâmid al-Marwarrûdhî Ahmad ibn 'Âmir (d. 973), a teacher of Abû Hayyân al-Tawhîdî and others.

16. al-Tanûkhî, *Faraj* 4: 349–51; German translation by Weisweiler 272–74.

A moneychanger called 'Abd al-Wâhid ibn Fulân sells his beloved slave-girl to Abû Bakr ibn Abî Hâmid, the treasurer, for 300 dinars. In the evening he is distraught and cannot sleep. In the morning he is unable to work. Taking the money with him, he goes to Ibn Abî Hâmid. He states his case and asks if the sale could be rescinded. The treasurer asks, If you loved her that much, why did you sell her? He explains that his capital of 1,000 dinars was quickly spent on buying the girl and satisfying her demands, while he neglected his job. She would make his life miserable if he resisted her wishes, so he sold her. But now he regrets his decision.

The treasurer says that he has not had sexual intercourse with her yet. He gives her back; he does not want the dinars and gives another 1,000 dirhams into the bargain. He tells her to buy what she wants and not press her owner for more. He pledges to give her 1,000 dirhams a year. The money is indeed given as promised until the treasurer dies.

17. al-Tanûkhî, *Faraj* 4: 352–53.

Al-Hasan ibn Sahl (d. 850–51) buys a slave-girl from a merchant in Fustât for 1,000 dinars. The merchant, having cashed his check, returns home and finds everything clean, nicely arranged, with scents and wine ready. He is told that the girl he has just sold did this. The merchant goes to al-Hasan's house, where he sees the girl, more beautiful than ever, driving him mad with love. He implores al-Hasan to make the sale undone. Al-Hasan explains that this is impossible, since no girl who entered his house has ever left it, but he finally relents and asks the girl what she thinks. She chooses her former master and is returned to him. He is allowed to keep the 1,000 dinars as a present.

In this exceptional version, the man falls in love only after the sale of the girl.

18. (pseudo-)Ibn Qayyim al-Jawziyya, *Akhbâr* 24; German translation by Bellmann 64-65; and Weisweiler 279. The story is told in the first person by the protagonist.

Muhammad ibn 'Ubayd Allâh al-Zâhid says: Once I sold a slave-girl. But I missed her very much. Together with a friend I went to her new owner, asking for the sale to be undone. He refused. I returned despondently. At night I could not sleep. The next morning someone knocked at the door; it was the same man, who was returning the girl and did not want his money back. He had dreamed that someone said to him: Return the girl and you will enter Paradise.

Bellmann (433) argues that the protagonist's name is incorrect and that probably Abû 'Umar Muhammad [ibn 'Abd al-Wâhid] al-Zâhid (d. 957) is meant, a pupil of the grammarian Tha'lab who was known as Ghulâm Tha'lab. This identification looks rather arbitrary.

19. *al-Hikâyât al-'ajîba* 25–44; German translation by Hans Wehr in Marzolph 40–66, cf. 638–39; see also Wehr's introduction to the Arabic edition (vi–vii).

Talha grows up in luxury. His father, the qadi of Cairo, buys him a slave-girl called Tuhfa. They fall in love. The father decides they ought to get married. (The girl should be freed for a proper marriage, but later on it turns out she is still a slave. Perhaps it is the concubinage that is celebrated as a "wedding.") Tuhfa is taught singing. The father dies and the son squanders all his wealth. The girl suggests that he should sell her. Talha reluctantly sells her to a slave dealer, with the right of rescinding within three days. Next day the agent of a rich young man from Damascus, searching for a slave-girl for his patron, is struck by her beauty, skills, and knowledge (including the Qur'an, astronomy, arithmetic, chess, backgammon, singing, and playing). The slave merchant has forgotten about the condition and sells her. (A lacuna in the text omits the departure and arrival in Damascus.) When the girl meets her new master, Muhammad ibn Sâlih, she tells her story. The man pities her and promises to give her up. After some time he departs for Egypt. (The girl stays behind, rather illogically.)

Meanwhile Talha, mad with love, has been committed to an asylum. Recognized and rescued by an old friend of his father's, he goes to Damascus in order to find Tuhfa. But his ship founders and he arrives penniless in Tyre. On the road to Damascus he offers bread and salt to a rider out hunting and tells his story. The hunter turns out to be the caliph 'Abd al-Malik, who promises to help him.

Ibn Sâlih, now in Egypt, is falsely accused by enemies, and the caliph gives order for his house to be plundered and for all the women to be brought out. Tuhfa flees to an adjacent house belonging to a weaver and puts herself under his protection. The caliph, not finding Tuhfa, repents of his rash command. He offers Talha ten virgin slave-girls in compensation, but the offer is turned down. Talha accepts a post in the land taxation department.

Tuhfa has found a considerable sum of money that was left in the house of her master and asks the weaver to take her to Egypt with the money. In Cairo she sees that Talha's old house is shut up and empty. She rents a house from a tailor and lives by herself. By a fanciful course of events both Ibn Sâlih, now a beggar, and Talha meet Tuhfa at the same moment. After a recognition scene they tell one another their various stories. Ibn Sâlih, still Tuhfa's owner, gives her back. Talha will write to the caliph on Ibn Sâlih's behalf and shares his wealth with him. The caliph indemnifies Ibn Sâlih, who returns to Damascus. The false witnesses are punished. Talha and Tuhfa live happily ever after.

Daiber (28, 59–60) has connected this story with another story, of which he discusses several versions in detail, of a mystic slave-girl also called Tuhfa, found in an asylum by the famous mystic al-Saqatî (d. 867). Freed by him, she dies soon afterward, returning to her master. The similarities are striking but superficial.

20. *Alf layla wa-layla:* Subayh edition 2: 217–35; Littmann 3: 207–58; Burton 3: 306–44; Lane 2: 387–425.

This is the wordy story of 'Alî Shâr, a rich merchant's son, who squanders his inherited fortune. He sees a slave-girl offered for sale and stays to see the outcome of the auction. The girl, Zumurrud, is asked for her view. Rejecting some rich but unattractive bidders, she sets her mind on having 'Alî Shâr as her owner. He is too poor to buy her, but the girl secretly gives him 1,000 dinars of her own money, 900 of which he spends on the sale. They live happily together for a year, living from her handiwork. She is abducted by some wicked Christians, but after many adventures is finally reunited with her owner. This is not due to 'Alî Shâr, who throughout the story is a silly and ineffective young man, in contrast to the resourceful Zumurrud, who always takes the initiative and has, crossdressing, even risen to royal power. Perhaps surprisingly she gives up her position in order to return to 'Alî's country to live with him.

Although falling under the broad category of the topic under consideration, this last story is very different from all the others given here. A wild elaboration of this story is the Story of Nûr al-Dîn and Maryam al-Zunnâriyya: *Alf layla* (Subayh) 4: 80–129; Littmann 5: 624–757; Burton 7: 1–99; see Gerhardt 142–44.

WORKS CITED

Alf layla wa-layla. 4 vols. Cairo: Maktabat Subayh, n.d.

al-Antâkî, Dâwûd. *Tazyîn al-aswâq bi-tafsîl ashwâq al-'ushshâq.* Ed. Muhammad Altûnjî. 2 vols. Beirut: 'Âlam al-kutub, 1993.

Bellmann, Dieter, trans. *Über die Frauen: Liebeshistorien und Liebeserfahrung aus dem arabischen Mittelalter.* Munich: C. H. Beck, 1986.

Bray, Julia Ashtiany. *"Isnâds* and Models of Heroes." *Arabic and Middle Eastern Literatures* 1 (1998): 7–30.

———. "Verbs and Voices." *Islamic Reflections and Arabic Musings: Studies in Honour of Professor Alan Jones.* Ed. Robert G. Hoyland and Philip F. Kennedy. Oxford: Gibb Memorial Trust, 2004. 170–85.

Burton, R[ichard] F[rancis], trans. *The Book of the Thousand Nights and a Night.* 12 vols. London: H. S. Nichols, 1897.

Chauvin, Victor. *Bibliographie des ouvrages arabes ou relatifs aux arabes publiés dans l'Europe chrétienne de 1810 à 1885.* 12 vols. Liège and Leipzig: H. Vaillant-Carmanne, 1892–1922.

Daiber, Hans. "Literarischer Prozess zwischen Fiktion und Wirklichkeit: Ein Beispiel aus der klassisch-arabischen Erzählliteratur." *Annals of Japan Association for Middle East Studies* 10 (1995): 27–67.

Eliséeff, Nikita. *Thèmes et motifs des Mille et une Nuits: Essais de classification.* Beirut: Institut Franáais de Damas, 1949.

Gerhardt, Mia I. *The Art of Story-Telling: A Literary Study of the Thousand and One Nights.* Leiden: Brill, 1963.

Gerresch, Claudine. "Un récit des Mille et une Nuits: *Tawaddud,* petite encyclopédie de l'Islam médiéval." *Bulletin de l'Institut Fondamental d'Afrique Noire,* series B, 35 (1973): 57–175.

al-Ghuzûlî. *Matâli' al-budûr.* 2 vols. Cairo: Maktabat Idârat al-Watan, 1881–82.

al-Hamdûnî. *al-Tadhkira al-hamdûniyya.* Ed. Ihsân 'Abbâs and Bakr 'Abbâs. 10 vols. Beirut: Dâr Sâdir, 1996.

Hamori, Andras. "Folklore in Tanûkhî: The Collector of Ramlah." *Studia Islamica* 71 (1990): 65–75.

al-Hikâyât al-'ajîba wa-l-akhbâr al-gharîba (Das Buch der wunderbaren Erzählungen und seltsamen Geschichten). Ed. Hans Wehr. Wiesbaden: Franz Steiner, 1956.

Ibn 'Abd Rabbihi. *al-'Iqd al-farîd.* 7 vols. Cairo: Dâr al-Kutub, 1940–53.

Ibn 'Asâkir. *Tahdhîb Tarîkh Dimashq.* 7 vols. Damascus: Matba'at al-Taraqqî, 1932.

Ibn Habîb, Muhammad. *al-Muhabbar.* Ed. Ilse Lichtenstädter. Hyderabad: Dâ'irat al-Ma'ârif al-'uthmâniyya, 1942.

Ibn Hazm. *Tawq al-hamâma.* Ed. Ihsân 'Abbâs. Beirut: al-Mu'assasa al-'Arabiyya, 1980.

Ibn Hijja al-Hamawî. *Thamarât al-awrâq.* Ed. Muhammad Abû l-Fadl Ibrâhîm. Cairo: Maktabat al-Khânjî, 1971.

Ibn al-Jawzî. *Dhamm al-hawâ.* Ed. Ahmad 'Abd al-Salâm 'Atâ. Beirut: Dâr al-Kutub al-'ilmiyya, 1987.

———. *al-Muntazam.* 10 vols. Hyderabad: Dâ'irat al-Ma'ârif al-'uthmâniyya, 1937–40.

————. *al-Muntazam.* 18 vols. Beirut: Dâr al-Kutub al-'ilmiyya, 1992.

Ibn al-Mu'tazz. *Tabaqât al-shu'arâ'.* Ed. 'Abd al-Sattâr Farrâj. Cairo: Dâr al-Ma'ârif, 1968.

(pseudo-)Ibn Qayyim al-Jawziyya. *Akhbâr al-nisâ'.* Cairo: Matba'at al-Taqaddum, 1901.

Ibn Qutayba. *al-Ma'ârif.* Ed. Tharwat 'Ukâsha. Cairo: Dâr al-Kutub, 1981.

Ibn Shâkir al-Kutubî. *Fawât al-Wafayât.* Ed. Ihsân 'Abbâs. 5 vols. Beirut: Dâr Sâdir, 1973–74.

al-Ibshîhî. *al-Mustatraf fî kull fann mustazraf.* 2 vols. Cairo: Maktabat Mustafâ al-Bâbî al-Halabî, 1952.

al-Isbahânî, Abu 'l-Faraj. *al-Imâ' al-shawâ'ir.* Ed. Jalîl al-'Atiyya. Sûsa and Tunis: Dâr al-Ma'ârif, 1998.

al-Isfahânî, Abu 'l-Faraj. *al-Aghânî.* 24 vols. Cairo: Dâr al-Kutub, 1927–74.

al-Kalbî, Hishâm ibn Muhammad. *Jamharat an-nasab (Das genealogische Werk des Hishâm ibn Muhammad al-Kalbî).* Ed. Werner Caskel. 2 vols. Leiden: Brill, 1966.

Lane, Edward William, trans. *The Thousand and One Nights, Commonly Called, in England, The Arabian Nights' Entertainments.* 3 vols. London: John Murray, 1859.

Littmann, Enno, trans. *Die Erzählungen aus den tausendundein Nächten.* 6 vols. Wiesbaden: Insel Verlag, 1966.

Marzolph, Ulrich, ed. *Das Buch der wundersamen Geschichten: Erzählungen aus der Welt von Tausendundeine Nacht.* Munich: C. H. Beck, 1999.

al-Marzubânî, Muhammad ibn 'Imrân. *Nûr al-qabas al-mukhtasar min al-Muqtabas fî akhbâr al-nuhât wa-l-udabâ' wa-l-shu'arâ' wa-l-'ulamâ' (Die Gelehrtenbiographien).* Ed. Rudolf Sellheim. Wiesbaden: Franz Steiner, 1964.

Parker, Margaret R. *The Story of a Story across Cultures: The Case of the Doncella Teodor.* London: Tamesis, 1996.

Sadan, Joseph. "Hârûn al-Rashîd and the Brewer: Preliminary Remarks on the *Adab* of the Elite Versus *Hikâyât.*" *Studies in Canonical and Popular Arabic Literature.* Ed. Shimon Ballas and Reuven Snir. Toronto: York P, 1998. 1–22.

al-Safadî. *al-Wâfî bi-l-Wafayât.* Wiesbaden: Franz Steiner, 1962–.

al-Sarrâj. *Masâri' al-'ushshâq.* 2 vols. Beirut: Dâr Sâdir, n.d.

al-Suyûtî. *al-Mustazraf min akhbâr al-jawârî.* Ed. Ahmad 'Abd al-Fattâh Tammâm. Cairo: Maktabat al-Turâth al-islâmî, 1989.

al-Tanûkhî. *Ende gut, alles gut: Das Buch der Erleichterung nach der Bedrängnis.* Selected and trans. Arnold Hottinger. Zurich: Manesse, 1979.

————. *al-Faraj ba'd al-shidda.* Ed. 'Abbûd al-Shâljî. 5 vols. Beirut: Dâr Sâdir, 1978.

————. *Nishwâr al-muhâdara.* Ed. 'Abbûd al-Shâljî. 8 vols. Beirut: n.p., 1971–73.

(pseudo-?)al-Tanûkhî. *al-Mustajâd min fa'alât al-ajwâd.* Ed. Yûsuf al-Bustânî. Cairo: Dâr al-'Arab, 1985.

Weisweiler, Max. *Arabesken der Liebe: Früharabische Geschichten von Liebe und Frauen.* Leiden: Brill, 1954.

Wesselski, Albert. "Die gelehrten Sklavinnen des Islam und ihre byzantinischen Vorbilder." *Archiv Orientální* 9 (1937): 353–78.

6

Siblings in *Alf layla wa-layla*

Hasan El-Shamy

Introduction

A folk narrative may be seen as a description of life and living—real or fictitious (El-Shamy, *Folk Traditions* 1: xiii). Social relations, especially among family members, constitute a major part of the tales. Thus, the nature of feelings among members of the social group that a narrative describes governs the development of the plot. Positive feelings lead to positive results while negative feelings lead to a negative outcome. This principle applies to expressive culture, folk as well as elite, and has been labeled by the present author the "structure of sentiments" (El-Shamy, *Traditional Structure* 53–74; El-Shamy, "Emotionskomponente"), sentiments being learned feelings or affect rather than "genetically" transmitted emotions (El-Shamy, *Folktales of Egypt* xlvi, n. 2).

Siblings play a variety of social roles in narrative traditions. As a set of behavioral expectations, a social role is never one-dimensional (El-Shamy, *Folkloric Behavior* 64–66). For example, a brother or a sister is an entity defined as such when he or she interacts with another sibling. The same entity becomes a son or a daughter when interacting with parents, or a maternal or paternal uncle or aunt when interacting with the child of a sibling.

This essay examines sibling relations as expressed in the narratives contained in a modern popular edition of the Arabic collection *Alf layla wa-layla*, commonly known in English as the *Thousand and One Nights* (henceforth: *Nights*). As postulated and demonstrated by the present writer, the "brother-sister syndrome" is of paramount importance in Arab cultures and plays dominant roles in social structure and elite as well as oral folk literatures. The core of this dyadic relationship is a stable pattern of sentiments involving the entire family. It may be summed up as follows: brother-sister mutual love; sister-sister rivalry; brother-brother rivalry; child-parent(s) hostility; husband-wife hostility (or lack of love and affection); brother-sister's husband hostility; sister-brother's wife rivalry; brother-sister's child affection; and brother-brother's son hostility (El-Shamy, *Brother-Sister Syndrome* 320). These familial conditions are generated by social values and associated child-rearing practices. "According to the codes of honor [modesty]—religious and otherwise—strict rules of separation between the sexes are observed among traditionary groups. Yet, maximum exposure is allowed among siblings. It is common, sometimes the rule, for brothers and sisters to share the same bed or at least the sleeping quarters." (El-Shamy, *Brother-Sister Syndrome* 319).

Studies based on contemporary Arab oral traditions indicate that expressions depicting the brother-sister bond are more recurrent among women than among men and among young men more than among older men. The reasons for this phenomenon seem to be that as males progress through life, they get more satisfaction (or, perhaps, less frustration) from their relations with females. Conversely, females appear to receive less satisfaction as they age. However, additional research is required before such reasons are ascertained. The present inquiry proceeds from the assumption that the edition of *Alf layla* selected for analysis contains the work of adult males. Thus, in spite of the paucity of the brother-sister themes, a significant number of cases seem to conform to the general pattern generated in other fields of expressive culture.

Tales Illustrating the Brother-Brother Relationship

Of sibling relations, the interaction between brother and brother is the most frequently encountered in the *Nights*. Besides the eight tales discussed below, the brother-brother theme also appears as a secondary detail in other narratives. One such story is the tale of al-Hasan al-Basrî, in which the hero acts as umpire between two brothers quarrelling over a magic rod and a magic invisibility cap. Although this scene conforms to the negative pattern of sentiments between brothers, this intrusive detail has no consequences for the brother-brother pattern of interaction in the tale under consideration (*Alf layla* 3: 302–19, 4: 2–55; Chauvin 7: 29, no. 212A).

1. *Shahriyâr and his Brother Shâhzamân* (*Alf layla* 1: 2–5, 4: 317–18; Chauvin 5: 188, no. 111). The frame story of the *Nights* accounts for the experiences of two brothers, Shahriyâr and Shâhzamân, each a powerful king in his own independent domain. When setting off to visit his elder brother, Shâhzamân accidentally witnesses his wife having sexual intercourse with a black slave. He subsequently spies the same affair exercised by Shahiryâr's wife and her male and female attendants. United in misery, the two brothers travel together to find out whether anyone else has had a similar affliction. Through experience, they reach the conclusion that women are capable of betraying their husbands at will. After returning to their respective homes, each brother kills his own wife and all those involved in the sexual misbehavior. To avenge himself on womankind, Shahriyâr marries a virgin every night and murders her the following day. In the end, Shahrazâd, the daughter of his vizier, offers herself to Shahiryâr so as to rescue her kind, with the presumed stipulations that she would not be obliged to talk once dawn has arrived. This interdiction of talk beyond a certain time may also be presumed to have been imposed by Shahriyâr. It may be inferred from the first use of the formulaic sentence: "wa adraka Shahrazâd al-sabâh fa-sakatat 'an al-kalâm al-mubâh" ("And dawn caught up with Shahrazâd, thus she stopped the permitted talk"). With this ruse, she survives the planned execution for 1001 nights.

Notably, killing his culprit wife is the last time the younger brother Shâhzamân is mentioned. The *Nights* concludes with a scene involving only the elder brother, Shahriyâr, who has learned to give up his murderous ways at the hands of his wife, Shahrazâd. Meanwhile, Shâhzamân was symbolically removed from the stage. Thus, it may be inferred that misery had united the two brothers only temporarily; one brother succeeded in treating his affliction while there is no mention as to whether the other also managed to overcome his emotional ailment. If we ignore the symbolic significance of the elimination of the younger brother, the nature of the interaction here may be characterized as neutral or faintly positive.

2. *The Story of the Old Man with Two Black Dogs (the Second Sheikh)* (*Alf layla* 1: 11–13; Chauvin 7: 129, no. 397); designated as new tale-type 551A: *Only One Brother Is Successful in Seeking Riches (Wealth)*. Other brothers are jealous (El-Shamy, *Types of the Folktale*). This story is an account of a personal experience by an old man who is accompanied by two female dogs. He tells the story so as to partly ransom a man held captive by a jinni. The dogs are actually the man's two transformed (elder) brothers.

Following the death of their father, the three brothers had divided the inheritance. Contrary to the advice of the third brother (the narrator), the other two pursued ruinous business adventures. He repeatedly rescued them from financial ruin. With his help and counsel, all three undertook a profitable business trip and returned with great profits aboard a ship. On their way back, a woman offered herself as wife to him. He accepted, took her aboard the ship, and fell in love with her to the extent of becoming too preoccupied with her to pay attention to his brothers. The brothers conspired against him, dragged him out of bed, and threw him into the sea. The woman, however, turned out to be a Moslem jinni. She rescued him, transported him back home, and informed him of her intention to kill the culprit brothers. While he begged her not to do so, she had her sister transform them into dogs with the stipulation that the spell cannot be undone before a ten-year period. Since that period has elapsed, the narrator is now looking for that jinni woman seeking to have his canine brothers restored to their natural form.

This story is an expression of fraternal strife. The declared reason for the jealousy and envy of the two elder brothers is material wealth. Yet, the fratricidal intentions are expressed at the same time as the narrator was preoccupied with his wife, who distracted him from his social obligations toward his brothers. The punishment the brothers received in having to live as a dog (in a culture in which a "bitch" is considered among the lowest of the low) must be considered a strong humiliation, even if constituting a deserved punishment. The sentiments expressed here between brother and brother(s) are negative.

3. *The Story of Vizier Nûr al-Dîn with Badr al-Dîn, His Brother* (*Alf layla* 1: 64–84; Chauvin 6: 102–5, no. 270). The main characters in this narrative are two cross-paternal cousins in love with each other. The story begins with two brothers daydreaming about the future marriage of their as yet unborn children and beyond. The ensuing friction sets the conditions for the main episodes of the story in which a young man finds himself supernaturally placed in bed with a young woman who proves to be his paternal cousin.

Two brothers were working as viziers for the king of Egypt, with the office of vizier rotating between them. They discussed plans to marry on the same night, father children on the same day, and then, when the children—a girl and a boy—became of age to marry the two paternal cousins to each other. After they had settled on this, they started a dispute about the girl's *mahr* (bride-wealth) that ended in severe discord. The younger brother was so deeply offended that he quit his country and traveled eastward to settle in al-Basrah in Iraq, where he married and became the father of a son. Although the elder brother regretted his harsh treatment of the younger brother, no actual reconciliation ever took place.

The introduction portrays a lurking antagonism between two brothers. Initially, there is considerable amity between them. Yet, in a manner that suggests seeking a pretext to disagree, they fall into a dispute over a matter that may be described as "imagined troubles for the unborn child." The sentiments expressed here between the two brothers are predominantly negative.

4. *The Story of the Princes al-Amjad and al-As'ad* (*Alf layla* 2: 112–32; Chauvin 5: 208–10, no. 120 [1]). This story may be seen as expressing truly positive feelings and friendship between two half brothers who fall victims to female seduction and treachery. The half brothers are the sons of the same father by two different wives. They were raised together in an environment of luxury and constantly kept each other's company. Eventually, their irresistible handsomeness made each stepmother fall in love with her stepson and actively seek to seduce him. When the young men rejected the advances, the stepmothers decided to cover their intentions by reversing the blame. They claimed that it was the boys who had assaulted and attempted to seduce them. The husband believed his wives, and ordered both of his sons executed. The sons were, however, spared by the appointed executioner who let them escape.

The story proceeds with both half brothers going through adventures involving mortal dangers. Finally, they meet again, and the concluding episode presents each of them marrying a maiden who had rendered them lifesaving favors. The sentiments expressed here are positive. Success is attained by both siblings together.

5. *Jawdar, Son of Merchant 'Omar, and his Two Brothers* (*Alf layla* 3: 177–201; Chauvin 5: 257–60, no. 154). The story of Jawdar revolves around two axes: one constitutes a continuous theme that deals with open fraternal conflict; the other is transitory and treats magical ritual practices associated with locating treasure troves and overcoming their protective supernatural guardians.

Jawdar is the youngest of a merchant's three sons; the other two are Sâlim, the eldest, and Salîm, the middle one. Although the text does not specify this point, the context leaves no doubt in the mind of the reader/listener that the brothers are by the same father and mother. Fraternal jealousy and open conflict dominate the course of action throughout the entire tale, as the father loved Jawdar more than either of his two brothers. In order to avoid dispute after his death, the father divided his fortune into four equal parts, one for each of his children and the fourth for his wife. Motivated by greed, the two elder brothers demanded more of Jawdar's share. They persisted in their unjust quest and repeatedly sought legal aid until all three of them were impoverished by the high cost of legal contendings. Jawdar worked as fisher and generated an income. He was dutiful toward his mother. Meanwhile, the two elder brothers became "vagabonds" and directed their villainous behavior toward their mother. They imposed themselves on her, consumed her food, usurped her money, and beat her (an unpardonable affront). Yet, she remained kind to them.

The tale's middle section deals with the acquisition by Jawdar of magic objects and with the effect these objects have on the lives of the three brothers. The treachery of the two elder brothers reached new heights when they arranged to sell Jawdar as a slave. When their mother served them food without going through the toil of cooking, they discovered Jawdar's magic saddlebags and disputed over how to divide them. As the king learned about the magic object, he imprisoned the brothers and usurped the saddlebags for himself.

Meanwhile, Jawdar had escaped the enslaved labor when a storm sank the ship on which he served. Subsequently, Jawdar met the magician who informed him of the fate of his two brothers and also furnished him with a magic ring. Jawdar instructed the ring's jinni to rescue his brothers from jail. This was accomplished, and Jawdar once more treated the two brothers magnanimously. As the king became aware of the power that Jawdar possessed, he feared for his own safety. He arranged for his daughter to marry Jawdar, and when the king died, Jawdar was selected king. He installed his two brothers as his viziers. The brothers, nonetheless, could not tolerate the idea of being subordinate to Jawdar. They murdered him and divided his property and political offices between the two of them. The elder brother, Sâlim, acquired the magic ring and ordered the jinni to murder his brother Salîm. Then, he frightened the army leaders into accepting him as their king. He also demanded to marry Jawdar's widow, but was told that he had to wait until the end of her *'iddah* (the waiting period required by religious law before a divorcee or widow may remarry;

new motif P529.5§ in El-Shamy, *Folk Traditions*). He mocked the law and refused to wait. Meanwhile, Jawdar's widow pretended to accept, killed Sâlim with poison, destroyed both the magic saddlebags and the ring, and asked the religious authorities to select a new king.

The narrative portrays Jawdar as noble, loving, forgiving, and dutiful. By contrast, his brothers are depicted as thoroughly vile, envious, hateful, vindictive, and undutiful. The events climax in dual fratricide and a tragic ending. The sentiments expressed here are totally negative. All three siblings lose their lives due to the conflict and rivalry that dominates the interaction initiated by the two elder brothers.

6. *The Story of the Jewish Judge and His Pious Wife* (*Alf layla* 3: 10–11; Chauvin 6: 154–55, no. 321). In this narrative, a brother covets his brother's beautiful wife and tries to seduce her. This situation is a recurrent cause of fraternal conflict in oral traditions. Although no overt antagonism between the two brothers is expressed in this tale, by inference, negative feelings may be assumed to exist.

A Jewish judge wanted to go on pilgrimage to Jerusalem. He left his brother in his place on matters of jurisprudence, and also asked him to look after his wife during his absence. The brother became enamored with her and tried to seduce her, but she rejected him and sought refuge in her piety. As the man feared that she might reveal his offense, he got false witnesses to testify to his brother's wife's adultery. The woman was consequently sentenced to death by stoning, and was buried under a hail of stones cast at her. She was, however, saved by a passerby. In the continuation, the woman suffered numerous injustices but was always able to remain faithful to her original spouse. When she finally became a healer, all culprits sought her assistance and were healed, forgiven, and became believers in her miraculous powers. She was reunited with her husband.

In this story, the sentiment expressed between the two brothers is negative.

7. *The Story of 'Abdallâh Ibn Fâdil with His Two Brothers* (*Alf layla* 4: 266–88; Chauvin 5: 2–4, no. 2). This story, told as a personal experience, is a more elaborate variant of no. 2 (above) and no. 12 (below). The negative roles played by the two elder brothers against their youngest brother are typical. In the present text, as in no. 5 above, the writer amplifies the negative sentiments of the elder brothers as well as the punishment they receive in the end.

A guest spied his generous host, named 'Abdallâh, severely whipping, then caressing and comforting two dogs. When the caliph was told about this bizarre event, he asked the host for an explanation. The host then told the following as a personal experience.

His father had three sons, named Nâsir, Mansûr, and 'Abdallâh. After the death of their father, the elder two insisted on the division of the inheritance and went their own way. As they returned broke, 'Abdallâh out of compassion divided his share of the inheritance with them. Together all three brothers set out on a trade voyage and made much profit. As the ship anchored at an island, the two brothers refused to join 'Abdallâh in exploring the island and stayed aboard. On the island 'Abdallâh saved a (female) viper from a (male) snake that was pursuing her. The viper proved to be a jinni woman. Then he came to a city of petrified people and found a beautiful young woman. 'Abdallâh took her with him aboard the ship. Each of the two brothers demanded to be given the girl as wife, but 'Abdallâh refused due to a vow he had made to the young woman. He also pledged to find wives for his brothers. Instead, the two brothers threw 'Abdallâh into the sea and usurped his property. 'Abdallâh was rescued by the jinni woman he had helped. The jinni woman intended to kill the two culprit brothers, but 'Abdallâh interceded on their behalf. Consequently, she transformed them into dogs and stipulated that they must be whipped every day. When 'Abdallâh once failed to beat his canine brothers, the jinni woman gave him a painful thrashing for his negligence.

The caliph (being the sovereign of humans and jinn) ordered the jinni woman to disenchant the dogs. He also asked 'Abdallâh to forgive his brothers, and appointed 'Abdallâh *wâlî* of Basra. Even though 'Abdallâh shared both his wealth and political office with his brothers, they plotted to kill him and threw his apparently dead body into the sea. A dolphin saved him and carried him to shore, where a desert caravan found him and cared for him. He was taken to a faith healer, who proved to be the maiden he had met in the city of stone. She told him that upon learning of his brothers' crime and their plans for her, she had thrown herself into the sea and had been saved by the saint al-Khidr. All involved testified before the caliph, and the truth was learned. The caliph ordered that the perfidious brothers be crucified in front of 'Abdallâh's palace. 'Abdallâh's marriage to the young woman from the petrified city was officiated by the caliph himself.

The sentiments expressed between brother and brother(s) in this story are highly negative. In two cases (5, 7), the noble conduct of one brother toward his other envious brothers did not lead to change in the vile brother's attitudes. In both cases the brothers met with violent death: by poisoning and by being killed by a demon at the brother's command on the one hand (5), by crucifixion on the other (7). Conversely, the good-hearted siblings met with happy fates.

Summing up, in the category of tales illustrating the brother-brother relationship, the overall ratio of sentiments between brother and brother(s) is as follows: positive: 1; neutral-positive: 1; negative: 6.

A Tale Illustrating the Brother-Brother and Brother-Sister Relationship

The following narrative seems to be the only case in the *Nights* where the collateral sets of relations between a brother and his brother and between a brother and his sister occur simultaneously. In the present essay, this text serves as a transition to the brother-sister pattern of interaction. The core theme for the present inquiry is designated as new tale-type 932: *Brother-Sister Incest: The Sethian Complex* (El-Shamy, *Types of the Folktale*).

8. *The Story of King 'Umar al-Nu'mân and His Two Sons Sharkân and Daw' al-Makân* (*Alf layla* 1: 162–261, 290–320, 2: 1–21; Chauvin 6: 116, no. 277). This lengthy and multilayered account is labeled a *sîrah*, a genre dedicated to heroic folk narratives often depicted as "epic." It coheres around a number of situations, each with a distinct set of actions. These situations are as follows: (a) An elder brother harbors murderous attitudes toward the younger. (b) Two cross-gender twins, Nuzhat al-Zamân and her brother Daw' al-Makân, treat each other with love and affection. Yet, the sister ends up in an unwitting incestuous marriage with her elder half brother, the self-declared enemy of her own twin brother. (c) The bulk of the narrative is a detailed description of armed strife involving Moslem Arab groups on one hand and Christian Rûmîs (Greco-Romans) on the other. Numerous side stories and events recur within the course of the transgenerational time expanse covered by the *sîrah*. At the close of this segment, the brother-sister theme resurfaces in the theme of a Christian Rûmî king proving to be the half brother from the father of the Moslem Nuzhat al-Zamân who is the twin sister of Daw' al-Makân, meanwhile deceased. (d) At the close of the narrative, an affectionate brother and sister constituting a lone household in the desert meet a tragic end at the hands of a treacherous Bedouin robber (see no. 9, below).

(a) Sharkân was the only son of king 'Umar al-Nu'mân. Even though it seemed his father would be unable to sire any more children, after many years one of his Rûmî slave women, Safiyyah, became pregnant. This news did not please Sharkân because he feared that a new son might challenge his succession to the rule. So he secretly decided to kill the child, if it be a son. Safiyyah first gave birth to a girl (Nuzhat al-Zamân), but a while later, a boy (Daw' al-Makân) was born. Sharkân knew only of the girl, as the news of the boy's birth was kept secret. Eventually, Sharkân learned about the boy, and the attention paid to the boy by their father caused vexation and anger in him. In order to appease his feelings, Sharkân was given the rule of a major region of his father's kingdom. Thus, his anger toward his siblings was kept under control. He went as a conqueror to the Rûm countries, where he established a chivalrous love relationship with the king's daughter named Ibrîzah. She converted to Islam and accompanied Sharkân to his father's domain so that they could be properly married. During Sharkân's absence, his father treacherously drugged and raped Ibrîzah. She became pregnant, blamed herself, and left to rejoin her own people. On the way she experienced labor pains and was murdered during delivery by a male slave hireling after having rebuffed his attempt at seduction. The infant was cared for by her accompanying slave-girl and, eventually, Ibrîzah's father. The baby boy, who was half brother to Nuzhat al-Zamân and her two brothers Sharkân and Daw' al-Makân, became the Rûmî king Rûmzân. His relationship with his Moslem half sister was positive. At a later stage, fighting the Christian enemies together generated a sense of rapprochement between the two half brothers Sharkân and Daw' al-Makân. However, each died at a different phase of action.

(b) During an absence of their father, the twins Nuzhat al-Zamân and Daw' al-Makân set out together on a pilgrimage to Mecca. On the way the brother became sick; the sister lovingly managed to nurse him back to health. However, the Bedouin Hammâd abducted the sister, abused her, and sold her to a merchant. The brother suffered until a poor laborer kindly cared for him. The merchant offered the beautiful and sophisticated sister as a slave-girl to king Sharkân, who did not recognize her as his half sister. As Sharkân felt a mystical connection to her, he bought her, freed her from her status as slave, married her, and consummated the marriage. She was impregnated by him that very night and later gave birth to a baby girl. When Sharkân informed his father about the news of his marriage and the birth of a girl, the reply came with the sad news that

Sharkân's half brother and sister were missing. Sharkân "was saddened by his father's sadness, [but] he was delighted for losing his sister and his brother" (*Alf layla* I: 207).

When it was time for Sharkân to name his daughter, her mother had placed around her neck a unique gem treasured by members of the family. When Sharkân recognized the gem, his grave mistake became evident to the couple. They considered their incestuous relationship a matter of Fate and named the baby girl accordingly: Qudiya Fa-Kân ("It Was Predestined and Thus Became"). To remedy the situation, Sharkân gave his sister-wife in marriage to a valet in his court, pretending that her marriage to him was not consummated. The valet did not know that she was the king's daughter. Coincidence brought the twins together when they happened to travel to Baghdad in the same caravan. Daw' al-Makân was bemoaning the absence of his beloved sister in love poems that he chanted aloud. Nuzhat al-Zamân overheard the poems and realized that the chanter was her brother. She told her brother the entire affair including her previous marriage to her half brother and the actual consummation of that marriage. Nuzhat al-Zamân's husband realized that he had unwittingly married the king's daughter and hoped to be appointed to a high political office. Significantly, no feelings of love or affection were expressed between the valet and Nuzhat al-Zamân. Meanwhile, the news that king 'Umar al-Nu'mân was murdered by poisoning reached the travelers. The younger brother Daw' al-Makân was chosen to succeed to the throne. The new king held his court session with his twin sister present behind a curtain.

(c) The two half brothers joined forces in fighting the Rûmîs and in seeking revenge for their poisoned father. Sharkân was slain in his sleep by the vicious old woman Dhât al-Dawâhî; the younger, Daw' al-Makân, died later. The valet became king. Justice was accomplished for all at the hands of the Rûmî Christian king Rûmzân, mainly in his role as brother to his half sister Nuzhat al-Zamân.

(d) See no. 10 below.

In this tale, the sentiments expressed between brother and brother are negative or neutral. The sentiments expressed between brother and sister are positive.

Tales Illustrating the Brother-Sister Relationship

Besides the above-mentioned incident, three additional texts revolve around brother-sister relationships. Occasionally, the brother-sister theme may also appear as a secondary detail in some narratives. One such story is the tale of Badr Bâsim and Jawharah that constitutes the second part of the tale of the mermaid Jullanâr (*Alf layla* 3: 247–70; Chauvin 5: 147–51, no. 73). In this story, a quarrel between Jullanâr and her brother Sâlih, both of whom originate from an underwater world, is cited as the reason why she endangers herself by getting out of the water and sitting on the seashore, where she is abducted and sold as a slave. Eventually, the human king Shâhramân marries her, and they beget a son, named Badr Bâsim. Later in the story, the quarrel is abandoned and the plot develops into the theme of the maternal uncle rescuing his sister's son and helping him marry the underwater princess Jawharah. It is interesting to note that no wife of Jullanâr's brother is mentioned. Similarly, after the death of her human husband, Jullanâr does not remarry (cf. El-Shamy, *Traditional Structure* 67). Thus, an exclusive reunion of brother and sister is indirectly actuated.

9. Another case of such implicit expression of brother-sister tie is found in the story of Ghânim ibn Ayyûb (Chauvin 6: 14–16, no. 188; Marzolph and van Leeuwen, no. 36), where a merchant who "lahu mâl wa lahu walad . . . yusammîhi Ghânim ibn Ayyûb . . . ; wa lahu ukht ismuhâ Fitnah . . . fatuwuffiya wâliduhumâ . . ." ("has wealth and has a son . . . whom he names Ghânim ibn Ayyûb . . . ; and *he [the son] has a sister named Fitnah . . .* The father of the two of them died . . .") (*Alf layla:* 2: 146, emphasis added). In this Arabic passage, the writer/narrator perceives the son in association with the father, while associating Fitnah (the daughter) only with her brother. Burton presents this cluster of kinship ties in a more specific but less accurate manner as that of a merchant who "had a son . . . named Ghânim . . . *He had also a daughter, own sister to Ghânim,* who was called Fitnah, . . ." (Burton 2: 45—emphasis added). Consequently, the brother-sister association and its psychological significance are dissipated in the English text.

In a parallel cultural sphere, a study of kinship ties among possessing *zâr*-spirits (labeled *asyâd el-zâr*) concluded that in a situation where a father-daughter-son are involved "the brother and sister relationship . . . overrides that of the daughter and father" (El-Shamy, "Belief Characters" 27; cf. Littmann 35–36).

The story of Ghânim is concluded with an exchange marriage recurrent in folktales that revolve around brother and sister: the caliph marries the sister (Fitnah) and the brother (Ghânim) marries the caliph's favorite concubine.

10. *The Story of Hammâd the Bedouin* (*Alf layla* 2: 16–20; Chauvin 6: 124, no. 1). The affective core of this narrative belongs to the new tale-type 971C: *Insanity (Death) from Death of Beloved Sibling (Brother or Sister)* and is also depicted as the "Khansâ' syndrome" (El-Shamy, *Types of the Folktale*). The theme of a brother and sister alone constituting a household is common in oral folk traditions (El-Shamy, *Brother and Sister* 11, 12, 13, 17, 18, etc.). The following account is given as one of the numerous aside stories in the *sîrah* of king 'Umar al-Nu'mân (no. 8, above). It is a personal experience account describing the marauding practices of a treacherous Bedouin.

During a raid on a lone Bedouin encampment, the chief marauder, Hammâd, discovered that a young man and a young woman were the only inhabitants of the site. Hammâd was instantly infatuated with the beautiful young woman and presented himself and his band as hunters who needed a drink of water. The lad presented the young woman as his sister. Hammâd demanded that either the brother surrender her to him in marriage willingly, or he would take her by force after slaying him. As the brother rode out to combat, the sister passionately bade him farewell, kissed him between the eyes, and recited a poem about him as her defender. She concluded the poem with a verse in which she declared her love (*hawâ*) for her brother (*Alf layla* 2: 17). The lad challenged Hammâd and his men to duels, and defeated all challengers one after another. When he was about to kill Hammâd, his final enemy, Hammâd pleaded for mercy. The lad granted him safety and hospitality. The young woman was proud of her brother's deed; she approached him and, again, kissed him between his eyes. The brother made a covenant of sincere friendship with Hammâd, addressed him as "my brother," asked his sister to be hospitable to him, and bestowed many valuable presents on him. As the brother fell asleep, Hammâd decapitated him. The sister rent her clothes, threw herself on her slain brother, and chanted a poem lamenting him. She also informed Hammâd that her brother had intended for him to return to his home with gifts, and that he also had decided to give her to him in marriage. Then, the sister drew a sword and killed herself.

The sentiments expressed between brother and sister in this story are highly positive.

11. *The Story of the First Calender, a King's Son* (*Alf layla* 1: 39–42; Chauvin 5: 196–97, no. 115). This is another case of the new tale-type 932 (as in no. 7, above). It is given as a personal experience narrative reporting a brother-

sister incest committed by mutual consent. The writer also alludes to the influence of childhood experiences on the fostering of brother-sister erotic attraction.

After being obliged to take an oath of secrecy, a young prince assisted his paternal cousin and a young woman to hide inside a tomb in a cemetery. Only later was the prince able to tell the father of the missing youth about the cemetery incident, and the two of them went searching for it. When they got inside the tomb they found both the cousin and the young woman reduced to pieces of coal, locked together in each other's bosom. The father was disgusted; he spat on his son's face and slapped him with his shoe, and told his nephew that his cousin's beloved was in fact the young man's own sister. The father/uncle felt that the two had received the deserved divine punishment for conducting their incestuous affair.

The brother-sister pattern of interaction, though conflicting with social norms and regarded as sinful, is positive.

12. *The Creation of Iblîs* (*Alf layla* 3: 18-81; Chauvin 7: 54, no. *77*). A story within the narrative complex about the adventures of Hâsib Karîm, Bulûqiya, and Janshâh accounts for the origin of Iblîs (Satan, Lucifer) in terms of his failure to comply with a paternal command for brothers to marry their sisters. Strangely, it seems that virtually all literary commentators ignored the significance of the incestuous nature of this narrative. As provided in the *Nights*, it is told by the mythical jinn character Sakhr to a human seeker of the ultimate truth. Sakhr explained that God had created two hybrid creatures named Khalit and Malit: "Then God commanded the tails of Khalit and Malit to couple and copulate a second time. The tail of Malit conceived by the tail of Khalit and bore fourteen children, seven male and seven female, who grew up and intermarried one with the other. . . . All were obedient to their Lord, save one who disobeyed him and was changed into a worm which is Iblîs" (*Alf layla* 3: 33; for details of the myth see El-Shamy, *Mythological Constituents*).

The brother-sister pattern of interaction here, though antisocial (sinful), is positive. This is true in the case of six pairs where twin brother-sister marriages actually took place; it is also true to a lesser extent in the case where the one young man refused the supposedly divine arrangement.

In the category of narratives illustrating the brother-sister relationship, the ratio of positive to negative sentiments between brother and sister is 3:0.

Tales Illustrating the Sister-Sister Relationship

The initial situation in the *Nights*, involving the two brothers Shahriyâr and Shahzamân, is echoed between the two sisters Shahrazâd and Dunyazâd. Although the two sisters seem to be in amicable relations, the younger Dunyazâd is frozen in one role. After serving as a sympathetic one-person audience for her sister's narration at the outset of the *Nights*, she appears only sporadically in that very role. While her elder sister continues her altruistic mission and finally manages to reform the king, there is no mention of the fate of her sister Dunyazâd.

Besides this situation of sororal interaction in the frame story of the *Nights*, the two texts mentioned below treat a sister's pattern of interaction with her sister. This theme also appears as a detail motif. In the story titled Abu 'l-Hasan al-Khorâsânî, the heroine is reunited with the man she loves through the aid of her own sister, and both sisters are concubines in the caliph's harem. This action has no consequences for the sister-sister relationship (*Alf layla* 4: 229–37; Chauvin 5: 218, no. 129). Conversely, in the story of al-Hasan al-Basrî, the fairy named Nûr al-Hudâ is initially cruel to her sister Manâr al-Sanâ, as punishment for marrying a human man (*Alf layla* 4: 40–42).

13. *The Story of Zubaydah* (*Alf layla* 1: 53–57; Chauvin 5: 4–6, no. 443). This personal experience narrative is the feminine subtype of two versions of a story about brother-brother rivalry and conflict. Although the sentiments expressed in this text are recurrent, especially in women's tales, the narrative is unique. It has not been reported from any source besides the *Nights*, nor has it been reported from oral folktales. Yet, the tale has been designated as new tale-type 551B: *Only One Sister Is Successful on Quest (Seeking Riches). Other sisters are jealous* (El-Shamy, *Types of the Folktale*).

Zubaydah had two half sisters from the same father. After his death and the division of inheritance, the two sisters got married and left for the homes of their husbands. As the husbands squandered the fortune of their wives, the sisters returned impoverished to live with their half sister. Zubaydah welcomed them back, and all three subsequently engaged in trade together. On one trading voyage Zubaydah decided to explore the place where their ship had made an emergency stop. She soon discovered a city whose inhabitants had all been petrified because of their disbelief. Only a handsome young man who happened to be a believer was spared. Zubaydah took the young man with her. She told her sisters that they might keep all the profit they had made but that she would take the young man as husband. The sisters grew jealous and threw both Zubaydah and the young man overboard. The young man drowned, but Zubaydah herself was washed ashore on an island. There she observed a female viper being pursued by a male snake. Taking pity on the viper, she crushed the snake's head with a rock. The viper grew wings and flew away. Zubaydah then fell asleep and woke up to find beside her a maid rubbing her feet. The maid was also holding two black bitches. She proved to be the jinni woman saved when in viper form by Zubaydah from a pursuing evil jinni in snake form. She further informed Zubaydah that the bitches were actually her sisters, whom she had punished by sinking their ship and transforming them. The grateful jinni woman carried all of them back home. Zubaydah was ordered to administer to each of the two dogs three hundred lashes with a whip daily. Later, in the presence of the caliph, Zubaydah summoned the jinni enchantress, and the caliph ordered her to disenchant the two bitches and reconcile with her sisters.

The sentiments expressed between sister and sister(s) are negative.

14. *The Story Told by the Jewish Physician (The Murderous Sister)* (*Alf layla* 1: 99–102; Chauvin 6: 89–90, no. 253). In this story, a jealous woman murders her sister over a transient illicit sexual relationship with a young man.

While staying in Damascus, a young man met a beautiful girl who readily feasted with him and dallied in sexual activities at his home. She even refused to accept money from him; instead, she offered him a handsome monetary gift to prepare for their next rendezvous. She also promised to bring along another girl "better and younger" than herself (*Alf layla* 1: 101). When at the next meeting the two women arrived, the host paid more attention to the younger guest. In the end, he went to sleep with her. However, when he awoke, he found his hands covered with blood and the head of his companion severed. When the young man later attempted to sell a necklace left by the murdered girl, he was accused of theft and punished by having his hand severed. As the governor, who happened to be the father of the murdered girl, was informed about the affair, he ordered that the young man be compensated for the loss of his hand. He told the young man that the two girls both were his own daughters. The elder sister betrayed the secret of her sexual relationship with the young man to her younger sister, who secured permission from her father to accompany her elder sister on her outing. The elder sister then became jealous and slew the younger.

The sentiments expressed in this tale in terms of sister-sister relationship are negative. No punishment is mentioned for the murderous sister.

In this category of narratives, the ratio of positive to negative sentiments between sister and sister is 0:2, that is, 100 percent negative.

Tales Illustrating Brother-Sister-Like Relations

The patterns of interaction among family members within the household reflect the lifestyle and child-rearing practices within a community. As I have indicated elsewhere, brothers and sisters enjoy maximum physical closeness to one another during childhood and adolescent years. In a significant number of cases, this pattern continues in later phases of their lives (El-Shamy, *Brother-Sister Syndrome* 319). Once children reach the age of maturation, their interests are directed mainly toward a favorite sibling. This is also true of paternal cousins in the patrilocal extended family where children of brothers live with their parents in the house of their fathers' father. Two stories in *Alf layla*, discussed below, illustrate some of the consequences of these practices of socialization. Whether the children involved are biological siblings or sociological ones (by adoption or similar practice), the outcome is the same. Psychologically affiliated themes occur in the depiction of the relationship between a human being and a foster jinn sibling. This type of the brother-sister-like relationship is vividly illustrated in the story of al-Hasan al-Basrî in which the hero is "bebrothered" by the youngest of seven jinn sisters (new motif F 302.0.3§: Jinn-mikhawiyyah (bebrothering): jinniyyah [fairy, jinn-woman] as a man's foster-sister) (El-Shamy, *Folk Traditions*). Not only did she protect him from her own sisters, she also dressed him in new clothes, wept when he expressed agony, swore by "the sanctity of the love between" the two of them (*Alf layla* 3: 318), carried him hugged to her bosom, and flew with him to where he had seen another jinni maiden with whom he fell in erotic love after spying her naked.

15. *The Story of the First Eunuch* (*Alf layla* 1: 147–48; Chauvin 5: 277, no. 160). One eunuch told others like him the reason for his castration. His account is given in the form of personal experience narrative.

He was brought from his country when he was about five years of age. His owner raised him together with his daughter until they grew up. One day he entered upon the girl while she appeared to be full of desire. As they engaged in risky nonpenetration sex initiated by her, due to the excitement and vigor of youth, the boy's erect penis ripped the girls underpants and penetrated her. The girl's mother concealed the news of this incident and arranged for her daughter to marry an unsuspecting barber. Afterward, the slave boy was castrated and assigned to serve the daughter in her new home.

The brother-sister-like pattern of interaction is intimate and positive.

16. *Nu'mah and Nu'm* (*Alf layla* 2: 132–47; Chauvin 6: 96–97, no. 263). This story illustrates a pattern of interaction between a male child and a slave-girl purchased in his name.

Action in this romance begins with a notable buying a slave woman along with her baby girl, Nu'm. He took them home, introduced them to his wife, who was also his paternal cousin and the mother of his infant son, Nu'mah. Nu'mah and Nu'm were raised together like brother and sister until they became ten years of age. When Nu'mah finally learned that Nu'm was not his sister but his slave-girl, he married her, and they spent nine years in that state of marital contentment. The rest of this story deals with the abduction of Nu'm, the extended troubles for her, and her subsequent restoration to her husband. In this segment, the caliph's sister plays a positive role as the helper of the loving couple. The brother-sister-like pattern of interaction is intimate and positive.

In this category of narratives, the ratio of positive to negative sentiments between brother-like and sister-like is 2:0, that is, 100 percent intimate and positive.

Conclusions

From the data presented above the following may be concluded:

1. The brother-brother relationship is predominantly negative and fraught with conflict. Negative sentiments cohere around feelings of jealousy over parental favors, financial advantages, or beauty of a brother's wife or female companion.

2. The sister-sister relationship is exclusively negative and fraught with conflict. Negative sentiments cohere around feelings mirroring those that dominate the brother-brother relationship. Naturally, the attractiveness of a sister's husband or male companion provides a strong cause of jealousy.

3. The brother-sister and brother-sister-like relationships are exclusively positive and may lead to sexual attraction.

This dyadic set of sibling relationships and the attitudes it generates govern the "structure of sentiments" of a significant portion of Arab (and non-Arab) kinship systems and consequent forms of expressive cultures.

WORKS CITED

Alf layla wa-layla. 4 vols. Cairo: Maktabat al-Jumhûriyyah al-'arabiyyah, n.d.

Chauvin, Victor. *Bibliographie des ouvrages arabes ou relatifs aux Arabes publiés dans l'Europe chrétienne de 1810 à 1885.* 12 vols. Liège: Vaillant-Carmanne, 1892–1922.

El-Shamy, Hasan. "Belief Characters as Anthropomorphic Psychosocial Realities." *Al-kitâb al-sanawî li-'ilm al-ijtimâ'* 3 (1982): 7–36, 389–93 (Arabic abstract).

———. "The Brother-Sister Syndrome in Arab Family Life: Socio-Cultural Factors in Arab Psychiatry: A Critical Review." *International Journal of Sociology of the Family* 11.2 (1981): 313–23.

———. *Brother and Sister. Type 872*: A Cognitive Behavioristic Text Analysis of a Middle Eastern Oikotype.* Folklore Monograph Series 8. Bloomington: Folklore Publications Group, 1979.

———. "Emotionskomponente." *Enzyklopädie des Märchens.* Vol. 3. Berlin: Walter de Gruyter, 1981. 1391–95.

———. "Folkloric Behavior: A Theory for the Study of the Dynamics of Traditional Culture." (A case study of the stability and change in the lore of the Egyptian community in Brooklyn, NY). Diss. Indiana U, 1967.

———. *Folktales of Egypt: Collected, Translated, and Edited with Middle Eastern and [sub-Saharan] African Parallels.* Chicago: U of Chicago P, 1980.

———. *Folk Traditions of the Arab World: A Guide to Motif Classification.* 2 vols. Bloomington: Indiana UP, 1995.

———. "Mythological Constituents of *Alf laylah wa-laylah.*" *The Arabian Nights and Orientalism: Perspectives from East and West.* Ed. Yuriko Yamanaka and Tetsuo Nishio. New York: I. B. Tauris, 2006. 25–46.

———. *Tales Arab Women Tell and the Behavioral Patterns They Portray: Collected, Translated, Edited, and Interpreted.* Bloomington: Indiana UP, 1999.

———. "The Traditional Structure of Sentiments in Mahfouz's Trilogy: A Behavioristic Text Analysis." *Al-'Arabiyya: Journal of the American Association of Teachers of Arabic* 9 (1976): 53–74. Rpt. in *Critical Perspectives on Naguib Mahfouz.* Ed. Trevor Le Gassick. Washington, DC: Three Continents P, 1991. 51–70.

———. *Types of the Folktale in the Arab World: A Demographically Oriented Tale-Type Index.* Bloomington: Indiana UP, 2004.

Littmann, Enno. *Arabische Geisterbeschwörungen aus Ägypten.* Leipzig: Otto Harrassowitz, 1950.

Marzolph, Ulrich, and Richard van Leeuwen, with the collaboration of Hassan Wassouf. *The Arabian Nights Encyclopedia.* 2 vols. Santa Barbara, Denver, and Oxford: ABC-CLIO, 2004.

7

Political Thought in the *Thousand and One Nights*

Robert Irwin

It is a preposterous title, of course. Should we also look for political thought in *Snow White and the Seven Dwarfs*? Or in the slapstick films of Laurel and Hardy? Or in Superman comics? Surely, whereas politics is "the art of the possible," the *Thousand and One Nights* (henceforth: *Nights*) is, in large part at least, the art of the impossible. Yet a moment's reflection allows one to realize that the title is not so very preposterous after all. To start with, the exordium to the *Nights*, with its references to doomed and vanished dynasties ("Thamûd, 'Âd and Pharaoh of the Vast Domain") and its promise to provide lessons based on "what happened to kings from the beginning of time," strongly suggests that political concerns were not wholly alien to those who contributed to the *Nights* (Mahdi 1: 56; Haddawy 2). In listening to Shahrazâd, Shahriyâr is supposed to be learning from past examples (even if the political philosopher, Michael Oakeshott, once described the study of history as something the historian loves "as a mistress of whom he never tires and whom he never expects to talk sense" [182]). In the light of the opening exordium, the whole of the *Nights* can be considered to be an overblown and out-of-control example of the literary genre of mirror-for-princes (German *Fürstenspiegel*). In the mirror-for-princes section of *Nasîhat al-mulûk*, a work spuriously attributed to the eleventh-century theologian and Sufi, al-Ghazâlî (d. 1111), the reading of stories about past kings is advocated as a royal duty: "He must also read the books of good counsel . . . just as Anûshîrvân . . . used to read the books of former kings, ask for stories about them and follow their ways" (Crone, "Did al-Ghazali Write a Mirror for Princes?" 184).

To look at the politics of the *Nights* from another angle, when Elie Kedourie, in a study of modern Middle Eastern politics, came to discuss the medieval and Islamic legacy to the politics of the modern Middle East, he touched on the despotic powers of the caliphs and specifically of Abbasid caliph Hârûn al-Rashîd, and he had this to say: "The emblem of his terrible power is the black executioner who, in the *Nights*, is shown to be in constant attendance on Hârûn al-Rashîd. Nearness to supreme power is perilous. The constant care of the ordinary subject is to avoid the attention of authority. A story in the *Nights* concerns a householder who, coming back from work in the evening, finds a corpse near his door. He is terrified to report his discovery to the police, lest they accuse him of murder." Having given (a slightly garbled) version of "The Tale of the Hunchback" with its migratory corpse, Kedourie made the point that for most people under a premodern Islamic regime, happiness was dependent on having as little as possible to do with the rulers, and he went on to quote Hârûn al-Rashîd's son and successor, the caliph al-Ma'mûn, who declared that "the best life has he who has an ample house, a beautiful wife, and sufficient means, who does not know us and whom we do not know" (15). Historically it was probably quite easy for middle- or lower-class Baghdadis to avoid the real Hârûn. But in the fictions of the *Nights*, humble folk were not so lucky, and for many of them, their story and their peril begin when they come up against the nocturnally prowling caliph and suddenly find themselves talking for their lives.

Modern political textbooks tend to be drab productions. This was not always the case in medieval times, when storytelling was an accepted way of transmitting religious, political, and moral ideas. Political treatises are not the only possible expressions of political thought (even if the academic prejudice inclines that way). Mobs and mob violence, carnivals and kings-for-a-day, shadow theater and storytelling can all furnish examples of the politics of the street. For all its apparent wildness, the politics of the street has tended to be conservative. Mobs in eighteenth-century England were more likely to riot against freethinkers and Roman Catholics than they were to demonstrate against the government (White 104–20; cf. Davis 152–87). In Mamluk times, the commonest targets of mob violence in Cairo and Damascus were Christians and Jews. Although there were occasional protests against individual sultans, viziers, or *muhtasibs*, people did not protest against the institutions as such. Moreover, protestors generally preferred to blame the sultan's evil councilors rather than the sultan himself (Shoshan, *Popular Culture* 62–66; Shoshan, "Grain Riots"; Grehan;

Irwin, *Middle East* 54, 94–95). As we shall see, the latent tendency of the politics of the stories of the *Nights* was to support the status quo.

Throughout the Islamic world, there was a strong tradition of transmitting wisdom and information through teaching stories. Consider the political agenda of Ibn al-Muqaffaʻ (d. ca. 760) in his Arabic version of the Indo-Persian collection of animal tales and fables, *Kalîla wa-Dimna*, where storytelling animals instruct a hypothetical ruler and his ministers in the duties and perils of governing (Ibn al-Muqaffaʻ). The Ismaʻîlîs and the Muslim Neoplatonist group of Ikhwân al-Safâ ("Brethren of Purity") frequently used stories and fables to make political or moral points (Netton 89–94). Later yet, from the late twelfth century onward, Sufi masters began to make use of the teaching tale. Moreover, the philosophers Ibn Tufayl (d. 1185), Ibn Sînâ (Avicenna; d. 1037), and Ibn al-Nafîs (d. 1288) all produced fantasies that dealt in part with political and social issues. The fifteenth-century historian and belletrist, Ibn ʻArabshah, produced the *Fâkihat al-Khulafâ'*, a story-collection with a strong political content (Irwin, "What the Partridge Told the Eagle"). To take one example, he includes the story of a king who wickedly thinks of violating a shepherdess. As soon as he does so, the milk of the animals runs dry. When he abandons his wicked thought, it flows again (El-Shamy 275–76; cf. 262–63). The message of the story is that the prosperity of the land is dependent on the moral health of the king. If the king strays, his land becomes a wasteland (a wasteland that may make us think of the Arthurian wasteland presided over by the wounded Fisher King).

Some of the stories in the *Nights* shed a rather odd sort of light on Islamic political thinking. Others, however, come very close to expounding the banal and somewhat servile ideas that can be found in mainstream political theory of the time as produced by scholars such as Ibn Jamâʻa (d. 1333) or the author of *Nasîhat al-Mulûk*. For example, in the "Tale of King Omar bin al-Nuʻuman and His Sons," the young woman Nuzhat al-Zamân, who has been enslaved and sold to King Sharkân, is asked to demonstrate her prowess to the *qâdîs*, so as to prove her worthiness to become the king's bride. "O King, to hear is to obey." She then gives a lecture on government that parrots most of the conventional Islamic thinking on the rights and duties of rulers and subjects (Burton, *Nights* 2: 156–71). Kingship and religion are inseparable (and here she is almost certainly quoting the Persian treatise *The Testament of Ardashir*, which was translated into Arabic by Ibn al-Muqaffaʻ in the early eighth century) (Lambton 45, 51). The king must govern justly, taking care of the weak and preventing robbery and dissention, so that all of his subjects may receive the just rewards of their labors. The king's pillars of government are his emirs and the religious scholars (*'ulamâ'*). There are three classes of king: kings of faith, kings who govern according to justice and protect the faith, and kings who govern according to their passions and selfish whims. Nuzhat al-Zamân's class one king is really a caliph. The class two king is a sultan who theoretically exercises authority as the executive agent of the caliph, and the class three king is a tyrant and perhaps an infidel as well. Nuzhat al-Zamân then alludes to virtuous examples of the pre-Islamic Persian kings, Ardashir and Chosroes. The general trend of her political wisdom is Persianate, as she presents justice as deriving from the will of the ruler, rather than from religious law (*sharî'a*). She advises her king to be neither too generous nor too stingy in paying his army, and to take advice from his chamberlains (the *hâjibs*). Beware of ostentation, beware of excess, beware of the advice of women, deal equitably with everyone. Nuzhat al-Zamân's speech, though it is no more than a hodgepodge of moralizing clichés and improving examples, draws great acclaim from Sharkân's courtiers. Nuzhat al-Zamân is just as tedious in her way as her rival in the world of tedious slave-girls, Tawaddud.

Shahrazâd herself attempts something of the same kind in Habicht's Breslau edition of the *Nights*, in which Shahrazâd, running out of stories perhaps, tells Shahriyâr his own story. (It appears in Burton under the title "Tale of Two Kings and the Vizier's Daughter.") Shahriyâr, in listening, recognizes his own cruel and unjust behavior and repents of it. Shahrazâd is then emboldened to lecture him on the duties of a just king. She points out (as if this may not have occurred to him before) that a strong king needs a strong army. He must deal justly with his subjects. The king is like a gardener. He must employ a virtuous vizier to deal justly with his people. The vizier is like a doctor. The king's subjects will serve him well if he serves them well, and, if he does not, then they will not. It is hardly surprising that Shahriyâr falls asleep at the end of all this (Burton, *Supplemental Nights* 2: 263–72). Similar banalities are uttered by the seven viziers who advise the king in "King Jali'âd of Hind and His Vizier Shimas." They give the monarch tedious lessons on virtue and moderation. Kings are necessary to dispense justice and protect their subjects from foreign enemies. A king who is merciful and wise is a good king. People should be content with their lot. There is a good deal more of such spiritless stuff, though leavened with fable and anecdote (Burton, *Nights* 9: 32–134). Incidentally, the Persian "national epic," the *Shâhnâme* by Firdousi, whose compilation was concluded toward the beginning of the eleventh century, is similarly infested with *andarz; andarz*, a Persian word, designates moral, political, or religious precepts that are usually attributed to famous people (Shaked). The monarchical lore of old Persia also features in "The Righteousness of King Anurshirwan" (Burton, *Nights* 5: 254–55).

It is one of the curious features of the *Nights* that villains, like the treacherous amazons in the *Tale of Omar bin Nu'uman and His Sons* or the evil stepmother in the Syntipas cycle are just as likely to deliver lectures on right rule and moral living as their more virtuous opponents. It seems that the wickedness of the messenger was not held to disqualify the virtue of the message. In this respect, the wicked but moralizing lecturers of the *Nights* can be compared to the evil but sententious jackal Dimna in Ibn al-Muqaffa''s *Kalîla wa-Dimna* and to the sermonizing rogue, Abû Zayd, in Harîrî's *Maqâmât* (Irwin, "Beast Fable" 45–46). It may be superfluous to remark that the readiness of the kings of the *Nights* to be lectured on politics by women is unlikely to be something that reflected historical reality.

Some of the moralizing about contentment with one's lot, avoidance of bad advice, and so forth in the *Nights* comes in the form of animal fables. One such group of fables follows "The Tale of the Birds and Beasts and the Carpenter" (Burton, *Nights* 3: 125–62). The general burden of these tales is minding one's own business, resorting to prayer, quietism, and resignation to one's fate. "The Tale of the Birds and Beasts and the Carpenter" is an abridged and adapted tale that derives ultimately from the tenth- or eleventh-century encyclopedia, the *Rasâ'il* of the Ikhwân al-Safâ, and one of the tales that follows, that of "The Cat and the Crow," concludes with an explicit message: "This story, O king showeth that the friendship of the Brethren of Purity delivereth and saveth from difficulties and from falling into mortal dangers" (Burton, *Nights* 3: 150). The second batch of animal fables, framed within the story of "King Jali'âd of Hind and His Wazir Shimas," are not explicitly linked with the doctrines of the Brethren of Purity, but they contain similar public service messages—trust in God, trust in those of one's fellow men who are worthy to be trusted, and so forth. Although these fables are notionally addressed to a king, it seems plain that their real target audience is much humbler folk.

To someone who has read Hobbes, Rousseau, Bakunin, or Oakeshott, the discourses of the viziers and storytelling slave-girls and the moralizing verbiage of the birds and the beasts will seem not so much examples of political thought as substitutes for it. Nevertheless, the naïve and servile sententiousness of the narrators cited above accurately reflects a great deal of mainstream political theory in the Islamic world, which was turgid, craven, and sometimes unrealistic. Formal writing on politics was the shared monopoly of the *'ulamâ'* and the pet essayists and scribes of the court, and it is their kind of writing that Nuzhat al-Zamân and other political lecturers in the *Nights* ultimately drew upon.

Apart from overt political lectures and *andarz* precepts that have been awkwardly inserted in the stories, the plotting and outcome of the story itself often have a latent political meaning. Jack Zipes, introducing a study of Grimms' *Märchen*, or fairy tales, remarked that "if we reread some of the tales with history in mind, and if we reflect for a moment on some of the issues at stake, it becomes apparent that these enchanting lovable tales are filled with all sorts of power struggles over kingdoms, rightful rule, money, women, children and land, and that their real 'enchantment' emanates from these dramatic conflicts whose resolutions allow us to glean the possibility of making the world, that is, shaping the world in accord with our needs and desires" (Zipes 20). This is largely true of the stories of the *Nights*, also. Only the last phrase, suggesting the possibility "of shaping the world in accord with our needs and desires," seems to me to have too overoptimistic and revolutionary a flavor to apply to many of the stories that circulated in the medieval Islamic world.

Submission to God, submission to Fate, and submission to the ruler dominate rather a large number of the stories. The political direction is determined at the outset, when Shahrazâd, rather than thinking of how to overthrow the tyrant Shahriyâr, instead proceeds to entertain him with stories. Incidentally, to be entertained by stories is one of the prerogatives of kingship. In the eleventh-century *Siyâsat-nâme*, the famous Persian mirror-for-princes treatise, its author, Nizâm al-Molk, states that the king cannot do without suitable cup-companions. And the cup-companion "must possess an ample fund of stories and strange tales both amusing and serious, and be able to tell them well" (89). And of course the need to entertain Hârûn al-Rashîd or some other ruler or prince by telling him the story of one's adventures is a recurring motif in the *Nights*. The political theorists of the medieval Islamic world were realists. Rather than waste their time thinking of alternatives to despotism, they preferred to concentrate on how to get the best despot. In political theory and in storytelling in the *Nights*, a despot could be improved by good servants who provided him not only with good advice but also with stories that were conducive to political virtue.

In the ideal kingdoms of the *Nights*, the wise prince, on the one hand, will beware of ghouls, wicked stepmothers, and apparently pointless interdictions (of the whatever-you-do-don't-go-through-that-door kind). On the other hand, the ideal ruler will listen to sagacious advice. He will be brave and generous. He will also be younger. Although the Arab tellers of tales unquestioningly accepted hereditary right, they did not accept primogeniture, as they shared the very general fairy-story teller's prejudice in favor of younger brothers. In addition to being younger, he will also be good looking. Good looks are certainly part of politics. The virtuous kings and heroes of the stories of the *Nights*, all of them good looking, are following (however unconsciously) the precept of Nizâm al-Molk's *Siyâsat-nâme*, in which he ruled that the sovereign must have physical beauty (10). Al-'Aynî (d. 1451) similarly, in the presentation chronicle he composed for the fifteenth-century Mamluk Sultan al-Mu'ayyad Shaykh, seems also to have regarded good looks as one of the desirable qualities of a ruler (234–37). Although many of the tales in the *Nights* either originated in the Mamluk period or were rewritten in that period, they fail to reflect the political realities of that age in two important respects. First, the stories stress hereditary right, something that was rather at a discount in the Mamluk period. Second, they commonly stress the power of the vizier and his great influence over the ruler, but the real authority of the vizier rapidly declined under the Mamluks, and David Ayalon has noted that by the fifteenth century the "principal and almost the only duty of the *wazir* was to supply meat to the army" (61).

It is easy to exaggerate the popular nature of the *Nights* and, because it is easy, I did so myself in my own book on the *Nights* (Irwin, *Companion*). Looking again at the inflated and editorially unpoliced corpus of the *Nights*, as it has come down to us in the Bulaq (1835) and Calcutta (1839–42) editions, I now think that I greatly underestimated the contribution of the literature of the boon-companions (*nudamâ'*) and belletrists of the court to that corpus. Material from al-Mas'ûdî (d. 956), al-Tanûkhî (d. 994), Abu 'l-Faraj al-Isfahânî (d. 967), and other respectable folk were recycled by scribes who produced manuscripts of the *Nights* from the fifteenth century onward. The conservative and monarchical tendency that pervades so much of the *Nights* reflects the fact that a great deal of popular literature derives ultimately from elite culture. In somewhat the same way, the chapbooks that were sold by colporteurs to French peasants in the seventeenth and eighteenth century celebrated old-fashioned virtues, magic, mystery, kingship, and knight errantry. Moreover, some of the authors of those chapbooks were quite substantial and highly educated people (Mandrou; Tenèze).

However, it is now time to turn to the alternative, adversarial, and anti-establishment themes in the *Nights*, for such themes are indeed occasionally present. Systematic oppositional texts and sketches of utopias or alternative societies seldom feature in Islamic literature. A rare example of an oppositional fable occupies a large part of one of the volumes of the encyclopedic *Rasâ'il* of the Brethren of Purity. The Brethren were a secretive group of philosophers in tenth- and eleventh-century Basra. They had Platonist interests and, perhaps, Isma'îlî sympathies. Their encyclopedia drew on Buddhist stories as well as other stories about kings and animals in order to make their points. Their main political fable has been mentioned already as the source of the *Nights* story "The Birds and Beasts and the Carpenter," and it has been translated under the title *The Case of the Animals versus Man before the King of the Jinn: A Tenth-Century Ecological Fable of the Pure Brethren of Basra* (Goodman). In this remarkable and quite lengthy story, which dominates the volume of the encyclopedia devoted to the subject "On How the Animals and Their Kinds Are Formed," the animals, birds, and fishes combine to bring a court case against humanity at the court of the King of the Jinn, seeking to have humanity condemned for its cruelty, waste of resources, and environmental heedlessness. But, while it is accurate to describe it as an ecological fable, this is only part of the story. A careful reading suggests that the Brethren of Purity were using their animal mouthpieces in this story to denounce not just human cruelty to animals but also human cruelty to humans. The fable amounts to an attack on society as it was constituted in the tenth century, as it denounces war, enslavement as a consequence of war, gross inequalities in wealth, lack of charity, overclever shyster bureaucrats, politically ambitious *'ulamâ'*, corrupt judges, and the tyrannical caliphs who commit all conceivable crimes—murder, debauchery, and robbery—driven by excessive greed. The animals, victims of mankind, also symbolize the blindly obedient masses (Enayat; cf. Nasr 95). Thus *The Case of the Animals* more closely resembles Orwell's *Animal Farm* than might appear at first sight. Incidentally, the Brethren made use of other fables to make less contentious points about the virtues of cunning and cooperation and so forth.

Fairy tales and tales from the *Nights*, most of them anyway, are one-man utopias—that is to say not really utopias at all. Aladdin, for example, gets the woman, the palace, the jewels, and the glory, but others do not, and the society from which he emerged remains unchanged. As Robert Darnton has observed in the context of a discussion of French folktales in the early modern period, "[t]o dream of confounding a king by marrying a princess was hardly to change the moral basis of the Old Regime" (59). However, outside the fantasy world of the *Nights*, the Brethren of Purity did put forward some inconsistent and incoherent ideas for a spiritual utopia, which they referred to as the *madîna fâdila ruhâniyya*—a term that clearly derives from the political philosophy of the tenth-century philosopher, al-Fârâbî. Utopias featured so rarely in medieval Arab conjectures that Pierre Versins, the splendid compiler of an encyclopedia of utopias, knew of only one such—al-Fârâbî's *Ârâ' ahl al-Madîna al-fâdila,* or "Ideas of the Inhabitants of the Virtuous City" (Farabi; Versins 57). This was a lightly Islamicized version of Plato's ideal republic, that was to be governed by a philosopher-king. En passant, it is noteworthy that al-Fârâbî and the Brethren of Purity after him both conceived of utopia as a city. Cities were places where power and wealth were to be found, and happiness too. Muslim philosophers and storytellers agreed on that point, and consequently they wasted no time on bucolic reveries. The woods and fields of the European fairy tale are almost completely absent from the *Nights*, as they are from Islamic political philosophy.

Although most tales of the *Nights* deal only with the fulfillment of individual wishes, there is one tale that essays a brief but striking sketch of an alternative society. This is "The Tale of Abdullah the Fisherman and Abdullah the Merman" (Burton, *Nights* 9: 165–88; cf. Miquel 111–42). In this story the fisherman is introduced by the merman to the marvels of the deep, including merfolk's society. The merfolk, who dwell in numerous underwater cities, do not buy or sell, they have no use for precious stones, and they practice free love. They are in effect communists. I hardly need to add that the communism of the merfolk was presented as something to be marveled at, one of many marvels of the deep, rather than something to be emulated. But any kind of reference to communism in premodern Islamic discourse is extremely rare, even if some writers in the Islamic period, most notably Ibn al-Muqaffa', were fascinated by Mazdak, a sixth-century (and therefore pre-Islamic) Persian communist insurgent who was alleged to have fought for communal access to women and property (Crone, "Kavad's Heresy"). Although there were Muslim anarchists in ninth-century Basra (Crone, "Ninth-Century Muslim Anarchists"), I have found no echoes of this in the *Nights*. It is also disappointing that the other underwater society to feature in the *Nights*, that of "Julnar the Sea-Born," seems to have been a conventional monarchy (Burton, *Nights* 7: 264–308).

"The Tale of Abdullah the Fisherman" also mentions a "City of the Women of the Sea." Amazon communities also appear in the "Tale of

Omar bin Nu'uman," "The Man Who Never Laughed during the Rest of his Days," "Hasan of Basra," and "The Lovers of Syria." But such tales are rather a reflection of erotic fantasy than of political concerns (feminist or otherwise). Women who rule get a bad press in the stories and are sometimes presented as sorceresses or man-eating ghouls, though there are a number of important exceptions.

The story of "Abu Kir the Dyer and Abu Sir the Barber" celebrates the superiority of medieval or early modern Egyptian commerce and technology over those of far-flung heathen parts (Burton, *Nights* 9: 134–65). But Sindbad is, of course, the most famous explorer of exotic parts. The sea that Sindbad of the Sea sets out on is a highway to the mysteries of alien societies, and Sindbad of the Sea instructs Sindbad of the Land about such exotic matters as the Indian caste system, suttee, cannibal tribes, the city of apes, and the city of flying men. Sindbad's sea is thus, to some extent, a political sea. And here I cannot resist quoting from Oakeshott again: "In political activity then, men sail a boundless and bottomless sea; there is neither harbour for shelter nor floor for anchorage, neither starting place nor appointed destination. The enterprise is to keep afloat on an even keel; the sea is both friend and enemy; and seamanship consists in using the resources of a traditional manner of behaviour in order to make a friend of every hostile occasion" (127). But the unfortunate Sindbad is no good at all at staying afloat, and he makes friends of hostile occasions (such as the Old Man of the Sea) only belatedly and with great difficulty. In the end, the narrated dangers of the exotic function as a kind of affirmation of all that is familiar and traditional in Islamic society.

The king wandering the streets in disguise in order to learn the secrets of his subjects is one of the most familiar themes in storytelling and historical folklore. Apart from Hârûn al-Rashîd, rulers such as al-Hâkim bi-Amrillâh, Qâytbây, Pedro the Cruel, James V of Scotland, and many others are reputed to have done so. In many of the stories of the *Nights*, the king perambulating the city in disguise, serves as no more than a perfunctory prelude or framing device to someone else's adventure. In two stories, however, real or pretended failure to penetrate the ruler's disguise licenses sociopolitical criticism. In "The Night Adventures of Sultan Mohammed of Cairo" (Burton, *Supplemental Nights* 5: 90–94), the sultan and his vizier in disguise are looking for a certain house within which the sultan has previously glimpsed a beautiful damsel. To that end, the vizier has advised the sultan to decree that no candles should be lit in the city after the evening prayer. Then they identify a house that is not observing the blackout and, sure enough, the damsel is inside. They present themselves as dervishes seeking shelter for the night, but the sharp-witted damsel who has penetrated their disguise and knows perfectly well who they are takes advantage of their supposed dervishhood to deliver an unusually acerbic political lecture: "O Darwaysh, verily the Sultan's order should not be obeyed save in commandments which be reasonable; but this proclamation forbidding lights is sinful to accept; and indeed the right direction wherein man should walk is according to Holy Law which saith, 'No obedience to the creature in a matter of sin against the Creator.' The Sultan (Allah make him prevail!) herein acteth against the Law and imitateth the doings of Satan." The damsel then goes on to explain that the ordinance against candles was making it difficult for spinners, like the women of her family, to continue to earn their living. When the vizier points out that obedience is due the sultan from all his subjects, she replies that he may be sultan, but how does he know whether his subjects are starving or not? And she reemphasizes the point that obedience is not due to a sovereign who is in breach of the *sharî'a*. The sultan in disguise takes her admonishment in good part and returns the following night to give the family money and hear their story.

"The History of al-Bundukani" (Burton, *Supplemental Nights* 7: 42–85) is another example of a story in which the disguise of the ruler licenses his subject to speak bluntly. The circumstances are different in that, though the caliph Hârûn al-Rashîd is in disguise, the old woman he encounters has not penetrated that disguise. Instead, she mistakes for him a robber and a captain of thieves. At a certain level however, this is no mistake as the caliph with his corrupt officers and oppressive taxes is indeed a kind of robber-king. In the naïve old lady's eyes, only his status as a terrible robber can explain the terror and obedience the man inspires in all around him, "for that Moslems one and all dread him and his mischief." Only successful thieving can explain his lavish fortune. Later on in this comedy of errors, the same woman talking to Hârûn whom she still believes to be a robber chief, denounces the caliph for having ruined her household and unjustly imprisoned her son. However, it would be a mistake to make very much of all this, as in the end the caliph uses his wealth and power to make everything right for the widow and free her son from his unjust imprisonment. In this and many other tales the values of the establishment are implicitly affirmed.

To hear is to obey! The fantastic stories of the *Nights* that were read or listened to by people living under Mamluk or Ottoman despotism offered

Robert Irwin

them no escape from the despotic solution. Fiction merely offered different despots, Shahriyâr, Hârûn al-Rashîd, Sultan Muhammad. . . . Some were better and some worse than the ones the audience actually lived under.

WORKS CITED

Ayalon, David. "Studies in the Structure of the Mamluk Army." *Bulletin of the School of Oriental and African Studies* 15 (1953): 203–28 (pt. 1); 448–76 (pt. 2); 16 (1954): 57–90 (pt. 3).

Al-'Aynî, Badr al-Dîn. *Al-Sayf al-muhannad fî sîrat al-Malik al-Mu'ayyad Shaykh al-Mahmûd.* Ed. Fahim Muhammad Shaltût. Cairo: Dâr al-Kâtib al-'arabî, 1967.

Burton, Richard. *A Plain and Literal Translation of the Arabian Nights Entertainments: Now Entitled the Book of the Thousand Nights and a Night.* 10 vols. Benares [i.e., London]: Kamashastra Soc., 1885–88.

———. *Supplemental Nights to the Book of the Thousand Nights and a Night.* 6 vols. Benares [i.e., London]: Kamashastra Soc., 1886–88.

Crone, Patricia. "Did al-Ghazali Write a Mirror for Princes? On the Authorship of *Nasîhat al-mulûk.*" *Jerusalem Studies in Arabic and Islam* 10 (1987): 167–91.

———. "Kavad's Heresy and Mazdak's Revolt." *Iran* 29 (1991): 21–42.

———. "Ninth-Century Muslim Anarchists." *Past and Present* 167 (2000): 3–28.

Darnton, Robert. *The Great Cat Massacre and Other Episodes in French Cultural History.* London: Allen Lane, 1984.

Davis, Natalie Zemon: *Society and Culture in Early Modern France.* Stanford: Stanford UP, 1965.

El-Shamy, Hasan, ed. and trans. *Folktales of Egypt.* Chicago: U of Chicago P, 1980.

Enayat, Hamid. "An Outline of the Political Philosophy of the *Rasâ'il* of the Ikhwân al-Safâ." *Isma'ili Contributions to Islamic Culture.* Ed. Hossein Nasr. Tehran: Imperial Iranian Academy of Philosophy, 1977. 23–49.

Al-Farabi on the Perfect State (Ârâ'ahl al-Madîna al-fâdila). Ed. and trans. R. Walzer. Oxford: Oxford UP, 1985.

Goodman, Len, trans. *The Case of the Animals versus Man before the King of the Jinn: A Tenth-Century Ecological Fable of the Pure Brethren of Basra.* 4th ed. Los Angeles: Gee Tee Bee, 1978.

Grehan, James. "Street Violence and Social Interaction in Late Mamluk and Ottoman Damascus (ca. 1500–1800)." *International Journal of Middle East Studies* 35 (2003): 215–36.

Haddawy, Husain, trans. *The Arabian Nights.* New York: Norton, 1990.

Ibn al-Muqaffa', Abû Muhammad 'Abd Allâh. *Kalîla wa-Dimna.* Ed. Louis Cheikho. Beirut: Imprimerie Catholique, 1905.

Irwin, Robert. *The Arabian Nights: A Companion.* London: Allen Lane, 1994.

———. "The Arabic Beast Fable." *Journal of the Warburg and Courtauld Institutes* 55 (1992): 36–50.

———. *The Middle East in the Middle Ages: The Early Mamluk Sultanate, 1250–1382.* Beckenham, Kent: Croom Helm, 1986.

———. "What the Partridge Told the Eagle: A Neglected Source on Chinggis Khan and the Early History of the Mongols." *The Mongol Empire and Its Legacy.* Ed. Reuven Amitai-Preiss and David O. Morgan. Leiden: Brill, 1999. 5–11.

Kedourie, Elie. *Politics in the Middle East.* Oxford: Oxford UP, 1992.

Lambton, Ann K. S. *State and Government in Medieval Islam: An Introduction to the Study of Islamic Political Theory: The Jurists.* Oxford: Oxford UP, 1981.

Mahdi, Muhsin, ed. *The Thousand and One Nights (Alf Layla wa-Layla): From the Earliest Known Sources.* 2 vols. Leiden: Brill, 1984.

Mandrou, Robert. *De la culture populaire aux 17e et 18e siècles: La bibliothèque bleue de Troyes.* Paris: Stock, 1964.

Miquel, André. *Sept contes des Mille et une Nuits, ou Il n'y a pas de contes innocents.* Paris: Sindbad, 1981.

Nasr, Hossein. *An Introduction to Islamic Cosmological Doctrines: Conceptions of Nature and Methods Used for Its Study by the Ikhwân al-Safâ', al-Bîrûnî and Ibn Sînâ.* Cambridge: Belknap P, 1964.

Netton, Ian Richard. *Muslim Neoplatonists: An Introduction to the Thought of the Brethren of Purity.* London: George Allen and Unwin, 1982.

Nizam al-Mulk. *The Book of Government; or, Rules for Kings: The Siyâsatnâma or Siyar al-Mulûk.* Trans. Hubert Darke. London: Routledge and Kegan Paul, 1960.

Oakeshott, Michael. *Rationalism in Politics and Other Essays.* 2nd ed. Indianapolis: Liberty Fund, 1991.

Shaked, Shaul. "Andarz. I: Andarz and andarz literature in pre-Islamic Iran." *Encyclopedia Iranica.* Vol. 2. London: Routledge and Kegan Paul, 1987. 11–16.

Shoshan, Boaz. "Grain Riots and the 'Moral Economy': Cairo 1350–1517." *Journal of Interdisciplinary History* 10 (1979–80): 459–78.

———. *Popular Culture in Medieval Cairo.* Cambridge: Cambridge UP, 1993.

Tenèze, Marie-Louise. "Bibliothèque bleue." *Enzyklopädie des Märchens.* Vol. 2. Berlin: Walter de Gruyter, 1979. 283–87.

Versins, Pierre. *Encyclopédie de l'utopie, des voyages extraordinaires et de la science fiction.* 2nd ed. Lausanne: L'Age de d'Homme, 1972.

White, T. H. *The Age of Scandal: An Excursion through a Minor Period.* London: Jonathan Cape, 1950.

Zipes, Jack. *Breaking the Magic Spell: Radical Theories of Folk and Fairy Tales.* London: Heinemann, 1979.

Framing as Form and Meaning

8

The Teacher and the Taught: Structures and Meaning in the *Arabian Nights* and the *Panchatantra*

Sadhana Naithani

The *Arabian Nights* and the *Panchatantra* are both works of Asian origin, and both have exercised their power over folkloric and literary imagination across continents for many centuries. The *Panchatantra* has been considered to be the older of the two, and it is supposed to have influenced the *Nights*, yet the narratives about the origin of each of these works do not supply clear evidence. Both of them exist in more than one native version, and both have become popular in modern times by way of their translations into European languages. Through the ages, in telling and retelling, in translations and annotations, versions of the stories have emerged and become the subject of many scholarly works. For a folklorist scholar today, the widespread distribution and popular reception of the two works present a particular situation for research. The *Arabian Nights* continues to be an extremely popular work and is presented in the newest media, including, most recently, computer-animated films and video games. The *Panchatantra*'s genre is classified as fable, and accordingly it appears most prominently in various forms of children's literature. At the academic level, constant and valuable research on the process of how the two works came into being has revealed how they were molded and "constructed" in a continuous process lasting for many centuries. And yet, though the existing research is quite exhaustive, numerous details of their history and character, particularly of the *Arabian Nights*, remain to be studied (Marzolph 19).

A folklorist is faced with this contrast between the popular renown and the academic conclusions about the *Nights*. If this essay, then, proposes to analyze the ending of the *Nights*, on which version should this analysis be based: on the famous but highly constructed one, like Richard Burton's, or on others regarded as closer to "native" or "authentic" versions? Considering the intense discussion on the subject of the construction of the *Nights*, none of the versions retains credibility. I see this as the particular situation of research today when we are aware of the "folklore" materials as they have emerged in the process of modernity and textualizing. With reference to the textualization of Asian folkloric works into European languages during the past five centuries, it is worth noting that the so-called constructs have acquired an identity that has its own authenticity, such as an identity across national boundaries. Galland's *Mille et une Nuits* or Burton's *Nights*, for example, are known to millions of readers across the world as the *Thousand and One Nights* or the *Arabian Nights*. The "constructs" exist and cannot be wished away. More important, they need to be treated as "folklore" materials of a very special kind. Indeed, the process of textualization of oral narratives is often complex and varied. Each textualized narrative is a version, and there are often various textualized versions prepared from different sources, which is exactly the situation in the case of the *Arabian Nights*. How, then, should these different textualizations be treated for interpretative and analytical studies? I think that they present a situation similar to the one offered by oral variants.

Global Folklore

The various European versions of the *Arabian Nights*, based on different manuscripts, may be seen as different textualized versions. At the same time, our academic understanding of the *Arabian Nights* as a Western construct should not prevent us from acknowledging their folkloric identity. If the "constructs" have become internationally renowned versions, then their analysis refers probably less to their native contexts and more to their acquired international meaning. At a more specific level, the process of the emergence of European constructs of Asian folklore and their travel across continents is intrinsically related to the geography of the colonial world. Folklore from different parts of the world traveled to various other parts in the languages of the colonial rulers with an unprecedented speed. The popular renown and identity they gained under these circumstances have transcended their contexts. While the science of folklore may reevaluate them as constructs, it cannot deny that the constructs have been received as authentic by millions of listeners and readers for centuries. This situation necessitates their acceptance as a kind of folklore generated by a new process and received by people in circumstances completely different from those of their "original" context. This kind of folklore also has identifiable authors—translators and collectors—who were, to a certain extent, also storytellers. Rather than repeat a critique of the concept of construct, I propose to identify these constructs as a kind of folklore that is transnational. Different rural and urban systems have all generated their own folklore, and this one too is a product of a certain time—when the first global networks of cultural communication emerged, when the need to communicate internationally influenced the lives of an ever-increasing number of people.

This type of folklore material has a close relation to geography. The titles of numerous works of a folkloric character refer to geographical, national, linguistic, ethnic, and religious contexts. For example, the *Thousand and One Nights* are commonly known as the *"Arabian" Nights*, hereby referring quite distinctly to a specific regional or geographical context of the narrative and narratives being presented. Simultaneously, however, the works were not primarily intended for the contexts implied in their titles, but rather for transnational contexts. They were published and read elsewhere. By now, they have become integrated in various geographical, national, linguistic, and religious contexts. This fact also frees them from the limitations set by the boundaries implied in their titles. They stop to refer to a particular geographic and ethnic cultural context, probably to impart a sense of direction and landscape to their global readers. Additionally, there are innumerable genuine and fake versions—constructs of constructs. By Vladimir Propp's method of identification, the popularity of the original constructs would place them in the category "folklore by transmission" (8–9); and Propp was ready to grant this status to works of literature that had found their way into the folk and gained "versions" in the oral culture. The European versions of the *Arabian Nights* and the *Panchatantra* fulfill all the above-mentioned criteria. At the same time, their transnational character does not stand in contradiction to the relative status of the known and unknown native versions, nor the search for those.

In the following, I have chosen Richard Burton's the *Thousand Nights and a Night* as the main reference. For the *Panchatantra*, I have chosen the recent edition by Vishnu Sharma that is based on a Sanskrit manuscript dating from the eleventh century. The translation and introduction to the volume by Chandra Rajan—a contemporary Indian academic who is aware of the discourse about orientalist constructs—take into consideration the postcolonial context and debates and present a text that is translated into English directly from a medieval Sanskrit manuscript and, hence, is not a European construct.

Who Teaches Whom?

The *Arabian Nights* and the *Panchatantra* have both been studied from various perspectives. Both contain a large number of stories grouped within an umbrella or frame story, and the umbrella story of each work has remained more constant through the ages than the set of stories contained within. The present essay is a comparative study of the two umbrella stories, both of which have an identity independent of the stories they shelter. The comparative study proceeds from the observation that the structures of the two frame stories are strikingly similar, though composed of different specific elements.

Both stories are built on the education of rulers. This does not involve the education of "normal" persons but those difficult to be taught. Both teachers accept the challenge voluntarily but in the interest of the populace who would otherwise suffer under bad rulers. Both teach through the narration of stories. Both the umbrella stories have happy endings, as the teachers are successful in transforming their pupils into wise rulers. These points suggest a twinlike similarity between the structures of the *Arabian Nights* and the *Panchatantra*. Yet if we look at the structures analytically, we find that similarities are mixed with interesting dissimilarities.

The umbrella story of the *Arabian Nights* is the story of Shahrazâd—a young and learned girl—who cures the great King Shahriyâr of his emotional trauma and mental illness. Shahriyâr, distraught by the betrayal of his wife, had become a murderer of virgins—both literally and metaphorically. His kingdom became depleted of marriageable girls, but his revenge was not over. Night after night, his ministers and servants would procure a girl for him to bed and then behead at the break of the dawn. The gruesome killings went on, until one day the elder of the two daughters of his vizier, named Shahrazâd, volunteered to spend the night with him—a night that was promised to end in her beheading. Not dissuaded by her father, she also took her sister along. Shahrazâd went, offered herself, and when only a few hours separated life from death, her sister in a planned stratagem asked her to tell a story. Shahrazâd started, and the hours flew by. The night ended, but the narrative had not come to an end, and Shahrazâd stopped narrating. On this morning, the king did not call the guard to take the girl for beheading. Nor did he free her. Shahrazâd lived the day and narrated again at night, and the next night and the next and so on, and her narratives brought the king back to sanity.

The umbrella story of the *Panchatantra* is the story of Vishnu Sharma—a matured teacher who was invited by a king to teach his three sons. The three young princes of the *Panchatantra* were notorious for being incapable of any learning, and many a teacher had failed in their attempt to teach the boys. The wise prescribed a twelve-year-long education, or else, they suggested that the renowned teacher Vishnu Sharma be asked if he could teach them. Vishnu Sharma not only accepted the task of educating the princes into learned and sensitive rulers but also promised to complete his task in six months time. "Panchatantra" or, literally, five stratagems, are contained in the large number of stories that he told to successfully transform the princes.

The most striking difference in the two umbrella stories is the gender identity of the two teachers. Shahrazâd of the *Arabian Nights* is a young woman. Vishnu Sharma, the teacher in the *Panchatantra*, is an aged male professional teacher. This difference, however, is contrasted by similarity at another level—both are extremely learned and both are quite confident. Shahrazâd is introduced as having "perused the books, annals and legends of preceding Kings. . . . She had perused the works of poets and knew them by heart; . . . studied philosophy and the sciences, arts and accomplishments" (Burton 15). The narrator of *Panchatantra* is introduced as "Brahmana, Vishnu Sharma, a scholar par excellence who, according to the reputation he has among the body of students here, has mastery over several fields of learning" (Vishnu Sharma 4).

The difference between the two teachers intensifies in the two situations of teaching: Shahrazâd is a volunteer, actually a gambler for her own life. She tells her father: "I wish thou wouldst give me in marriage to this King Shahriyâr; either I shall live or I shall be a ransom for the virgin daughters of Moslems and the cause of their deliverance" (Burton 15). She gambles with her life because she believes in her tales. After instructing her sister to demand a story at night, she says: "I will tell thee a tale which shall be our deliverance, if so Allah please, and which shall turn the King from his bloodthirsty custom" (24). Shahrazâd must come to the palace, wed the king, and trick him into hearing stories that are meant to transform him: "when it was midnight Shahrazad awoke and signaled to her sister Dunyazad who sat up and said: 'recite to us some new story, delightsome and delectable'" (24). Shahrazâd seeks the king's permission and begins to narrate.

In the *Panchatantra*, Vishnu Sharma is a confident, almost arrogant teacher: "If I do not teach your [the king's] sons in such a manner that in six months time they do not have complete mastery over all the wide expanse of political and practical wisdom, then let my name be thrown away and forgotten. . . . In six months time, your sons will possess unsurpassed knowledge of all branches of practical wisdom. Hear! This is my lion-roar" (5). Vishnu Sharma is invited and employed by the father of the princes and has the students in his charge. The king, father of his students said: "Do me a favour, sir, and take the princes in hand; teach them, instruct them, so that they become unsurpassed in their mastery over all matters relating to practical wisdom" (5); "Vishnu Sharma took charge of them and took them home with him" (5).

This comparison again reveals an interesting mix of dissimilarities and oblique similarities: Shahrazâd stakes her life, while Vishnu Sharma stakes the respect and honor he has earned through his life. Almost universally, the two stakes would be considered of equal importance. Shahrazâd's role as teacher is neither declared, nor predefined, nor articulated in the process, but hidden behind her role as storyteller and entertainer. Vishnu Sharma's identity as a teacher is of supreme importance, and yet he disappears behind his stories. Both the teachers are, however, extremely confident of the power of their knowledge and their method of communicating this knowledge. In accepting their respective tasks, they are as alone as each other.

The listeners of these tales, or those who were to be taught by these teachers, build another curious set of target audience. The most obvious is the difference in their age and state of mind. The target listener of Shahrazâd's tales—King Shahriyâr—is an adult male whom personal experience has changed from being a good and just ruler to a murderer, and he had sworn himself "by a binding oath that whatever wife he married he would abate her maidenhead at night and slay her next morning" (Burton 14). The three princes in the *Panchatantra*, listeners of the stories told by Vishnu Sharma, are young boys, described by their father as "obstinate fools" (Vishnu Sharma 3) and as "all dunces of the first water, each one more dull-witted than the other" (4). Moreover, they do not have any say in the matter of their education. Thus, while Vishnu Sharma is called to inscribe his tales on clean slates, because "their intelligence has to be awakened" (4), Shahrazâd's tales must awaken her listener in a different sense, her tales must, first of all, possess the power to erase prior experience and knowledge.

The differences between the identities of the narrators and recipients are two sides of a triangle whose base line is constituted by the narratives themselves. The narratives of the *Arabian Nights* and the *Panchatantra* belong to two radically different genres. Ferial Ghazoul's comparative study of the two works is concerned with the different types of tales contained in the two works. She locates the following reasons for the apparent discrepancy: Vishnu Sharma, in creating fables for his young pupils, told tales of human society through animal characters; Shahrazâd's tales are meant for an adult listener and explore dark recesses of human psychology. Thus, Ghazoul concludes that "the elements of the poetic logic of the Indian classic converge in order to *mean* while the narrative logic of the Arabian classic works in order to *be*." (21) Her insightful conclusion of the "difference" between the types of tales in the two works, and the way each work effectively creates its own situation, nonetheless misses the point that Vishnu Sharma is telling these tales to educate irresponsible young boys into becoming responsible adults, while Shahrazâd is working to bring the king back from depravity to a balanced adult approach to life. Both teacher-narrators succeed in bringing their royal pupils back to the humanly acceptable rational social world, albeit from two opposite extremes of "ignorance."

Within a comparative study of the two works, one is faced with a complex set of structural similarities and meaningful differences. The similarity in the purpose of narration and its successful completion through decisively different kinds of narratives suggests the hypothesis that there are different levels of the communication of knowledge from the teacher to the taught, a specific and an abstract level. The gender identities of the narrators, their relation to their listeners, and their narratives belong to the specific level. An integral relationship between the kind of knowledge communicated and the form of its communication belong to the abstract level.

What Is Being Taught?

In the following I will explore the hypothesis that there is a relationship between the specific and the abstract levels of the two works under consideration. In other words: what do Vishnu Sharma's narratives expose the princes to beyond the stated morals of the stories? Are the nonhuman protagonists such as animals and plants only props to reveal the machinations of human society? Why do Shahriyâr's narratives have the power to transform Shahriyâr if "the aim is plain living, *survivre*" (Ghazoul 17)? If it is as difficult to locate any "moral" in Shahrazâd's tales as it is impossible to miss it in Vishnu Sharma's tales, then what exactly is being communicated that transforms Shahriyâr?

To answer the above questions, I will leave aside the morals deducible from the *Panchatantra* narratives and their possible interpretations toward the construction of socioethical codes. Instead, I will take into consideration what the *Panchatantra* communicates beyond the machinations of human society through the use of nonhuman protagonists. In the context of the *Arabian Nights*, I ignore the existential quality of Shahrazâd's narratives as strategies for survival in order to see her as a teacher and more. For the sake of analysis, and because of the mystery regarding the original narrators of the two works, I consider Shahrazâd and Vishnu Sharma as filling equivalent roles. If they are creations of some other narrators—which is most likely—then each unknown narrator idealized herself or himself through them.

Shahrazâd's tales are tales of human characters and society—be they king or beggar, master or slave, man or woman, virtuous or vile, realistic or magical, thief or saint. They are stories about human beings and their relationships, their capabilities, their desires, their true and false sense of values, their powers and their weaknesses. The jinnis and other creatures appear to regulate, change, and facilitate human affairs, but they either do not belong there (like the jinnis), or they are not independent characters of a story. Shahrazâd weaves a magical charm of real and imaginary landscapes and cityscapes, but these are peopled. Mother nature and her ways become matters of observation and juxtapositions through which Shahrazâd portrays contradictions that cannot be avenged by one or the other: "See'st not when blows the hurricane, sweeping stark and striking strong / How many trees earth nourisheth of the dry and of the green" (Burton 25).

The conflicts between justice and injustice, kindness and cruelty, loyalty and deceit, the banal and the wondrous, joy and sorrow are constituents that are closely related to each other in nature itself, and yet, the one is not necessarily responsible for the downfall of the other. The hurricane blows, and trees get caught in it, but the hurricane is not responsible for the fate of the trees, nor can it be blamed because of its blowing, independent of the effects. The like contradictions do not intend to argue that one is better than the other, and therefore, ultimate and final judgments are not possible. In

Shahrazâd's narratives, human nature is a reflection of Mother Nature herself, containing all shades of emotions that collide with each other due to their own laws of motion. The collision, however, is not always intentional, nor controllable, but it exists. The acceptance of its existence, especially where it cannot be controlled, is the first step toward finding one's own place in the scheme of things. And one's own place is caught between "natural" contradictions, the contradictions relating to emotions, beliefs, deeds, and knowledge. The subject of these contradictions can neither judge nor be judged on any absolute scale. Knowledge is the realization of mystery, deeds never have only a singular effect, beliefs stand to be corrected, and emotions need to be accompanied by compassion for the mystery. These interconnections in Shahrazâd's weltanschauung are transformative.

Shahrazâd plays her role in opposition to her listener Shahriyâr. She remains an invisible narrator who knows everything but is "only" narrating. Magic and adventure are the two most widely prevalent elements in the *Arabian Nights*, though Shahrazâd actually shows her listener the joys and sorrows of the entire humanity. In her play with magic and adventure, I see a relation between the abstract and the specific level of communication: Shahrazâd's types of tales are essentially related to the real purpose of her narration. Shahriyâr's mind is afflicted with experience, and Shahrazâd takes him on unbelievable journeys, creates magical scenarios with such a craft that he can believe in these shimmering illusions. What Shahrazâd's magical adventure stories do is to create a counterhypnosis to the one afflicting Shahriyâr, and in this state of mind she can speak to him directly, as she eventually does in the end. Still, it took almost three years for Shahriyâr to see the light and Shahrazâd to reveal her purpose—six times more than it took the great teacher in the *Panchatantra* to teach his pupils.

The question of the end is an important one in the context of the multiple texts of the *Arabian Nights*. Heinz Grotzfeld's article on the "neglected conclusions" of the *Nights* discusses the different conclusions of the umbrella story of the *Nights*, particularly in the less well known versions. Grotzfeld says: "The original conclusion of the *Nights* seems to be lost" (75). And yet, his references go back to a "*Nights* recension which circulated in Baghdad" in the tenth century. Grotzfeld compares the well-known versions like that of Galland with "forgotten and overlooked recensions" prepared from different sources and languages. Three important classifications emerge: one, that Shahrazâd pleads for mercy in the name of the child or children she has had from Shahriyâr; two, that Shahrazâd "converts" Shahriyâr over a period of a thousand and one nights into reevaluating his act of beheading the girls; and three, that Shahrazâd weaves into her narratives Shahriyâr's own story as the last tale before revealing her true purpose. We then have different versions of the end of the *Nights* for analysis, but how different are these versions? There are more common elements in them than different ones. Common elements are: Shahrazâd has had children with Shahriyâr, she reveals the true purpose of her narratives, he concedes her intelligence and accepts her as his wife. The differences consist of minor details: whether one or more offspring, whether Shahrazâd holds forth at the end in grand style or not, whether Dînâzâd is married to Shahriyâr's brother or not. In consequence, the differences do not make significant difference to this analysis. None of the different versions in the manuscripts contradict or dilute Shahrazâd's success and Shahriyâr's acceptance of her role in his transformation.

In Burton's text, Shahriyâr does not offer forgiveness on his own. He remains in his role as the ruler, and Shahrazâd in her gender and status role must ask for redemption most indirectly: "these thousand nights and a night have I entertained thee with stories of the folk. . . . May I then make bold to crave a boon of Thy Highness" (Burton 508). When permitted, she brings her children to the fore and says: "I crave that thou release me from the doom of death, as a dole to these infants; for, if thou kill me, they will become motherless and will find none among women to rear them as they should be reared" (Burton 508). In this manner, Shahrazâd hints at her role as a teacher to her children, and as soon as the boon is granted, the teacher in her speaks directly to the pupil who has never before admitted to being one: "Thou marvelledest at that which befell thee on the part of women; yet there betided the Kings of the Chisroes before thee greater mishaps and more grievous than that which hath befallen thee, and indeed I have set forth unto thee that which happened to Caliphs and Kings and others with their women, but the relation is lonesome and hearkening groweth tedious, and in this is all sufficient warning for the man of wits and admonishment for the wise" (Burton 508–9). This Shahrazâd reminds us of the younger Shahrazâd who volunteered to go to the murderous king believing in herself and her knowledge. Shahrazâd was not only narrating to postpone her death—sufficiently evidenced in her definite act of stopping narration at the break of each dawn. She reveals her true purpose to him and is as confident of the value of her narratives as Vishnu Sharma was at the beginning of his project. Again a dissimilar similarity—both know and declare that they are teachers because those they teach or taught will be or were transformed into new human beings.

The *Panchatantra* is supposed to have been authored by Vishnu Sharma. Still, the question remains: who was Vishnu Sharma? When did he live? There are no definite answers to these questions. Chandra Rajan offers various possibilities: Vishnu Sharma probably was a folk narrator, or maybe a court personage who had keenly observed the ways of the kings and the courtiers. He may also be a fictional character. Seen in the context of Indian tradition, the anonymity of artists and authors is a regular feature. Vishnu Sharma may also be the name of more than one person who were his direct or indirect followers and who contributed to the growth of the work. Whatever Vishnu Sharma's historical identity is, it is his identity as integrated in the *Panchatantra* that is relevant for our analysis. Whoever it was that chose to teach through animal stories, chose its characters within larger narrative traditions and cosmological conceptions, he appears determined to reveal the place of all things alive—including the plant kingdom. The larger narrative tradition dates back to the *Rig Veda* and the prevalence of animal characters on a par with humans. In the subsequent development of philosophical thought on the Indian subcontinent, there is no essential difference between the human and nonhuman forms of life. The conception of time as circular and life and death as transitions from one form of life to another in rebirth obliterates the differences between the various species at the metaphysical level. However, it would be factually incorrect if this evaluation were to suggest that the narrator of the *Panchatantra* only used the narrative techniques available to him. No work of Indian literature prior to the *Panchatantra* made such an exclusive use of animals in storytelling. The stories contained in the Jatakas, didactic tales about Buddha's various rebirths that are considered to be more ancient than the *Panchatantra*, use animals in their interaction with human beings and also delve into their human traits. They do not proceed from the sameness of the soul in all living beings but elaborate the principle itself. The *Panchatantra* assigns no explanations for the way its animal characters are. They occupy center stage with an unprecedented obviousness that goes far beyond the usage of a particular narrative technique. The narrator of *Panchatantra* also keenly observed and appreciated the animal and plant kingdoms. The lessons in social ethics and propriety are loud, but there is a sublime level of teaching—the knowledge about animals and plants.

The reason for Vishnu Sharma choosing to narrate through animal characters seems to reflect a particular philosophical plane. The *Panchatantra*'s first book apparently states a reason for this attitude: "Any creature understands what is plainly said," because the "intellect sees clearly revealed another's true intent and purpose, gains knowledge from expression of face and eyes, from gesture and deportment" (Vishnu Sharma 1: 18). Not only are animals like human characters, but the human being in the *Panchatantra* also has animal traits. "Princes are like serpents" (1: 23), the narrator teaches his royal pupils. All characteristics and traits—bravery, honesty, deceit, and cruelty—are actually subject-neutral, as they are present not only in humans. It is the characteristic reflected in the deed that defines or differentiates the good and the evil:

> A crow named Lightwing . . . saw a fowler approaching the tree. . . . He was a man of fierce appearance with splayed hands and feet, bloodshot eyes, bulging genitals; thickset, with a very rough, gnarled frame and swarthy complexion; his hair was knotted in a bunch on top of his head. Why describe him at great length? Suffice it to say that he appeared a second god of destruction, noose in hand; the very incarnation of evil and the soul of unrighteousness; prime instructor in crime and bosom friend of Death. (2: 194)

Crow is the witness to the acts of a "fowler." Life on planet earth is a theatre where everyone is simultaneously an actor and audience, but

> Sun and Moon, Fire and Wind, Heaven and Earth!
> The Waters, Death and the Self! Day and Night,
> and both the Twilights! You all watch the round
> of Man's existence and see if it is right. (1: 170)

The "intelligent art of living" that the *Panchatantra* has set out to teach needs to be based on the perception of this play. Observations of this kind, whereby animals are not performing their humanlike roles, abound in the *Panchatantra* and give the impression that the teacher was teaching his pupils not only about the human beings that they were to rule but also about the flora, fauna, and animal populations of their kingdom. This hypothesis is supported by many examples that do almost nothing for the movement of the story or do not give a social moral but are almost an environmentalist's verses. Book 2 of the *Panchatantra* opens with a verse on the banyan tree—a native Indian tree:

> Deer recline in its shade;
> birds in multitude gather to roost
> darkening its dark-green canopy of leaves;

troops of monkeys cling to the trunk;
while hollows hum with insect-throngs,
flowers are boldly kissed by honey-bees;
O! What happiness in every limb showers
on assemblages of various creatures;
Such a tree deserves all praise,
others only burden the earth. (2: 193)

This is a lively description of a living tree and the meaning of its existence to so many different beings, noticeably nonhuman. The banyan tree is the great community tree of every village society in India, and it is never cut down. It is quite likely, though not always provable, that the *Panchatantra* has had its influence in the formation and continuance of this folk belief and practice. One of the most remarkable features of the *Panchatantra* is the absence of any divine being, though it does talk of soul and destiny and indirectly subscribes to the idea of God. What it does not subscribe to is the institution of religion and the hierarchy of any commandments—it rather constructs its own sense of good or evil, right or wrong, and high or low. This sense does not distinguish between species and forms of life, but between characteristics, attributes, and compulsions, the combination of which can vary from individual to individual, yet they may also be definable as group characteristics (such as, for example, "princes are like serpents"). The study and presentation of society to princes who ought to become rulers is at a level as abstract as that of diminishing the difference between man and other forms of life. Every character is like a personification of an abstract principle, pure as essence. The *Panchatantra* teaches through the portrayal of an abstract but pure hypothesis and through the creation of "ideal" types. It is necessary to repeat here that these "ideal" types are not divine—not even divine mythological birds. There is a gradation of beings as high and low, but as characteristics that are high or low, or as useful in different contexts. The play should be fair, and no character has a right over the life of another except in self-defense or as a naturally determined way of survival. Kings too, the narrator ends up showing, are part of this larger natural schema—as possessors of certain natural instincts and of a learned discretion through which they remain in a position of power. This position, however, is not a permanent state but needs to be retained by the creative application of the rules of the larger game, which means a general acceptance of others as players in the game. There are different characteristics, combining with each other, grouping themselves and disintegrating into uselessness. The *Panchatantra* plays out at such a level of abstraction that it merges the boundaries between the fictional and the realistic.

Teaching and Storytelling

The *Arabian Nights* is similar to the *Panchatantra* in its structure of an umbrella story holding many others, but these umbrella stories are made of a different fabric resulting, to stay within the metaphor of umbrella, in different responses to light and rain. Vishnu Sharma's education process entails using ideal types—pure, crystallized characteristics. Corresponding to the narrative situation, it is like formal education: what should one be? Shahrazâd's narratives, on the contrary, come from a politically marginalized narrator who shows the listener: what could one be? Shahrazâd does not have the opportunity of formalized teaching to present high and lofty ideals in an authoritative manner, but the power to informally relativize the listener's place in this world. She not only makes him see himself with reference to others but also to accept and respect another—a woman—as "teacher" and thereby himself as the taught. She erases distortion not by justification but by replacing it with a realistic image. Her use of magic is symbolic of the need—that her own task can be accomplished only through magic. The image that replaces distortion is produced by magic but is itself very realistic. In this manner, Shahriyâr can see his real place in this world of human beings. Shahrazâd is not a magician but a teacher who reveals the true purpose of her magic without fearing that its effect may evaporate. Shahrazâd practices what Vishnu Sharma had set out to teach: the intelligent art of living.

There are two essential similarities between the umbrella story of the *Arabian Nights* and that of the *Panchatantra:* one, that they are both stories about storytelling; and two, that they are both stories about the relationship between the teacher and the taught. The storyteller is the teacher in the *Nights*, and the teacher is the storyteller in the *Panchatantra*. There is no similarity between the various listeners or the various characters being taught, but that difference itself proves the shared feature: the relationship between the teacher and the taught does not proceed from or end at a stasis. It is a journey in which the person who "shows" the other the colors of life is the teacher, and the other person or persons whose eyes subsequently see the world—and consequently his or their own self—in a new light is the taught. The experience is transformative for both the teacher and the taught. It is a process whereby "teaching" is a challenge, and the identity of the teacher and the taught are established in the process of teaching and learning. Initially, other power structures between the teacher and the taught, like those of status, gender, and age, may be conducive or not for this relationship, but the position of the teacher and the taught emerges in spite of those.

The attraction of the *Arabian Nights* and the *Panchatantra* for the European translators also hints at the power of the original texts. The history of their popularity and influence across the world proves their own thesis: that the teacher and the taught will both be identified in the communication of knowledge, and that all other power structures between them will be redefined in the intellectual theater of life. In spite of versions and constructions, they have taught recipients across the globe the art of storytelling: from Galland to Hollywood, the attraction of the *Nights* has not diminished; from Aesop to contemporary comics—the voice that the *Panchatantra* gave to nonhuman living beings continues to be heard.

WORKS CITED

Burton, Sir Richard. *Tales from 1001 Arabian Nights: Selected from the Original Sixteen Volumes of The Thousand Nights and a Night.* Mumbai: Jaico, 2002.

Ghazoul, Ferial. "Poetic Logic in the *Panchatantra* and the *Arabian Nights*." *Arab Studies Quarterly* 5 (1983): 13–21.

Grotzfeld, Heinz. "Neglected Conclusions of the Arabian Nights: Gleanings in Forgotten and Overlooked Recensions." *Journal of Arabic Literature* 16 (1985): 75–87.

Marzolph, Ulrich. "Re-Locating the *Arabian Nights*." *Orientalia Lovanensia Analecta* 87 (1988): 155–63.

Propp, Vladimir. *Theory and History of Folklore.* Trans. Ariadna Y. Martin and Richard P. Martin. Ed. Anatoly Liberman. Manchester: Manchester UP, 1984.

Vishnu Sharma. *The Panchatantra.* Trans. and intro. Chandra Rajan. New Delhi: Penguin Books India, 1993.

9

Framing in Narrative

Lee Haring

Sir Arthur Conan Doyle is credited with reengineering something Shahrazâd did not tinker with: the relation between "the chronology of the story to be told and the ordering and presentation of that chronology" (Chabon 14). As Conan Doyle's faithful fans know, he frames the Sherlock Holmes stories in a "larger, ongoing macro-story" of the lives of Holmes and his companion Dr. Watson, which is analogous to Shahrazâd's framing narrative in the *Arabian Nights*. "Set within this frame is the story of a client who has sent up a card or blustered in to see Mr. Holmes, and has now sat down to tell it" (Chabon 14). The client's story takes the reader into "the story of the investigation conducted by Holmes and Watson. . . . The investigation in turn produces the story of how the crime was committed"; other stories are often nested into Doyle's piece as it continues. Thus Conan Doyle invented "a way to tell stories about the construction of stories without the traditional recourse to digression, indirection, or the overtly self-referential" (Chabon 14). He could have devised this sophisticated technique only because long before, the nesting technique had been implanted in English literature by the framing in the *Arabian Nights*. Ultimately it was derived from oral performance.

Had he visited the west of Ireland, Conan Doyle (whose Scottish origin did not conceal his Irish name) could have heard an Irish narrator practice the ancient technique. "I'll tell you what I'll do," says one character, a smith, to the Irish mythological hero Cúchulainn. "I'll fix your sword for you tomorrow, if you tell me a story while I'm doing it" (O'Sullivan 75, 264). Cúchulainn complies. Right in the middle of his story, the smith's wife violates his interdiction against eavesdropping, Cúchulainn breaks off, the framed story is incomplete, and the smith, his helper, and his wife are all punished by the curtailment of Cúchulainn's performance. The Irish story-teller's performance is fully completed: "They went by the ford, and I went by the stepping stones. They were drowned, and I came safe" (O'Sullivan 79). The formulaic ending of this performance corrects the disorderly curtail-ment inside the frame. Conan Doyle might have been pleased; so might King Shahriyâr. Folktale scholars label the piece "Story-Teller Interrupted by Woman" (Aarne and Thompson [henceforth AT] 1376 A), or "How a Hus-band Cures His Wife of Fairy Tales" (Uther 2: 180–81) and call it a frame story (Thompson, *Folktale* 415; Blackburn 496).

The world knows frame stories from the *Arabian Nights;* literary scholars conceive them as belonging to a genre; performance critics con-ceive them as manifestations of a process. To conceive the frame story as a genre makes it an entity, a product, a kind of story (Irwin); to conceive "framing" as a device or skill makes it a strategy, one element of the story-teller's range of techniques, which he or she can invoke in multiple ways (Mills, this volume). "Frame" is one metaphor; the banyan tree and the umbrella are others (Naithani, this volume). Irish, ancient Indian, and Arabian storytellers found it endlessly useful. It's the "umbrella" that makes the *Panchatantra*, which was drawn from scattered oral perfor-mances, neat and readable. The *Arabian Nights*, taking up the technique, imitates oral framing as a means of standardizing Shahrazâd's movement from one story into the next.

What is this device, so familiar in writing, so beloved of European readers of the *Nights*, but a formal stylization of people's habit of interrupt-ing their oral discourses and going to another level? It is a human habit; it is probably a cultural universal, preferred in certain story traditions, losing visibility in others (Bacchilega, Geider, this volume); it is the manifestation of an abstract, general structure, the laws of which call for formulation (Todorov 15); it is a part of the grammar of narrative, influencing "each tale that filters through it" (Naddaff 7), "part of the total narrative context of the oral tale, [supplying] clues for its interpretation" (Blackburn 505); it is an artistic superstructure erected upon a basic cognitive cultural instrument which may well be panhuman (Fauconnier and Turner 250). Conceived so diversely, visible in so many more settings of performance than Shahrazâd's demonstration that story can subdue aggression (Enderwitz, Birkalan, this volume), framing requires multiple modes of interpretation.

If each tale, like the Irish one I began with, is a thing, an au-tonomous whole, and if the frame story is a genre, it is not an autonomous one, because it requires other genres to live on. It is also highly variable culturally. Afghanistan, like Ireland, knows oral framing (Mills 123), perhaps under literary influence (Belcher 16-18). In Africa, the frame story is not everywhere an oral genre, but African and Malagasy performers link their pieces, in a technique that is certainly related: they often tell trickster tales in clusters or chains, alternating trickster's success with his defeat, thereby leading the audience toward a sense of cosmic order (Paulme, "Quelques procédés"). The audience's memory supplies another sort of frame from their familiarity with trickster's predictable behavior.

What criticism, then, is appropriate for it? Because, after reading Chaucer and Boccaccio, I came upon framing in the course of oral narrative research in the islands of the Southwest Indian Ocean, the hybrid cultures there have impelled me to adopt a hybrid critical method. In the region I study, multiple languages, traditions, and interactions are the rule. In Mauritius, it is normal for a speaker to break informally out of one lexical, grammatical, syntactic, or reference unit into another. The storyteller Nelzir Ventre, a Kreol *séga* singer whom I recorded at length in Mauritius, gave some of his characters an incomprehensible lingo, especially in their songs, which he called *langaz*. In the Comoros, another multilingual culture, folktales declare that a person's ability to understand an arcane language confers power. In many Comoran tales, a character's linguistic ability brings him high rank. If she is a woman, her speaking ability saves her from danger, quite like Shahrazâd. Such code switching, a linguistic kind of framing, points beyond creole linguistics to cultural creolization. Everywhere nowadays, a hybridized interpretive method seems the only instrument to disentangle the interconnectedness of meanings, symbols, images, money, and power that we call globalization (Haring, "Cultural Creolization").

Hybrid interpretation assembles several critical orientations familiar in literary study (Abrams). What a narratologist calls embedding a creole linguist recognizes as code switching. If framing is conceived as an attribute of message-form, the critic will look for the genre "frame story." If it is an attribute of code, say a bit of fixed-phrase folklore popping up in the middle of free-phrase narrating, the creolist will perceive code switching, and the rhetorician will perceive the prestige value of the alternate code. If framing, say the insertion of song into speech, is conceived as an attribute of the channel of communication, the historical critic will see a continuity between ancestral and modern styles (Haring, "African Folktales" 189–91).

Framing by Formula

Every listener knows the most obvious sort of framing in oral narrative: the opening or closing formula, like "They were drowned, and I came safe," "Once upon a time," and "They all lived happily ever after." Storytellers in Mauritius, and its dependent island Rodrigues, will open with *"Sirandan!"* The formula demands a response, *"Sampek!"* In Mauritian Kreol, the first word literally means riddle. Opening a story with *"Sirandan!"* preserves the association of riddling with storytelling, which creoles inherited from their African ancestors. The second, answering word is apparently no more than a rhetorical device; lexicographers find its other meaning, a kind of fish, irrelevant (Baker and Hookoomsing 283). For his closing formula, Henri Lagarrigue, of the neighboring island of Réunion, remembered one well known in Madagascar: "If it's a lie, it's not my fault, the old ones were the liars" (Decros 149–59; Carayol 7: 19–21; Renel 1: 45, 1: 49, 1: 88–89, 1: 153). But being a true creolizer, with the Malagasy formula he combined with it a characteristically Mascareigne *"Kriké!"*

Formulas are not always an aesthetically neutral formality, not "absolutely independent of the rest of the story," as Charles Renel thought in Madagascar (Renel 1: lviii). In some traditions at least, they have a thematic affinity with what is coming (Sokolov 302). In an Arab-influenced society like the Comoros (as in Ireland far away), they have a refinement and elaboration all their own, reminiscent of the stunning wedding costumes and gold jewelry women bring out for *le grand mariage*.

Nipetraka ampanjaka, nipetraka tajiry, nipetraka oaziry, zanaka
    angano tsàre ela.
Nikomokomoko ka Ravoalavo,
Sôla ny lohany,-Rafaraka, Rafaraka!
Ino nankadilanuaua vanihanao?
—Fanaovam-bango mandeha doany.—Voankôy!
Ino nankamena forinao?
—Fipetraha an-tany mena. (Blanchy et al. 99)

Kings were living, rich people were living, viziers were living.
Things happen fast in tales.
Mr. Rat is gargling,

he has a bald head.

"Hey, wasp, hey wasp!

What made your head so pointy?"

"Tying up my hair to go to The Place."

"Hey, spider!

What made your bottom so red?"

"Sitting on the red ground."

Dady ny Saidy, of the village of Poroani in the Comoran island of Mayotte, is speaking in Malagasy to Sophie Blanchy. At the end of her long,
elaborate tale, her closing formula resembles the Irish one quoted above:
"Nengako ao reo, zaho niply navy ato. Tsy haiko koa kabaron-dreo afara
añy, I left them there I came back here. I don't know what happened to
them after that" (Blanchy et al. 130). But it also recalls other formulas in
use in the Southwest Indian Ocean, for instance in the Seychelles: "I was
passing by there, I said to Soungoula 'Give me a bit to drink'; he gave me
a kick that threw me here, and I fell to St. Louis" ("Creole Stories" 49).

Once framed material is analytically separated from what frames it
(Meletinsky), even the formula, like any frame, can be seen as a metalan-
guage, a variable and semantically loaded way of commenting on what's
inside. A correlation between framing formulas, content, and thematic
grouping has shown up, for instance, in Spain (Ramos 67). Sociohistori-
cally, the formula is a culturally approved frame, as variable internationally as plots or characters. Rhetorically, to restore the words of an opening
formula to the context of performance invites a mode of criticism that
looks to their effect on a hearer (Lüthi 92). Speech-act criticism will call a
formula a "performative" utterance, a part of the verbal interaction. By
saying, "I am a frame," the formula becomes a "perlocutionary" act, affecting the mind-set of the audience (Austin 94–101). The collaboration of
disciplines is needed to understand such devices fully.

Opening and closing formulas frame oral performances "from the
outside." On the inside, a performer may insert equally fixed phrases. Are
these "formulas"? In Irish storytelling, they are called "runs." Performed poetry offers many opportunities to use such fixed phrases for composition
(Lord; Foley, *Immanent Art;* Foley, *Traditional*). In prose narratives, the
fixed phrase stands out by being "framed" by the free phrases around it. No
one can miss it (O'Sullivan 40). Even a transitional formula, "it was well
and it wasn't ill," stands out from the context that frames it. Paradoxically,

through its very familiarity and repetition, the "run" exemplifies defamiliarization—the concept that Russian formalist critics held out as the core of perception and the source of artistic values (Shklovsky). It also changes pace for the performer and audience.

The Formula Personalized

Exceptional oral performers personalize their interventions. Gérose Barivoitse, of Sainte-Suzanne in Réunion, acquired enough fame in the 1970s to be called *le roi*, the King, to be invited to festivals of traditional culture, and to appear on French national television. For his interviewer Mr. Barivoitse explains and performs the technique of the opening formula.

> GÉROSE BARIVOITSE: *Kriké!*

> CHRISTIAN BARAT: *Kraké* the king!

> GÉROSE BARIVOITSE: The key in your pocket, the shit in my bag! Always that's the habit with us, don't you find anything surprising in that? Only if people don't know, they say we seem to be talking shit. Go see if it is. Not true! Those are the words in Kreol to begin a story. (Barat et al. 51)

Then he goes into his Kreol version of one of the best-known European folktales, "The Brave Tailor" (AT 1640; Uther 2: 342–44; Grimm and Grimm 80–86). To adapt it to Southwest Indian Ocean tradition, Mr. Barivoitse brings in the region's familiar ogre character, Gran Dyab, as an adversary for the hero.

He personalizes more than the formula. Throughout the performance, he intervenes in his own voice. Introducing his main character, Mr. Barivoitse points to his injured leg, creating a piquant connection among his hero, himself, and another regional folktale hero, the scabrous Ti Zan who rescues his sister from her disastrous marriage to a wolf-man (Görög-Karady and Seydou; Baissac 146–61).

> Well, there was one guy, he had—he was cleaning a big sore on his foot. Not like this, 'cause I'm already cured. I got cut, I did—I couldn't have a daughter. I couldn't go to the king to marry the king's daughter. What the fuck am I gonna do with that stuff? I'd rather cut him and cure myself.

Viewed as rhetorical gestures or perlocutionary acts, Mr. Barivoitse's shifts of voice serve to maintain his personal connection with his audience.

Mr. Barivoitse knows the difference between the two frames well enough to play with them. Rather than hide behind a depersonalized formula (or disappear for many minutes at a time, as Shahrazâd does for her survival), Mr. Barivoitse remains onstage throughout, continually interrupting the fictional world to speak from the performance situation. In the end, the hero traps Gran Dyab, brings him to the king, and gets the princess. By the end, Mr. Barivoitse will have done considerable personalizing. It is his kind of framing. Twice he compares himself unfavorably to the hero because he's not an eligible suitor; he mocks the hero's shamming; in one breath, he praises and deflates the hero's strength.

> I was standing there looking, I said, "Fuck your mother," I said, "that bugger is strong!" What kind of strong, with that big sore? Poor bugger. Don't say it!

Structuralist criticism would fasten on this contradiction between a narrator's attitudes toward his hero, and look behind it for more basic oppositions in the life-situation of Réunionnais *petits blancs*. If to some readers structuralism has seemed antipolitical or even inhuman (Diamond), it is this mode of criticism that declares the framing or "embedding" of narrative to be the image of all storytelling (Todorov 70–73). In the complex plotting of the *Arabian Nights*, like that of a Mauritian storyteller we shall see below, "the embedding narrative is the *narrative of a narrative*" (Todorov 72). But phenomenologically, this narrator achieves a final triumph of shifting between frames in a quadruple closing formula. For its portrayal of the hero's victory, its fusion of two realities, and its reframing of Gran Dyab into the twentieth century, it merits full translation.

> He said, "Forward march!" Gran Dyab marched marched, got to the sea, turned over—rrr! Back on the road! The people cleaned his sores well. The guy was well decked out, he gave the orders. I found him and said, "Hey, I know everything that you've done."
>
> *Kriké!*
>
> CHRISTIAN BARAT: *Kraké mésyé!*
>
> GÉROSE BARIVOITSE: A nice story! The key in your pocket, the shit in my bag! I said, "Give me a little something, give me—"

"A little something? Get out!" Baf! I got sores there. If I hadn't been cut there, kaf! I got a nice sore. Well, what king's daughter am I going to kill flies for? King's daughters, there aren't any more. So I came here and told you the story. But be careful about getting sores. Try and cure them. I'm not saying you have them. If you get sores on your feet, try and cure them, because you're gonna do that, you're gonna kill seven flies, you're gonna wound fourteen! But what king's daughter will you find, what Gran Dyab either? You won't find them, because nowadays Gran Dyab goes around in his little airplane. Gran Dyab's plane goes around, he comes down at night, his two claws on his hand. People try to catch him, he gets 'em, gives 'em a hit in the face, they fall down. He takes his plane and *rrip!* That's Gran Dyab these days! Be careful!

Well, that's it. (Barat et al. 51–53)

His "coda" lies "just outside the story in the realm of conversation, thus layering a third frame onto the boundaries of the story" (Young 36). His editors interpret his framing phenomenologically: "Not only do we get episodic intrusion of the discourse into the narrative, incursions regulated by the teller and his audience by '*Kriké-kraké*'; the whole narrative enters *explicitly* into the narrator's [personal] history" (Barat et al. 101). In the terms of narratological criticism, his closing formula converges two "moments." In one, he narrates into a microphone; in the other, the scabrous hero battles Gran Dyab. Suddenly Mr. Barivoitse forces a temporal "isotopy" between the story and himself (Genette 221).

Multiple Descriptions

"Two descriptions are better than one," remarked Gregory Bateson (Bateson 67). Framing requires more than two. Phenomenology, narratology, and structuralism describe Mr. Barivoitse's technique. Comparison to literary narrative provides another mode of description. Where his linguist editors use words like *intrusion* and *incursion*, a literary critic would see Gérose Barivoitse as crossing the boundary between the genre frames called fiction and autobiography. His interruptions resemble the practice of novelists like Cervantes, Laurence Sterne, Thackeray, or Dickens, who often interrupt their narratives to address their reader directly—a device cast into the shade by Flaubert and Henry James (Lubbock 156–202). Genre theory in folkloristics will point out that he creates a new "ethnic genre" (Ben-Amos). Then creolization theory would find an affinity between Mr. Barivoitse's mixing of genres, or modes of discourse, and the convergence of African, Malagasy, and European cultures in his island of Réunion. He appropriates elements of them all, to perform an equivalent in narrative lexicon of the mixing of languages. Through verbal art, he takes a rearguard action against cultural and linguistic standardization.

His register switching is only a tiny part of Mr. Barivoitse's framing. More relevant is his transformation of attitude. In the Southwest Indian Ocean as in the Caribbean, where cultures clash, transformation with a satiric purpose comes quickly to such an artist. So complex are Gérose Barivoitse's interventions that a mythological motif (*Periodic sacrifices to a monster*, motif S262 in Thompson, *Motif-Index* [henceforth Mot.]); his etiological tag, "That's when signing with your thumb began"; and his closing formulas themselves become parodic uses of narrative convention (Haring, "Parody").

Finally, a rhetorical criticism would notice that Mr. Barivoitse uses the formula *Kriké-kraké* as a cue to demand reassurance that his listener is attending. Far from relinquishing his turn at speaking, he is reinforcing his turn by means of the formal deference of his hearer's reply. "In performances of all kinds," says Erving Goffman, "the obligation to provide continuity for the audience, that is, constant guidance as to what is going on, accounts considerably for the manipulation of participation status and the enactment of channels" (Goffman 234). For any less audacious performer, Mr. Barivoitse's incursions and intrusions would not be a performance option. They might even not be accepted by an audience. After all, there are rules for such things, which are a prominent topic in folkloristic analysis and receive much attention from theorists of performance (Gossen; Ferry; Bauman; Kapchan; Calame-Griaule).

Evidently multiple descriptions are better than two.

Framing One Channel in Another

Repeatedly in the *Arabian Nights*, poetry, or song, is inserted into the prose of narrative; the narrator shifts channels (Haring, "Techniques" 25–26). Whether indicating its oral ancestry or attesting to the influence of the literary collection, this cherished practice of storytellers too is a kind of framing. A typical example, from the Islamic society of Ngazidja (Grande Comore), in the Comoro islands: an abused youngest daughter, Nyandje, is helped by a speaking tree she finds floating by the seashore.

I'm sent to you by the mother of this child
Nyandje Nyandje
This Nyandje wanting her father's blessing
Nyandje Nyandje
Wanting her mother's blessing, may she get it
Nyandje Nyandje. (Ahmed-Chamanga and Ali Mroimana 132-33)

Later the song is repeated; with this donor's help, the young woman will prevail. The shift would be called channel switching by a linguist. A literary critic might merely call it quotation, especially if the source could be identified. Quotations or allusions that are perfectly recognizable to an audience may look to an outsider only like framing one channel in another. Quotations from Saint-Simon, in Proust, "obviously constitute a first, formal level of embedding"; the author's allusions to the *Arabian Nights* reside at a second level, a kind of metonymy. Never forgetting his *Arabian Nights*, Proust also uses "embedding" as a metaphor, for example when he introduces the *petite bande* of blooming young girls as encroaching on the adults (Jullien 101). But none of these involve a shift of channel.

Framing as a Device of Narrative Grammar

Psychologically, framing is part of a performer's learning, his acquisition of "a grasp of the structures and functions of the genre" (Hymes, "The 'Wife'" 50). With that knowledge, he or she can judge which episodes and which digressions will be appropriate to bring to an audience. Oral performers have been quite articulate about that learning process, none more so than Sydney Joseph of Mauritius. In "The Siren-Girl," which he recorded for me in 1990, Sydney Joseph combines five distinct plots. His skill in combining them reveals a mastery of narrative grammar, in the structuralist sense: "a set of rules for the creation of artifacts mutually accepted by the members of the culture producing them" (Deetz 108–9). As a comment on his learning process, Sydney Joseph told me,

> In the old days, when people told stories, you would listen to them. If you have a bit of intelligence, you remember the story completely. In the old days when people told stories, I would remember them gradually so I could tell them the same way. Now when I tell stories, I invent them, to see if they are the same style, if they "rhyme" [*rime*] (Joseph).

Sydney Joseph's creations, then, are built on the models he has observed. Part of his past comes from Africa, where riddling and storytelling go together, and indeed for him, inventing stories resembles playing with riddles (which he calls *zedmo,* puns): "Just like when you make riddles, it's the same. There are riddles that people give, but when they ask for the answers, that's hard, and no one can get the answers." To *rime* means to fit his production in to traditional stylistic expectations, to create the future out of the past (Glassie 395).

Imagine being such a storyteller. If your first unit isn't enough for you, what to do?

> Right away he goes into a second part, which is actually another story, conforming to a different formal type from the first. Yet he has retained the same hero. So he finds himself obliged, if his tale has been moving upward, to reverse direction in this second part and move downward. This he manages either by having his hero violate an interdiction previously unknown, or by dropping that very hero into a trap that has been laid, most often, by a new adversary. . . . The listener cannot foresee the particular nature of the peril awaiting the hero, or the misdeed he will commit. (Paulme, *La Mère* 43–44)

Denise Paulme's description of West African framing uncannily anticipates a complex story Sydney Joseph recorded for me. The contrasting episodes he combines, in the tale he called "The Siren-Girl," continually surprise the listener. The piece also demonstrates that for a gifted narrator, "rhyming" goes far beyond inventing something that looks like a familiar traditional tale. It includes framing. Of course it does mean giving his audience "rhyming" elements, which are known elsewhere in the region, as well as in Africa and India: a submarine palace where the hero will find his girl; a second palace, which will later be disenchanted; animals who give him parts of their bodies so that he can later summon their aid (Mot. F 725.3, D 705.1, and B 501). Seen from the narrator's point of view, should his inclusion of these motifs also be thought of as a kind of framing? Isn't all narrative creativity, ultimately, the combining of motifs? But when he goes from one plot into another, he exercises framing at the level of narrative grammar, a practice quite different from the mechanical switching of the *Arabian Nights* (which I think Sydney Joseph has not read). I disentangle the five plots.

"Well," he begins with an almost invisible formula, "there was a man and a woman in a house. They had one son." This son will be Sydney Joseph's "Man on a Quest for His Lost Wife," in a story known all round the world (AT 400; Uther 2: 231–33), with three analogues in the *Arabian Nights*, three treatments by the Grimms (Grimm and Grimm 338–47, 605–13), and a version in Madagascar (Renel 1: 65–76). All the elements warranted by folktale scholars as necessary elements of this international plot appear in "The Siren-Girl": a father promises his son to a sea creature; the boy finds a princess with whom he sleeps chastely; the hero is allowed to visit home on condition that he does not reveal the secret; he loses the princess by breaking a prohibition; he sets out in search, gets help, and acquires magic objects; and with their aid he retrieves and marries the princess. But as Denise Paulme predicted, that first plot is not enough. Sydney Joseph's second plot comes in at a point when the hero has violated an interdiction.

> As she put her head on his arm, to sleep, the boy just lit a match. He lit the match and saw her face at night. Well, at night, when he saw her, he just grabbed her and kissed her, and he got a big shock. According to the rules, he has no right to kiss that young siren. In that castle, the mother instantly knew, and she made that castle disappear, that very night, under the sea— vanished.

Banished from her underwater world, yet still detached from human society, he arrives on land; he finds a *ponyar*, dagger, which enables him to catch octopus as food; and Sydney Joseph now inserts his second plot, the "Grateful Animals" tale (AT 554). He wanted me to note that he was following traditional epithets for his animal characters in folktales (Baker and Hookoomsing 155): "These animals, what are they? As the story goes, apparently, we call these the *komper*. There was Komper Lion, there was Komper Eagle, and there was Komper Ant, black ant."

With his knife the hero carves a deer for the three. Each grateful animal gives him a whisker or feather, which will summon the animal when the hero is in danger. These motifs are as traditional as the word *komper* (Mot. B 392, B 431.2, B 455.3, B 481.1, B 501, and D 1421).

Combining "The Grateful Animals" and "The Man on a Quest for His Lost Wife" is evidently a bit of traditional framing in the Southwest Indian Ocean. Both stories are especially well known in Madagascar, where one narrator combined them in the 1870s (Dahle 250–58). Madagascar was a trans-shipping point from which many Africans arrived in Mauritius. That Malagasy precursor, however, did not poise his hero between two equally desirable women, as Sydney Joseph does for suspense.

Now for a third plot and a new sort of rhyming. If the hero wants this new girl, his first task will be to protect the king's goats from a marauding lion. This he accomplishes by summoning the grateful lion from the preceding episode and staging a duel between the two, so as to move toward the classic folktale outcome where he gets his girl (Propp 63–64). The duel of lions "rhymes" creatively with one of this region's favorite animal stories, the false tug-of-war, which is unquestionably of African origin (AT 291; Uther 2; 168–69; Crowley) and much beloved of East African and island storytellers (Werner 268–69; "Creole Stories" 64–65; Baissac 25–33). This piece of dramatic irony narrates a deception: a small animal deceives two large animals into pulling against each other. "Rhyming" on this model, Sydney Joseph creates a lengthy duel. The one lion loses; it looks as if the hero must marry her and acquire half the kingdom.

To get his hero out of this marriage, Sydney Joseph rather awkwardly reconnects him to the siren-girl and draws in a fourth plot, "The Ogre's Heart in the Egg" (AT 302; Uther 2: 180–81). The hero, who turns himself into an ant with the help he has received from the grateful animals, learns how to find the life of the siren-girl's father; following her information, he kills him. A similar episode, perhaps with a common source, occurs in a nineteenth-century Mauritian tale (Baissac 358–89; "Creole Stories" 19–20). But the outraged siren-girl disenchants the castle. What listener could foresee that she will now abandon fairyland, venture into the "real" world, and enter the cash economy by opening a village pharmacy? In the end, Sydney Joseph manages the hero's recovery by a fifth plot, which spins off from Madagascar's favorite legend of marriage between a mortal and a water-spirit (Haring, "Water-Spirits"). The siren-girl cleans him up and hears his story of refusing the other girl.

> The siren said to him, "Well, what have I got now? I only have this shop, I have people who work here. Well, if you agree, we'll make a *kondisyon*. We will get married. Those who live here do not know that I am a siren. You are the only one to know this, and you don't tell anybody about this, or else I'll leave."
> They got married.

In the Malagasy legend, marriage between the underwater woman and a mortal on land leads to a catastrophic violation of taboo and dissolution of the marriage (Haring, *Index* 358–60). But in "The Siren-Girl," a marriage between these two enables Sydney Joseph's tale to "rhyme" with folktales that award their hero a wife and a place in society. Sydney Joseph ends his story as modestly as he began it: "So this means I am telling you this story now. Finished." Is any story in the *Arabian Nights* more complex? Does any story in the *Nights* combine so many motifs?

The sort of critical orientation that emphasizes the artist's personality will attribute the merits of Sydney Joseph's extraordinary narrative to his "peculiarities" (Okpewho 39). Structuralism, going to the a-psychological opposite extreme, will see the framing as "the *narrative of a narrative*." Narratology will call what Sydney Joseph does a special instance of *recursivity*, a temporal concept "that makes it possible to describe the structure of expectations created by the process of self-replication" (Ryan 121). Rhetorical criticism, attending to the expectations of an audience, will see the listener being asked to participate in an alternative experience of time. Sociohistorical or contextual criticism will see the formal configuration of "The Siren-Girl"—its combining of plots from different languages and traditions—as mirroring Mauritian creolization. Especially it mirrors the parodic strain so characteristic of creole culture. The unexpected episodes that Sydney Joseph inserts into the fairytale's usual movement toward marriage and prosperity have a deflating effect, as if the performer is both upholding and deflating the folktale genre. Gérose Barivoitse's interruptions have the same effect. People like these—creoles in Mauritius, *petits blancs* in Réunion, people in marginal cultures, people oppressed by the encroachment of international capitalism—often make use of traditional verbal art as a means of deconstructing dominant ideologies through remaking their expressive forms (Bauman and Briggs). Their thinking is hybridized.

Analyzing Sydney Joseph's text in this way assimilates the combining of tale motifs to framing. Does this make sense, or does it extend the concept too far? Doesn't all narrative creativity come down, ultimately, to the combining of what scholars call motifs? To discover its principles, we fasten upon *words:* the storyteller's text, the scholar's motif. Hence the method is not only hybrid but also logocentric and materialist. All folkloristics is necessarily logocentric; it ignores deconstructive thought. The criticism of verbal art by folklorists explicitly subscribes to "a belief in a *logos* or *phonè,* a self-present word constituted not by difference but by presence" (Kneale 186). Folkloristics postulates a system "structured by a valorization of speech over writing, immediacy over distance, identity over difference, and (self-)presence over all forms of absence, ambiguity, simulation, substitution or negativity"—the sort of system challenged by deconstruction (Derrida, *Dissemination* 4, n. 1). The transcendental signified, which this system requires, is denoted among American scholars as a moment of situated social communication, which is witnessed and captured by an observer. "The communicative event is the metaphor, or perspective, basic to rendering experience intelligible" (Hymes, "Introduction" 18). Thus folkloristics keeps returning to the words of that communication, first spoken, then transcribed, transliterated, and translated—in writing.

There is a materialist alternative, too complex to be properly expounded here. People's capacity for making up and performing narratives, like their capacities for comprehending genres, judging performances, adapting genres to occasions, and incorporating novelty, is "no doubt derived from innate abilities. . . . [S]uch innate abilities, however, are almost certainly not specific to folklore" (Hymes, "The 'Wife'" 53). The new field of cognitive linguistics offers a base for understanding, at last, what philosophers have meant by those "innate abilities." Cognitive linguists are exploring the connection between expressive culture and the activity of neurons. They avow that they know a great deal about "how specific neural structures of the kind found in the brain can learn the specific kinds of concepts that are central to human language" (Lakoff and Johnson 570). According to cognitive linguists, conceptual metaphors are our principal tool of thought, which we derive from our physical experience, and from the messages of our society and culture. The metaphors and symbols of poetry, fiction, drama, and folklore are based on these conceptual metaphors, so that, for example, the journeys of Sydney Joseph's folktale hero are recognizable because everyone knows that life is a journey (Lakoff and Johnson 59–72). A few scholars have begun to explore the terrain lying between conceptual metaphor and poetic thought; much remains to be done (Turner, *Death Is the Mother*; Turner, *Reading Minds*; Hart).

Finally, what correlation might exist between framing, as a component of "the formal configuration of the artwork[,] and the structure of the social system" (Hohendahl 172)? Do certain societies favor frame stories, or foster the habit of subordinating one plot to another? Do certain societies look for symbolic structures that speak to their own stratification? When Antoine Galland was translating the *Arabian Nights*, his contemporary Colbert was striving to make France economically self-sufficient. Just when Galland was domesticating Oriental narratives, France took possession of Mauritius (1715), renaming it Isle de France; just then too, the French navy, merchant marine, and modern police organization were being created. What subtext lay behind these moves? If folk narrative is the overcoming of a contradiction (Lévi-Strauss 434), is framing part of the attempt to resolve or overcome contradictions in the unspoken reality? Does framing enact the syntax of social hierarchy? A hybrid critical method is called for. Its theory will adopt both the multiple assumptions of postmodernism and the openness to major sociohistorical change inherited from Marxism.

NOTE

Four of the five islands mentioned are independent nations; Île de la Réunion is an overseas department of France. Research there has been supported by the United States Information Agency, the Wolfe Humanities Institute of Brooklyn College, and the John Simon Guggenheim Memorial Foundation, and assisted by innumerable cordial persons in all the islands. Dorothy Noyes, Regina Bendix, and Dörte Borchers have given me the benefit of critical readings of this article. All translations are my own.

WORKS CITED

Aarne, Antti, and Stith Thompson. *The Types of the Folktale: A Classification and Bibliography.* 2nd rev. ed. Helsinki: Academia Scientiarum Fennica, 1961.

Abrams, M. H. "Orientation of Critical Theories." *Twentieth Century Literary Criticism: A Reader.* Ed. David Lodge. London: Longman, 1972. 1–26.

Ahmed-Chamanga, Mohamed, and Ahmed Ali Mroimana. *Contes comoriens de Ngazidja, au-delà des mers.* Paris: L'Harmattan, 1999.

Austin, J. L. *How to Do Things with Words.* Oxford: Oxford UP, 1962.

Baissac, Charles. *Folklore de l'île Maurice.* Paris: G. P. Maisonneuve et Larose, 1887.

Baker, Philip, and Vinesh Y. Hookoomsing. *Morisyen-English-Français; Diksyoner kreol morisiyen; Dictionary of Mauritian Creole.* Paris: L'Harmattan, 1987.

Barat, Christian, Michel Carayol, and Claude Vogel. *Kriké kraké: Recueil de contes créoles réunionnais.* Travaux de l'Institut d'Anthropologie Sociale et Culturelle de l'Océan Indien. Paris and Saint-Denis: CNRS, 1977.

Bateson, Gregory. *Mind and Nature: A Necessary Unity.* New York: Dutton, 1979.

Bauman, Richard. *Verbal Art as Performance.* Prospect Heights: Waveland P, 1977.

———, and Charles L. Briggs. "Poetics and Performance as Critical Perspectives on Language and Social Life." *Annual Review of Anthropology* 19 (1990): 59–88.

Belcher, Stephen. "Framed Tales in the Oral Tradition: An Exploration." *Fabula* 35.1–2 (1994): 1–19.

Ben-Amos, Dan. "Analytical Categories and Ethnic Genres." *Folklore Genres.* Ed. Dan Ben-Amos. Austin: U of Texas P, 1976. 215–42.

Bendix, Regina. *In Search of Authenticity: The Formation of Folklore Studies.* Madison: U of Wisconsin P, 1997.

Blackburn, Stuart. "The Brahmin and the Mongoose: The Narrative Context of a Well-Travelled Tale." *Bulletin of the School of Oriental and African Studies* 59.3 (1996): 494–507.

Blanchy, Sophie, Zaharia Soilihi, Noël J. Gueunier, and Madjidhoubi Said. *La maison de la mère: Contes de l'île de Mayotte.* Paris: L'Harmattan, 1993.

Calame-Griaule, Geneviève. *Ethnologie et langage: La parole chez les Dogon.* Paris: Gallimard, 1965.

Carayol, Michel. "La littérature orale réunnionaise." *L'encyclopédie de la Réunion.* Gen. ed. Robert Chaudenson. Vol. 7. Saint-Denis: Livres-Réunion, 1980. 9–36.

Chabon, Michael. "The Game's Afoot." *New York Review of Books* 52.3 (Feb. 24, 2005): 14–17.

"Creole Stories from Various Contributors, Vol. 1." *Creole Stories from Various Contributors.* Unpublished, 1978. In Seychelles National Archives.

Crowley, Daniel J. *Folktale Research in Africa.* Legon: Ghana UP, 1971.

Dahle, L[ars]. *Specimens of Malagasy Folk-Lore.* Antananarivo: A. Kingdon, 1877.

Decros, Marie Christine. *Contes réunionnais, textes et traductions.* Mémoire de maîtrise, Centre Universitaire de la Réunion, 1978.

Deetz, James. *In Small Things Forgotten: The Archaeology of Early American Life.* Garden City: Anchor, 1977.

Derrida, Jacques. *Dissemination.* Trans. and ed. Barbara Johnson. Chicago: U of Chicago P, 1981.

———. *Of Grammatology.* Trans. Gayatri Chakravorty Spivak. Baltimore: Johns Hopkins UP, 1976.

Diamond, Stanley. "The Myth of Structuralism." *The Unconscious in Culture: The Structuralism of Claude Lévi-Strauss in Perspective.* Ed. Ino Rossi. New York: Dutton, 1974. 292–335.

Dumont, Louis. *Homo hierarchicus: Essai sur le système des castes.* Paris: Gallimard, 1966.

Fauconnier, Gilles, and Mark Turner. *The Way We Think: Conceptual Blending and the Mind's Hidden Complexities.* New York: Basic, 2002.

Ferry, Marie-Paule. "Telling Folktales—Why?" Trans. Lee Haring. *Southwest Folklore* 6.1 (1986): 1–16.

Foley, John Miles. *Immanent Art: From Structure to Meaning in Traditional Oral Epic.* Bloomington: Indiana UP, 1991.

———. *Traditional Oral Epic: The Odyssey, Beowulf, and the Serbo-Croatian Return Song.* Berkeley: U of California P, 1990.

Genette, Gérard. *Narrative Discourse: An Essay in Method.* Trans. Jane E. Lewin. 1972. Ithaca: Cornell UP, 1980.

Glassie, Henry. "Tradition." *Journal of American Folklore* 108 (1995): 395–412.

Goffman, Erving. *Frame Analysis: An Essay on the Organization of Experience.* 1974. Harmondsworth: Penguin, 1975.

Görög-Karady, Veronika, and Christiane Seydou, comp. and ed. *La fille difficile: Un conte-type africain.* Paris: CNRS, 2001.

Gossen, Gary H. "Chamula Genres of Verbal Behavior." *Journal of American Folklore* 84 (1971): 145–68.

Grimm, Jacob, and Wilhelm Grimm. *The Complete Fairy Tales of the Brothers Grimm.* Trans. Jack Zipes. New York: Bantam, 1987.

Haring, Lee. "African Folktales and Creolization in the Indian Ocean Islands." *Research in African Literatures* 33.3 (2002): 182–99.

————. "Cultural Creolization." *Acta Ethnographica Hungarica* 49.1–2 (2004): 1–38.

————. *Malagasy Tale Index.* Helsinki: Academia Scientiarum Fennica, 1982.

————. "Parody and Imitation in Western Indian Ocean Oral Literature." *Journal of Folklore Research* 29.3 (1992): 199–224.

————. "Techniques of Creolization." *Journal of American Folklore* 116.459 (2003): 19–35.

————. "The Water-Spirits of Madagascar." *Cross Rhythms* 2 (1985): 157–75.

Hart, F. Elizabeth. "Cognitive Linguistics: The Experiential Dynamics of Metaphor." *Mosaic* 28 (1995): n.p.

Hohendahl, Peter Uwe. *Prismatic Thought: Theodor W. Adorno.* Lincoln: U of Nebraska P, 1995.

Hymes, Dell. "Introduction: Toward Ethnographies of Communication." *American Anthropologist* 66.6, pt. 2 (1964): 1–34.

————. *Now I Know Only So Far: Essays in Ethnopoetics.* Lincoln: U of Nebraska P, 2003.

————. "The 'Wife' Who 'Goes Out' Like a Man: Reinterpretation of a Clackamas Chinook Myth." *Structural Analysis of Oral Tradition.* Ed. Pierre Maranda and Elli Köngäs Maranda. Philadelphia: U of Pennsylvania P, 1971. 49–80.

Irwin, Bonnie D. "The Frame Tale East and West." *Teaching Oral Traditions.* Ed. John Miles Foley. New York: MLA, 1998. 391–99.

Jameson, Fredric. *The Political Unconscious: Narrative as a Socially Symbolic Act.* Ithaca: Cornell UP, 1981.

Joseph, Sydney. Interview. Grand Bel Air, Mauritius, 1990.

Jullien, Dominique. *Proust et ses modèles: Les Mille et une Nuits et les Mémoires de Saint-Simon.* Paris: José Corti, 1989.

Kapchan, Deborah A. *Gender on the Market: Moroccan Women and the Revoicing of Tradition.* Philadelphia: U of Pennsylvania P, 1993.

Kneale, J. Douglas. "Deconstruction." *The Johns Hopkins Guide to Literary Theory and Criticism.* Ed. Michael Groden and Martin Kreiswirth. Baltimore: Johns Hopkins UP, 1994. 185–92.

Lakoff, George, and Mark Johnson. *Philosophy in the Flesh: The Embodied Mind and Its Challenge to Western Thought.* New York: Basic, 1999.

Lévi-Strauss, Claude. "The Structural Study of Myth." *Journal of American Folklore* 78 (1955): 428–44.

Lord, Albert B. *The Singer of Tales.* Cambridge: Harvard UP, 1960.

Lubbock, Percy. *The Craft of Fiction.* 1921. New York: Viking, 1957.

Lüthi, Max. *The European Folktale: Form and Nature.* Trans. John D. Niles. 1982. Bloomington: Indiana UP, 1986.

Meletinsky, Eleazar. "Structural-Typological Study of Folktales." *Soviet Structural Folkloristics.* The Hague: Mouton, 1974. 19–51.

Mills, Margaret. *Rhetoric and Politics in Afghan Traditional Storytelling.* Philadelphia: U of Pennsylvania P, 1991.

Naddaff, Sandra. *Arabesque: Narrative Structure and the Aesthetics of Repetition in the 1001 Nights.* Evanston: Northwestern UP, 1991.

Okpewho, Isidore. *African Oral Literature: Backgrounds, Character, and Continuity.* Bloomington: Indiana UP, 1992.

O'Sullivan, Sean, ed. and trans. *Folktales of Ireland.* Chicago: U of Chicago P, 1966.

Paulme, Denise. *La mère dévorante: Essai sur la morphologie des contes africains.* Paris: Gallimard, 1976.

———. "Quelques procédés du conteur africain." *La statue du commandeur: Essais d'ethnologie.* Paris: Le Sycomore, 1984. 79–97.

Propp, Vladimir. *Morphology of the Folktale.* Trans. Laurence Scott. 2nd rev. ed. Austin: U of Texas P, 1968.

Ramos, Rosa-Alicia. "Opening and Closing Formulas and Patterns in Galician Oral Narrative." *Southern Folklore* 46.1 (1989): 53–69.

Renel, Charles. *Contes de Madagascar.* Collection de Contes et Chansons Populaires. Paris: Ernest Leroux, 1910.

Ryan, Marie-Laure. "Cyberage Narratology, Computers, Metaphor, and Narrative." *Narratologies: New Perspectives on Narrative Analysis.* Ed. David Herman. Columbus: Ohio State UP, 1999. 113–41.

Shklovsky, Victor. "Art as Technique." *Russian Formalist Criticism: Four Essays.* Trans. Lee T. Lemon and Marion J. Reis. 1917. Lincoln: U of Nebraska P, 1965. 3–24.

Sokolov, Y. M. *Russian Folklore.* 2nd ed. Trans. 1950. Catherine Ruth Smith. Hatboro, PA: Folklore Associates, 1966.

Thompson, Stith. *The Folktale.* New York: Holt, 1946.

———. *Motif-Index of Folk-Literature.* 6 vols. Rev. and enl. ed. Bloomington: Indiana UP, 1955–58.

Todorov, Tzvetan. *The Poetics of Prose.* Trans. Richard Howard. Ithaca: Cornell UP, 1977.

Turner, Mark. *Death Is the Mother of Beauty: Mind, Metaphor, Criticism.* Chicago: U of Chicago P, 1987.

———. *Reading Minds: The Study of English in the Age of Cognitive Science.* Princeton: Princeton UP, 1991.

Uther, Hans-Jörg. *The Types of International Folktales: A Classification and Bibliography.* 3 vols. Helsinki: Academia Scientiarum Fennica, 2004.

Werner, Alice. *Myths and Legends of the Bantu.* 1933. London: Frank Cass, 1968.

Young, Katherine G. *Taleworlds and Storyrealms: The Phenomenology of Narrative.* Dordrecht: Martinus Nijhoff, 1987.

IV

Translation, Adaptation, and Reception

10

The *Arabian Nights* in the *Kuokoa*, a Nineteenth-Century Hawaiian Newspaper: Reflections on the Politics of Translation

Cristina Bacchilega and Noelani Arista

The history and influence of European-language translations and adaptations of *Alf layla wa-layla* are both momentous and spread out into more than one thousand and one episodes. Robert Irwin, Jorge Luis Borges, Pier Paolo Pasolini, Salman Rushdie, and Mary Zimmerman have been, within different genres and traditions, the best twentieth-century tellers of this tale of transformations. In turn, the feminized representation of the Orient in these Western-language texts has provided another productive critical framework for the study of the *Arabian Nights* in translation, as shown in the works of Rana Kabbani, Fedwa Malti-Douglas, and Eva Sallis.[1] But what of translations of the *Arabian Nights* into non-Western languages? It is safe to say that they have not yet been a major focus of inquiry for scholars of the *Arabian Nights* (Geider). In this essay we begin to address the above question by focusing on a specific case, the 1874–75 translation of a selection from the *Arabian Nights* into the Hawaiian language. Sharing the "discovery" of such a text is an obvious but hardly simple step: *how* to approach this Hawaiian-language translation and with what *goals*? Our essay grapples with these questions by articulating the dialogue between two scholars who—with different disciplinary knowledge, linguistic competence, and questions about translation—seek to read *He Kaao Arabia* in ways that, we hope, will make it of interest to several communities. Our goals, therefore, are to show how the study of non-Western translations can be of use in the project of "re-locating" the *Arabian Nights* (Marzolph); to promote a better understanding of Hawai'i in the nineteenth century; and to participate in a larger discussion of translation and colonialism (Bassnett and Lefevere; Haring; Naithani; Spivak, *Politics of Translation*; Venuti). To put it differently, our project necessarily involved taking a collaborative, interdisciplinary, and historical approach to *He Kaao Arabia*'s politics of translation; it also involved confronting in a dialogic form how this nineteenth-century translation of the *Arabian Nights* from English into Hawaiian *and* its twenty-first-century translation back into English for this essay could mean something different to each of us and the communities we belong to.

CB: When I realized that the University of Hawai'i at Mānoa library had a photocopy of a Hawaiian-language translation of selections from the *Arabian Nights*, my first reaction, as a fairy-tale scholar with a special interest in gender politics, was "Indeed Shahrazâd's prowess as a storyteller would be understood and valued in Hawaiian culture. *'I ka 'ōlelo nō ke ola, i ka 'ōlelo nō ka make,*' the Hawaiian *'ōlelo no'eau* or proverb goes: 'Life is in speech; death is in speech,' meaning 'Words can heal; words can destroy' (Pukui: no. 1191). And this is what the *Arabian Nights* is about." My subsequent research showed I had a lot to learn about the politics of translation in nineteenth-century Hawai'i. Hawai'i was an independent kingdom and internationally recognized nation then; following the violent overthrow of the Hawaiian monarchy in 1893 by Euro-American businessmen, it would be annexed to the United States in 1898 against the will of most Hawaiians. As Lawrence Venuti states, "[a]lthough the history of colonialism varies significantly according to place and period, it does reveal a consistent, no, an inevitable reliance on translation" (Venuti, *Scandals of Translation* 165): translation, even the translation of the *Arabian Nights*, was a part of these historical dynamics. Once I moved from the photocopied text to the microfilmed newspaper pages of *Ka Nupepa Kuokoa*, I entered a public sphere that not surprisingly, if we take Jürgen Habermas's definition (14–26), played out dynamics among heterogeneous social groups: I am referring to Hawai'i's nineteenth-century bilingual newspaper production that addressed Hawaiians, Euro-American settlers, and to a much lesser extent, late in that century, Asian immigrants. I thus set out to read the translation of the *Arabian Nights* within the context of this public sphere, and our work is still in progress.

I say *our* work because, given my rudimentary knowledge of the Hawaiian language, upon locating the text I asked Noelani Arista if she would translate at least some portions of the text back into English. Our subsequent interaction showed I had a lot to learn about contemporary, early twenty-first-century politics of translation as well; fortunately, Noelani Arista agreed to join me in the interpretive and reflective endeavor of writing this essay.

NA: When Cristina Bacchilega approached me to translate portions of *Kaao Arabia*, I looked on the work as a challenge but also as an opportunity to attempt translation in a literary genre that I had yet to apply my abilities to. As a graduate student in history and a translator of Hawaiian-language documents, I try to cultivate a sense of the language that is indigenous to a given form. I have experience translating nineteenth-century Hawaiian legal documents, the letters of Hawaiian and foreign missionaries, and other types of writings generated by the American Board of Commissioners for Foreign Missions in Hawai'i. I also have a lot of experience reading and translating one specific class of chants, *kanikau*, or Hawaiian laments. But I had yet to apply myself to translating a story whose origins were far removed from Hawai'i. So for me an intriguing component of the challenge came from the recognition that elements that made the *Arabian Nights* exciting and entertaining to Arabic-speaking audiences would not necessarily have spoken to a Hawaiian audience. Because of these considerations we needed to be attentive to alterations in tone, emphasis of a certain theme, or the omission of specific characters and episodes. How does a translator proceed when she is translating a work previously translated more than twice before? The readers of *Kuokoa* were informed that *"He Kaao Arabia no ke Keiki Alii Bedera o Peresia . . ."* was *"Unuhiia no ke 'Kuokoa,' mai ka Olelo Arabia a i ka Olelo Haole, a mai ka Olelo Haole a i ka Olelo Hawaii,"* or "Translated for the *Kuokoa* from Arabic into English and from English into Hawaiian." For me the act of retranslating the tales into English was, regardless of its utilitarian dimension, an exploration of historically charged negotiations of difference. Expectations that Arabic-speaking audiences would have had about the roles of women in society, the duties of a king, and what constituted correct and incorrect behavior toward others in society differed radically from what Hawaiian audiences learned from *mo'olelo* (stories). Characters and expectations in the nineteenth-century English language version of the *Arabian Nights* also differed from Hawaiian *mo'olelo* and cultural practices. I became particularly attentive in my own translation to the agency and mediation of the *Kuokoa* Hawaiian-language translators.

Texts

The longest section of *He Kaao Arabia* (literally: "An Arabian [Fictional] Tale") was published in the weekly Hawaiian-language newspaper *Ka Nupepa Kuokoa* in 1875, from May 1 to July 3, in ten installments telling the story *"He Kaao Arabia! No ke Kanaka Lawaia! Ke Kumu o ka Pomaikai,"* which translates as "An Arabian tale about the Fisherman! The source of Good Fortune"; this is the text that was photocopied in 1990 for the Hawaiian and Pacific Collection of the Hamilton Library at the University of Hawaiʻi at Mānoa as part of a "Hawaiian Language Project" supervised by Hawaiian language professor Larry Kimura. However, as Cristina Bacchilega found going back to the microfilms, the very first installment of *He Kaao Arabia* had appeared in that same newspaper on September 26, 1874, and two more stories or cycles had followed: *Keiki Alii Bedera o Peresia,* which appeared in four installments from October 3 to October 24, and the seven *Huakai Holomoku a Sinibada Ka Luina,* which the *Kuokoa* ran from October 31 to December 12, 1874, in six installments. It is possible to say then that the following selections from the *Arabian Nights* were translated for the *Kuokoa* specifically during the 1870s: a section of the frame tale with no title, "The Story of Bedr Bâsim and Jôharah," the seven voyages of Sindbad the Sailor, and "The Story of the Fisherman."

What else can we assert with some certitude? The introductory note in the *Kuokoa* tells us that the tales were translated specifically for that newspaper and from "ka Olelo Haole," that is, the English language. (Please note that no diacritical marks are used in these nineteenth-century Hawaiian-language texts, while it is standard use to include them in contemporary Hawaiian writing; following such practice, *olelo* will be *ōlelo* when we refer to it.) From Noelani Arista's translation of *"No ke Kanaka Lawaia!"* back into English, it is clear that its English-language source is "The Story of the Fisherman" in Edward William Lane's 1839–41 translation of *Alf layla wa-layla,* the *Arabian Nights,* that more or less follows the Bulaq edition.[2] The source of the other Hawaiian-language translations is not as obvious because these tales are rendered in abbreviated form or adapted, while *He kaao Arabia No ke Kanaka Lawaia!* or "The Story of the Fisherman" is fully translated from Lane's text. Bacchilega speculates that all of the *Kuokoa* tales are from Lane. Given the strong "civilizing" or moralizing mission of the *Kuokoa*, Lane's bowdlerized rendition of selected tales would seem the appropriate choice. No illustrations from Lane's text are included in the Hawaiian-language translations.

The *Kuokoa* provides one more piece of information: the translator of "The Story of the Fisherman" signed the text and made some introductory comments. We know, then, that S. K. Ulele translated that cycle in 1875, but we do not know who translated the three tales that appeared in 1874. Arista's preliminary hypothesis is that those translations were not Ulele's because the text of these three tales in Hawaiian is distinctive in several ways. At the end of each newspaper installment, the formula telling readers that there is more to come is *"pipi holo kaao"* (sprinkled, the tale runs) rather than the more standard *"aole i pau"* (to be continued, not done) that we find in Ulele's text. The translator of King Shahriyâr's story removed significant sections of the plot, while Ulele's translation follows Lane's translation "faithfully." The Hawaiian syntax of the 1874 texts differs from Ulele's, and so do their rhythm and style. At this point, we do not know who S. K. Ulele was, but it is quite possible (Fukushima, personal communication) that Ulele is a pen name—a common convention in Hawaiian newspapers of the time—since one of its meanings is "to set, as type" (Pukui and Albert 368).

Contexts

We hope to have communicated how difficult it is to ascertain what one would consider to be "basic" information: the what, when, and who of these translations. These Hawaiian-language texts then seem to fit quite well in the complex and convoluted history of the *Arabian Nights*, in its transformations before and after its first translation into a Western language in the early eighteenth century. But there are Hawai'i-specific historical factors that should inflect the reading and discussion of the Hawaiian translations of the *Arabian Nights*, and we offer for consideration that taking these factors into account as we examine the Hawaiian texts can contribute a particular variation to the story of Orientalism and the *Arabian Nights* in translation. The historical factors we want to foreground as having affected the politics of translation in Hawai'i during the second half of the nineteenth century are interrelated: on the one hand, the Hawaiians' voluminous production of newspapers during that time; on the other, the ongoing suppression of the Hawaiian language and culture, which became more overt after the 1893 overthrow of the Hawaiian monarchy.

Hawaiians had been communicating orally for centuries when missionaries came to Hawai'i in 1820 and sought to develop a written Hawaiian language with the purposes of disseminating Christianity among the natives. In 1834, the first two Hawaiian-language newspapers appeared, both of them strongly tied to missionary interests: *Ka Lama Hawaii* (founded by Lorrin Andrews for the Lahainaluna Seminary) and *Ke Kumu Hawaii* (see Mookini iv–v, 22, 24–25 for further information). "By 1853, nearly three-fourths of the Native Hawaiian population over the age of sixteen years were literate in their own language" (Lucas 2). From 1834 to 1861, newspapers were issued by Protestant or Catholic institutions or by the Hawaiian government. The year 1861 marked the advent in the public sphere of two "new" kinds of newspapers. One, *Ka Nupepa Kuokoa* (The Independent), was issued by an independent printer, Henry Martyn Whitney; he was the son of a missionary, started the English-language newspaper that under various titles has been running in Honolulu since 1856, and explicitly wanted to establish a "free press" in Hawai'i. (He also published the first tourist guide to the islands in 1875.) The other, *Ka Hoku o ka Pakipika* (The Star of the Pacific), was the first newspaper to be published by a native Hawaiian (Mookini vi–vii; see Silva for further discussion).

As the "English-mainly" campaign (Lucas 2–8) and the annexation debate mounted, the number of Hawaiian-language newspapers multiplied, which indicates that Hawaiians clearly recognized the power of the printed word and actively participated in the public sphere. Hawaiian writers took an active role as writers, editors, and publishers in the press by 1861, producing approximately 120,000 newspaper pages through seventy different papers over the next eight decades (Nogelmeier 8). Hawaiian-language newspapers were in print from 1834 to 1948; over this span of 115 years, approximately 168 different Hawaiian-language newspapers were published, some running for decades and others a few months. While during the 1874–78 period only two were being printed (*Ka Nupepa Kuokoa* and the missionary *Ka Lahui Hawaii*), Hawaiian-language newspaper production reached a high of fourteen concurrent publications in 1896 (Mookini ix, x). It is precisely in 1896—three years after the overthrow of the Hawaiian monarchy and two years before the official annexation of Hawai'i as a Territory of the United States—that English was mandated by law as the only official language of instruction in all public and private schools in Hawai'i, thereby institutionalizing the suppression of Hawai'i's indigenous language. During that same time, fostered by Hawai'i's immigration and sugar plantation economy, "Pidgin" or Hawai'i Creole English became the preferred alternative to the English language, allowing Hawaiians, Japanese, Chinese, Portuguese, and Filipinos to communicate in noninstitutional settings. By 1929, only three Hawaiian-language newspapers were in circulation and by 1944 there was one, which closed in 1948. As scholar of Hawaiian literature, Ku'ualoha Ho'omanawanui, remarks: "Most Hawaiians in the first half of the twentieth century turned away from their language and social customs to blend into the 'melting pot' propaganda" of the time (165). It is only in the late 1950s, after statehood, that Hawaiian cultural and political activism resurfaced and brought about a revival of the Hawaiian language, hula, music, navigation, education (Hawaiian immersion schools), religion, and a sovereignty movement. Within the context of rereading history as told in the Hawaiian language by Hawaiians, scholars in a number of disciplines are turning to those Hawaiian-language newspapers that are now accessible primarily in microfilm. Nogelmeier's and Silva's work have called attention to how Western approaches to the study of Hawai'i have dismissed this immense Hawaiian-language archival repository of Hawaiian self-representation and knowledge. The ongoing digitization of these resources holds much promise. "The purpose of *Ulukau*, the Hawaiian Electronic Library, as its younger sister, the *Hawai'i Digital Library*, is to make these resources available for the use, teaching, and enhancement of the Hawaiian language and for a broader and deeper understanding of Hawai'i" (http://www.nupepa.org).

It should be clear that in the nineteenth century, when Euro-American settlers were speaking and reading Hawaiian and when Hawai'i was still a sovereign nation, Hawaiian-language and English-language newspapers constituted an important site not only for providing information but also for educating and galvanizing the people of Hawai'i. In this hotly contested public sphere, settlers and Hawaiians struggled for competing systems of governance, land development, language, and culture. As Hawaiian-language scholar Puakea Nogelmeier recently stated, every Hawaiian who had a strong opinion—whether it was about politics or a published story—wrote to the newspapers, which recorded the voices of the people (*nā leo*), their narratives and counternarratives. These narratives included current events, but also *mo'olelo* (history/story) and *ka'ao* (fictional tales). Among the Hawaiian *mo'olelo*, we find stories about Pele, the goddess of the volcano, and Kamapua'a, the pig-god, along with tales about chiefs and legendary places. The categories of *mo'olelo* and *ka'ao* were applied in the newspapers both to Hawaiian tales that had previously circulated orally *and* to foreign texts in translation.

Several newspapers regularly featured these *moʻolelo* and *kaʻao* on the front page, and that is where we find *He Kaao Arabia*. So it is important to consider its publication as part of a large-scale production of translations into Hawaiian that appeared in these nineteenth-century newspapers. The selections in the 1874-75 issues of the *Kuokoa* are not the only *Arabian Nights* translations to be found in Hawaiian-language newspapers. So far (August 2005), thanks to the assistance of Hawaiian newspaper researcher Sahoa Fukushima, we know of twelve other such tales: four published in *Ka Hoku o ka Pakipika* starting in 1861; one in the *Kuokoa* in 1863 ("No Ke Keiki Alii Opio Camalazamana, A Me Ke ʻLii Wahine Opio Badoura" [Story of the Prince Kamar-ez-Zeman and the Princess Budûr]); four more in the 1865–66 issues of *Ke Au Okoa* (The New Era), a weekly that merged with the *Kuokoa* in 1873; two "Aladdin" tales published in 1884 in *Ka Nupepa Aloha Aina* (The Patriot) and *Ke Ola o Hawaii* (The Life of Hawaiʻi); and one, titled "He Moolelo Kaao Mazewana, Ke Keikialii o Persia" in 1891, a "Jullanar" translation. At least two of the *Arabian Nights* stories then were translated *twice* into Hawaiian, in the 1860s first and then in the 1870s: the frame tale and the story of Bedr Bâsim and Jôharah.[3] "Aladdin" and "Jullanar" also appeared in different newspapers in the longer 1861–91 span. It is quite likely that more of the *Arabian Nights* tales were translated and published. For the purposes of this essay, we are focusing on the cluster of 1870s translations in the *Kuokoa* as a meaningful, though limited, starting point for reflecting on the politics of translation in nineteenth-century Hawaiʻi; but the translation of the *Arabian Nights* selections must be understood within the context of the *Kuokoa*'s publication of other narratives, both Hawaiian and foreign.

Ka Nupepa Kuokoa, "the longest running and most influential of the Hawaiian-language newspapers, was published from October 1861 to December 29, 1927" (Forbes 296; see also Hori; Silva 80–82). In addition to recording local news and history as well as current events from foreign countries (*no Amerika, no Cuba, no Beritania Nui, no Geremananui, no Peresia, no Rusia, no Italia, no Kina*, and more; from Cuba, from Great Britain, from Great [*sic*] Germany, from Persia, from Russia, from Italy, from China), the *Kuokoa* aimed to disseminate "foreign ideas as regards mode of life, habits, business, and industry" and to "stand firmly on the side of truth and religion" while avoiding "religious disputations" (from

Whitney's editorial statement in the first issue, as transcribed in Forbes 296). The *Kuokoa* published Hawaiian *moʻolelo* (e.g., "a series on the Hawaiian chief Umi" that began in 1862), Hawaiian *kaʻao* from the oral tradition (like Moses Manu's rendition of *Keaomelemele* in 1884–85), and new or literary Hawaiian tales such as the Cinderella-like story of *Laieikawai* by S. N. Haleole (which was then issued in book form in 1863). It also published a large number of translated fictions or *kaʻao*. These included very early on in 1861 some European fairy tales: "The Twelve Brothers," "Snow White," "Puss in Boots," and "The Frog Prince" (Schweizer). In the 1870s specifically, the *Kuokoa* offered its readers translations of German wonder tales such as "Ka Wai o ke Ola" ("The Water of Life") and "Kanani Hiolanikanahele" ("Sleeping Beauty"); a tale from China *"na Raianahu ka huhui hoku nani o Pekina,"* about the beautiful cluster of stars of Peking; our selections from the *Arabian Nights; "He Iwakalua Tausani Legue malalo o ke kai . . ."* ("Twenty Thousand Leagues under the Calm Sea . . ."), an adaptation of Jules Verne's popular narrative; and a multivolume fictional work translated from English that we have yet to identify, *He Moolelo Kaao o Robiana Lo, Ka hiwahiwa o ke koa* ("The Fictional Tale of Robiana Lo, the Choicest of Warriors"), which the newspaper ran from November 1871 to August 1874.[4]

We will venture to make a generalization at this point: translation in Hawaiʻi's public sphere in the latter part of the nineteenth century served very different sociopolitical purposes depending on whether it was translation into or from Hawaiian. Hawaiians translated a wide variety of texts from English into Hawaiian for Hawaiian-language newspapers, taking a cosmopolitan approach to different narrative conventions and cultures, just as their King Kalākaua would be doing in the 1880s when upon returning from his world tour he brought novelties such as the telephone, the flush toilet, and electrical lights to Iolani Palace.

This open-minded use of translation was a sign of confidence in the Hawaiian language and culture, and as such an inclusive practice; it was also a sign of acculturation into the settlers' worldview and cultural codes. In contrast, translation from the Hawaiian language into English became increasingly, though not exclusively, symptomatic of a dismissal of Hawaiians and their language as not essential to the workings of business and politics in Hawaiʻi (see Lucas 2–8 for examples in the courts). This close-minded use of translation was a sign of the settlers' sense of superiority, and as such an exclusionary practice; it was also a sign of the making of colonialism in the islands. There were indeed instances of assertive uses of translation into English that Hawaiians themselves made as well, but the point of the contrast here is to sketch the dynamics of translation in Hawaiian-language newspapers as a context within which to read *He Kaao Arabia.*

Translations

Moved by our different questions about *He Kaao Arabia* and enabled in different ways by Noelani Arista's reverse translation, we offer specific, textual observations about these nineteenth-century Hawaiian-language translations of selections from the *Arabian Nights.*

CB: While the story of Shahriyâr and his brother Shâhzamân is presented to the readers of the *Kuokoa,* it is not, however, part of the frame tale that in Lane's English-language version introduces Shahrazâd (Sheherazade) as the brave and savvy teller of the *Arabian Nights.* This means that in the Hawaiian version there is no Shahrazâd to tell the tales in sequence and for a purpose, and there is no life-or-death tension to the telling of the tales. It is true that Lane's translation reduced Shahrazâd's role and that its serialized pamphlet edition "omits Sheherazade's formal division of nights with its intrusion of the tale-teller's voice" (Sallis 51), but the character of Shahrazâd the storyteller was there in Lane's edition. In the *Kuokoa* text there is no trace of her. While it is not possible to know the reasons for this choice, I note several effects of it.

One, the gender dynamics of *He Kaao Arabia* are not as complex as they are in the *Arabian Nights* where, as scholars have pointed out, the agency and artistry of Shahrazâd control the misogyny of some of the tales and eventually the misogyny of King Shahriyâr.

Two, the powerful connection between repetition and variation in storytelling and sex that is at the heart of the *Arabian Nights* is not there in the Hawaiian text or is definitely downplayed. Shahrazâd as lover and teller is not there to make that link. Another excised episode within the first tale would seem to confirm this translation strategy. When the beautiful woman who has been kept locked up in a chest by the jealous jinn shows Shahriyâr and his brother that she has nevertheless cheated on the jinn many a time, Lane's text intimates that the two kings also have sexual relations with her: "The damsel . . . made signs to the two Kings, as though to say, Come down, and fear not this 'Efreet. . . . So, being afraid, they came down to her; and, *after they had remained with her as long as she required*, she took from her pocket a purse, and drew out from this a string, upon which were ninety-eight seal rings." She asks the two kings for their rings to add to her collection for "the owners of these rings, said she, have, all of them, been *admitted to converse with me, like as ye have*, unknown to this foolish 'Efreet" (Lane 9, my emphasis). The sexual intercourse is quite explicit in other English-language versions. But in the Hawaiian, we find:

> A o na keiki alii hoi, eia no laua ke kau nei iluna o ke kumu laau, a hiki i ka wa a ua akua lapu nei i ala ae ai, a ho-o iho la i ua wahine nei iloko o ka pahu aniani, a kau ae la iluna o ke poo, a luu aku la iloko o ke kai. (*Kuokoa* September 26, 1874)

> And as for the youthful kings, here they were atop the tree, up until the time when the troublesome spirit awoke and thrust the woman into the glass coffer, placed it upon his head, and dove into the sea.

The two brothers do not participate themselves in the cuckolding of the jinn; they remain safely at the top of the tree, which marks the purely verbal nature of their "conversing" with the woman.

Three, the Hawaiian translation is not fettered by the frame tale, thus allowing for the publication of a few, selected tales. Since *He Kaao Arabia* follows in the *Kuokoa* the publication of *Robiana Lo*, with its several hundred installments, there is a possibility that the translator or editor made the decision not to create the expectation of a long and evolving text in the *Kuokoa* readers. The absence of the frame tale may also be related to my next point.

Four, the translator focuses on King Shahriyâr as the protagonist of the tale and on his role as king, not as betrayed individual. The Hawaiian text immediately introduces Shahriyâr as a monarch of "he nui kana mau hana pono," "many . . . good deeds," but "o ka huhu ino hikiwawe loa kona hewa" (*Kuokoa* September 26, 1874), "his flaw was that he was quick to get intensely angry." The Hawaiian adaptation ends when the King has taken to the quotidian habit of marrying a virgin and then having her executed the next day. The translator comments that because of "this cruel activity, he [the King] became a person scorned by his people. This is the fate of unprincipled [*kolohe*] Kings, they are defeated and persecuted by their own people—sprinkled, the tale runs." The king's actions are not presented as a warning or punishment for women to control their sexuality; rather, the people's reactions to the king's actions function as an implicit warning to any leader, including of course the Hawaiian monarch. The focus on a leader's righteousness and his taking care of the people and the land is a common and significant topos in Hawaiian *moʻolelo*, as exemplified in so many stories including those of the "good" ruling chiefs Umi and Kawelo. But it is interesting to note that 1874, when this tale was published, was also the year in which David Kalākaua became the second *elected* Hawaiian monarch and that the election itself was highly contested.

The hypothesis I draw from these observations is that the absence of Shahrazâd and the frame tale in this Hawaiian text allows for downplaying the *Arabian Nights'* sexuality and for making Shahriyâr's tale assume a localized, possibly political, function in 1874 Hawaiʻi. Since their arrival in the islands in 1820, the missionaries had set out to change the Hawaiians' "management of the body" and affect a "redefinition of family" (Merry 230); the further bowdlerization of Lane's already tame text can be ascribed to this christianizing process. The Hawaiian-language translation does not, in this sense, reflect Hawaiian sexual norms. At the same time, since the story in Hawaiian emphasizes what is expected of a king or chief, this translation perhaps indirectly reflects the Hawaiian understanding that sexuality among high-ranking chiefs was to be viewed within the context of political and genealogical considerations (see Malo).

I should note that in the 1862 tale, "Moolelo no Samesala Naeha," published in the *Au Okoa* there *is* a Shahrazâd figure: Samesala Naeha was, in Sahoa Fukushima's draft translation, "the most choice of all the women in Arabia. She had no equal" for wisdom, storytelling, and song.

> O ua Samesala Naeha nei, oia ka wahine maikai loa ma Alabia a puni, aole kona like ma ka aina, aole hoi i na la mamua aku. . . . Aole no hoi he wahine naauao i puka mai e noho maluna iho keia honua.

> Samesala Naeha, was the most choice of all the women in Arabia, there was no one like her in all the land, certainly not in those days. . . . There was no other woman as wise who lived on earth.

Proof of her wisdom is that she and her sister train themselves for battling Shahriyâr's violence:

> O ka laua hana mau, mai ka manawa i hoomaka mai ai naʻlii e pepehi i na wahine, o ka haku i mau kaao, a me na mele, o ke ao i ka hula, nolaila, ua akamai loa laua ma ia mau hana.

The constant pastime [she and her younger sister, Haikanaau, had] from the time the king started to kill off the women, was to become skilled at composing stories and songs, and also learning to dance.

The tale ends with the following statement:

Nolaila, e ike lea kakou e na hoa, o na keaka a pau e puka aku ana ma keia hope aku, e olelo ia ana ua unuhi ia noloko mai o na po hookahi tausani a me kumamakahi o Alabia, o keia wahine no ka mea nana i haku ia mau mea a pau loa. E laa, o Hesini, ka Lauolioli, a me na mea e ae he nui loa i koe.

Therefore, my friends, the stories we see published hereafter, were taken from the thousand and one nights of Arabia. This is the woman who composed them all. For instance, Hesini, Ka Laauolioli, and many others. She is identified as the poet, but her sister Haikanaau's dance plays an important part in the storytelling.[5]

Does the existence of this Hawaiian Shahrazâd in *Ka Hoku o ka Pakipika* invalidate my hypothesis about the downplaying of sexuality and gender dynamics in *He Kaao Arabia* as it appears in the *Kuokoa*? I don't think so, because this is Samesala Naeha's or Shahrazâd's only appearance. Readers are told of the happy ending to her story, her marriage to the king, and the royal status granted to her three children. But the story itself never does function as a frame tale. Given that other Hawaiian traditions function as story cycles, omitting or isolating the scene of storytelling from the *Arabian Nights* selections that are translated seems deliberate. Furthermore, the heroine's name in Hawaiian is not as one would expect a transliteration of Shahrazâd, but Samesala *Naeha*, which associates her with "pain," multiple pain (*nā* indicates plural; *ehā*, "hurt, in pain" Pukui and Elbert 37). Within Naeha is the pain of women, those women the king has murdered and those he would murder if he were to continue in his serial killing; within Naeha is the pain of men like her father who are losing their loved ones to Shahriyâr's vengeful violence. The thematic focus even in this Hawaiian version of the frame story is not so much on gender or storytelling, but on the two brothers as kings and on the contradiction between them being "He mau alii ma ka hooponopono aupuni ana, a he mau kane make wahine no hoi," "rulers who cared for their kingdom as well as men who murdered women"; and, as Arista reminds me, the theme of chiefs taking proper care of their people was popular with Hawaiian audiences and would have resonated deeply with Hawaiian tales and histories of chiefs. In the 1862 version, this tension is resolved as the violence proves to be an aberration in the ruler's behavior. As a name, Naeha may be a symbolically suggestive choice, but it did not become, the way Shahrazâd did, a signature name for the power of storytelling.

NA: The master storyteller Shahrazâd is introduced to a Hawaiian audience as Samesala Naeha in the 1862 *mo'olelo* bearing her name. What inspired the name Samesala is unclear; however, Naeha may be readily translated as pains, sorrow, or suffering. The woman's name marks her affliction and that of the other women in the frame story. Naeha stands in for the plight of all the women before her who experienced the tortuous knowledge of impending death as well as her own psychic trauma, as she and her sister must always devise stories compelling enough to stave off execution for another day. Shahrazâd's name, which means "of noble appearance or origin" (Marzolph and van Leeuwen 702), points to her suitability as future mate for the king, Shahriyâr, while Naeha's name is freighted with the burden of woman's condition, often as the victim of murderous jealousy and life without justice.

Naeha's sister in the story is Haikanaau, which translates as "to the guts" or "heart speaks." In Hawaiian the *na'au* is the seat of knowing, and moral nature (Andrews 408). Her name more than her sister's is a foreshadowing of what is to come. In this context, Haikanaau can also be translated as "conscience," or as "justice." Haikanaau is the female witness to what passes between Naeha and the king, and in the Hawaiian story she symbolizes the presence of justice in the midst of an ongoing unjust situation. Haikanaau takes on an additional meaning since, as the dancer who gives life to her sister's chanted words, Haikanaau also contributes to conveying messages to the king's own *na'au*. Unlike the sister pair in the original frame story, Naeha chants stories accompanied by an instrument while Haikanaau dances hula—providing hand and foot motion to illuminate the chanted stories. In hula chanted words are just as important as the hand and foot motions and other bodily movements that a dancer employs. We are told in the story that "the constant pastime of the women from the time the kings began to murder women was to become skilled at composing stories and songs and learning to dance." The women were so well trained and skilled at their respective talents that according to the text, "there was no other woman as wise" as Naeha who "lived upon the earth," while Haikanaau had "no match when it came to hula." The description of their skill and the manner in which the sisters work together is reminiscent of other Hawaiian famed female pairs, like the sisters Pele and Hiʻiaka, and Hiʻiaka and her protégé and ʻaikane, the famed dancer Hopoe.

Returning to the main focus of our analysis, omissions in the Kuokoa translation of Shahriyâr's story remove the tale's focus on the woman who has sexual relations when she pleases. This kind of female power that is associated with sexuality—and that in Western translations of the *Arabian Nights* is particularly associated with the Orient—may have been carefully removed from stories published for Hawaiian audiences because American missionaries so deeply influenced the production of literacy in early nineteenth-century Hawaiʻi. Their disapproval of Hawaiian lifestyle and its "lasciviousness" worked openly as censorship and also internally as self-censorship, even in an "independent" or nonmissionary newspaper.

However, whatever his intentions, the translator's interventions also have a subversive effect. In the same episode of that story, the Hawaiian translator changes a key item in the encounter between the two kings and the woman who has been taken captive by the Efrit:

> A ike nae ua wahine nei, ua ka ia loa ia ua akua nei e ka hiamoe nui, hapai ae la ia i ke poo mai kona uha ae, a hookuu iho la i ka honua, a ku ae la a hele aku la i ka pahu aniani, a lawe ae la he pokaa kaula, a helu iho la ia lakou me ka nana pono, a huli ae la i keʻkua lapu, oiai no oia e moe ana, a pane iho la me ka leo ano hoohie, "Naaupo maoli no ka manao, o ka lili ka mea e hoopaaia ai ka ui; me ka manao ole i kau paa ana iaʻu, ke ike nei au, o keia mau kaula a pau, naʻu wale no ia mai na ipo mai aʻu he kanahiku kumama-lima." (*Kuokoa* September 26, 1874)

> And the woman realized that the troublesome spirit was struck deeply by great sleep, and she lifted his head from her thigh, and placed it on the ground, and stood and went over to the glass coffer and brought out a ball of string, and counted them off carefully and turned to the troublesome spirit as he slept and said in a dignified voice, "Truly ignorant is the idea that jealousy is the thing which could master beauty; without considering your imprisonment of me, I see, all of these strings belong solely to me, given to me by all of my lovers, some seventy-five."

In the Hawaiian version of this tale the woman counts off seventy-five strings from a ball of string to signify the number of lovers she has had, unbeknownst to the Efrit. But in Edward Lane's text, as quoted earlier in this essay, she "took from her pocket a purse, and drew out from this a string, upon which were ninety-eight seal rings." Perhaps the Hawaiian translator was inspired by Lane's mention of "string" when he made the shift from rings to string.

Sporadic mention is made in historical records to the practice of Hawaiian genealogists and chanters who used knotted cord as a memory aid to keep track of the names of individuals and generations that they were responsible for remembering when chanting lengthy genealogical chants belonging to the *ali'i* (chief, ruler; Pukui and Elbert 20). The rings that the woman collects as mementos of her liaisons have in the Hawaiian translation been replaced by a counting device from the Hawaiian past. This instance of substitution undercuts once again the woman's power by making her means of keeping a record of her betrayals more impersonal, while in the English-language version the illicit nature of the woman's impersonal sexual encounters is emphasized by the fact that she remembers, savors them over and over again, thanks to the very personal memento that each man has given to her. Yet omitting the seal ring provides its own illicit "ring" in the Hawaiian translation. By substituting a counting device from the censored if not "outlawed" Hawaiian past, a device used by those whose responsibility it was to *remember,* the translator provided his Hawaiian reading audience with their own moment of illicit recollection. Thus, while the sexual power of the woman over her male conquests is downplayed, the feeling of participating in illicit activity, which both texts encourage readers to respond to, is maintained.

NA AND CB: In the other two tales published in 1874, "the Story of Bedr Bâsim and Jôharah" and "Sindbad the Sailor," just as in the story of Shahriyâr, condensation and omission are at work for the purposes of adaptation. But in *"He Kaao Arabia! No Ke Kanaka Lawaia! Ke Kumu O Ka Pomaikai"* ("An Arabian Tale! About the Fisherman! The Source Of Good Fortune"), the translator's strategies are different, and that is probably because a different translator was at work in 1875.

NA: As a translator, I am always interested in the process of translation, in considering what pains a translator endures to produce a "faithful" translation. We were lucky because S. K. Ulele, the translator of "The Fisherman's Tale" gave a brief glimpse into his process when he introduced the first of ten installments in the May 1, 1875, issue of *Ka Nupepa Kuokoa:*

> I ka poe heluhelu Kaao o ke *Kuokoa:*—Aloha oukou: He malihini no au imua o oukou ma keia manawa a kakou e kamailio nei. I ka hoao ana nae e alakai ia kakou mamuli o ka nani a me ka maikai o ka Moolelo mai na Buke Moolelo Haole mai. A he mea mau no hoi i ka poe hoopuka Kaao a Moolelo ka hoaui iki ana ae i na hopuna olelo kupono ole i ka hoike ana aku imua o

ka lehulehu, a ma na wahi pamaloo hoi i wahi nani, alaila e nani a maikai auanei ke Kaao, o keia mau hoololi nae, he mau mea liilii wale no, aka o ka hapa nui e unuhi pololei ia no, a aole no hoi e oi aku na huaolelo lealea ma o aku o na palena kupono.

To the readers of *Kaao* in the *Kuokoa:*—Greetings to you: I am a stranger before you now as we converse, as I attempt to lead us after the beauty and the charm of the story from English language storybooks. It is the habit of the people who publish *Kaao* and *Moolelo* to slightly shorten passages that are not suitable to share before the masses, and in the places which are dull and lack beauty, to embellish until the *Kaao* is satisfying[;] these changes however, are simply trifles, the bulk of it is translated faithfully, and entertaining words do not exceed the bounds of propriety.

Here Ulele admits that the *Kaao* is edited in places for content, with words that he deemed unsuitable removed. "Dull" (*pāmaloʻo* literally means "dry" and "rainless," as in "to thunder without rain"; Pukui and Elbert 313) portions of the story would be energized to speak directly to Hawaiian sensibilities. Thinking how to-this-day popular translations into English of Hawaiian *moʻolelo* and *kaʻao* have often been "free" to represent an imaginary or fantastic Hawaiʻi, most interesting perhaps is Ulele's statement that faithful translation is of importance to him as well as to his audience.

CB: S. K. Ulele's Hawaiian translation follows the English-language plot "faithfully," as he promises in his above-cited preamble. The translator's focus, however, is not as it was in Lane's text on ethnography (Schacker) or even on whatever makes these tales "Arabian." In the tale of "King Yûnân and the Sage Dûbân," for instance, the king remains unnamed and is identified as Greek (which is what Yûnân means in Arabic). Allah (*Alahe* in *Kuokoa* May 8, 1875) and the prophet Mohammed (*Mahometa* in *Kuokoa* May 15, 1875) are mentioned, but so is God (*Akua Nui* in *Kuokoa* May 1, 1875). ʻEfrît and jinni are translated as *akua lapu*, a term that identifies a spectral being or ghost, an evil spirit, already present in the Hawaiian worldview, and Lane's other term of jinn, *Mârid*, is translated as a title, *ka Merida*, and used only to address the jinn directly (for several examples see *Kuokoa* May 1, 1875).

In their new context, these are domesticating choices that shift attention from the tales' cultural milieu to their narrative mode and purpose. These are, as the translator's note suggests, his focus: rendering the charm of English-language stories and the moral of good fortune in the fisherman's tale. To support this reading of the translation, I can point to the inclusion in the Hawaiian translation of all tales that are part of "The Story of the Fisherman" cycle as demonstration that Ulele was cognizant and appreciative of the internal logic of this cluster of stories, in particular the mirroring of or thematic link among them (for instance, as David Pinault noted, "just as the fisherman is threatened by the demon, so is the sage threatened by the ungrateful king," 230). In addition to the translator's preamble, his focus on "good fortune" is evidenced in his direct address to the readers and commentary following the tale of the Sage Dûbân:

> Here, oh readers, shall we regard and look upon our sources of good fortune, since we have indeed seen the things about the Greek King who was fooled by the deceitful words of his prime minister who looked for faults and loved honors, but the wrongdoer in all his actions was not victorious. Therefore, oh dear friends, don't take up the attitude of the Prime Minister, but be careful, with good intentions, not to claim honors not rightfully due, and be satisfied with the position that you have, since the motto [*moto*] of this story is this, "from little things big things are obtained"; so it is with the position that you have, from the humble all the way to those advanced in age, therefore let us all accept the same [what we have] and take care.

Ulele will not allow his readers to miss the point of this tale-within-the-tale and further takes the initiative to draw a specific warning from it: "don't take up the role of the Prime Minister." I have not followed this cue yet, but exploring the politics of King Kalākaua's court may point to the translator's foregrounding of the prime minister as a reference with direct bearing on the political dynamics of 1875 Hawai'i.

NA: The passage that Cristina Bacchilega just quoted from *"Ka Pau Ana o ka Moolelo o ke Alii Helene—Kana Kuhina—Me ke Kanaka Naauao Dubana,"* "The Ending of the Story of the Greek King—His Minister—and the Sage Dûbân" (*Ka Nupepa Kuokoa* June 5, 1875) is one of the points in *Kaao Arabia* at which the Hawaiian translator includes his own commentary on the story. This is how it appears in the sixth installment of *Kaao Arabia*:

> Maanei kakou e ka poe heluhelu e haliu ae ai a e nana no ko kakou kumu o ka pomaikai, oiai ua ike 'la no kakou i na mea e pili ana no ke Alii Helene puni wale i na olelo pahele a kona Kuhina imihala a puni hanohano, aka, aole e lanakila ka mea hana hewa ma kana mau hana a pau. Nolaila, e na makamaka, mai noho a lawe i ke kulana o ke Kuhina, aka, e malama me ka manao maikai piikoi ole i ke kulana i loaa ia oe, oiai, o ka moto o ko kakou nei kaao, oia no keia, "mailoko mai o na mea liilii i loaa ai he mea nui," pela

no me ke kulana i loaa ia oe, mai ka haahaa mai no ia a kau loa aku i ka puaneane, nolaila e lawe like kakou a e malama. (*Kuokoa* June 5, 1875)

Commentaries like this one show the extent to which, in a new context, translated narratives could be made to highlight a moral that the original story may have pointed to, but was secondary in importance to its greater themes. Hawaiian audiences in 1875 would have been accustomed to the missionary-tinged moralizing the translator interjected, since much of what was published in translation was geared to "teaching" Hawaiians about the superiority of life lived and imported *mai ka ʻāina ʻē mai*, "from foreign lands." In his extensive introduction to the first issue in 1861, Henry M. Whitney, publisher of *Ka Nupepa Kuokoa*, wrote that the newspaper would be devoted to many things but, most importantly, it would "endeavor to furnish from week to week such reading matter as may tend to develop and enlarge the Hawaiian mind, and enable Hawaiians to think, feel, act and live more like foreigners." This production of translated literature to build Hawaiian "literacy" in *haole* or foreign cultures (*haole* in Hawaiian is commonly used to refer to Caucasians, foreigners of European or American origin), then, while seemingly attempting to blur the boundaries between Hawaiians and *haole*, in fact also solidifies their difference—their separateness and the power relations supporting it. In similar ways, this story and its appended moral are utilized to keep Hawaiians in check and in their place, satisfied with their lot in life as the inheritors of foreign and much greater traditions, religious beliefs, and ways of living. In such places, *Kaao Arabia* is used to further the project of producing the "native-*like*-foreigner."

CB: Did the Hawaiian translators recognize the double-edged fascination that the Orient exercised on Lane and so many other European translators of the *Arabian Nights* as paralleling the Euro-American settlers' representation of Hawaiians as the most noble of the primitive people of the Pacific, an inflection of what Paul Lyons has recently called Pacificism? It is difficult to tell. But I noted with interest, thanks to Noelani Arista's translation, that some of the elements that served to exoticize the *Arabian Nights* for a Euro-American readership—blackness and sexuality—are downplayed in the Hawaiian version. The Hawaiian translation does not portray Shahriyâr's wife's lover as a "black slave" (Lane 5) but as a "*Keonimana i makemakeia*" (*Kuokoa* September 26, 1874), "Gentleman whom she desired"; similarly, his younger brother finds his own wife with a "*kauwa kuapaa*," a "slave" but not a "male negro slave" (Lane 4). The English-language text's implicit discourse of class is downplayed and the one on race is excised, either because the translator found the latter unacceptable or because its inclusion would make the story less palatable to Hawaiian readers. Similarly, as mentioned earlier, sexuality and gendered expectations are also downplayed in the translation into Hawaiian. These were not only aspects of the *Arabian Nights* that titillated the Euro-American imagination but matters in general over which Hawaiian culture and the missionary-settler culture diverged quite radically. A different kind of translation could have told Hawaiian readers more about these problematic aspects of the imagination that produced European translations of the *Arabian Nights*, but that is not what we have.

He Kaao Arabia reads as an example of the Hawaiians' rather generous representation in the public sphere of a foreign imagination and as an effort to make positive and entertaining domestic uses of it. Given the ensuing colonization and feminization (Trask) of Hawai'i, it would appear that this practice of translation in the Hawaiian-language newspapers contributed primarily to the Hawaiian readership's acculturation into the ways and mentality of Euro-American settlers, an acculturation that by the end of the nineteenth century would give way to the political subordination of the Hawaiian people and culture to another nation. "*I ka 'ōlelo nō ka make*": "death is in speech" or language—"words can destroy."

However, something else about *He Kaao Arabia* strikes me as a student of fairy tales and folklore. What the different translation strategies adopted by the anonymous 1874 translator(s) and by Ulele have in common is skillful storytelling. The art of Hawaiian storytelling through song, dance, chant, and other oral forms continued to serve them well in the new medium of the newspaper: remembering can work as resistance. In the case of the *Arabian Nights*, the translators were in print doing what dancers and chanters would do in performance. They would not, for instance, perform the entirety of the Pele and Hi'iaka epic poetry, but select a narrative cluster or minicycle that seemed most appropriate to the situation or most effective in conveying a message indirectly. They were making use of a tradition—indigenous or foreign—to negotiate the present through story. In *He Kaao Arabia*, there is no Shahrazâd, but we do "hear" the voices of the Hawaiian translators retelling the tales to Hawaiians. In their words, these are tales of doing the right thing and making things right: the cruel leader will lose the people's following; the small and humble can achieve more than the treacherous Prime Minister. Thus, in these translators' words, as in the words of the absent Shahrazâd's, "*aia nō ke ola*," there is life.

NA: In some places, *He Kaao Arabia* utilized idioms and images that were clearly a link to the Hawaiian past, showing that not only did S. K. Ulele, the Hawaiian translator, know enough to produce "faithful" translations, but also that he could for himself and Hawaiian readers produce something more satisfying, a foreign tale speaking in a native tongue.

> Lawaia moewaa
> Ka upena ume iki
> Anu hewa i ke Ao
> Ke kuuna ia ole
>
> Unlucky fisherman
> The net that attracts little
> Bitterly cold in the day
> The cast that snares no fish
> S. K. Ulele (*Kuokoa* May 1, 1875)

As if to show with pride that he has composed this little piece, S. K. Ulele appends his name to the poem that follows his translator's introduction and precedes the text of "The Story of the Fisherman." Ulele had many choices for the word I have translated as "unlucky." He could have used something very conventional like *pōʻino*, "unfortunate or bad luck"; *pōmaikaʻi ʻole*, "unlucky or ill fated"; or even the gloss/transliteration of the English words "bad luck," *pakalaki*. Instead Ulele decided to illustrate his knowledge of the cherished past when he chose the word *moewaʻa*, literally "a dream of a canoe," which in former times was considered bad luck (Pukui and Elbert 250), a portent of disappointment or even death. Hawaiian audiences craved such flourishes of expression from writers and translators, I would imagine, especially because during those years they were being bombarded by the dichotomy between *ka wā kahiko*, "the past" and *kēia mau lā*, "these days," with the positive emphasis on the present. Hawaiian newspapers, including the *Kuokoa*, were rife with articles, observations, and news comparing the dark past with the enlightened present. In an odd way foreigners were making the Hawaiian past of recent memory, the still living past, into something negative and anti-quated. This is evidenced by the common translation to this day of *"i ka wā kahiko"* as "in ancient times," which has a different connotation from "in the old times" (Pukui and Elbert 112) or "in the past." Similarly, Davida Malo's book *Ka Moolelo Hawaii* (literally: Hawaiian History) was translated as *Hawaiian Antiquities,* even though Malo—who was writing about the beliefs and practices of his own times—had died in 1853, not long before Nathaniel Emerson translated the book in 1898. What brings me to believe that Ulele's words would be welcome as an act of cultural "re-membering" (Stillman) is that Hawaiians would often write to the newspapers in defense of Hawaiian ways of knowing, insisting on their ef-ficacy and relevance to the times. Perhaps to counter the relegation of their culture to the distant past, Hawaiian writers and translators were happy to impress the audience with their knowledge, the way S. K. Ulele is in his poem. Sharing such tidbits here and there throughout the stories would establish his reputation among Hawaiians, that he was knowledgeable and could share this knowledge in ways that were clever and hidden.

NA and CB: Our preliminary reading of *He Kaao Arabia* in the *Kuokoa,* then, is that this nineteenth-century Hawaiian translation of the *Arabian Nights* for the newspapers has little to do with the (re)production of Orientalism as sexual and exotic fantasy and much more to do with the Hawaiian transla-tors' benevolent representation of a foreign imagination, that of "English-language stories," and their transformation of it for specific localized uses. We say this *not* to undermine the importance of Orientalism as a framework for reading the *Arabian Nights* in its many translations; rather, the Hawaiian example indirectly confirms the reading of the *Arabian Nights* as a Western fantasy of the "Orient" and thereby can constitute an interesting variation within that interpretive narrative. The Hawaiian translation presents the tales as stories translated from the English language; yes, they were once in Arabic, but the focus of the Hawaiian translation is located much more in its relation to the West than to the fantastic Orient. As such, *He Kaao Ara-bia* is an instance of colonial translation in nineteenth-century Hawai'i. But it is more than that. Our focus on the rhetoric of *He Kaao Arabia* as trans-lation and on its allusions to the "protocol" of Hawaiian literature and cul-ture seeks to foreground, as both Spivak (*Critique of Postcolonial Reason, Death of a Discipline*) and Silva suggest in different contexts, the translators' indigenous agency within the larger politics of translation at the time; and it is our understanding that, for Hawaiian translators and readers, *He Kaao Arabia* took the form both of acculturation and resistance.

NOTES

1. See Stephen Benson's book for a recent and significant scholarly take on the influence of the *Arabian Nights*. For two specific case studies that speak to these larger issues of Orientalism, see Jennifer Schacker's chapter on Edward Lane's translation of the *Arabian Nights* in her book *National Dreams* (2003) and John Stephens's and Robyn McCallum's chapter "The Idea of the Orient" in *Retelling Stories, Framing Culture* (1998).

2. Like the Hawaiian translation, Lane's text had also initially appeared in serialized form in thirty-two pamphlets, but then it was bound in three volumes.

3. When we published an earlier version of this essay in *Fabula* 45.3–4 (2004): 189–206, we did not know of these texts; Sahoa Fukushima's research and translations were funded through a 2004–5 Research Relations grant from the University of Hawai'i at Mānoa that Bacchilega received.

   There is also one more story, titled "He Moolelo Hoonanea No Ali Hiba Ke Ahikanana A Me Ka Lua Ole O Ke Koa O Ka Aina Kupua" [An Entertaining Story of Ali Hiba the Fierce Warrior Second to None of the Land of the Supernatural], in the 1898 *Ka Lei Rose O Hawaii*.

   The tales in *Ka Hoku o ka Pakipika* are "He Kaao no Hesini" [Story of Hasan] (November 28, 1861–April 3, 1862); "He Wahi Kaao no ka Manu Olelo, ka Laauoli, a me ka Wai Olenalena" ["A Tale of the Talking Bird, the Singing Tree, and the Golden Water"; a version of "Two Sisters Who Envied Their Cadette"] (April 3–17, 1862); "Moolelo no Samesala Naeha! O ka Moolelo keia o ka Mea nana i haku i na Kaao Arabia" signed by S. K. Kaai ["Story of Samesala Naeha! This is the story of the person who composed the Arabian Tales"; a version of the frame story with highly unusual details]; and "He Moolelo no Aladana a me ka Ipukukui Kupanaha" ["Story of Aladdin and the Wonderful Lamp"]. The *Au Okoa* featured "Rose Mohala! He Kaao Arabia" [Blooming Rose] (September 25–October 9, 1865; "Ali Sera & Kumuruda. He Kaao Arabia" [Story of Ali Shâr and Zumurrud] (October 16–30, 1865; "Bedera Basima & Giohara, He Kaao Arabia" [Bedr Bâsim and Jôharah] (November 6–December 4, 1865); and "Ke Kaao o Habiba! He Kaao Arabia" [The Story of Habiba] (December 11, 1865–March 26, 1866).

   While Lane's edition of the *Arabian Nights* would seem to be the principal source for the 1874–75 translations, it is more complicated to ascertain the source of the 1860s and 1890s texts. The story of Aladdin, for instance, was not part of Lane's popular volumes. In addition to Lane's, there were only a few English-language translations available at the time (e.g., Jonathan Scott's 1811 translation adapting Antoine Galland's French text; George Lamb's 1826 translation of selections from Joseph von Hammer's German edition), but manifold editions and selections from them (Chauvin). It is quite plausible to look to Galland as the (mediated-through-English editions) source for some of the stories, especially since "Aladdin" is part of Galland's repertoire of "orphan stories" (Marzolph and van Leeuwen 82–85). Some of the stories, however, include episodes that are not recognizable from well-known editions: in the "Moolelo no Samesala Naeha," the younger brother cross-dresses, pretending to be an old woman healer in order to save his brother who has been held captive by his treacherous wife and her black lover; in the 1898 "He Moolelo Hoonanea No Ali Hiba" the hero is born as a *mo'o* or lizard, a *kupua* (being who can take many forms) commonly featured in the Hawaiian *mo'olelo*. More information is needed to state whether these are free translations or original adaptations.

4. We will be pleased to know if this Hawaiianized name, Robiana Lo, rings a bell with any of our readers.

5. S. K. Kaai is named as the translator of the Samesala Naeha story and three more in the 1860s. His initials are the same as those of the 1875 translator, S. K. Ulele, opening up the possibility—if Ulele is a pseudonym—that they may be the same person (Fukushima, personal communication).

WORKS CITED

Andrews, Lorrin. *A Dictionary of the Hawaiian Language.* (1865). With an Introduction to the New Edition by Noenoe K. Silva and Albert J. Schütz. Honolulu: Island Heritage, 2003.

Au Okoa (Ke). The New Era. Honolulu: April 1865–March 1873. Bishop Museum Library.

Bassnett, Susan, and André Lefevere, eds. *Constructing Cultures: Essays on Literary Translation.* Philadelphia: Multilingual Matters, 1998.

Benson, Stephen. *Cycles of Influence: Fiction, Folktale, Theory.* Detroit: Wayne State UP, 2003.

Borges, Jorge Luis. *Seven Nights.* Trans. Eliot Weinberger (Siete noches. Lectures delivered in Buenos Aires in 1977.) New York: New Directions, 1984.

Chauvin, Victor. *Bibliographie des ouvrages arabes ou relatifs aux Arabes.* 12 vols. Liège: Vaillant-Carmanne, 1892–1922.

Forbes, David W. *Hawaiian National Bibliography, 1780–1900.* Vol. 3: 1851–80. Honolulu: U of Hawai'i P, 2002.

Fukushima, Sahoa. Personal communication. September 2004.

Geider, Thomas. "*Alfu Lela Ulela: The Thousand and One Nights* in Swahili-speaking East Africa." *Fabula* 45.3–4 (2004): 246–60.

Habermas, Jürgen. *The Structural Transformation of the Public Sphere: An Inquiry into a Category of Bourgeois Society.* Trans. Thomas Burger. Cambridge: MIT P, 1991.

Haring, Lee. "Pieces for a Shabby Hut." *Folklore, Literature, and Cultural Theory.* Ed. Cathy L. Preston. New York: Garland, 1995. 187–203.

Hoku o ka Pakipika (Ka). The Star of the Pacific. Honolulu: Sept. 1861–May 1863. Hawaiian Historical Society Library.

Hoʻomanawanui, Kuʻualoha. "Ka Ola Hou ʻAna o ka ʻŌlelo Hawaiʻi i ka Haʻi ʻAna o ka Moʻolelo i Kēia Au Hou" (The Revival of the Hawaiian Language in Contemporary Storytelling). *Traditional Storytelling Today: An International Sourcebook.* Ed. Margaret Read MacDonald. Chicago: Fitzroy Dearborn, 1999. 160–70.

Hori, Joan. "Background and Historical Significance of *Ka Nupepa Kuokoa.*" Online Hamilton Library UHM resource. Sept. 26, 2006. http://libweb.hawaii.edu/digicoll/nupepa_kuokoa/kuokoa_htm/kuokoa.html#rival.

Irwin, Robert. *The Arabian Nights: A Companion.* Harmondsworth: Penguin, 1994.

Kabbani, Rana. *Europe's Myths of Orient: Devise and Rule.* Bloomington: Indiana UP, 1986.

Lane, Edward W. *The Thousand and One Nights, or, Arabian Nights Entertainments.* London: Chatto and Windus, 1930.

Lucas, Paul F. N. "E Ola Mau Kākou I Ka ʻŌlelo Makuahine" (Hawaiian Language Policy and the Courts.) *Hawaiian Journal of History* 34 (2000): 1–28.

Lyons, Paul. *American Pacificism.* London: Routledge, 2005.

Malo, David. *Hawaiian Antiquities (Moolelo Hawaii).* Trans. Nathaniel B. Emerson. 2nd ed. 1898. Honolulu: Bishop Museum, 1951.

Malti-Douglas, Fedwa. *Woman's Body, Woman's Word: Gender and Discourse in Arabo-Islamic Writing.* Princeton: Princeton UP, 1991.

Marzolph, Ulrich. "Re-Locating the Arabian Nights." *Orientalia Lovanensia Analecta* 87 (1998): 155–63.

———, and Richard van Leeuwen, with the collaboration of Hassan Wassouf. *The Arabian Nights Encyclopedia.* 2 vols. Santa Barbara, Denver, and Oxford: ABC-CLIO, 2004.

Merry, Sally Engle. *Colonizing Hawaiʻi: The Cultural Power of Law.* Princeton: Princeton UP, 2000.

Mookini, Esther K. *The Hawaiian Newspapers.* Honolulu: Topgallant, 1974.

Naithani, Sadhana. "Prefaced Space: Tales of the Colonial British Collectors of Indian Folklore." *Imagined States: Nationalism, Utopia, and Longing in Oral Cultures.* Ed. Luisa Del Giudice and Gerald Porter. Logan: Utah State UP, 2001. 64–79.

Nogelmeier, Puakea M. *Mai Paʻa I Ka Leo: Historical Voice in Primary Materials, Looking Forward and Listening Back.* Diss. U of Hawaiʻi at Mānoa, 2003.

Nupepa Kuokoa (Ka). The Independent Press. Honolulu: October 1861–December 1927. Microfilm consulted at the U of Hawaiʻi-Mānoa Hamilton Library.

Pasolini, Pier Paolo. *Il fiore delle mille e una notte: Arabian Nights.* Screenplay by and directed by Pier Paolo Pasolini. Produced by Alberto Grimaldi. Italy, 1974.

Pinault, David. *Story-Telling Techniques in the Arabian Nights.* Leiden: Brill, 1992.

Pukui, Mary K. *ʻŌlelo Noʻeau: Hawaiian Proverbs and Poetical Sayings.* Honolulu: Bishop Museum, 1983.

———, and Samule H. Elbert. *Hawaiian Dictionary: Hawaiian-English, English-Hawaiian.* Rev. and enl. ed. Honolulu: U of Hawaiʻi P, 1986.

Rushdie, Salman. *Haroun and the Sea of Stories.* London: Granta, 1990.

Sallis, Eva. *Sheherazade through the Looking Glass: The Metamorphosis of The Thousand and One Nights.* Richmond: Curzon P, 1999.

Schacker, Jennifer. *National Dreams: The Remaking of Fairy Tales in Nineteenth-Century England*. Philadelphia: U of Pennsylvania P, 2003.

Schweizer, Niklaus R. "Kahaunani: Snow White in Hawaiian: A Study in Acculturation." *East Meets West: Homage to Edgar C. Knowlton*. Ed. Roger L. Hadlich and J. D. Ellsworth. Honolulu: U of Hawaiʻi P, 1988. 283–89.

Silva, Noenoe. "Ka Hoku o ka Pakipika: Emergence of the Native Voice in Print." *Aloha Betrayed: Native Hawaiian Resistance to American Colonialism*. Durham: Duke UP, 2004.

Spivak, Gayatri C. *A Critique of Postcolonial Reason*. Cambridge: Harvard UP, 1999.

———. *Death of a Discipline*. New York: Columbia UP, 2003.

———. "The Politics of Translation." *Outside in the Teaching Machine*. New York: Routledge, 1993. 179–200.

———. "Questioned on Translation: Adrift." *Public Culture* 13.1 (2001): 13–22.

Stephens, John, and Robyn McCallum. *Retelling Stories, Framing Culture: Traditional Story and Metanarratives in Children's Literature*. New York: Garland, 1998.

Stillman, Amy K. "Re-Membering the History of the Hawaiian Hula: Cultural Memory." *Reconfiguring History and Identity in the Postcolonial Pacific*. Ed. Jeannette M. Mageo. Honolulu: U of Hawaiʻi P, 2001. 187–204.

Trask, Haunani-Kay. *From a Native Daughter: Colonialism and Sovereignty in Hawaiʻi*. Rev. ed. Honolulu: U of Hawaiʻi P, 1999.

Ulukau: The Hawaiian Electronic Library. Hoʻolaupaʻi. Hawaiian Nūpepa Collection. Sept. 26, 2006. http://www.nupepa.org.

Venuti, Lawrence. *The Scandals of Translation: Towards an Ethics of Difference*. London: Routledge, 1998.

———. "Translation, Community, Utopia." *The Translation Studies Reader*. Ed. Lawrence Venuti. London: Routledge, 2000. 468–88.

———, ed. *The Translation Studies Reader*. London: Routledge, 2000.

Zimmerman, Mary. *The Arabian Nights: A Play*. Evanston: Northwestern UP, 2005.

11

Alfu Lela Ulela: The *Thousand and One Nights* in Swahili-Speaking East Africa

Thomas Geider

The *Thousand and One Nights* (henceforth: *Nights*) venture into a multitude of geographical directions, including the sources of the tales and the geographical references within the tales (Henninger) as well as their translation into various languages. While the preserved manuscripts of the *Nights* originate from the Arab world, its stories derive from Indian, Greek, Jewish, Iranian, and Turkish sources. Antoine Galland's French translation of 1704–17 introduced the tales to Europe, and they were subsequently translated into most European (and several non-European) languages. As for the repertoire of the *Nights*, most compilers or editors individually selected stories from varying sources either labeled as or imagined to represent the *Nights*. Consequently, a solid corpus of *Nights* stories does not exist, and one should rather speak of "a broad network of texts" and "an amalgam of types of stories" (van Leeuwen 90, 98). In particular, the arrangement of the post-Galland manuscripts and translations often followed European ideas about the Arab world that resulted from and contributed to a specific kind of "Orientalism" (Marzolph, "Relocating"). Meanwhile, the marvelous tales of the *Nights* continue to inspire hosts of European and American writers, filmmakers, and other creative artists (Walther 160–65; Irwin 237–92). Moreover, the *Nights* are being reenacted within new contexts of orality and reformulated in modern Arabic literature.

In addition to Arab and Western tradition, the world of the *Nights* also includes those African cultures that were Islamized centuries ago and that have continued to remain in close contact with Arabic culture and literature. Indeed, the geographical distance between the Arabian Peninsula and Africa is quite short. There are westward land routes from Sudan leading through the Bilâd al-Sûdân up to Senegal (Triaud and Kaye). From southern Somalia, the maritime "Swahili Corridor" (Horton) extends to the coastlands of Kenya and Tanzania, with the adjacent islands of Lamu, Zanzibar, and others. As connections between the Arab and Swahili narrative traditions have rarely been discussed in previous research, in the present essay I provide a survey of the existence of the *Nights* in the Swahili-speaking regions of East Africa.

The Swahili are an African-based Bantu-speaking community inhabiting the East African coastal and insular lands. They have been in maritime contact with Arabia, Iran, and India since the second century CE and have been Islamized since at least the ninth century. In consequence, the Swahili population is composed of African and Oriental peoples, and their culture integrates elements from both continents into a new distinct entity (Nurse and Spear; Allen; Mazrui and Shariff). An Oriental influence is clearly visible in loanwords from the Arabic, Persian, and Indian languages (Lodhi). This influence can also be identified in elements of the normative, expressive, and material cultures. Swahili literature is partly related to the oral literature of the Bantu-speaking peoples (e.g., in the animal and ogre stories). Swahili literature also contains elements of Arabic origin, such as those visible in sophisticated forms of poetry or in the terminology of the prose genres (Rollins). During the nineteenth century, European influence in the field of literature gained significance particularly through language studies and Western book culture. Earlier studies on the intercultural composition of Swahili narratives that also take the Swahili *Nights* into consideration include those by Inge Hofmann, who discusses single texts in view of their Arabic and Indian origins, and Marina Tolmacheva, who is more general in her argumentation.

The tales of the *Thousand and One Nights* and other Oriental stories quite certainly reached the Swahili-speaking world by sea. When, how, and where this happened remains unknown, as precolonial Swahili writers did not pay attention to folktales. Likewise we lack general historical information about storytelling. The autobiography of Princess Salme (1844–1924), who was born and raised in Zanzibar as the daughter of Sultan Sayyid Said and a Circassian mother, is a rare document of the nineteenth century. Princess Salme's book was published under her German married name, Emilie Ruete, in Berlin in 1886. Ruete offers vivid accounts of the multicultural life in the palace in Zanzibar, where the Sultan insisted that everybody talk Arabic, while, as soon as he turned his back, a "Babylonian mess" broke out with people speaking Persian, Turkish, Circassian, Swahili, Nubian, and "Abyssinian" (Ruete 35). Ruete mentions storytelling only in connection with "the black nurses," who are said to have narrated "fables" and "hair-raising stories and tales" to their charges, tales whose frequently occurring lions and sorcerers would even startle adults (30, 66–67). Ruete does not mention whether stories of the *Nights* were also told, but her awareness of this corpus is indicated by her enthusiastic depiction of the colorful celebrations and amazing environment of the healing spring of Chemchem, which would "fully accord to the descriptions in the '1001 Nights'" (180). Whether Ruete acquired the notion of these stories in Zanzibar or in Germany is not clear. If the sultan's palace with its members, servants, slaves, and concubines was a model for the communities in the smaller homes of the wealthy social class, we could assume that such a multicultural setting provided an adequate milieu for the diffusion and reception of stories from various origins.

Literacy was a constituent feature of the Swahili learned class of the nineteenth century (Pouwels 84–85). In 1909 this fact was documented in a peculiar way when the German administration at that time confiscated the private libraries of six Swahili political opponents, whose holdings the German scholar Carl Becker undertook to register. Besides books on religion, law, grammar, and astrology, Becker encountered booklets with stories and tales, among them single tales from the *Nights* such as the stories of Tawaddud, Ajîb and Gharîb, and Hasan of Basra (Becker 51). Although Becker neither specified which editions he saw, nor where they came from, an import of Arabic books from Cairo is generally indicated. At any rate, this incidence proves that the *Nights* could have reached the East African coast not only by oral communication but also by way of (Arabic) books. While Becker's record is representative for the two decades of German colonial rule in East Africa, it is also possible that such Arabic booklets had already reached East Africa shortly after they were printed, that is, before the era of European colonialism. The *terminus post quem* for stories from the *Nights* would be the date of their first complete printed Arabic editions (Bulaq I, 1835; Calcutta II, 1838–42). The presence of manuscripts of the *Nights*—current in the Arabic-speaking world since the fifteenth century (Grotzfeld 25)—cannot be excluded in East Africa, but it will be difficult to prove.

Traces of the *Nights* in "Classic" Collections of Swahili Folktales

A study of the precolonial distribution of the *Nights* in East Africa must start from the early colonial sources. Edward Steere (1829–82) presented the first collection of East African tales as *Swahili Tales* (1870). Steere, who worked as a missionary for the Universities' Mission to Central Africa in Zanzibar from 1864 to 1882, was a pioneer in the study of Swahili, the language he used for his work of evangelization (Miehe). His collection presents eighteen folktales collected from six named Zanzibari male narrators. For three of these tales, Steere himself noted connections to the *Nights*. The first is "The History of Mohammed the Languid" (Steere, *Swahili Tales* 149–89), which Steere had found in Edward Lane's translation as "Aboo-Mohammad the Lazy" (Lane 2: 362–80). The tale was first dictated to Steere by Mohammed bin Abdallah, and then by "another Mohammed, who unfortunately died when he had got as far as p. 180"; it was then continued by the first storyteller. Both narrators related the tale "in the court dialect, which is more Arabic in its forms and vocabulary than the rest [of the edited tales], and is characteristically represented by a strict translation of an Arab story" (Steere, *Swahili Tales* ix). Although the Swahili text has only been published in an abridged form, the correspondence of wording to the Arabic original is striking, even more so when one considers two different storytellers at work (see also Hofmann 3). This fact might indicate a general esteem of verbatim memorization; furthermore, the oral telling of stories from the *Nights* appears to have been (at least sometimes) closely connected to a certain degree of literacy in the Arabic language.

The second tale from the *Nights* published by Steere is "Hasseebu Kareem ed Deen and the King of the Snakes" (Steere, *Swahili Tales* 329–59). Steere marks it as "not included in Lane's translation," but Hofmann (3) has shown the tale to be contained in Enno Littmann's translation (3: 762–71; 4: 7–97), where it is rendered according to the Calcutta II edition. In comparison to the version of the *Nights*, the Swahili version is heavily abridged, and the names of the protagonists appear to be adapted to Swahili pronunciation (e.g., Tighmûs > Taighamusi). As an example of the difference between the two versions, the Swahili tale mentions a king of snakes, whereas the Arabic has a queen (Hofmann 3). Steere remarks that "we have an Arabic manuscript in the Mission library at Zanzibar, containing the story of 'Hasseebu,' but differing in many of the names and circumstances from the form given in the Arabian Nights"

(Steere, *Swahili Tales* vi). Whatever version of the text this manuscript might have contained, its existence once more indicates the interaction between oral and written tradition.

The third tale mentioned by Steere as being related to the *Nights* is "The Cheat and the Porter" (409–13), which Steere (vi) again does not see included in Lane's translation. The anecdote-like story tells of a trader who promises to pay his porter with three wise counsels. These counsels turn out to be most trivial ("Don't believe someone saying that slavery/ poverty/hunger is better than freedom/riches/satisfaction"). Upon hearing the last one, the porter drops the chest he has been carrying, saying that he has a wise counsel to offer, too: "Don't believe anyone saying that there is one glass left unbroken in the box." While this story is frequently documented in classical Arabic literature (Marzolph, *Arabia ridens* 2: no. 949; Marzolph, "Lehren" 887), it is not contained in any edition or translation of the *Nights* (see Köhler 519; Hofmann 3).

Several early collections of tales were aimed at school instruction. Three years prior to his *Swahili Tales*, Steere had published the booklet *Hadithi za Kiingereza* (1867), presenting four "English Stories" in the Swahili language (see Spaandonck 47, nos. 700, 704). The source of these tales is Charles Lamb's *Tales from Shakespeare* (1807), which contains prose summaries of plays by Shakespeare. In the Swahili reader, the tales rendered are *The Taming of the Shrew, The Merchant of Venice, The Tragedy of King Lear*, and *The Life of Timon of Athens*. Some twenty years later, the three anthologies *Mambo na Hadithi* (Affairs and Stories; 1884), *Mashujaa: Hadithi za Wayonani* (Heroes: Stories of the Greeks; 1889; after Charles Kingsley), and *Hadithi za Esopo* (Stories from Aesop; 1890) introduced Swahili translations of classical Greek and Roman narratives (see Spaandonck 47, nos. 701-3). Interestingly, the very same authors who presented European tales in Swahili also organized the transfer of Arabic tales and parts of the *Nights* into Swahili literature. A point in case is the anonymous collection *Swahili Stories from Arab Sources*, published by the Universities' Mission Press in Zanzibar in 1886. This collection presents sixteen Arabic tales in both Swahili and English without quoting their original source. "The War of the Camel" tells of a sultan who drives off a camel that had disturbed the birds in his garden. A fervent young warrior kills the sultan, and many people die in subsequent fights and battles. This continues until one day another sultan, whose son had been killed, finds the warrior and forgives him for the love of God Almighty. Other stories are "An Anecdote of a Prophet," "The Times of the Prophet David," and "Alms Are True

Wealth"; the story "The Cat That Was a Devotee" is a variant of the international tale-type of Aarne and Thompson (henceforth AT), AT 113 B: *The Cat as Sham Holy Man*. All of the tales in this collection share some moral message that the missionaries obviously found adoptable to their Christian teachings.

Swahili tales were also published in the context of the German colonial endeavor, and the first item is the bilingual *Anthologie aus der Suaheli-Litteratur* (Anthology of Swahili-Literature, 1894), compiled by Carl Gotthilf Büttner (1848–93), a missionary and first German professor for Swahili (Dammann, "Büttner"). This book's section "Hekaya na visa" (Tales and Stories) presents eighteen folktales that were written down or dictated by the Swahili lecturers Sleman bin Said and Amur bin Nasur in Berlin (Büttner 1: 77–130; 2: 77–137). Sleman and Amur probably adopted their stories from other published works rather than relying on oral tradition. Büttner himself remarked that "we can find stories of Arabic, Indic, African origins. Some of them are old acquaintances, which perhaps were told already in Noah's ark." He did not, however, feel well equipped to search for their origins (1: xi). Büttner's anthology does not show any direct relations to the *Nights*, but rather to Arabic oral tradition in general. *Hekaya nya nabii Musa na kipofu* (Story of the Prophet Moses and the Blind; 1: 79–80; 2: 75–79) tells how "Moses prays to Allah that He may cure a man of his blindness, but his alteration of the man's destiny ends in disaster" (Bertoncini 13). The "Story of Miss Matlai Shems" is apparently an extract from a longer novel (Büttner 1: 106–15; 2: 113–25) that so far has not been identified. Other stories serve etiological functions: the origins of treasures in the earth, of bananas, and of high and low tide.

The two Berlin Swahili lecturers obviously had an inclination toward tales of clever and cunning characters. Among them we find the earliest documentation of Swahili stories of Abû Nuwâs (Büttner 1: 87–95; 2: 86–94). This character derives from the personality of the historical Abû Nuwâs (757–814), a famous poet in Baghdad during the time of the caliph Hârûn al-Rashîd (786–808). Abû Nuwâs also makes his appearance in the *Nights* (Littmann 3: 298–304, 425–31; see Schade, "Zur Herkunft" and "Weiteres"). He is usually portrayed as a libertine character with a particular inclination toward wine and young men (Wagner 45–46). In Swahili oral tradition, Abû Nuwâs has changed into an arbitrator who judges in favor of the poor against the rich and powerful, as a punisher of criminals, and sometimes as a trickster acting for his own sake. His power is based on intelligence and verbal wit and sometimes shows spiritual and mystic tendencies (Knappert 6), with the strategy of "proving the absurd" prevailing (Ranke). Büttner's Abû Nuwâs stories reappeared in the canonical edition of *Hekaya za Abunuwas na Hadithi Nyingine* (1-22; preceded 1915 by a Swahili edition attributed to Samwil Chiponde and G. B. Broomfield that was translated into English by William Harold Ingrams 48–85). Other collections published new anecdotes of *Abunuwasi* (e.g., in Velten, *Märchen und Erzählungen*). Abû Nuwâs became a prominent character in Swahili oral tradition, and tales about him still are told today (Russell 204–8).

The third "classical" edition of Swahili folktales was published by Carl Velten (1862–after 1935). Velten, a student of Büttner's, served as colonial translator in Dar es Salaam (1893–96) and later held the chair of Swahili studies in Berlin (Dammann, "Velten"). Both his Swahili text edition and the separate German translation bear the title *Märchen und Erzählungen der Suaheli* (Fairy-Tales and Narratives of the Suaheli). The sixty-five tales in this collection were recorded from the oral performance of fourteen male narrators whose individual characteristics are briefly described (text edition xii-xiii; not in the German translation). While many of the stories are animal tales, others deal with relationships between men and women. In Hofmann's opinion (17–18), the dilemma tale *Mchumba na ndugu watatu* (The Lover of the Three Brothers; Velten, *Märchen und Erzählungen* [text] 44–45; [translation] 71–73) is partly related to the story of "Prince Ahmed and the Fairy Perî Banû" in the *Nights* (Littmann 3: 7–85, at 29–31), particularly in the motif when three young men are asked for their most decisive contribution to reviving the dead lover (AT 653 A). Connecting this motif to the *Nights* is not, however, mandatory, as recent Africanist research has shown this type of dilemma story to be widely attested in Africa (Reuster-Jahn). The story *Nguvu za uganga* (The Power of Witchcraft; Velten, *Märchen und Erzählungen* [text] 92–94; [translation] 148–52) forms the second episode in the "Story of the Third Royal Mendicant" in the *Nights* (see Lane 1: 160–61; Littmann 1: 162–85). While in the Arabic version the murderer is not recognized and continues onto his next adventure, the Swahili tale closes with the father of the killed youth pardoning the culprit (Hofmann 3f). Velten (*Märchen und Erzählungen* [text] xii–xiii) states that the stories were recorded by oral dictation from narrators, who are said to have possessed a *mittlerer Bildungsgrad*, or "medium degree of education," implying that they were to some extent literate.

The fourth "classical" edition of Swahili tales, also published by Velten, is *Prosa und Poesie der Swahili* (Prose and Poetry of the Swahili).

Besides historical and poetic texts, it documents a total of forty-two tales in the Swahili language. Again we find animal tales but also ogre tales. The collection's only story that Hofmann (16–17) relates as "thoroughly congruent" with a tale in the *Nights* (see Littmann 1: 27–32) is the "Story of a Man Who Learned the Animal Language" (Velten, *Prosa und Poesie* 35–39). Again, this relation appears questionable when we look at the wide and independent distribution of the tale in Africa as exemplified for Madagascar (Haring 30) and thirty-nine ethnic groups in the Congo area (Maalu-Bungi).

When Tanganyika became part of the British Empire in 1919, the school system was modernized, and the Swahili language was then standardized in 1925–30 (Whiteley 59–61, 79–96). In the following years, there was a need of Swahili material for reading matter and also as a medium to propagate the modern way of life in a world ruled by Britain. An important medium was the monthly journal *Mambo Leo* (Today's Affairs), founded by the Education Department in Dar es Salaam in 1923. The journal published essays and news of all kinds and also contained entertaining texts, among them translations of foreign literature. These entertaining texts were usually issued in serialized form. Issues from the initial period of 1923–32 include adaptations of literary tales such as "The Voyages of Sindbad the Sailor" (1923–24), "Aladdin and the Wonderful Lamp" (1925–26), "Ali Baba and the Forty Thieves" (1926), Longfellow's *Tale of Hiawatha* (1927), and Daniel Defoe's *Robinson Crusoe* (1928). All of these stories were published without any introduction, source reference, or further comment. The three well-known tales, belonging to the most popular tales of the *Nights* in the post-Galland translations, thus appeared in a kind of paradigmatic linkage to Western narratives. This conjunction becomes further evident from the fact that from 1928 onward, Swahili translations of foreign literature were published as separate books. In the following listing I intend to convey an impression of how the stories of the *Nights* became part of a corpus of "new Swahili literature." We read Stevenson's *Kisiwa chenye hazima* (Treasure Island, 1929), Haggard's *Mashimo ya Mfalme Sulemani* (King Solomon's Mines, 1929), Kipling's *Hadithi za Maugli, Mtoto Aliyelelewa na Mbwa Mwitu* (The Story of Mowgli, the Child Who Was Raised by a Wild Dog [The Jungle Books], 1929), Swift's *Safari za Gulliver* (Gulliver's Travels, 1932), Harris's *Hadithi za Mjomba Remus* (Tales of Uncle Remus, 1935), and again the abovementioned tales by Defoe and Longfellow. These items were translated by Frederick Johnson, who was occasionally supported by Edwin W. Brenn (see Spaandonck 48, nos. 707, 712, 713, 716, 718). For the contemporary author Canon Hellier (255), the years 1925 to 1930 were "the beginning of the 'modern period'" of Swahili literature, a period later marked by Rajmund Ohly (74) as the "transition from the Oriental to the Western cultural hemisphere." Even though these "classics" of world literature were praised for their "very good" Swahili translations (Harries 28–29), they were also criticized for containing abridged versions addressing juvenile readers, a form that would impede an adequate appreciation of their literary qualities. The Zanzibarian writer and literary historian Abdulrazak Gurnah (born 1948), who integrates oral storytelling into his postcolonial novels of exile and migration, would later mention that stories, such as those of Gulliver, *Romeo and Juliet*, and the *Arabian Nights*, at first became part of his introduction to literature through the oral narration of illiterate elderly women who had heard these stories from others, among them at least one literate person (Gurnah 229–30).

Looking for a reason for the strong presence of foreign literary texts in Swahili, Wilfred Whiteley (245) has pointed out "a conspicuous lack of original writing" at the time, implying that the Swahili people were not regarded as possessing an appealing prose of their own. Apparently, the many dozens of Swahili and other African folktales that had been published in scholarly documentation up to that time were not regarded as deserving the same kind of popular and educative attention. Scholarship still has to account for this negligence. Did the African oral tales not fit into the system of literacy and education as propagated by Western teachers who were often attached to Christian missions? Was this due to their supernatural symbolism and their messages focusing on ancestor worship, which sometimes dominated the tales? Were the African tale texts thought to carry unrecognized subtexts of criticism and subversion that were deemed offensive by the colonial establishment? Notably, even Arabic stories might have carried a potential of subversion and Oriental-Islamic solidarity. Yet the stories of the *Arabian Nights* were so well known among the Europeans that this potential was not significantly considered.

Translations of the *Thousand and One Nights* in Swahili

In the context of school literacy, language standardization, and the building of the Empire in the period from the 1920s to the 1930s, the tales of the *Nights* enjoyed a second career in the Swahili-speaking world, now based on modern mass production of books in Roman letters, aimed at reaching both Swahili native speakers and Swahili second language speakers. The 1929 edition *Mazungumzo ya Alfu-Lela-Ulela, au Siku Elfu na Moja* (Entertainments of the Thousand and One Nights) presented the translation by Edwin W. Brenn as edited by Frederick Johnson and was published in two volumes. The well-known Swahili lexicographer and translator Johnson (d. 1937; Whiteley 16, 84) served as the first secretary of the Inter-Territorial Language Committee. Brenn, who worked as a senior clerk in the Education Department (Iliffe 266), was not an Englishman, as his name might suggest, but an East African. This becomes evident from two clues: first, the qualification "Educated C.M.S. Rabai, Mombasa" (which does not appear in the reprints) is added to his name, meaning that Brenn had been a student at the school of the Church Missionary Society at Rabai near Mombasa. This school exclusively educated Africans, among them many former slaves who sometimes took a new name after their liberation. The second clue is given by Diedrich Westermann (429), who terms Brenn a "native" (*Eingeborener*). Hence, the first Swahili translation of the *Nights* was not produced by coastal Swahili native speakers but by "Europeans," as Swahili speakers would say, because a man such as Brenn was locally classified as European (*mzungu*) by virtue of his Christian name, the modern education he had received, and his career within the British colonial administration.

The 1929 edition contains a selection of thirty-four stories. The preface, dated January 1, 1928, is signed by Brenn. In addition to some general remarks, the preface informs the readers that the stories originate from Indians, Arabs, and Persians, and were originally told during the reign of Abbasid ruler Hârûn al-Rashîd. Even though the source text of the translation is not mentioned, we might assume an English source rather than any of the available Arabic editions. The edition includes these stories:

> vol. 1 (1929) = vol. 1 (reprints): no. 1. *Mwanzo* (Beginning = The beginning of the frame story of Sultan Shahriyâr and the narrator Shahrazâd).—2. *Mfanyaji Biashara na Jini* (The Merchant and the Jinn).—3. *Mzee wa Kwanza na Mbuzi* (The First Elder [Sheykh] and the Goat [Gazelle]).—4. *Mzee wa Pili na Mbwa wawili Weusi* (The Second Elder and the Two Black Dogs).—5. *Mvuvi* (The Fisherman).—6. *Mfalme wa Kiyonani na Douban, Mganga* (The King of Yûnân and the Healer Dûbân).—7. *Mtu na Kasuku* (The Husband and the Parrot).—8. *Waziri Aliyeadhibiwa* (The Punished Vizier = The Envious Wezeer and the Prince and the Ghooleh [Lane]).—9.

Mfalme kijana wa Visiwa Vyeusi (The Young King of the Black Islands).—10. *Mawalii watatu waana wa Wafalme, na Wanawake watano wa Bagdadi* (The Three Saints [Mendicants] and the Five Women of Baghdad).—11. *Walii wa Kwanza, Mwana wa Mfalme* (The First Royal Mendicant).—12. *Walii wa Pili, Mwana wa Mfalme* (The Second Royal Mendicant).—13. *Mtu mwenye Kijicho na yule aliyeomwonea Kijicho* (The Envier and the Envied).—14. *Walii wa Tatu, Mwana wa Mfalme* (The Third Royal Mendicant).—vol. 2 (reprint), 15–22. *Safari ya saba za Sindbad, Baharia* (The Seven Voyages of Sindbad the Sailor).—23. *Mbilikimo mwenye Kinundu* (The Pygmy with the Hunchback).—24–25. *Nduguye Kinyozi wa Tano/wa Sita* (The Barber's Story of his Fifth/Sixth Brother).

vol. 2 (1929) = vol. 3 (reprint): 26. *Mambo yaliyompata Kamaralzaman na Badoura Binti Mfalme* (The Adventures of Kamaralzaman and Princess Badoura).—27. *Nurdin na Mwajemi Mzuri* (Nurdin and the Good Persian).—28. *Aladdin na Taa ya Ajabu* (Aladdin and the Wonderful Lamp).—29. *Mambo yaliyompata Harun Rashidi, Khalifa wa Bagdadi* (The Adventures of Harun Rashidi, caliph of Baghdad).—vol. 4 (reprint): 30. *Baba-Abdalla Kipofu* (Abdalla the Blind).—31. *Sidi-Nouman.*—32. *Ali Kogia, Mfanyaji Biashara wa Bagdadi* (Ali Kogia, the Merchant of Baghdad).—33. *Farasi wa Uchawi* (The Magic Horse).—34. *Ndugu wawili wanawake waliomwonoea kijicho Dada yao Mdogo* (The Two Sisters Who Envied Their Younger Sister).

The Swahili edition ends without the concluding part of the frame story. The arrangement of the text more or less follows the sequence as given by Lane (nos. 1–27, 33); the remaining stories appear in Richard Burton's translation. Compared to the verbosity of many of the stories in the English translations, the stories in the Swahili translation appear heavily abbreviated. Probably neither Lane nor Burton provided the source text, but rather any one of the numerous available popular editions of the time. The abridgements bear particular characteristics: passages of direct speech are much shorter and hardly formulaic; epic backgrounds and descriptions with highly specified adjectives are lacking; on the whole, the language and action of the stories is much more straightforward. While the personal and geographical names appear in a reduced form that has at times been adjusted for Swahili pronunciation, there are no striking features of adaptation to the African environment. Each story basically aims at telling a tale of adventure, morality, and cleverness, and philosophical or erotic components are absent. Thus the adultery of Sultan Shahriyâr's wife in the opening of the frame story is reduced to a mere mention:

Hata siku moja . . . kwa bahati akatambua kuwa mkewe alikuwa akimdan-ganya, na matendo yake yote yaligeuka kuwa maovu hata Sultani akapen-dezewa kutwaa sheria, na kumwamuru waziri wake mkuu amwue (Brenn and Johnson 1: 1–2).

until one day . . . he discovered by chance that his wife had beguiled him and that her acting turned out to be so wicked that the Sultan preferred to call upon the law and ordered his first vizier to kill her.

The two-volume edition of 1929 was reprinted several times (1947, 1951, 1960, etc.) in four small volumes. Sixty-five drawings signed by H. I. Ford illustrate the books. By employing features of nineteenth-century European realism, Orientalism, and fantasy (in particular for the spir-its), the artist projected the scenery, action, and protagonists with their Oriental appearance and dress into an undefined historical period, per-haps the Middle Ages. The numerous reprints prove the book's success, even though secondary data on sales figures or the channels of book trading, let alone local voices expressing appreciation and/or criticism, are lacking. While the text of the new edition (Brenn and Saidi; Brenn and Yahya) is still based on Brenn's translation, it has been revised con-siderably by O. Saidi (vol. 1) and A. S. Yahya (vols. 2–4). At times, their versions appear to be even more abbreviated. In some words, the orthog-raphy has been modernized. Four of the former thirty-four stories have been skipped (nos. 6, 7, 8, and 29). In the new edition, the simplified il-lustrations prepared by K. K. Abdalla depict Oriental and African char-acters. Spirits and uncanny scenes are no more to be seen. These charac-teristics clearly document children to be the new edition's intended audience.

Hassan Adam from Tanga, Tanzania, is currently undertaking a new translation project. As Swahili lecturer at the University of Cologne, Adam initiated the cultural and literary journal *Jua* (Sun), which has been issued as a bimonthly desktop publication since 1996. It particularly attracts sub-scribers in East Africa and among Swahili people residing in "the cold lands" of Europe and America. From the first issue on, Adam serialized the stories of the *Nights* under the title *Hadithi za Alfu Lela U Lela* (Stories from the Thousand and One Nights). In letters to the editor, readers ex-press their great appreciation and enjoyment to "have the lost stories back." This reaction prompted Adam to publish his translation in book form in East Africa. Two volumes are currently in print with the publishing house

Mkuki na Nyota in Dar es Salaam and were released with the title of *Alfu Lela Ulela* in 2004; further volumes are in preparation. Adam (1998) considers the *Nights* to be quite popular among the Swahili people, as they are always curious about spirits (*majini*) and the supernatural, creatures that abound in the stories and can somehow be referred to in actual life. Swahili people also enjoy the stories from the *Nights* because, as a people oriented toward the sea, they like to read about sea travel adventures: Sindbad is their hero. Many people understand *Sindibada* etymologically as deriving from *Siendi baada*, "I don't go after (anybody else)," meaning "I am always there before everybody else" (Adam; see also Knappert 9).

Contemporary readers relish Adam's withdrawal from the previous youth-oriented style of writing and his use of older illustrations. Adam recycles Ford's illustrations from the Brenn and Johnson translation and freely combines them with other nineteenth-century illustrations by Henri Baron, Horace Castelli, Gustave Doré, and others, taken from a recent reissue of German translations of French popular printings from 1860 to 1865 (Pinson). Adam's preference for peculiar "Oriental" images and a new "coastal" language in contrast to the somewhat mechanistic standard Swahili is obviously connected to a process of restoring the identity of coastal Swahili that had become blurred during the era of Tanzanian *Ujamaa* politics (in effect until 1985). These politics had thoroughly attempted to submit the nation to Swahili dominance and, in consequence, to level the cultural peculiarities of the country's ethnic diversity.

A second reason to reconsider Swahili cultural identity through the help of stories concerns the estranging effects by Western media productions (see *Jua* 2.3 [1998] 3). In addition, readers appreciate the fact that Adam also translates tales of the *Nights* hitherto unknown to them. Adam's source texts are the editions by Burton and Gustav Weil (1865). Swahili readers now read stories such as the *Kisa cha Mzee wa Tatu na Nyumbu* (The Story of the Third Sheikh with the Mule), *Kisa cha Shamsuddin Ali wa Qahira na Badruddin Hassan wa Basrah* (The Story of Shamsuddin Ali of Cairo and Badruddin Hassan of Basra), *Kisa cha Matufaha Matatu* (The Story of the Three Apples), the four stories of the Barber's four brothers, the *Kisa cha Mkristo* (The Story of the Christian Broker), the *Kisa cha Mganga wa Kiyahudi* (The Story of the Jewish Doctor), and others. Adam is not too scrupulous in translating certain details that might or might not be regarded as offensive, such as Sindbad's hearing of God's voice in heaven, or erotic elements. In his translation, the sultan, "when he entered the house, good heavens!, he found his wife embraced in love with one of his slaves" (*Alipoingia ndani, la haula! Akamkuta mkewe amekumbatiwa kimapenzi na mtumwa wake mmoja!*) (*Jua* 1 [1996] 16). In the previous editions, this passage had been paraphrased as if by a prude. Regardless, full renderings of the more erotic tales of the *Nights* are still regarded as unsuitable for inclusion in the Swahili publication (Adam).

Conclusion

While the *Thousand and One Nights* definitely are part of the Swahili-speaking world, it remains unknown when they were introduced to the region. Although oral tradition may be assumed for the period of contact between the Arab world and East Africa since about 900 CE, the nineteenth century deserves particular attention. Evidently, literacy in Arabic played a major role in the transfer of some of the tales to East Africa. Swahili private libraries around 1909 have been shown to contain Arabic printed books rather than manuscripts (Becker). Arabic editions of the *Nights* were widely available at least since 1835, hence it was presumably the period 1835-50 in which both the *Thousand and One Nights* and Abû Nuwâs stories experienced an increased popularity in East Africa. In this period, the shift of the Omani rule to Zanzibar brought a steep increase in Arab immigrants, thus resulting in new impacts upon the Swahili lexicon and literature. While the stories then recorded in Swahili were orally narrated in an abbreviated form, they remain visibly close to the Arabic original with only minor adaptations to the African environment. Whether the Swahili narrators were aware of a distinct corpus called *Alf layla wa-layla*, which is not mentioned by Steere (*Swahili Tales*), Büttner, or Velten, but ambiguously alluded to in Ruete, is an open question. Likewise, it remains unknown whether the increased popularity of the *Nights* was peculiar to Zanzibar or whether it also spread to other parts of the Swahili coast.

The European literary influence in the twentieth century led to a second career for the *Nights* among Swahili-speaking recipients. The title of the new edition of 1929, *Alfu Lela Ulela*, has created a general consciousness of the tales as parts of a specific body of narratives originating from the Arab world. Still today, this edition remains canonical in Swahili literature through its numerous reprints and its use in primary and secondary instruction. Just as inherent European curiosity allowed the *Nights* to receive a fertile reception in Europe since 1704, the more recent European interference in East Africa has also firmly established the *Nights* in this part of the world. Their further appreciation in East Africa is an ongoing process, documented above all by creative writing, such as Abdulrazak Gurnah's novel *By the Sea* (2001), and the new translation prepared by Hassan Adam. Future research, in addition to numerous topics suggesting themselves for fieldwork in East Africa, will also have to take into account translations of stories from the *Nights* into Western African languages such as Hausa (Nigeria; *Dare dubu da d'aya*, 1924), Ewe (Ghana, Togo; *Zâ akpe deka kple deka*; 1946) and Duala (Cameroon; *Ikolo a bulu na bulu bo*, 1983).

NOTE

This essay is dedicated to Mwalimu Hassan Adam on the occasion of his retirement as Swahili teacher at the University of Cologne in summer 2004.

WORKS CITED

Aarne, Antti, and Stith Thompson. *The Types of the Folktale: A Classification and Bibliography.* 2nd rev. ed. Helsinki: Academia Scientiarum Fennica, 1961.

Adam, Hassan, ed. and trans. "Hadithi za Alfu Lela U Lela." *Jua* 1 (1996)–4.6 (2000).

———. "The Popularity of 'Alfu Lela Ulela' (1001 Nights) in Swahili Society." Paper read at the Symposium Einblicke in die Swahiliforschung, Institut für Afrikanistik, University of Cologne, April 16, 1998.

Allen, James de Vere. *Swahili Origins: Swahili Culture and the Shungwaya Phenomenon.* London: J. Curry, and Athens: Ohio UP, 1993.

Becker, Carl H. *Materials for the Understanding of Islam in German East Africa.* 1909. Ed. and trans. B. G. Martin. *Tanzania Notes and Records* 68 (1968): 31–61.

Brenn, Edwin W., trans, and Frederick Johnson, ed. *Mazungumzo ya alfu-lela-ulela, au siku elfu na moja (The Arabian Nights Entertainments in Swahili).* 2 vols. London: Longmans, 1929.

———, trans., and O. Saidi, rev. *Alfu lela ulela au siku elfu na moja.* New ed. Vol. 1. Nairobi, Dar es Salaam, and Kampala: Longmans, 1973.

———, trans., and A. S. Yahya, rev. *Mazungumzo ya alfu lela ulela au siku elfu na moja.* New ed. Vols. 2–4. Nairobi, Dar es Salaam, and Kampala: Longmans, 1974.

Burton, Richard. *A Plain and Literal Translation of the Arabian Nights Entertainments: Now Entitled the Book of the Thousand Nights and a Night.* 10 vols. Benares [i.e., London]: Kamashastra Soc., 1885–88.

Büttner, Carl G. *Anthologie aus der Suaheli-Litteratur. Gedichte und Geschichten der Suaheli.* Vol. 1: Texte. Vol. 2: Übersetzungen. Berlin: Felber, 1894.

Dammann, Ernst. "Büttner." *Lexikon der Afrikanistik.* Ed. Herrmann Jungraithmayr and Wilhelm J. G. Möhlig. Berlin: Reimer, 1983. 57–58.

———. "Velten." *Lexikon der Afrikanistik.* Ed. Herrmann Jungraithmayr and Wilhelm J. G. Möhlig. Berlin: Reimer, 1983. 257.

Enzyklopädie des Märchens (henceforth EM). Vols. 1ff. Berlin: Walter de Gruyter, 1975ff.

Grotzfeld, Heinz, and Sophia Grotzfeld. *Die Erzählungen aus "Tausendundeiner Nacht."* Darmstadt: Wissenschaftliche Buchgesellschaft, 1984.

Gurnah, Abdulrazak. "Literatur: Eine durchwachsene Geschichte." *Früchte der Zeit: Afrika, Diaspora, Literatur und Migration.* Ed. Helmuth A. Niederle, Ulrike Davis-Sulikowski, and Thomas Fillitz. Vienna: WUV-Universitäts-Verlag, 2001. 227–38.

Harries, Lyndon. "Translating Classical Literature into Swahili." *Swahili* 40.1 (1970): 28–31.

Hekaya za Abunuwas na Hadithi Nyingine: Swahili Stories Told and Written Down by Africans. London: Macmillan, 1935.

Hellier, Canon A. B. "Swahili Prose Literature." *Bantu Studies* 14 (1940): 247–57.

Henninger, Josef. "Der geographische Horizont der Erzähler von 1001 Nacht." *Geographica Helvetica* 4 (1949): 214–29.

Hofmann, Inge. "Zur Herkunft einiger Swahili-Erzählungen." *Afrika und Übersee* 53.1 (1969): 1–37.

Horton, Mark. "The Swahili Corridor." *Scientific American* 257.3 (1987): 76–84.

Iliffe, John. *A Modern History of Tanganyika.* Cambridge: Cambridge UP, 1979.

Ingrams, William Harold. *Abu Nuwas in Life and Legend.* Port-Louis: Privately printed, 1933.

Irwin, Robert. *The Arabian Nights: A Companion.* London: Allen Lane, 1994.

Knappert, Jan. *Myths and Legends of the Swahili.* Nairobi: Heinemann, 1970.

Köhler, Reinhold. "Steere, Swahili Tales." *Kleinere Schriften zur Märchenforschung.* Vol. 1. Ed. Johannes Bolte. Weimar: Felber, 1898. 514–20.

Lane, Edward W. *The Thousand and One Nights, Commonly Called, in England, The Arabian Nights' Entertainments.* 3 vols. New ed. Ed. Edward Stanley Poole. 1838–41. London: Routledge Warne, 1865.

Leeuwen, Richard van. "Traduire Shéhérazade/Translating Shahrazad." *Transeuropéennes* 22 (2002): 89–99.

Littmann, Enno. "Alf layla wa-layla." *The Encyclopaedia of Islam.* 2nd ed. Vol. 1. Leiden: Brill, 1960. 358–64.

———. *Die Erzählungen aus den Tausendundein Nächten.* 6 vols. Wiesbaden: Insel, 1976.

Lodhi, Abdulaziz Y. *Oriental Influences in Swahili: A Study in Language and Culture Contacts.* Göteborg: Acta Universitatis Gothoburgensis, 2000.

Maalu-Bungi, Lungenyi L. "Observation sur le thème du langage des animaux dans les contes zairois." *Annales Aequatoria* 1.2 (1980): 635–61.

Mambo Leo, 1–16 (Journal), 1923–38.

Marzolph, Ulrich. *Arabia ridens: Die humoristische Kurzprosa der frühen adab-Literatur im internationalen Traditionsgeflecht.* 2 vols. Frankfurt: Klostermann 1992.

———. "Lehren: Die drei L. des Vogels." EM 8 (1996): 883–89.

————. "Re-Locating the Arabian Nights." *Orientalia Lovanensia Analecta* 87 (1998): 155–63.

Mazrui, Alamin M., and Ibrahim Noor Shariff. *The Swahili: Idiom and Identity of an African People.* Trenton: Africa World P, 1994.

Miehe, Gudrun. "Steere." *Lexikon der Afrikanistik.* Ed. Herrmann Jungraithmayr and Wilhelm J. G. Möhlig. Berlin: Reimer, 1983. 228–29.

Nurse, Derek, and Thomas Spear. *The Swahili: Reconstructing the History and Language of an African Society, 800–1500.* Philadelphia: U of Pennsylvania P, 1985.

Ohly, Rajmund. *Swahili, the Diagram of Crises.* Vienna: Afro-Pub, 1982.

Pinson, R. W., ed. *Märchen aus 1001 Nacht: Die berühmten Geschichten aus dem Morgenland.* Bindlach: Gondrom, 2001.

Pouwels, Randall L. *Horn and Crescent: Cultural Change and Traditional Islam on the East African Coast, 800–1900.* Cambridge: Cambridge UP, 1987.

Ranke, Kurt. "Ad absurdum führen." EM 1 (1977): 79–85.

Reuster-Jahn, Uta. "Mantel, Spiegel und Fläschchen (AT 653 A)—eine afrikanische Dilemmageschichte." *Märchenspiegel* 14.4 (2003): 18–20.

Rollins, Jack D. *A History of Swahili Prose.* Vol. 1: *From Earliest Times to the End of the Nineteenth Century.* Leiden: Brill, 1983.

Ruete, Emilie. *Leben im Sultanspalast: Memoiren aus dem 19. Jahrhundert.* Ed. Annegret Nippa. Frankfurt: Athenaeum, 1989.

Russell, Joan. *Communicative Competence in a Minority Group: A Sociolinguistic Study of the Swahili-Speaking Community in the Old Town, Mombasa.* Leiden: Brill, 1981.

Schaade, Arthur. "Weiteres zu Abû Nuwâs in 1001 Nacht." *Zeitschrift der Deutschen Morgenländischen Gesellschaft* 90 (1936): 602–15.

————. "Zur Herkunft und Urform einiger Abû Nuwâs-Geschichten in Tausendundeiner Nacht." *Zeitschrift der Deutschen Morgenländischen Gesellschaft* 88 (1934): 259–76.

Spaandonck, Marcel van. *Practical and Systematical Swahili Bibliography: Linguistics, 1850–1963.* Leiden: Brill, 1965.

Steere, Edward. *Hadithi za Kiingereza.* Zanzibar: Universities' Mission P, 1867.

————. *Swahili Tales, as Told by Natives of Zanzibar.* London: Bell and Daldy, 1870.

Swahili Stories from Arab Sources, with an English Translation. Zanzibar: Universities' Mission P, 1886.

Tolmacheva, Marina. "The Arabic Influence on Swahili Literature: A Historian's View." *Journal of African Studies* 5 (1978): 223–43.

Triaud, J. L., and A. S. Kaye. "Sûdân, Bilâd al-." *The Encyclopaedia of Islam.* 2nd ed. Vol. 9. Leiden: Brill, 1997. 752–61.

Velten, Carl. *Märchen und Erzählungen der Suaheli* (Lehrbücher des Seminars für Orientalische Sprachen 18). Stuttgart and Berlin: Spemann, 1898 (Swahili texts).

————. *Märchen und Erzählungen der Suaheli.* Stuttgart and Berlin: Spemann, 1898 (German translation).

————. *Prosa und Poesie der Suaheli.* Berlin: Published by the author, 1907.

Wagner, Ewald. "Abû Nuwâs." EM 1 (1977): 43–48.

Walther, Wiebke. *Tausendundeine Nacht: Eine Einführung.* Munich and Zurich: Artemis Verlag, 1987.

Westermann, Diedrich. "Literatur in Eingeborenensprachen." *Völkerkunde in Afrika.* Ed. Hermann Baumann, Richard Thurnwald, and Diedrich Westermann. Essen: Essener Verlags-Anstalt, 1940. 423–33.

Whiteley, Wilfred H. *Swahili: The Rise of a National Language.* London: Methuen, 1969.

———. "The Work of the East African Swahili Committee, 1930–1957." *Kongo-Overzee* 23 (1957): 242–55.

12

The *Thousand and One Nights* in Turkish: Translations, Adaptations, and Issues

Hande A. Birkalan-Gedik

The *Thousand and One Nights,* also known as the *Arabian Nights,* have captured the imagination of numerous audiences all over the globe for generations. Introduced to world literature through Antoine Galland's French translation *Les Mille et une Nuits* at the beginning of the eighteenth century, the *Arabian Nights* have inspired Western literature and creative arts in innumerable ways. Some of the tales might already have been known in the Middle Ages and early modern times by such authors as Chaucer, Boccaccio, Voltaire, and Montesquieu, who may have used them as a source of inspiration for their own works. While the first European translations of the *Arabian Nights* were aimed at an adult audience to be entertained in the parlor, later editions were adapted to match the interests of families who wanted to use the tales as children's stories.

In Turkish culture, familiarity with the *Arabian Nights* was common long before Western audiences came to know these tales. As the territory of the Ottoman Empire included most of the Arab lands, the stories of the *Arabian Nights* were known and told among a great number of people. Long before the Ottoman Empire became influenced by modern issues such as language simplification, westernization, or the modernization attempts in the nineteenth century, the people in Anatolia spoke a much simpler language than Ottoman Turkish, a kind of "vox populi" known as *Türkî* (Turkish) or *Lisan-ı Türkî* (Turkish language).[1] Many of the tales and motifs included in the *Arabian Nights* had become a part of Turkish oral tradition. Turkish storytellers knew the tales of the *Arabian Nights* and shared them with an audience fascinated by the form, medium, and content of the tales. The first Turkish translation of the *Arabian Nights,* usually known as *Binbir Gece* (Thousand and One Nights), was prepared by Abdî in the fifteenth century, and since then, its stories continue to be translated for Turkish readers.[2]

Even though the first translation of the *Arabian Nights* dates back to the fifteenth century, the collection has long maintained a marginal position in the study of both Turkish folklore and literature. In consequence, a disparity exists between the stories and the critical attention devoted to their analysis. An exception is perhaps the work of literary critic Şinasi Tekin, who focused on translation and *gazels,* or love poems in the *Arabian Nights* (Tekin, "Binbir Gece"; Tekin, "Elf leyle"). Despite the long tradition of storytelling and reciprocal efforts of translating in both the Turkish and Arab worlds, it is hard to find any critical study focusing on issues of translation and editing of the *Arabian Nights* beyond scattered references in the forewords of the respective translations. In most Turkish translations, the original source text is not identified, and for some of the earlier translations, either the source text or the name of the translator, and in most cases both, are still being disputed. For other translations, the translator is unknown or not identified. In particular, critical remarks about the efforts to eliminate "obscene" or "sexual" elements in order to purify the text for the popular audience have not been discussed by literary critics or folklorists.

Considering these shortcomings, in the following I propose to discuss some particular aspects of the *Arabian Nights.* First, I will focus on the reciprocal influence between the Arabic language and culture and the impact of Ottoman language and culture as seen through the *Arabian Nights* in order to demonstrate the degree of intercultural exchange between the two cultures. This section will discuss linguistic similarities between the two languages concerned as well as the impact of oral literature. Second, I will move into the realm of manuscripts, printed editions, and processes of translation of the *Arabian Nights.* Here my aim is to link the issue of translation to the cultural politics and historical milieu of the Ottoman Empire and the modern Turkish state.

I argue that translating the *Arabian Nights* into Turkish is more about literary politics than about the literary text itself. Modernity and westernization projects both had an impact on how the various translations were prepared. In addition, the translation of different texts in their turn influenced the visions of modernity and westernization. This relationship has both been produced by and further contributed to a peculiar perception: on the one hand Ottoman-Turkish perception of Arab culture, and on the other Arab perception of Ottoman-Turkish culture. In particular, the attempts of westernization in the Ottoman Empire, and later in Turkey, shaped the image of the Turk as being oriented toward the West, equipped with rational ideas and more advanced. In contrast, the Arabs were portrayed as oriented toward the East and combined with an image of Eastern sentimentality and backwardness. This dual depiction also influenced the Turkish attitude toward the *Arabian Nights* as a "love/hate" relationship. While popular audiences in Turkey showed a great interest in the tales, elements that did not fit into the "new" Turkish culture were considered detrimental by cultural politicians. In consequence, many translators turned to Western translations instead of Arabic texts as sources for their translations of the *Arabian Nights.*

For my current work on the *Arabian Nights,* I have aimed to examine Turkish translations available in Ottoman manuscripts and also in printed editions in Latin characters. During my examination of the *Thousand and One Nights* in Turkish, I was able to see some of the manuscripts with special permission, whereas I was not granted official permission to do research in some other libraries. In some cases, the rejection of my formal application indicated that "the library does not house this particular item," although some scholars have pointed out the location of certain manuscripts in specific libraries (Onaran, *Binbir Gece Masalları* 2001; Tekin; Acaroğlu).

The *Arabian Nights* and Turkish Oral Tradition

The mutual influence between the *Arabian Nights* and Turkish oral tradition can be explained by way of the sociohistorical developments in the Middle East and the continuing exchange among the Turkish, Persian, and Arab cultures. Since the eleventh century, Iran, Mesopotamia, and Syria have been influenced first by the Seljuks, and later on by the Ottomans. The impact of the extended historical presence of Turks in the region has created a stock of cultural and linguistic elements common to these cultures. According to some scholars, the influence of Turkish culture on the *Arabian Nights* is already shown in the collection's title. The tales are known in Turkish as *Binbir Gece Masalları,* or literally "Tales from a Thousand and One Nights." The term *binbir* in its popular alliteration does not imply the exact number of a thousand and one, instead it suggests an innumerable amount of tales. Moreover, some researchers regard the Turkish *binbir* as a powerful symbolic term, as the origin of the numeric denomination the *Arabian Nights* later gained in both Arabic (*Alf layla wa-layla*) and Persian (*Hezâr-o yek shab*) and, hence, in many European translations (Littmann 362; Miquel 8).

Besides the title, there are other influences originating from Turkish culture, such as the name *Ali Baba* suggests. (Even though the tale of Ali Baba is a late addition to the collection, it originates from the "authentic" performance of a Syrian storyteller). Vehbi Belgil boldly, yet not scholarly, even argues that there is more than a name to the Turkish origin of Ali Baba, as in his opinion the actual geographical place where the tale of Ali Baba and the forty thieves took place is located in Eastern Anatolia (Belgil 67–68). The tales of clever thieves and rogues included in the *Arabian Nights* mirror numerous details of social and popular life during the Mamluk period and Turkish rule in Egypt (Littmann 362–63; Grotzfeld; Perho). The cycle of stories related to Abbasid caliph Hârûn al-Rashîd is commonly regarded as an addition from the late medieval Arabo-Islamic period, that is, the period of Mamluk and Ottoman reign (see Gerhardt 419–70). In some ways, the representation of this ruler in the *Arabian Nights* reflects the Arab imagination of how a Turkish sultan in the fifteenth century might have lived.

Numerous Turkish folktales reveal a relation to tales in the *Arabian Nights*. The appearance of Hârûn al-Rashîd as a *Keloğlan* (baldheaded), a character often depicted as lazy, clever, skillful, and witty (Eberhard and Boratav no. 303) probably gives the Turkish perspective of the Arab caliph. In another tale, however, the mild and just caliph is depicted more or less as a historical character showing his care for his subjects by helping a poor woman (Eberhard and Boratav no. 301). Some of the most popular tales of the *Arabian Nights* have also been documented from Turkish oral tradition, such as the tale of "Ali Baba and the Forty Thieves" and the tale of "Aladdin and the Magic Lamp" (Eberhard and Boratav nos. 179, 180). Even the mythical region of Mount Qâf is encountered in Turkish folktales (Eberhard and Boratav no. 58 III 4): in the tale of "The Grateful Cat and Dog" a man rescues a snake, a cat, and a dog, and receives a magical object from the dog that enables him to marry the princess. Later, the magical object is stolen and he is sent to a far-off place whose remoteness is indicated by its name "Mount Kaf." As the motif of Mount Qâf is well known from Arabic learned and popular tradition, its mention does not necessarily suggest the influence of the *Arabian Nights* (Streck and

Miquel). The tale of Polyphemus, known in Turkish as *Tepegöz* (Eberhard and Boratav no. 146), is originally Greek, but is also contained in the *Arabian Nights* as one of the adventures of Sindbad the Sailor (Conrad). The tales of Sindbad, even though they are not contained in the early Arabic manuscripts of the *Arabian Nights,* had already been incorporated into the collection prior to Galland's translation, namely in a seventeenth-century Turkish manuscript that contains the Sindbad tales as part of a highly individual choice of tales differing from the Arabic manuscripts (Chauvin 201). A final example for the "oral connection" between the *Arabian Nights* and Turkish popular tradition is the appearance of the phoenix (Turkish *anka*) in various folktales (Eberhard and Boratav nos. 36, 72, 136, 140, 206, 226, and 239; see Birkalan and Lenz).

Turkish Translations of the *Thousand and One Nights*

In addition to the general impact of the *Arabian Nights* on Turkish oral tradition and linguistic borrowings, the *Thousand and One Nights* were influential by way of translations into both Ottoman and modern Turkish. In order to contextualize the social and historical framework, it is useful to divide the translations roughly into five periods: the Ottoman Period (fourteenth–eighteenth centuries), the Tanzimat Period (early nineteenth century), and three different stages of the Republic Period (1922–50; 1950s–80s; 1980s to present). In this last period, a few critical essays about translation and editing issues were published.

Long before the Western fascination with the *Arabian Nights,* some of the tales in the collection were translated into Ottoman Turkish and became available either as manuscripts or printed books. The first known translation is the one prepared by Abdî in 1429, of which manuscripts exist at least in four different locations (Istanbul, Archeological Museum, no. 237; Ankara, Millet Library, no. 1202; Ankara, Public Library, no. 239; Leiden, University Library, no. 1558). In his book *Osmanlı Müellifleri* (Ottoman authors), Mehmet Tahir (1972–75) mentions a certain Hevesi of Skopje as a second early translator, but no manuscript of that work is available. Several other manuscripts of different translations exist in libraries outside of Turkey, including a manuscript in the British Library in London, and four in the Bibliothèque Nationale in Paris; some of these works comprise more than one volume. Abdî translated only a section of the *Arabian Nights* under the title of *Cemasbname* (Book of Cemasb); it includes fifty-five nights and has so far not been published. One of the most popular tales included in this version is *Cemasp,* or *Şahmaran.* The tale is about the king of serpents and is widespread in Turkish popular tradition (Eberhard and Boratav no. 57). Turkish folklorist Pertev Naili Boratav indicates that the motif of the serpent king is among the motifs introduced to Turkish narrative tradition through the *Arabian Nights.*

Another manuscript translation preserved at the Istanbul Ayasofya Library probably goes back to the thirteenth or fourteenth century. Previous research has pointed out that the appearance of this translation coincided with the visits of German orientalist scholar Hellmut Ritter, and doubt has been voiced as to the manuscript's authenticity. This translation contains five stories.

The seventeenth-century Beyânî manuscript (1636), comprising ten volumes, presents several interesting problems. The first of these problems is concerned with the date of the manuscript's acquisition. Tekin (2001) argued that the manuscript's original copy, which was bought and sent to France by Galland just about fifty years after its preparation, is currently housed at the Bibliothèque Nationale in Paris. He pointed out that Galland had probably acquired the manuscript when he was appointed to Istanbul as an assistant to the French ambassador, that is, between the years 1672 and 1675. Hermann Zotenberg, however, notes that the Turkish ms. no. 356 in Paris consists of eleven volumes that had been joined together by error in the Royal Library as if constituting one set. Volumes 2–10, which actually constitute a set, had been purchased as early as about 1660 for Cardinal Mazarin's library and following Mazarin's death in 1662 had been transmitted to the Royal Library in 1668. He also argues that the first volume constitutes an independent translation from the Arabic—quite different from that in the second volume. If we are to follow Tekin's argument, we find a logical mistake. Galland's journey to Constantinople did not begin until 1670, or according to some sources, not until 1672. If the Royal Library had acquired the translation as early as 1668, Galland could not have been the person who brought the copy to France. On this issue, Heinz Grotzfeld (personal communication) has recently argued that volumes 2–10, which were translated as late as 1636, reflect a recension of the *Nights* prior to that published by Muhsin Mahdi, which has not been compiled before ca. 1450. In comparing the stories and their order in the repertoire of the Turkish translation with the stories and their order in the Syrian and Egyptian branches of the *Nights,* Grotzfeld suggests that the archetype of these recensions might have been derived from a repertoire close to that of this Turkish translation. While roughly retaining the order of the stories, the author of the archetype has selected certain tales, joined together other ones, and has also added new material (such as the tale of the barber and his brothers). These characteristics could result from the publication of "unfinished" material that was being circulated while the text was still in draft form.

Grotzfeld's argument about the purchase of the Turkish manuscript deserves further investigation as he notes an important point: Since Galland had access to the Royal Library—why did he not search for a copy of *Alf layla wa-layla* there? If the copy in the Bibliothèque Nationale dates back to as early as ca. 1660, and if it has not been brought to the library by Galland—then who brought this manuscript to Paris? The issue of how these manuscripts were taken abroad from Turkey (Acaroğlu 14) constitutes a promising area for future investigation. As for the present, we might speculate the Turkish manuscript at the Bibliothèque Nationale to constitute a possible "bridge" between the Oriental and the Western traditions.

The other interesting point is about the social and historical milieu of the seventeenth century and the choices Beyânî had made as a translator. Beyânî translated the *Arabian Nights* upon the order of Sultan Murad the fourth. The original Arabic source text has neither been indicated nor identified by later research. From historical research we know that Beyânî's translation was available for rent at the old bookshops (*sahaflar*) in Istanbul (Tekin, "Elf leyle" 208). If the text was translated upon the order of Sultan Murad the fourth, then for what reason did the manuscript leave the Ottoman palace? Did the manuscript belong to the palace, in the first place? Did Murad the fourth, known for his prohibition of tobacco and alcohol in public places, enjoy reading the stories in private? Was the translation discharged from the palace after the sultan's death in 1640? While these questions remain unanswered, it is possible to characterize the choices Beyânî made as a translator. Quite obviously, Beyânî enjoyed a certain degree of liberty in relation to the original, at times adding explanatory sentences or explicit scenes and dialogues about sex and sexuality written in the sociolect of seventeenth century middle-class Ottoman Turkish (Tekin "Elf leyle" 278).

The first printed translation of the *Arabian Nights* in Turkish appears to have been undertaken by Ahmet Nazif. Nazif was a poet and *kadı* (religious judge) during the reign of Sultan Abdulaziz. He had translated the first volume of the *Arabian Nights* in 1842, and the remaining five volumes were published together in 1851 (Acaroğlu 14). The second edition of this translation was published in 1870 as a four-volume work. While a copy of volumes 3 to 6 of the first edition are currently housed at the Beyazıt Library in Istanbul, no copies of the first two volumes appear to be preserved in publicly accessible libraries. Like some of the Western translators, Nazif also wanted to prepare a book that literally contained a thousand and one nights. According to Alim Şerif Onaran, the beginning of the first volume indicates "Esmaî" as the work's original Arab author, and he is quoted to have named his work *Elf leyle ve leyle*. This would make the *Arabian Nights* the work of the Arabic philologist al-Asma'î (d. 828), a fact that is most unlikely, even though it corresponds to his reputation as a gifted teller of stories. The same passage also mentions that the Arabic work has been translated into Turkish under the title of *Binbir Gece,* or *İbretinüma* (literally: Supplier of Wise Counsel), and the translator was indicated as Lamii Çelebi, a famous Ottoman author who died in 1531 (Onaran, *Binbir Gece Masalları* 2001. 18).

In 1869, French orientalist Charles Clermont-Ganneau, who had held positions at the Foreign Ministry of France, published "The Story of Khalifa and Khalifa" from the *Arabian Nights* in both Turkish and French. As the author knew Arabic as well as Turkish, he might have translated the tales himself (Acaroğlu 15). Another Turkish translation in four volumes was published in Armenian script. The first volume was translated by Hovannes Tolayan in 1891, and the remaining three volumes by M. B. Arabacıyan in 1892 (Onaran, *Binbir Gece Masalları* 2001. 18).

Cultural Politics, Literature, and History

The Tanzimat Period (1839–76) ushered in a series of reforms that were to cure the outdated Ottoman institutions by what was perceived to be the *elixir vitae*—a westernization cognate to modernization. As part of the new project, the Tanzimat reforms also reinforced the usage of a language simpler than previous Ottoman Turkish, which had relied on "Turkish syntax and Arabo-Persian in all else" (Silay 19). This era of reforms called for a different medium of communication because both Arabic and Persian signified the rejected and outdated culture. At the same time, the heightening interest in Turkish nationalism in the nineteenth century fashioned an intellectual movement opposed to Ottoman cosmopolitanism. Therefore, the hybrid Ottoman language needed to be simplified to suit a larger audience. These new attempts were significant for the present topic insofar as the idea of returning to the "Turkish folk" was tantamount to a latent rejection of translating the "Arabian" tales. During the Tanzimat Period, the Ottoman-

Turkish elite was influenced by French culture and maintained close contact with France. Particularly in the nineteenth century, translations of the *Arabian Nights* into Turkish were derived from French, instead of from the original Arabic source. This decision might be due to various reasons. Above all, the elite had already abandoned the "high" language of the Ottomans that relied heavily on Persian and Arabic borrowings. Moreover, the attitude of turning to Western sources, such as French versions of the *Arabian Nights,* corresponded to the predominant mimicry of the West and Western culture. Meanwhile, no endeavor was made to translate the tales from Arabic into Turkish.

Parallel to the new directions of the political mainstream, many scholars showed a nascent interest in Turkish language and literature. Their focus also included the life of the ordinary people and their culture, aiming to discover the "folk" and the lore within. Therefore, the Turkish people became the true source of culture and the fundamental agent for the formation of a national identity. While this supposedly "Turkish" folk culture was being revived and began to replace the previously dominant Ottoman high culture, the symbols of national identity were drawn from a romanticized view of folk life.

During the Tanzimat Period, the distinguished journalist Şinasi (1826–71) under the title of *Durub-ul Emsal-i Osmaniye* (Ottoman Proverbs; 1863) published a collection of 1,500 Ottoman proverbs selected from written sources. In the work's second edition, the number of proverbs was increased to 2,500; and in the third edition, Şinasi included 4,004 units, albeit without a clear distinction as to which of them were and were not actual proverbs (Oy). Şinasi's main intent lay in proclaiming that the spirit of the nation was best expressed through the national language. Similarly, Rıza Tevfik (1868–1949; see Zarcone) understood literature as the pure and wise product of the *vox populi*. For Ottoman literary works, he concluded that "in Ottoman literature, the form and the style, thus, the taste is Iranian, and it is alien to the Turkish culture" (Tevfik 74). Ziya Gökalp (1876–1924)—a leading figure in sociology, a mystic poet, and the forefather of Turkish nationalism—emphasized the products of the ordinary people as revealing their pure, good, and natural side. For Gökalp, Turkish folktales, anecdotes, and epics were imbued with this "national spirit." He considered folk materials as belonging to the original and pure things that reveal the character of great genius (Kaplan 219). In consequence, Gökalp argued for the collection of stories, anecdotes, songs, and proverbs, so that they might be presented to other nations in order to demonstrate the richness of Turkish folklore (Gökalp

68–69). Aiming to show the degree of Turkishness in folklore materials, he emphasized originality and authenticity as fundamental for the study of art and aesthetics (Berkes 262). Believing in authenticity and originality, he sought to obtain the best and unspoiled form of the folklore materials (Gökalp 69; Bayrı 178).

In this manner, republican scholars, artists, and literati were actively engaged in discovering the "folk" within Turkey. Ziya Gökalp's involvement with folk aesthetics, Rıza Tevfik's interest in folk philosophy, and Fuat Köprülü's involvement with the Central Asian origin of the Turkish folk literature all sought to discover the values of the "folk." Given their focus, these scholars neither considered translating the *Arabian Nights* nor studying the influence of the *Arabian Nights* on Turkish oral tradition or vice versa. In the same vein, as early as 1920, Yusuf Ziya and Musa Süreyya, administrators of the Darülelhan (Music Conservatory), attempted to establish a nationwide collection of folk songs. In 1925, Hamid Zübeyr Koşay published an article titled "Halk Edebiyatı ve Ananelerini Toplamanın Usulü" (The Methodology of Collecting Folk Literature and Traditions) in *Muallimler Mecmuası* (Journal of Teachers). Türk Halk Bilgisi Derneği (Turkish Folklore Society), the first folklore organization of the Republican period, was founded in 1927 by director of national education İshak Refet Işıkman, education inspector İhsan Mahvi, and sociologist Ziyaettin Fahri Fındıklıoğlu (Birkalan).

Despite these sentiments rooted in the rejection of Arab influence in Turkish language and culture, translations of the *Arabian Nights* continued to be prepared well beyond the Tanzimat Period. Between 1910 and 1928, during the early years of the Turkish Republic, five translations were published in Turkish in the Ottoman script. Vedat Örfi Bengü's edition *Binbir Gece Hikayeleri* (Tales of the Thousand and One Nights) demonstrates a stark contrast to the nascent interest in Turkish folklore materials. Bengü adapted selected translations from the *Arabian Nights* and published his work in the Ottoman script. The same work, with minor changes, was published in Latin script in 1943, and again in 1990. Only in the short preface to the 1943 edition, Bengü mentions that he wrote his book upon the recommendation of Ivan Mujukin, who had challenged him saying, "You are from the Eastern culture, why don't you write a screen-play?" Upon this suggestion, Bengü wrote a screenplay because he would not rely on the *Thousand and One Nights* as translated by foreign writers; furthermore, he aimed to "accentuate action and description" in the stories. He goes on to say that he wanted to show the importance of Shahrazâd "as a pure hearted woman who protected her fellow 'citizens' " (Bengü, *Binbir Gece*). At the same time, not a single one of Bengü's tales corresponds to those in the standard corpus of the *Arabian Nights,* so his work can at best be considered as a creative adaptation of the *Arabian Nights.*[3]

Just as was the case with Western translations of the *Arabian Nights,* the translation of the *Arabian Nights* into Turkish implied many different efforts. The popular magazine *Resimli Ay* (Illustrated Monthly) presented selections from the *Thousand and One Nights* between 1927 and 1928 in the form of twelve pamphlets. The translator of these texts, the last translations to appear in the Arabic script, is not indicated. Even though the translations in *Resimli Ay* are not complete, in terms of translation, they present a language and context easily understood by the Turkish audience. *Resimli Ay* was distributed in small pamphlets among the old bookshops around the Beyazıt area in Istanbul.

Between 1928 and 1930, five translations of the *Arabian Nights* had appeared in Turkish, of which only one was aimed at children. In contrast, only one translation of the *Arabian Nights* was published between 1930 and 1939. The lack of translations in this period might be related to the fact that language reforms in Turkey officially began in May 1928; on January 1, 1929, it became unlawful to use the Arabic alphabet to write Turkish. From the mid-1930s until the mid-1940s, as part of the nationalist project, Turkey saw the height of enthusiasm for language reform, and some of the suggested reforms were so extreme as to endanger the language's intelligibility. By the late 1940s, considerable opposition to the purification movement had risen among teachers, writers, poets, journalists, and editors, who began to complain in public about the instability and arbitrariness of the officially sanctioned vocabulary. In 1950, the Turkish Language Society lost its semiofficial status, and eventually some Arabic and Persian loanwords began to reappear in government publications. By the early 1950s, Ottoman Turkish was completely out of use. The young republic's aspirations to present itself as secular and Western were at the root of the reform. Conservatives viewed this attitude, whether political or religious, as a provocation to their ideals.

When the oppositional Democrat Party came to power in 1950, the political history of Turkey changed from a one-party state to the direction of greater individual freedom. A tendency to resist official interference in matters of private concern grew, and the government's role in language matters was reduced. At the same time, the new period witnessed a revivalist tendency with respect to some cultural and religious terms and phrases and a growing internationalization of some vocabulary. Between the late 1940s and the early 1960s, a total of ten Turkish translations of the *Arabian Nights* appeared, including those by Rıfat Necip, Selami Münir Yurdatap and Rakım Çalapa, Muharrem Zeki Korgunal, Nihat Yalaza Taluy (*Binbir Gece Masalları*), Hüseyin Başaran, Halit Fahri Ozansoy, Suat Taşer, Ferid Namık Hansoy, and Raif Karadağ. Selami Münir Yurdatap and Rakım Çalapa's joint work is a translation from Arabic into Turkish. While Yurdatap translated the tales, Çalapa adapted the translation to a folktale style. Taluy's (*Binbir Gece Masalları*), Başaran's, and Ozansoy's translations are particularly aimed at children. Hansoy's translation of the *Arabian Nights* is based on Paul de Maurelly's French adaptation of the stories for the young. As a matter of fact, most of the translations that appeared in Turkish after the 1950s continued to be intended for children. Rather than translating anything like an "authentic" or complete corpus of the *Arabian Nights,* these translations focused on stories such as "Ali Baba and Forty Thieves," tales of marvel, the adventures of Sindbad, and the tale of Aladdin's Magic Lamp. One out of several reasons for choosing these tales was probably their entertaining character and the fact that they were free of sexual allusions and, thus, appropriate for children.

Suat Taşer's work is an adaptation of the *Arabian Nights* for broadcasts in the Ankara and Cyprus radio programs. Parts of his book were published in the newspaper *Vatan* (Homeland). Taşer altered the structure of the *Arabian Nights* by moving the stories around. The frame story, for example, appears as the first night. Taşer himself numbered the stories as different nights up to night thirty-two. He also inserted a *gazel* by the Ottoman court poet Fuzulî into his text (Taşer 276). Taşer neither indicates the criteria for his selection nor the foreign text that served as his model.

After the 1980s, there is a tremendous increase in the number of translations. Between 1980 and 1985, more then twenty translations of parts of the *Arabian Nights* into Turkish appeared, all of which were directed at children. The most often translated stories are those of Sindbad and Aladdin. While language reform and modern usage were pushed forward during periods of liberal governments, they were de-emphasized under conservative ones (Heyd; Lewis). These translations, however, used "proper" Turkish according to the official guidelines, and at the same time in terms of style, content, and form aimed to create an aura of a "happier" environment and a more effective social system as well as to solidify mores for the next generation through representing strong and determined male characters. With these characteristics, the tales might be regarded as some sort of "opium" against the social repercussions of the coup d'état in 1980.

In the 1990s, one of the most important translations was that of Alim Şerif Onaran, published in 1993 and 2001, respectively. Onaran translated the *Arabian Nights* as *Binbir Gece Masalları* (Tales of the Thousand and One Nights). Onaran states that he did not value the translation prepared by Galland, because Galland expurgated and bowdlerized the original tales. In contrast, Onaran preferred and took as his source text the translation prepared by Joseph Charles Mardrus (1899–1904), because in his opinion Mardrus left the stories "as they were"; this also meant that stories mentioning sexuality were retained, albeit cleaned from their "obscene" elements (Onaran, *Binbir Gece Masalları* 2001: 17).

Literary historian Şinasi Tekin has criticized Onaran for translating the tales from French, as he would certainly neglect colloquial speech, the style of the folktale, and sayings or proverbs in Turkish. One example mentioned in Tekin's discussion concerns the Arabic expression "Selamun aleykum." This expression, constituting the standard formula of greeting and welcome, literally means "Peace be upon you." Even though the Arabic saying is being utilized in modern Turkish in exactly the same wording, Onaran translated the French wording to Turkish, thus more or less producing an unintelligible result (Tekin, "Ely leyle" 77). In a similar vein, Onaran goes to great lengths to explain almost every Arabic and Persian word in footnotes.

The Influence of the *Arabian Nights* on Modern Turkish Literature

Besides translations and adaptations, a strong influence of the *Arabian Nights* is apparent in modern Turkish literature. Poets and writers such as Orhan Veli Kanık, Behçet Necatigil, and Hulki Aktun were attracted by the tales. Orhan Duru's short story "Şişe" (Bottle) ends with the tale-number 1,002, the tale of Shahrazâd herself. Güneli Gün's novel, *Bağdat Yollarında* (On the Road to Baghdad [1987]) is a postmodernist project. It plays with the role of the storyteller Shahrazâd by adding historical characters from the Ottoman Empire and subverting the notion of storyteller and storytelling. While Gün acknowledges that she had "stolen" the tales from the *Thousand and One Nights* and adapted them to the taste of Turkish readers, it is interesting to note that she herself calls the source text a "picaresque novel." This subversion is apparent in her creation of the "feminist" storyteller Hürü. Marrying a woman first, and then an Ottoman sultan, Hürü presents the weakest possible connection to any text of the *Arabian Nights*.

The Treatment of Offensive Language in Turkish Literature

The translations of the *Arabian Nights* in Turkish add up to a great number. At the same time, they present various issues to be discussed. The first point relates to the source and originality of the translated material. It is common opinion in *Arabian Nights* scholarship that a complete standard version of the *Arabian Nights* most probably never existed. Instead, the tales were chosen and added according to the demands of the audience, whether Arabic or European, who took the idea of a "thousand and one" nights literally. Similarly, Boratav comments on the nature of the Turkish translations. Boratav points out that the tales of the *Arabian Nights* are not the products of a single individual author, but rather a combination of both oral and written sources. Accordingly, from time to time, new tales were added to versions of the *Arabian Nights*. The same attitude of treating the corpus of tales included in the *Arabian Nights* was applied when they entered Turkish tradition, sometimes to such a degree that the line between a literal translation from the source text and the tales added later remains totally obscured. Since no text of the *Arabian Nights* can claim to represent the one "original" or "authentic" version (or, in other words, any text may rightfully voice that claim), it is not possible to find out to which degree the translations were faithful to their source text. In this respect, literary critic Şinasi Tekin's juxtaposition of the fifteenth-century Egyptian manuscript edited by Mahdi, the oldest Arabic manuscript of the *Arabian Nights* preserved, to Beyânî's translation in the seventeenth century is pointless. Moreover, it also appears from Mahdi's investigations that European demand had, to a certain degree, influenced the Arabic manuscripts prepared in the eighteenth and nineteenth centuries (Mahdi; see also Marzolph), a point that to a large extent also applies to the different translations in Turkish.

At first, the Turkish translations of the *Arabian Nights* were prepared from the original Arabic. Later translations did not rely upon Arabic and chose to translate from a European language, in particular French. Tekin, who favors the translation from Arabic into Turkish, heavily criticizes the translation of the *Arabian Nights* from languages other than the original Arabic. Besides not drawing on an "original" text, he believes that in those translations the language has been obscured, most of the tales have been censored, and the style of the folktales has been altered.

Can translating from "Western" languages be regarded as part of Turkey's long-term modernity project, as an example of orientation toward the West? After all, this project is somewhat problematic itself. The language reform created a drastic and permanent estrangement from the literary and linguistic heritage of the Ottomans. By replacing the Arabic with the Latin alphabet, Turkey consciously turned toward the West and effectively severed a major link with a part of its Islamic heritage. By providing the new generation with no need or opportunity to learn Arabic letters, the alphabet reform cut off Turkey from its Ottoman past and culture.

Another element of alienation is inherent in the increased number of translations after 1980. As these translations aimed to satisfy the curiosity of both children and a wider general audience, they were low in cost as well as widely distributed. These translations are characterized by traces of "puritanism" and linguistic interference, betraying editors' and publishers' codes of morality. Even in academic research, in the name of purifying texts, many of the tales were presented in changed style, content, and meaning. While "cleaning up" issues related to sexuality made the translators' ideologies more visible, they stabbed a knife into the heart of the *Arabian Nights,* because in the original collection, sexuality was a means for expressing desire—the desire to live and to narrate.

In this regard, Beyânî's handling of sexuality in his seventeenth-century Ottoman manuscript is quite revealing. Tekin remarks that, in comparison to both the fifteenth-century Ottoman manuscript and the fourteenth-century Arabic manuscript, Beyânî's text is full of explicit sexual statements (Tekin, "Elf leyle" 78). According to Tekin, Beyânî enters the text not only as a visible translator, such as when he inserts long explanatory sentences, but he also adds other sentences dealing with the sexual scenes of the *Arabian Nights,* even reaching the degree of obscenity. Tekin believes that the "original" *Arabian Nights* did not contain this kind of explicit statements, but that Beyânî had inserted them himself. Although his argument about the "purity" of the *Arabian Nights* is far from being likely, Beyânî might well have adapted or "distorted" the language in the translation. For example, the *adab* genre of Arabic literature includes ready wit and sexual discourse, offering criticism of social institutions and men's control over the female body. In Ottoman literature, equivalent satirical and humoristic genres exist, such as *latife, mülatafa* (jokes), *hiciv* (satire), and *tehzil* (ridicule) (Özkırımlı 1: 292). Sexuality was expressed in oral tradition by way of jokes about Nasreddin Hodja, folktales, or similar genres. Besides, Ottoman love poems commonly mention the "desire" toward a woman or a man. The eighteenth-century Ottoman court poet Nedim, a rebel to the existing poetic conventions, expressed homosexual sentiments, although these have been argued to stand in lieu of mystical overtones (Silay). Folklorist İlhan Başgöz notes the common occurrence of obscene stories in collections of Nasreddin Hodja stories compiled before the seventeenth century (Başgöz, *Nasreddin Hoca* 115). In other words, verbal transgressions of moral boundaries that today are regarded as unquestionably accepted were treated in a different manner. By inserting obscene words and descriptions into his translation, Beyânî might have acted along a similar line argued by Fedwa Malti-Douglas for the attitudes of male narrators in medieval Arabic texts. Malti-Douglas notes that in virtually all medieval Arabic texts, the generators of discourse—who were basically men—were obsessed with the female body and woman's access to discourse (Malti-Douglas 87, 111). This attitude later continued in men's control over editions, translations, and adaptations of these texts. Against this backdrop, Beyânî's translation could well betray his desire to introduce his voice into the translations by adding obscene elements to the original. While it is difficult to ascertain whether Bayânî did or did not follow this intention, the ways in which later readers accepted his text is quite revealing.

Ottoman culture had a more tolerant attitude toward obscene elements in manuscripts until the mid-sixteenth century, be that original Ottoman texts or translations. From the seventeenth century onward, Ottoman authors adapted more bourgeois ethics, where most discourses on sexuality different from the mainstream were dismissed, while some were tolerated in the name of mysticism. Later on, with the introduction of Western ideas into Turkish culture in the eighteenth century, literature was increasingly identified as a medium of education, and therefore, a stricter code on sexuality was observed. The Ottoman penal code of 1858 aimed at preventing offensive and obscene language material from reaching the public. The penal codes of 1864, 1876, and 1909 even granted the government the right to censure all publications before printing. The republic of Turkey carried on a similar mission to punish the "indecent and obscene" (Başgöz, *I, Hoca Nasreddin* 17). In the years to follow, this bourgeois ideology about controlling the materials became all the more apparent, and literature was increasingly used to promote a certain state ideology.

At present, after the *Arabian Nights* have been translated into Turkish for centuries, we face two camps. Both scholarly and lay translators have attempted to adapt the *Arabian Nights* to bourgeois ethics by appropriating the tales and by adapting new styles and meaning to serve their interests and needs. Their attitude was especially prevalent at the end of seventeenth and the beginning of the nineteenth century. Some of those translators—in accordance with the dominant ideology—sought to maintain stylistic, semantic, and ethical power in their translations by eliminating elements that were regarded as sexual, vulgar, or otherwise offensive for middle-class sensibilities. Others, represented by authors like Beyânî, challenged the norms either by keeping the language as encountered in the original source text or by introducing even more obscene elements into the translation. None of the early translators attempted to produce translations faithful to the original. In consequence, complete translations of the *Arabian Nights* from Arabic into modern-day Turkish for the popular audience and also a critical text for academic purposes are still missing. Besides the cultural politics of the Turkish translations, there is also the need for a detailed study of the manuscripts, particularly considering the complexity of issues related to Galland's translation and the impact of Turkish translations on other European editions. While the translations prepared in the Republican Era profited from Western sources for translating the *Arabian Nights,* we may now surmise from Zotenberg's notes as well as from Grotzfeld's assertions that the Ottoman Turkish translations from the Arabic might have affected the translations of the *Arabian Nights* into Western languages.

NOTES

I would like to thank Professor Heinz Grotzfeld for providing valuable comments and for directing my attention to the important article by Zotenberg.

1. Historically speaking, the development of the Ottoman language can be divided into three periods: Old Ottoman, or Old Anatolian Turkish (thirteenth to fifteenth centuries); Middle Ottoman, or Classical Ottoman (sixteenth to nineteenth centuries); and Modern Ottoman (nineteenth to twentieth century). The term *Osmanlıca* (Ottoman) was first coined by the elites of the Tanzimat Period (1839–76) to denote the hybrid language of the Ottoman court.
2. In the following, I will speak of the *Thousand and One Nights* when referring to a work in Turkish, and of the *Arabian Nights* when the general topic is considered.
3. The book contains the following tales: Gülnihal Sultan and the Oath of Shehriyar; Prince Solomon; Vizier Abraham; Noah, the Second Vizier; A Miracle-Like Event. The second book contains the following stories: In the Land of Horrors;

Caravan; Toward Happiness; The Woman Magician; Semender Shah; The Female Rival; Evening Preparations; Little Donkey. The third book has the following sections: Alive Graveyards; The Pond with a Green Marble; The Rage of the Sultan; The Advice of Hanife; Kismet; Poor Gülnihal Sultan; In the Grave; Discovery of the Murder; Salvation; End of a Bloody Reign.

WORKS CITED

Acaroğlu, Türker. "Türkçe'de Binbir Gece Masalları Kaynakası" (A Bibliography of the 1001 Nights in Turkish). *Masal Araştırmaları.* Ed. Nuri Taner. Istanbul: Art-San, 1988. 13–24.

Başaran, Hüseyin. *Binbir Gece Masalları.* Ankara: Kültür Matbaası, 1957.

Başgöz, İlhan. *Geçmişten Günümüze Nasreddin Hoca* (Hodja Nasreddin from Past to Present). Istanbul: Pan Yayıncılık, 1999.

———. *I, Hoca Nasreddin, Never Shall I Die.* Bloomington: Indiana UP, 1998.

Bayrı, Mehmet H. "Ziya Gökalp ve Türk Folkloru" (Ziya Gökalp and Turkish Folklore). *Türk Yurdu* 26.5–6 (1942): 175–79.

Belgil, Vehbi. "Binbir Gece Masallarının Sonsuz Gençliği" (The Eternal Youth of the Thousand and One Nights). *Halk Kültürü* 3–4 (1985): 55–76.

Bengü, Vedat Ö. *Binbir Gece.* Istanbul: Uğur Kitabevi, 1946.

———. *Binbir Gece Hikayeleri* (The Stories of Thousand and One Nights). Istanbul: Cihan-Cemiyet Kitaphaneleri, 1922.

———. *Binbir Gece Masalları.* Istanbul: Burak Yayınevi, 1990.

Berkes, Niyazi, ed. *Turkish Nationalism and Western Civilization: Selected Essays of Ziya Gökalp.* London: Allen and Unwin, 1959.

Beyânî. Bibliothèque Nationale, Paris, ms. Turc. 356/2, 1636.

Birkalan, Hande. "Pertev Naili Boratav, Turkish Politics and the University Events." *Turkish Studies Association Bulletin* 25.1 (2001): 39–60.

———, and Millicent Lenz. "Mythical Birds." *Archetypes and Motifs in Folklore and Literature: A Handbook.* Ed. Jane Garry and Hasan El-Shamy. Armonk: M. E. Sharpe, 2005. 80–87.

Chauvin, Victor. *Bibliographie des ouvrages arabes ou relatifs aux arabes.* Vol. 4. Liège: Vaillant-Carmanne, 1900.

Clermont-Ganneau, Charles. *Story of Khalifah and Khalifah.* Jerusalem: Typographie de Terre Sainte, 1869.

Conrad, JoAnn. "Polyphem." *Enzyklopädie des Märchens.* Vol. 10. Berlin: Walter de Gruyter, 2002. 1174–84.

Eberhard, Wolfram, and Pertev Naili Boratav. *Typen türkischer Volksmärchen.* Wiesbaden: Franz Steiner, 1953.

Gerhardt, Mia I. *The Art of Story-Telling. A Literary Study of the Thousand and One Nights.* Leiden: Brill, 1963.

Gökalp, Ziya. *Principles of Turkism.* Trans. Robert Devereux. Leiden: Brill, 1968.

Grotzfeld, Heinz. "Contes populaires de l'époque Mamlouke dans les Mille et une Nuits." *Aram* 9–10 (1997–98): 43–54.

———. Personal communication. Letter dated September 23, 2004.

Gün, Güneli. *Bağdat Yollarında* (On the Road to Baghdad). Istanbul: Simavi Yayınları, 1993.

Hansoy, Ferid N., trans. *Binbir Gece Masalları.* Istanbul: İnkılap Kitabevi, 1959.

Heyd, Uriel. *Language Reform in Modern Turkey.* Jerusalem: Israel Oriental Society, 1954.

Kaplan, Mehmet. *Türk Edebiyatı Üzerine Araştırmaları* (Research on Turkish Literature). Istanbul: Dergah Yayınları, 1987.

Karadağ, Raif. *Binbir Gece Masalları.* 4 vols. Istanbul: Ak Kitabevi, 1959–61.

Korgunal, Muharrem Z. *Binbir Gece Hikayeleri* (Stories of The Thousand and One Nights). Adana: Ayyıldız Kitabevi, 1954.

Lewis, Geoffrey. *The Turkish Language Reform: A Catastrophic Success.* Oxford: Oxford UP, 1999.

Littmann, Enno. "Alf layla wa-layla." *Encyclopedia of Islam.* Vol. 1. Leiden: Brill, 1960. 358–64.

Mahdi, Muhsin. *The Thousand and One Nights (Alf Layla wa-Layla): From the Earliest Known Sources.* 2nd ed. 3 vols. Leiden: Brill. 1984–94.

Malti-Douglas, Fedwa. *Woman's Body, Woman's Word: Gender and Discourse in Arabo-Islamic Writing.* Princeton: Princeton UP, 1991.

Marzolph, Ulrich. "Re-Locating the Arabian Nights." *Orientalia Lovanensia Analecta* 87 (1988): 155–63.

Miquel, André. "The Thousand and One Nights in Arabic Literature and Society." *The Thousand and One Nights in Arabic Literature and Society.* Ed. Richard G. Hovannisian and Georges Sabagh. Cambridge: Cambridge UP, 1997. 6–13.

Nazif, Ahmet, trans. *Tercüme-i Elf leyle ve leyle* (Translation of the Thousand and One Nights). 6 vols. Istanbul: Matbaa-ı Amire, 1851?

——— *Tercüme-i Elf leyle ve leyle.* 4 vols. Istanbul: Matbaa-ı Mekteb-i Sanayi, 1870?

Necip, Rıfat. *Binbir Gece Hikayeleri.* 2 vols. Istanbul: Hilmi Kitabevi, 1946–48.

Onaran, Alim Şerif. "Binbir Gece." Trans. from Jean Gaulnier's French text. *Argos* 17 (January 1990): 70–73.

———. *Binbir Gece Masalları.* Istanbul: AFA Yayınları, 1992.

———. *Binbir Gece Masalları.* 8 vols. Trans. from the French. Istanbul: Yapı Kredi Bankası Yayınları, 2001.

Oy, Aydın. "Tanzimat Yazarları ve Atasözleri" (Authors and Proverbs of the Tanzimat Period). *Türk Dili* 93 (1959): 500–503.

Ozansoy, Halit F. *Binbir Gece Masalları.* Istanbul: Doğan Kardeş Yayınları, 1957.

Özkırımlı, Atilla. "Cinsellik." *Türk Edebiyatı Ansiklopedisi.* Vol. 1. Istanbul: Cem Yayınevi, 1987. 291–99.

Perho, Irmeli. "The *Arabian Nights* as a Source for Daily Life in the Mamluk Period." *Studia Orientalia* 85 (1999): 139–62.

Silay, Kemal. *Nedim and the Poetics of the Ottoman Court: Medieval Inheritance and the Need for Change.* Bloomington: Indiana UP, 1994.

Streck, M., and André Miquel. "Ḳāf." *Encylopaedia of Islam.* 2nd ed. Vol. 4. Leiden: Brill, 1978. 400–402.

Tahir, Mehmet Bursalı. *Osmanlı Müellifleri* (Ottoman authors). Ed. A. Fikri Yavuz. 3 vols. Istanbul: Meral Yayınevi, 1972–75.

Taluy, Nihat Y. *Binbir Gece Masalları.* Istanbul: Varlık Yayınevi, 1954.

————. *Binbir Gece Masalları: Alaeddin'in Lambası.*Istanbul: Varlik Yayınları, 1962.

Taşer, Suat. *Binbir Gece Masalları.* Ankara: Emek Basım-Yayınevi, 1975.

Tekin, Şinasi. "Binbir Gece'nin İlk Türkçe Tercümeleri ve Bu Hikayelerdeki Gazeller Üzerine" (On the First Turkish Translations of the *Arabian Nights* and the *Gazels*). *Türk Dili Araştırmaları* (1993): 23.

————. "Elf leyle ve leyle'nin 17: Yüzyıl Yazması Nasıl Yayımlanmalı? Bu Metin ne Kadar Müstehcen?" (How Should a Seventeenth Century Manuscript of the Arabian Nights Be Published? How Obscene Is This Text?). *Tarih ve Toplum* 208 (April 2001): 77–80.

Tevfik, Rıza: "Folklore-Folklor." *Türk Folklor Araştırmaları Yıllığı* 15.301 (1914): 7057–59.

Yurdatap, Selami M., and F. Yaylalı. *Binbirinci Gece* (The Thousand and First Night). Istanbul: ca. 1939–48.

————, and Rakım Çalapa. *Binbir Gece Masalları* (The Stories of the Thousand and One Nights). Istanbul: Türkiye Basımevi ve Yayınevi, 1950–54.

Zarcone, Thierry: *Mystiques, philosophes et francs-maçons en Islam: Riza Tevfik, penseur ottoman (1868–1949). Du soufisme à la confrérie.* Paris: Institut français d'études anatoliennes d'Istanbul, 1993.

Zotenberg, Hermann: "Notice sur quelques manuscrits des Mille et une Nuits et la traduction de Galland." *Notices et Extraits des Manuscrits de la Bibliothèque Nationale* 28 (1887): 167–235.

I3

The Persian *Nights:* Links between the *Arabian Nights* and Iranian Culture

Ulrich Marzolph

The *Thousand and One Nights*—or, as I prefer to call them in the following for purely practical reasons: the *Arabian Nights*—as we perceive them three hundred years after Antoine Galland's epochal French adaptation bear a distinct Arabic imprint. Meanwhile, the commonly accepted model for their textual history acknowledges various stages in the conceptualization and effective formation of both the collection's characteristic frame story and the embedded repertoire. The vast majority of tales in the preserved manuscripts of the *Nights* has been integrated into the collection during two periods of Arabic influence, the so-called Baghdad and Cairo periods (Gerhardt 115–374). These "Arabic" stages are preceded by an Iranian version, probably dating to pre-Islamic times, which in its turn profits from structural devices and narrative contents originating from Indian tradition. Considering the eminent position that Iran and Iranian culture hold in the early stages of the textual history of the *Arabian Nights*, surprisingly few details are known concerning the collection's relation to and its actual position within the Iranian cultural context. In the following, I propose to discuss links between the *Arabian Nights* and Iranian culture on several levels. In surveying these links, I will treat five major areas: (1) the Iranian prototype of the *Nights;* (2) tales of alleged Persian origin; (3) Persian characters within the tales; (4) Persian translations of the *Arabian Nights*; and (5) the position of the *Arabian Nights* in modern Iran.

The Iranian Prototype *Hazâr afsân*

The title of the commonly acknowledged Iranian prototype of the *Arabian Nights* is given in the tenth century by various Arab authors in a more or less identical spelling as *Hazâr afsân[e]* (Abbot 150–51). Both the Arab historian al-Mas'ûdî (d. 956) and the Baghdad bookseller Ibn al-Nadîm (d. after 988) mention the book and its content in some detail; short references to the book's title are also contained in Abû 'Abdallâh Muhammad al-Yamanî's *Kitâb Mudâhât Kalîla wa-Dimna* (Book of Tales Similar to Those in Kalîla wa-Dimna; written in 969) and Abû Hayyân al-Tauhîdî's (d. 1023) *Kitâb al-Imtâ' wa'l-mu'ânasa* (Book of Delight and Cordiality) (see Marzolph and van Leeuwen 588). While this title is usually understood to mean "A Thousand Stories," the Persian term *afsân[e]* is semantically close to terms like *afsun* and *fosun*, both denoting a magic spell or incantation, and, hence, an activity linked in some way or other to magic. In consequence, Persian *afsân[e]* may be understood as not simply a narrative or a story, but more specifically a "tale of magic." The Persian title was translated into Arabic as *Alf khurâfa*, the Arabic term *khurâfa* denoting a genre of fantastic and unbelievable narratives. The eponym of the literary term is Khurâfa, said to have been a man of the Arabian tribe of Banû 'Udhra who was carried off by demons and who later described his experience. His tale is recorded on the authority of the prophet Mohammad who himself vouched for the existence of the character and the authenticity of his statements (Drory). *Alf khurâfa* was not, however, necessarily the title of the Arabic translations of *Hazâr afsân[e]*, since al-Mas'ûdî further specified that those were usually known as *Alf layla* (A Thousand Nights). Ibn al-Nadîm mentions that the Arabic version of the book continues through a thousand nights and contains less than two hundred stories. At the same time, the content of the collection in any of its early versions, whether Persian or Arabic, is unknown. The oldest preserved Arabic manuscript dates from the fifteenth century and is the first document to inform about the content of the medieval *Alf layla wa-layla* (Grotzfeld).

Ibn al-Nadîm's summary of the opening passages of the frame story is short. While he mentions the king's ritual behavior of marrying and killing a woman night after night, he neither states a reason nor elaborates on the previous events, such as the two kings witnessing the faithlessness of their wives, or their being violated by the tricky woman kept in a box by a demon (Horálek). Either Ibn al-Nadîm had not bothered to actually read the introductory passages—given his judgmental verdict on the

Nights as a "worthless book of silly tales" (Abbott 151) this appears to be quite probable—or whatever he had seen did not correspond to the refined and structured frame story known today. Moreover, Ibn al-Nadîm claims to have seen the book "in its entirety several times," thus indicating that complete copies containing the conclusion of the frame story were available in his day, even though they might have been rare. At the same time less than a dozen manuscripts that can reliably be related to the period predating Antoine Galland's French translation (1704–17) have been preserved. These manuscripts appear to indicate that the collection in its historical development was regarded as an open-ended concept with the potential to integrate an undefined number of tales, not necessarily comprising either a thousand nights or a thousand tales, and maybe not even aiming or requiring to close the frame opened at the beginning (Marzolph, "Re-Locating the *Arabian Nights*").

As for the authorship of the Persian *Hazâr afsân*, Ibn al-Nadîm reports the opinion that the book was composed for (or by?) Homâ'i, the daughter of King Bahman; al-Mas'ûdî, according to whom a certain Humâya was the daughter of Bahman, the son of Isfandiyâr and Shahrazâd, regards Humâya as the sister of the Achaemenid emperor Darius who reigned before him; this information is corroborated by various other Arabic historians (Pellat). While the earliest preserved document of the *Arabian Nights*, an Arabic fragment dated 266/879 (Abbott), testifies to the popularity of the collection in the Arab world in the first half of the ninth century, most conjectures as to its early history remain speculative. Both al-Mas'ûdî and Ibn al-Nadîm were inclined to attribute a Persian or Indian origin to fictional narrative in general, and modern scholarship agrees on an Indian origin for the frame story or at least certain elements in it (Cosquin). The Persian names of the main characters in the frame story of the Arabic version—Shahrazâd, Shahriyâr, Dînâzâd, or similar forms—are taken to indicate an early familiarity with the Persian prototype, most probably dating back to pre-Islamic times. The Persian text might then have been translated into Arabic as early as the eighth century. A number of intriguing similarities between the frame story of the *Arabian Nights* and the historical events narrated in the biblical book of Esther even led Dutch scholar Michael J. de Goeje to presume a Jewish (or Judeo-Persian) author as the compiler of the original version of the *Nights*. De Goeje's thesis has been refuted in great detail by Emmanuel Cosquin.

Various reasons have been suggested for the change of the original number of a thousand (tales) into a thousand and one (nights) (see Barth).

Most prominently, German scholar Enno Littmann ("Zur Entstehung" 664) has supported the hypothesis that the latter number gained its superior position because of the prominence of the Turkish alliteration *bin bir*, meaning "a thousand and one." Scholars of Persian literature tend to refute this opinion, quoting as their argument a number of instances from as early as the twelfth century, in which the number 1001 appears in Persian prose and poetry (as *hezâr-o yek*) to denote an undefined and indefinite amount. The mystical poet Farîd al-Dîn 'Attâr (d. 1201) in his biographical work on famous mystics quotes Hakîm Tirmidhî (d. ca. 910) as saying that he saw God in his dreams a thousand and one times (Meier; Ritter 461). In his poetry, 'Attâr himself used the phrase "a thousand and one persons must be set in order ere thou canst properly put a morsel of food into thy mouth" (Boyle 46). The poet Nezâmî (d. 1209) even chose his pen name deliberately so as to allude to the thousand and one secrets hidden in his tales (Barry 87–88; Nezâmî 586–90), as the numerical value of its letters add to the amount of 1001 (n = 50, z = 900, â = 1, m = 40, i = 10). Although these instances indicate a strong position of the number 1001 in medieval Persian culture, it remains to be studied whether or not the Persian usage might have influenced the collection's general denomination in Arabic.

While it is possible to estimate the date of the first Arabic translation of the Persian *Hazâr afsân[e]*, it is not altogether clear until what time the Persian book survived. Munjîk of Tirmidh, a highly literate poet of the tenth century, is quoted as having "read heroic tales and listened to their narration from written sources: 'Many versions of the tales of the Seven Trials, and the Brass Fortress did I read myself, and heard recited [to me] from the book [called] *Hazâr afsân*.'" (Omidsalar 329). Similar evidence is said to abound in the verse of the poet Farrokhi who lived in the early eleventh century (329). And still Nezâmi in a passage of his romance *Khosrou and Shirin* alluded to the collection under its ancient Persian name of *Hazâr afsân* (Barry 87). The tales of the Seven Trials (Persian *haft khvân*) and of the Brass Fortress mentioned by Munjîk belong to the genre of mythical history and are also contained in the Persian national epic, the *Shâh-nâme* or "Book of the Kings" compiled by Munjîk's contemporary Ferdousi (d. 1010). In consequence, the *Hazâr afsân* alluded to by Munjîk appears to denote a collection of mythical or historical narratives rather than a precursor of the *Arabian Nights*. Driving this argument somewhat further, one might speculate that the term *Hazâr afsân* in medieval Persian poetry did not even mean a specific book or compilation. Probably the

Hazâr afsân was similar to the concept of *arzhang* (or *artang*), a denomination linked to the notion of a mysterious colorful masterpiece of art produced by the legendary Persian artist Mâni. While the exact characteristics of this masterpiece are not clear, some sources mention his house, and others refer to a lavishly illustrated manuscript (Sims 20). By analogy, *Hazâr afsân* might have implied a fictitious concept of a truly wonderful and unsurpassedly inspiring collection of narratives.

Tales of Alleged Iranian Origin

Jiří Cejpek, in the chapter on "The Iranian Element in the *Book of a Thousand and One Nights* and Similar Collections" in Jan Rypka's *History of Iranian Literature*, is quite apodictic as to the extent of the Iranian material in the *Arabian Nights*. In an extensive passage devoted to this problem, he regards the "core of the *Book of a Thousand and One Nights*" as "undoubtedly Iranian" and speaks of its being "modeled on the Middle Persian prose folk-book *Hazâr afsânak* which was Iranian throughout in character" (663). Accordingly, he also claims that the frame story, including its embedded stories, is of Iranian origin. Next Cejpek supplies a list of stories "all of which form part of the Iranian core in the *Book of a Thousand and One Nights*, i.e. the original *Hazâr afsânak*"; the stories listed by him include "the stories of the Merchant, the Ghost and the Three Old Men [. . .], The Fisherman and the Ghost, The Three Apples [. . .], The Porter, The Three Ladies and the Three Qalandars [. . .], The Magic Horse, Hasan from Basra, Prince Badr and Princess Jauhar from Samandal, Ardashîr and Hayât an-nufûs, Qamar az-zamân and Queen Budûr." In addition, Cejpek mentions what he calls the "[d]efinitely Iranian" tales about "Ahmad and the fairy Parîbânû, and the Story of the Jealous sisters," conceding, however, that it is "doubtful and in fact unlikely" that these stories were part of the original Persian collection (664).

While Cejpek relies on previous research (such as Østrup 42–71; see also Elisséeff 43–47), in terms of evidence to support his evaluation, it is interesting to note his arguments. Cejpek says: "Proper names are a great help and rarely let one down when determining the origin of a story. If they are Persian it means that they are original and prove the subject in question to be of Persian origin too. On the other hand, if one finds Arabic names in Iranian stories (which happens particularly in the magic fairy-tales), they have been invented and substituted for the Iranian ones later on" (664). As detailed arguments are missing, this statement ought to be considered a fairly general one. In fact, in view of the other evaluations in Cejpek's writing, it appears to be highly biased in favor of Iran. On a general level, comparative folk-narrative research has shown that the names that are not constitutive for a given folktale are as susceptible to change as numerous other ingredients or requisites (Nicolaisen). Moreover, it remains unclear why Cejpek denies Arabic names the very quality he previously claims for Persian ones.

Enno Littmann, who has also dealt in some detail with the various national or ethnic components in the *Arabian Nights*, argues in terms of content. In his evaluation, relying on Johannes Østrup, those tales in which benevolent ghosts and fairies interact independently with human characters are of Persian origin (Littmann, *Tausendundeine Nacht* 18; Littmann, "Zur Entstehung" 677–95). The most prominent tales he regards as Persian according to this evaluation are the tales of Qamar al-zamân and Budûr, Ahmad and the Fairy Perî Banû, The Ebony-Horse, Jullanâr the Mermaid, and The Two Envious Sisters.

To name but a third source surveying the Iranian element in the *Arabian Nights*, Jean-Louis Laveille in his recent study of the theme of voyage in the *Arabian Nights* (189–93) also concedes a Persian character to about ten stories, including the already named ones of Qamar al-zamân and Budûr, the Ebony-Horse, and Ahmad and the Fairy Perî Banû.

Interestingly, at least two of the tales mentioned by the above-quoted authors—those of Ahmad and the Fairy Perî Banû and of the jealous sisters—belong to the stock of what Mia Gerhardt has termed the "orphan tales" (12–14). Those tales are not included in the fifteenth-century Arabic manuscript used by Galland. Their outlines were supplied to him by the Syrian Maronite narrator Hannâ Diyâb, and the tales Galland constructed on the basis of Hannâ's narration only became part of the traditional stock of the *Arabian Nights* after Galland had introduced them into his publication when his original manuscript material had been exhausted. This fact leads one to ponder about the feasibility of using the geographical or ethnical approach to identify the Persian element in the *Arabian Nights*, in fact about the very justification of any attempt to identify ingredients supposed to be constituted against or derived from a specific ethnical or national backdrop. Persian narrative literature at any given state, and certainly at the stage in which it might have contributed discernibly to the narrative repertoire of the *Arabian Nights*, was of a hybrid character, incorporating numerous elements originating from other national or ethnic cultures; besides the Indian narrative tradition, the Greek (Davis) is most notable. Cejpek aims to compensate this hybridity by pointing out the fact that "the Indian material [in the *Arabian Nights*] was so completely iranized that there can be no question of the *Thousand and One Nights* being a direct descendant of an Indian model" (665).

Yet readers such as Laveille correctly point out that Iran in a number of tales in the *Arabian Nights* serves as nothing more than an imaginative matrix, a "never-never land of collective memory constituted by the legends" ("un pays de cocagne dans la mémoire collective constituée par les légendes") (Laveille 189; see also Djebli 205-06; Henninger 224). While this evaluation certainly holds true for the two "orphan tales" mentioned above, its impact for the earlier history of the Iranian contribution to the *Arabian Nights* should also not be underestimated. Already in the early Islamic period, Iran had gained renown as a place of legends, similar to the manner in which Babylon—according to a Koranic allusion (2,102) and subsequent Islamic legend about the angels Hârût and Mârût—was invariably linked to the concept of magic. Altogether, the present knowledge about this level of a Persian link to the narrative stock of the *Arabian Nights* includes little direct Persian influence and relies on general evaluations that have not been subjected to detailed scrutiny.

Persian Characters in the Nights

Besides the standard Persian kings and princes, serving—somewhat like the kings of European fairy tales—to illustrate the acme of royal (and, by analogy, permanent) rule, Persian characters in the *Arabian Nights*—quintessentially named Bahrâm—figure in two distinct categories: the merchant and the Magian (Arabic *majûsî*), the latter corresponding to the Persian Zoroastrian (Marzolph and van Leeuwen 629).

Appearing frequently, the Persian merchant is essentially a neutral role supporting two major aspects. First, it indicates the cultural impact of medieval trade between Iran and the Arabic lands. This impact is already documented in storytelling by the famous anecdote of Nadhr ibn al-Hârith, the Arab merchant who challenged the prophet Mohammad by promising to narrate Persian legends (Omidsalar 328–29). Second, it stresses the general character of the *Arabian Nights* as being what Aboubakr Chraïbi has labeled a "mirror for merchants" (6; see also Coussonnet). Since the merchant is an unobtrusive and unsuspicious character, villains would at times dress up in disguise as a Persian merchant, a motif figuring most prominently in the tale of Hasan of Basra.

The Magian denotes a lay member of the Zoroastrian community rather than a Zoroastrian priest. In contrast to the neutral merchant, the Magian is one of the standard villain characters of the *Arabian Nights*. In medieval Arabic narrative literature, the Magians are imagined as infidels practicing a number of strange customs, including the worship of fire, human sacrifice, and incestuous relations, specifically between grown-up sons and their mothers (Marzolph, *Arabia ridens* 2: nos. 28, 706, 738; Marzolph, *Das Buch der wundersamen Geschichten* no. 1; see also van Gelder 37–77). Practicing a different belief and rituals that were in stark contrast to the basic Islamic tenets, the Magians were vulnerable to being portrayed and stereotyped as a highly dubious ethnic Other. Besides customs conflicting with public morals, such as a certain Magian's homosexual preferences in the tale of 'Alâ' al-din Abû al-shâmât, Magians in the *Arabian Nights* invariably practice magic and kill the true believers. Magians figure most prominently in the Tale of As'ad and Amjad (Sironval) which in turn is embedded in the tale of Qamar al-zamân, when As'ad is kidnapped and held prisoner to be presented as a human sacrifice on the Mountain of Fire. Magians are furthermore encountered by Sindbad on his fourth voyage, when his comrades are killed by a tribe of cannibal Magians ruled by a *ghûl*. Magian adversaries are mentioned in the story of Gharîb and his Brother 'Ajîb. And, finally, Badr Bâsim, the son of Jullanâr the mermaid and her human husband, is shipwrecked during his adventures on an island inhabited by Magians whose queen is the vicious sorceress Lâb. In all cases in which an ethically good (and hence, by extension, Muslim) protagonist falls victim to the Magians, the only means to save him is through the help of a Muslim (and hence, by extension, ethically good) man who often spends his life in the city or country of the Magians without professing his true belief. The practice of hiding or even denying one's true belief in time of imminent personal danger constitutes a legally accepted practice in Islam known as *taqiyya*. This practice is particularly linked to the Persian context by the fact that the adherents of the creed of Shiism, which only became the dominant creed in Iran from the Safavid period onward, were often subjected to severe persecutions and practiced *taqiyya* in order to both survive and remain true to their belief (Meyer).

It would be interesting to study the reception (and hypothetical change) of the image of Iranian characters in Persian translations of the *Arabian Nights*. After all, Persian authors and readers might justly be supposed to be more sympathetic toward their fellow countrymen than the ethnically different Arabs, regardless of the formers' religious creed. Historical circumstances make it, however, obvious that the image of Iranians in Persian translations of the *Arabian Nights* is unlikely to be different from that of the Arabic version. The outlook and worldview of the *Arabian Nights* is not defined by the language of the tales, be it Arabic, Persian, or any other language, but rather by the cultural background. This cultural background is dominated by (Islamic) religion, which in turn is the same for Muslim Arabs and Muslim Iranians. And it is Muslims that constituted the overwhelming majority of the country's population soon after the Islamic conquest and certainly the main category of readers at the time when the Persian translations of the *Arabian Nights* were prepared.

The implications of the image of the Magians in Persian versions of the *Arabian Nights* may in some way be compared to the development the image of Alexander the Conqueror underwent in Persian and general Islamic tradition. In historical Persian sources originating against a Zoroastrian backdrop, Alexander is an evil destroyer, a conqueror annihilating traditional values—such as he had, in fact, experienced in history (Yamanaka). In contrast, later Islamic sources transformed him not only into a triumphant conqueror but also into a just ruler, and eventually into a sage and a prophet (Waugh). Regardless of the language in which later sources were compiled, the common religious perspective determined the evaluation of Alexander in the Islamic sources. Since Iran's Arabic conquerors were in a similarly alien and hostile position toward Iran as had been Alexander, it was tempting for them to propagate his image in a similarly sympathetic way as Greek and Hellenistic sources did. By analogy, a Persian translation of the stereotype image of the pre-Islamic fire worshipers pictured in the Arabic sources would not result in any major changes, as the religious perspective of Islam was and still is shared by both Muslim Persians and Arabs, and Magians despite their national or ethnic proximity to their fellow Iranians would be—and in fact often are—alienated because of their religious creed.

At any rate, the negative image of the Magian is characteristic of Arab sources, and no truly Persian version of a given tale would—for various reasons—employ the character of the Magian as a villain. Whereas narratives rooted in ancient Iranian belief would resort to fictitious characters such as evil demons or sorcerers, the standard ethnical villain characters in modern Persian folktales are the Jew, the black man, and the gypsy (Marzolph, *Typologie* 29).

Persian Translations of the *Nights*

When and where the *Arabian Nights* were first translated into the Persian language is not known exactly. While Turkish translations from the Arabic, some probably enlarged, already existed before Galland's French adaptation (Chauvin 23, 201), Persian translations apparently were not prepared before the beginning of the nineteenth century. As is well known, the British colonial enterprise exercised a decisive influence on the textual history of the *Arabian Nights*, particularly as two of its early printed editions were published in Calcutta (1814–18, 1839–42). In a similar vein, the attention generated by the publication of the printed editions might have given rise to suggesting a version of the *Arabian Nights* in Persian, a language that continued to hold its position as the local lingua franca of all of India. The catalogues of Persian manuscript collections worldwide list at least four early nineteenth-century versions of the *Arabian Nights* in Persian, variously known as *Alf leile va-leile, Hezâr-o yek shab,* or—in a curious distortion of its Arabic name—as *Alf al-leil.* None of these manuscript versions has so far been studied in detail. While Ahmad Monzavi's *Union Catalogue of Persian Manuscripts* (3659) lists two manuscripts presently not available for inspection in Madina and Tehran, the *Catalogue of the Arabic and Persian Mss. in the Oriental Public Library at Bankipore*, India, mentions a manuscript "collection of one hundred tales from the Alf laylah," compiled in satisfaction of his friends' request by a certain Auhad ibn Ahmad Bilgrâmî and completed on Dhû 'l-qaʿda 15, 1251, corresponding to March 3, 1836 (Muqtadir 195, no. 767). The content of this manuscript, comprising some 102 folios, is not known.

The Berlin Staatsbibliothek possesses yet another Persian translation, the only manuscript whose text is available to me at present (Pertsch 967–68, no. 998; Nabavinezhâd). The text of this manuscript comprises 118 folios covering eighty-one nights, and containing the opening of the frame story up to a part of the tale of Nûr al-Dîn ʿAlî and His Son Badr al-Dîn Hasan. The sequence of tales reminds one of the Breslau edition prepared by Maximilian Habicht (and, after his death, continued by Heinrich Leberecht Fleischer; 1824–43). The manuscript is written by different hands, suggesting its production as the copy of an already existing manuscript through the collective effort of different scribes. The manuscript's language both in terms of syntax and vocabulary indicates its origin from northeastern Iran. This evaluation is also corroborated by the name of the translator/compiler that is given as Mirzâ Zein al-ʿâbedin

Khân Neishâburi (fol. 29b/1-30a/1: *motarjem-e in ketâb*, "the translator of this book"), that is, a person originating or living in the town of Neishâbur. As the manuscript is not complete, it does not contain a colophon mentioning the date of compilation; the circumstances would, however, suggest a production in the first half of the nineteenth century. The text of this Persian manuscript version is particularly curious inasmuch as both its wording and division into nights differ considerably from both contemporary printed editions of the Arabic text, Bulaq I (1835) and Calcutta II (1839–42). Further research is needed in order to determine the Arabic text used as the basis of translation, most probably a manuscript, and its relation to other versions of the *Arabian Nights*.

The only existing version of the *Arabian Nights* in Persian presenting the full number of 1001 nights was prepared by Mollâ 'Abd al-Latif Tasuji together with the poet Mirzâ Sorush of Esfahan and was completed in 1259/1843. Soon after, the translation was published in a two-volume lithographed edition, the calligraphic work of which was accomplished in 1259/1843 and 1261/1845 respectively.[1] After his accession to the throne in 1264/1847, young Nâser al-din Shâh, who was an avid reader of the Persian translation (Amanat 49-50, 66)[2] and is said to have yearned for a finely illustrated copy of the book ever since he first listened to the stories, ordered the calligrapher Mohammad Hosein Tehrâni to copy the text. When this job was achieved on a total of some 570 text folios in 1269/1852, a team of more than forty leading artists under the supervision of the famous Abu 'l-Hasan Khân Ghaffâri Sani' al-molk supplied an equal number of folios containing illustrations, besides preparing the bookbinding that is lavishly embellished by lacquerwork. The working conditions in the chambers of the polytechnic school (the Majma'-e Dâr al-sanâye') appear to have been "cramped" (Zokâ' 33), as numerous people had to work together in modest quarters. The resulting work, preliminary sketches of which are preserved in an album kept in the British Library (Titley 221–22), was finished only seven years later in 1276/1859 and is now preserved in the library of the Golestân Palace in Tehran. It comprises a total of 2279 pages in large folio format that are bound in six exuberantly decorated volumes (see Âtâbây; Zokâ' 33–38, 83–105, plates 12–34). This manuscript represents the last outstanding specimen of the traditional art of the book in Qajar Iran. According to a recently published document (Bakhtiyâr), the cost of preparing its illustrations and illumination totaled the sum of 6,850 *tumân*. This amount was equivalent to a sixth of the total amount spent to construct and decorate the contemporary multistoried palace in Tehran known as Shams ol-'emâre, itself the most sumptuously decorated royal building of the Qajar period. A painting by Abu 'l-Hasan Khân Ghaffâri depicts Dust-'Ali Khân Mo'ayyer al-mamâlek, head of the polytechnic school, presenting a volume of the manuscript to the ruler (Zokâ' 134, no. 69; Bakhtiyâr 130).

Except for two places in the manuscript, the text folios alternate with those containing illustrations. The space on the illustrated folios has been divided into at least three and up to as many as six images per page, the individual images being framed and separated from one another by a band of illumination that also includes a caption indicating the content. The illustrations, which have recently been studied in some detail as a "bridge between East and West" (Buzari; see also Khânsâlâr), number a total of 3,600 different scenes. In the course of restoration in recent years, making a photographic documentation and reproduction of this manu-script has repeatedly been discussed, as doing so would serve both conser-vatory functions and make this monument of Qajar art available to na-tional and international scholarship. In view of the uninhibited and outspokenly playful illustration of the sexual scenes particularly at the manuscript's beginning, such a reproduction contradicts the presently propagated values in Iran and is unlikely to happen soon. Even so, the manuscript's published images contain a wealth of information about popular customs and material culture of the Qajar period.

One of the most fascinating images illustrates a scene from the story of Ghânim ibn Ayyûb in which, as the caption says, the caliph Hârûn al-Rashîd, who in the *Nights* embodies the quintessence of just rule (Marzolph, "Hârûn al-Rashîd"), speaks to his vizier Ja'far al-Barmakî (Zokâ' 85, no. 12). The fact that the Abbasid caliph and his vizier are ren-dered in the likeness of the young Qajar ruler Nâser al-din Shâh and his prime minister Amir Kabîr add a tragic touch to this image. Amir Kabîr, who was an extremely able and powerful prime minister as well as the Shâh's favorite, had suddenly been dismissed by the Shâh in late 1851, and was subsequently executed on Rabî' I 17, 1268, corresponding to January 9, 1852. In this manner, he had suffered a similar tragic fall from the ruler's favor and untimely death as had been experienced by Hârûn al-Rashîd's vizier Ja'far and the Barmakid clan. If it holds true that the manuscript's il-lustration was not begun before the year 1269, the image rather than un-knowingly foreshadowing the tragic event probably represents a late tribute by the artist (and the ruler, who undoubtedly approved of the illustrations in person) to the once powerful and highly esteemed politician.

When the first lithographed edition of the *Arabian Nights* was prepared in 1259–61/1843–45, lithographic illustration had not yet become a regular phenomenon. Soon after the preparations for illustrating the luxurious royal manuscript had begun, a second lithographed edition was ordered, this time containing illustrations. As the effort of preparing the lithographed book was considerably easier, the task was achieved much faster than the manuscript, and the result was published in 1272/1855. This first illustrated lithographed edition of the *Arabian Nights* in Persian, in fact the first ever Oriental edition of the *Nights* containing a regular set of illustrations, includes seventy illustrations executed by Mirzâ 'Ali-Qoli Kho'i, an eminent artist of the day (Marzolph, "Mirzâ 'Ali-Qoli Xu'i"), and two of his apprentices, Mirzâ Rezâ Tabrizi and Mirzâ Hasan (see Marzolph, *Narrative Illustration* 232). This edition in turn appears to have created an increased popular demand, since only three years later Mirzâ Hasan, the son of the well-known court painter Âqâ Seyyed Mirzâ, illustrated another edition on his own, albeit with a slightly reduced iconographical program (ibid.). A total of at least seven additional lithographed editions of the *Arabian Nights* in Persian were published between 1289/1872 and 1357/1938 (Safi-nezhâd), all but two of which—the editions of 1292–93/1875–76 and of 1357/1938—contain illustrations that are usually modeled on either of the two early illustrated editions.[3]

The translation prepared by Tasuji and Sorush is regarded as an exceptional piece of literature (Bahâr 369) in the formative period of the modern Persian language. Its textual basis has never been discussed in previous scholarship, and a close comparison between the translation and the Arabic original constitutes a promising field for future study. In theory, both the editions of Bulaq and Calcutta II would have been available, even though the publication of the latter one was probably just finished when the Persian translation was already under way. Fortunately, both editions differ considerably in wording, and a particularly peculiar lacuna proves the Bulaq edition beyond reasonable doubt to constitute the basis for the Persian translation. The Bulaq edition offers a highly reduced version of the Third Qalandar's tale that is narrated within The Story of the Porter and the Three Ladies of Baghdad. In its full version, this tale consists of three episodes: The destruction of the talisman on the Magnetic Mountain, the fateful slaying of the youth in the underground palace, and the protagonist's adventures with the forty maidens. While the Calcutta edition contains the tale's full text, the Arabic manuscript serving as the basis for this particular passage of the Bulaq edition must have suffered from a lacuna of several folio occurring shortly after the beginning of the second episode and affecting the text of the third episode up to the point at which the protagonist is about to break the taboo of opening the forbidden door. In order to mend the break, the compiler of the printed edition has merged the originally distinct second and third episodes: As in the second episode, the hero watches a group of people preparing an underground mansion. As soon as they have left, he uncovers the mansion's lid, enters, and then, as toward the end of the third episode, wanders through thirty-nine beautiful gardens. When opening a door, he finds the magic horse that brings him to the ten mournful youths and hits out one of his eyes. This version by way of its Qajar period Persian translation was also popular as a separate chapbook under the title of *Se gedâ-ye yek-chashm* (The Three One-Eyed Beggars) in mid-twentieth-century Iran (Marzolph, *Dâstânhâ-ye shirin* no. XLIV) and lingers on as far as the modern study of the *Arabian Nights* in Iran, when the tale's summary simply reads: "By accident, [the hero] in an underground city mounts a horse whose tail makes him blind. [. . .]" (Samini 392).

Two further Persian-language adaptations of the *Arabian Nights* need to be mentioned. One is a heavily abridged illustrated chapbook version published in pocketbook format in 1280/1863 (Chauvin 23, no. 20 zz; Edwards 129); the other one is a versified version, comprising the full number of 1001 nights, prepared by the Persian poet Seif al-sho'arâ' Mirzâ Abo 'l-Fath Dehqân (d. 1326/1908), published under the title *Hezâr dâstân* (One Thousand Stories), in a folio-sized lithographed edition in 1317–18/1899–1900. The latter edition contains a set of fifty-nine illustrations prepared by the contemporary popular artists 'Ali-Khân and Javâd (Marzolph, *Narrative Illustration* 243).

The *Arabian Nights* in Modern Iran

As a final point, the position of the *Arabian Nights* in modern Iran deserves to be mentioned. Reliable and extensive information about international *Arabian Nights* scholarship is available to Persian readers through two studies published by Jalâl Sattâri (1368/1989, 1382/2003) as well as through the Persian translation of Robert Irwin's *Companion* (Irwin 1383/2004). A first edition printed in movable type had been prepared by Mohammad Ramazâni, head of the famous publishing house Kolâle-ye khâvar as early as 1315–16/1936–37. This edition also contained a learned introduction by the scholar 'Ali-Asghar Hekmat. While Ramazâni's edition appears to reproduce major parts of Tasuji's nineteenth-century translation faithfully, even a superficial comparison reveals various editorial changes that were obviously deemed necessary to adjust the content and wording to contemporary taste. Several printed editions in Persian circulate since the 1990s, all of them presenting adapted, if not censored versions following Ramazâni's edition. One of the editions available to me is a typical "Bazaar edition." It is presented in the traditional style of Persian chapbooks as *Hekâyat-e shirin-e Alf leile va-leile shâmel-e barkhi as hekâyât-e Hezâr va yek shab* (The Sweet Story of the [Arabic] "Thousand and One Nights," containing some of the stories of the [Persian] "Thousand and One Nights"). The fact that this booklet, dating from the 1980s, is printed as "gray literature" without the obligatory mention of publication details might indicate that the publisher was not sure whether the book's content might cause him trouble. Mitrâ Mehrâbâdi's one-volume edition of "Tasuji's translation" follows Ramazâni's edition quite closely inasmuch as she includes the preface by 'Ali-Asghar Hekmat and even reproduces most of the illustrations from the former edition. At the same time, her short introductory notice makes it perfectly clear that some of the disputable passages could not be reproduced in a "society paying respect to moral values" (*yek jâme'e-ye akhlâq-garâ*) (Tasuji 1380/2001, 4). In contrast to most other recent editions, Mehrâbâdi's adapted reprint footnotes difficult passages and at the end of each of the five volumes of the original edition has a glossary of terms unfamiliar to modern Persian readers.

Particularly the sexually pronounced passages of the frame story and the introductory set of tales of the *Nights* are bound to conflict with the moral standards propagated in today's Iran (Marzolph, "Zur Lage der Erzählforschung") and have been adjusted accordingly. As a case in point, I have compared in detail two passages in various available editions. The first one is the introductory passages in which Shâhzamân surprises both his own and his brother Shahriyâr's wife committing adultery and in which later on both men are violated by the beautiful woman kept in a box by a demon; the second one is the joyful discussion of the various denominations of the female and male sexual parts celebrated by the porter and the three ladies in the story of the same name.

Both Tasuji's (1275/1858, fol. 1b–2b) and—reproducing Tasuji's wording verbatim—Ramazâni's (1315–16/1936–37, vol. 1, 3–8) texts present the sexually pronounced elements of the frame story in a manner closely following the wording of the Arabic text. Ramazâni even includes an uninhibited (European) illustration of the scene in which Shâhzamân spies on Shahriyâr's wife and her servants as they embrace their male lovers in the garden just after Shahriyâr has left to go hunting (1: 5). While the same text is also reproduced in the Bazaar edition and one of the modern editions (Tasuji 1379/2000, vol. 1, 1–6), Mehrâbâdi in her edition of "Tasuji's translation" has opted to replace the three instances of extramarital sexual relations with an all-embracing summary in a wording reminiscent of Tasuji's style: "Yet, there came a time when those two brothers due to the filthy and disagreeable character of their wives killed them . . ." (*lik zamâni farâ resid ke ân do barâdar be-sabab-e khu-ye zesht va nâ-pasandi ke as hamsarân-e-shân bedidand, ânhâ-râ koshtand . . .*). The sentence is then continued with Tasuji's words: ". . . and from then on, Shâhzamân chose to live in celibacy . . ." (. . . *va az ân pas, Shâhzamân, tajarrod gozide . . .*) (Tasuji 1380/2001, 22).

The version published under the title *Dâstânhâ-ye Hezâr va yek shab* (The Stories of the "Thousand and One Nights," 1377/1998) contains a modern retelling that follows Tasuji's text to some extent while justifying the rendering of the reprehensible action by additional comments aiming to illustrate the psychological conflict experienced by Shâhzamân. Whereas Shâhzamân in the older versions, including the Bulaq edition and Tasuji's translation, have Shâhzamân return to his wife simply because he has forgotten something,[4] this version (vol. 1, 11) states that Shâhzamân loved his wife dearly (*nesbat be hamsar-e khod delbastegi-ye besyâr dâsht*) and for that reason wanted to see her one more time before he left. As he approached her bedroom, he was hoping that his unexpected appearance would make the queen even happier. In consequence, the loving husband Shâhzamân was shocked even deeper than in the previous versions to discover his wife's adultery. As a further digression motivating his following action, instead of straightaway slaying the sinful lovers, he could not believe his eyes and went into an inner dialogue about how this situation was possible at all before he finally killed them. Probably this version is not so much indicative of the restraints experienced by publishers in modern Iran than by the requirements of motivating the action so that juvenile readers—at whom this edition is apparently directed—were given a better chance to understand.

The joyful sexual discussion between the porter and the three ladies has been translated by Tasuji in minute detail (Ed. 1275, fol. 11–12). When their party reaches its climax, the text first says: "In short, they spent their time drinking wine, reciting poetry and dancing until they got drunk . . ."

(*al-gharaz be-mei keshidan va ghazal khvândan va raqs kardan hami-gozarândand tâ inke mast shodand*...). Then follows the scene in which they undress one after the other, take a bath in the pool, and tease the other sex with proposing to guess the name of their private parts. Soon after Shahrazâd has resumed her narrative in the eleventh night, it is time for the characters in her story to have dinner, and the young ladies ask the porter to leave (... *tâ hangâm-e shâm shod dokhtaregân goftand aknun vaqt ân-ast ke az khâne birun ravi*). In Ramazâni's text (1315–16/1936–37, vol. 1, 54–56) and, following him, in one of the modern editions (Tasuji 1379/2000, vol. 1, 35), the beginning of this scene is just the same, and the three ladies one after the other take a bath, sit close to the porter, and "have fun with each other" (*beshukhi va-lahv mashghul shodand*). While the playful slapping in the original version is justified by the fact that the porter does not guess the "correct" denomination for the women's sexual parts, in this version it is motivated by sheer joy, if anything, before—with the wording of Tasuji's text—the women ask the porter to leave.

It is interesting to note that the unrestricted sexual joy of this particular passage has also been regarded as revoltingly obscene in some of the European translations. While Richard Burton, renowned for his particular delectation of obsessive sexuality, renders the passage in detail (1: 89–93), Edward William Lane in his puritan manner has the following wording:

> The wine continued to circulate among them, and the porter, taking his part in the revels, dancing and singing with them, and enjoying the fragrant odours, began to hug and kiss them, while one slapped him, and another pulled him, and the third beat him with sweet-scented flowers, till, at length, the wine made sport with their reason; and they threw off all restraint, indulging their merriment with as much freedom as if no man had been present. (1: 124–25)

At the end of this passage, and before the ladies ask the porter to leave, Lane has inserted a footnote titled "On Wine, Fruits, Flowers, and Music, in Illustration of Arab Carousals." He begins by mentioning that in his translation he has passed over "an extremely objectionable scene, which, it is to be hoped, would convey a very erroneous idea of the manners of Arab *ladies*; though I have witnessed, at private festivities in Cairo, abominable scenes, of which ladies, screened behind lattices, were spectators. Can the same be said with respect to the previous carousal? This is a question which cannot be answered in a few words." He then delves into an extended and most learned discussion of the mentioned subjects occupying more than twice the space a translation of the actual passage would have required (193–204).

Mehrâbâdi has again opted for an even more condensed and less objectionable wording than the one given by Ramazâni. In her version, there is neither wine, nor dance, nor even poetry, and—needless to mention—even less bathing or nudity. Instead, the porter is accepted by the ladies as an educated boon-companion with whom they spend some time in pleasant conversation (*hammâlrâ be-nadimi bar-gozide be-sohbat ne-shastand*) before sending him away at dinnertime (Tasuji 1380/2001, 38–39). Again, the related illustration in Ramazâni's edition has not been reproduced. Similarly, in the modern retelling the original drink of wine (Persian *mei* or *sharâb*)—whose consumption is strictly forbidden under the present interpretation of Islamic laws in Iran—has been replaced by an act beyond reproach, namely passing around a cup of *sharbat*, or sweet juice (*Dâstânhâ* 1: 137), and the company spends their time reciting love poetry, a pastime "all of them sincerely enjoyed" (*hame-ye ânhâ az in bazm samimâne lezzat mi-bordand*) before, once more, the porter is asked to leave.

Since Iran has contributed decisively to the genesis and character of the *Arabian Nights*, it appears natural that this body of world literature is appreciated in today's Iran as part of the country's literary heritage. However, a sound appreciation of the collection's original character appears more jeopardized than ever before, as the treatment of the text passages just discussed demonstrates. The consumption of alcoholic beverages and the indulging in extramarital sexual relations, both of which are frequently encountered in the *Nights*, contradict the moral values presently propagated in Iran, and publishers opt for different strategies to adjust the text so as to eliminate reprehensible components. As both Ramazâni's Persian edition and Lane's English rendering prove, similar strategies have been at work in different periods as well as different cultural contexts, albeit with varying success. Whereas the Western world has grown accustomed to regarding the *Nights* as a monumental and uninhibited affirmation of the joy of life in all its manifestations, Iranian readers are restricted to textual versions that have been adapted to their present political circumstances.

Yet the *Arabian Nights* throughout their history have proven to be highly capable of adjusting to a diversity of cultural contexts. Two announcements in a recent issue of the Iranian journal *Farhang-e mardom* (Folklore) indicate some of the directions into which the future reception of the *Arabian Nights* in Iran develops (Vakiliyan 164–65). The Iranian writer Mohammad Bahârlu is preparing a new Persian edition. The text of his edition, comprising a total of 1,400,000 words, will be completely adapted to the grammar and style of the modern Persian language while remaining faithful to Tasuji's translation. Moreover, the edition is to contain an annotated index of the Koranic verses and prophetic utterances as well as of other Arabic and Persian expressions that might need to be explained to the modern readers. The second publication mentioned, by the folklorist Mohammad Ja'fari Qanavâti, and since published, presents versions of tales from the *Nights* collected from recent oral tradition in Iran. Besides documenting a renewed interest in the *Nights,* both publications indicate the degree to which official guidelines determine how this part of the country's literary heritage is to be dealt with. At any rate, this is an unfinished chapter in the collection's history that is still being written.

NOTES

1. Early Persian lithographed books do not contain a regular date of publication. As they constitute the direct successors of previous manuscript production, their dating is to be inferred from the book's colophon, in which the calligrapher would often state his own name and the name of the person who ordered or paid for the preparation of the book together with the year (and sometimes the day and month) of completion of the written text that served as the basis of lithographic reproduction.

   There is some confusion in Iranian studies concerning the completion of the manuscript and the publication of the first lithographed text. Mohammad Ja 'far Mahjub in his influential study still holds the work of translation to have begun in 1259; in consequence, he considers the data concerning the printed editions of 1259, 1261, and 1263 as faulty (48). He quotes the Islamic date 1263 with reference to Chauvin (23) who lists a lithographed edition Tehran 1847; this edition cannot be verified. For copies of the Persian *editio princeps*, said to be "the best printing ever made of this work" (Zokâ' 33), and later editions see Marzolph, *Narrative Illustration* 231–32.

2. The Iranian National Library contains a total of six copies of the *editio princeps*. As the National Library also incorporates the holdings of the former library of the royal palace, this comparatively large amount to some extent also indicates the ruler's interest.

3. Two editions printed in Lahore are listed by Naushahi 1: 552–53.

4. While the Bulaq text (1252, vol. 1, 2) has a simple "something" (Arabic: *hâjja*), Tasuji argues that Shâhzamân had forgotten to take along a precious jewel (*gouhari gerânmâye*) intended as a present for his brother.

WORKS CITED

Alf layla wa-layla. Al-tabʿa al-ûlâ. muqâbala [wa-]tashîh al-Shaykh Muhammad Qitta al-ʿAdawî. Alif Laila wa-Laila. The Book of a Thousand and One Nights. Reprint of the Original Copy of the Bulaq edition of 1252, AH. 2 vols. Baghdad: Maktabat al-Muthannâ, ca. 1965.

Amanat, Abbas. *Pivot of the Universe: Nasir al-Din Shah Qajar and the Iranian Monarchy, 1831–1896.* Berkeley: U California P, 1997.

Âtâbây, Badri. *Fehrest-e divânhâ-ye khatti-ye Ketâbkhâne-ye saltanati va ketâb-e Hezâr va yek shab* (Catalogue of the Manuscript Collections of Poems in the Royal Library and the Book of "The Thousand and One Nights"). Tehran, 2535/1976.

Bahâr, Mohammad Taqi Malek al-shoʿarâ'. *Sabk-shenâsi* ([Persian] Stylistics). 3 vols. Tehran: Amir Kabir, 42535/1977.

Bakhtiyâr, Mozaffar. "Ketâb-ârâ'i-ye 'Hezâr va yek shab' (noskhe-ye ketâbkhâne-ye Golestân)" (The Illumination of the "Thousand and One Nights" [the manuscript preserved in the Golestân palace museum]). *Nâme-ye Bahârestân* 5 (1381/2002): 123–30.

Barry, Michael. "Le conte de la princesse du maghreb sous le pavillon turquoise par nezâmî de gandjeh (1141–1209)." *Horizons Maghrébins* 42 (2000): 83–89, 97–99.

Barth, John. *Don't Count on It: A Note on the Number of The 1001 Nights.* Northridge: Lord John P, 1984.

Boyle, John Andrew, trans. *The Ilâhî-Nâma or Book of God of Farîd al-Dîn 'Attâr.* Manchester: Manchester UP, 1976.

Burton, Richard F. *Arabian Nights with Introduction & Explanatory Notes.* Reprinted from the Original Edition Issued by the Kamashastra Society for Private Subscribers only. Benares [i.e., London]: 1885. 16 vols. Beirut: Khayat 1966.

Buzari, ʿAli. "*Hezâr-o yek shab-e* Sani' al-Molk: Poli bein-e sharq va Gharb" ("The Thousand and One Nights by Sani' al-Molk: A Bridge between East and West"). *Farhang-e mardom* 3.11–12 (1383/2005): 49–60.

Cejpek, Jiří. "The Iranian Element in the *Book of a Thousand and One Nights* and Similar Collections." Jan Rypka. *History of Iranian Literature.* Ed. Karl Jahn. Dordrecht: Reidel, 1968. 607–709.

Chauvin, Victor. *Bibliographie des ouvrages arabes ou relatifs aux arabes publiés dans l'Europe chrétienne de 1810 à 1885.* Vol. 4. Liège: Vaillant-Carmanne, and Leipzig: Harrassowitz, 1900.

Chraïbi, Aboubakr. "Situation, Motivation, and Action in the *Arabian Nights.*" *The Arabian Nights Encyclopedia.* Ed. Ulrich Marzolph and Richard van Leeuwen. Santa Barbara, Denver, and Oxford: ABC-CLIO, 2004. 1: 5–9.

Cosquin, Emmanuel. "Le Prologue-cadre des Mille et une Nuits." *Revue Biblique* 6 (1909): 7–49; also in *Études folkloriques.* Paris: Édouard Champion, 1922. 265–347.

Coussonnet, Patrice. *Pensée mythique, idéologie et aspirations sociales dans un conte des Mille et une nuits.* Cairo: Institut français d'archéologie orientale du Caire, 1989.

Dâstânhâ-ye Hezâr va yek shab (The Stories of the Thousand and One Nights). 2 vols. 1377/1998. Tehran: Eqbâl, 1382/2003.

Davis, Dick. *Panthea's Children: Hellenistic Novels and Medieval Persian Romances.* New York: Bibliotheca Persica P, 2002.

Djebli, Moktar. "Cités d'Orient dans les *Mille et une Nuits.*" *Les Mille et une Nuits: Contes sans frontière.* Ed. Edgard Weber. Toulouse: Amam, 1994. 195–211.

Drory, Rina. "Three Attempts to Legitimize Fiction in Classical Arabic Literature." *Jerusalem Studies in Arabic and Islam* 18 (1994): 146–64.

Edwards, Edward. *A Catalogue of the Persian Printed Books in the British Museum.* London: British Museum, 1922.

Elisséeff, Nikita. *Thèmes et motifs des Mille et une Nuits: Essai de classification.* Beirut: Institut Français de Damas, 1949.

Enzyklopädie des Märchens (henceforth EM). 11 vols. Berlin: Walter de Gruyter, 1977–2004.

Gerhardt, Mia I. *The Art of Story-Telling: A Literary Study of the Thousand and One Nights.* Leiden: Brill, 1963.

Goeje, Michael J. de. "De Arabische nachtvertellingen." *De Gids* 50 (1886): 385–413.

Grotzfeld, Heinz. "The Age of the Galland Manuscript of the Nights: Numismatic Evidence for Dating a Manuscript?" *Journal of Arabic and Islamic Studies* 1 (1996–97): 50–64.

Henninger, Josef. "Der geographische Horizont der Erzähler von 1001 Nacht." *Geographica Helvetica* 4 (1949): 214–29.

Horálek, Karel. "Frau im Schrein." *EM* 5 (1987): 186–92.

Irwin, Robert. *Tahlili az Hezâr-o yek shab.* Trans. Fereidun Badre'i. Tehran: Farzân, 1383/2004.

Ja'fari Qanavâti, Mohammad. *Revâyathâ-ye shafâhi-ye Hezâr-o yek shab* (Oral versions of [tales from the] *Thousand and One Nights*). Tehran, 1384/2005.

Khânsâlâr, Zahrâ. "Hezâr-o yek shab-e Sani' al-Molk" ("The *Thousand and One Nights* of Sani' al-Molk"). *Zenderud* 37–38 (1384–85/2006): 73–92.

Lane, Edward William, trans. *The Thousand and One Nights, Commonly Called, in England, The Arabian Nights' Entertainments.* Reprint of the edition 1859. 3 vols. London: East-West Publications, and Cairo: Livres de France, 1979.

Laveille, Jean-Louis. *Le thème de voyage dans Les Mille et une Nuits: Du Maghreb à la Chine.* Paris: L'Harmattan, 1998.

Littmann, Enno. "Anhang: Zur Entstehung und Geschichte von Tausendundeiner Nacht." *Die Erzählungen aus den Tausendundein Nächten.* Vollständige deutsche Ausgabe in sechs Bänden. Wiesbaden: Insel, 1953. Vol. 6: 648–738.

———. *Tausendundeine Nacht in der arabischen Literatur.* Tübingen: Mohr, 1923.

Mahjub, Mohammad Ja'far. "Dâstânhâ-ye 'âmmiyâne-ye fârsi. 11: Tarjome-ye fârsi-ye Alf leile va leile" (Popular Persian Tales. 11: The Persian Translation of the Thousand and One Nights). *Sokhan* 11 (1339/1960): 34–53.

Marzolph, Ulrich. "Alf leile va leile (Hezâr-o yek shab)." *The Beginning of Printing in the Near and Middle East: Jews, Christians and Muslims.* Ed. Lehrstuhl für Türkische Sprache, Geschichte und Kultur, Universität Bamberg, Staatsbibliothek Bamberg. Wiesbaden: Harrassowitz, 2001. 88.

———. *Arabia ridens: Die humoristische Kurzprosa der frühen adab-Literatur im internationalen Traditionsgeflecht.* 2 vols. Frankfurt: Klostermann, 1992.

————. *Dâstânhâ-ye shirin: Fünfzig persische Volksbüchlein aus der zweiten Hälfte des zwanzigsten Jahrhunderts.* Stuttgart: Franz Steiner, 1994.

————. *Hârûn al-Rashîd.* EM 6 (1990): 534–37.

————. "Mirzâ 'Ali-Qoli Xu'i: Master of Lithograph Illustration." *Annali (Istituto Orientale di Napoli)* 57.1–2 (1997): 183–202, plates I–XV.

————. *Narrative Illustration in Persian Lithographed Books.* Leiden: Brill, 2001.

————. "Re-Locating the *Arabian Nights.*" *Orientalia Lovanensia Analecta* 87 (1998): 155–63.

————. *Typologie des persischen Volksmärchens.* Beirut: Deutsche Morgenländische Gesellschaft; Wiesbaden: Franz Steiner, 1984.

————. "Zur Lage der Erzählforschung im nachrevolutionären Iran." *Spektrum Iran* 8.3 (1995): 39–51; English version "Folk-Narrative and Narrative Research in Post-Revolutionary Iran." *Folklore in the Changing World.* Ed. Jawaharlal Handoo and Reimund Kvideland. Mysore: Zooni, 1999. 299–305.

————, ed. *Das Buch der wundersamen Geschichten: Erzählungen aus der Welt von 1001 Nacht.* Munich: C. H. Beck, 1999.

————, and Richard van Leeuwen. *The Arabian Nights Encyclopedia*, with the collaboration of Hassan Wassouf. 2 vols. Santa Barbara, Denver, and Oxford: ABC-CLIO, 2004.

Meier, Fritz. Unpublished notes about the Persian contribution to the *Arabian Nights.* Ms. University Library Basel NL 0323:D5.16. (no date).

Meyer, Egbert. "Anlaß und Anwendungsbereich der taqiyya." *Der Islam* 27 (1980): 246–80.

Monzavi, Ahmad. *Fehrest-e noskhehâ-ye khatti-ye fârsi* (Catalogue of Persian Manuscripts). Vol. 5. Tehran: Mo'assasse-ye farhangi-ye manteqe'i, 1349/1970.

Muqtadir, Maulavi Abdul. *Catalogue of the Arabic and Persian Manuscripts in the Oriental Public Library at Bankipore. Vol. 8: Persian Manuscripts. Biography, Romances, Tales and Anecdotes.* Patna, 1925.

Nabavinezhâd, Hosâm al-Din. "Qesse-ye shab-e Hezâr-o yek shab: Tarjome-ye Mirzâ Zein al-'âbedin Khân Neishâburi" ("The Early History of the *Thousand and One Nights*: The [Persian] Translation by Mirzâ Zein al-'âbedin Khân Neishâburi"). *Zenderud* 37–38 (1384–85/2006): 15–28.

Naushahi, S. Arif. *Catalogue of Litho-Print and Rare Persian Books in Ganj Bakhsh Library, Islamabad.* 2 vols. Islamabad: Markaz, 1986.

Nezâmî. *Le Pavillon des Sept Princesses.* Trans. from Persian be Michel Barry. Paris: Gallimard, 2000.

Nicolaisen, Wilhelm F. H. "Name." EM 9 (1999): 1158–64.

Omidsalar, Mahmoud, and Teresa Omidsalar. "Narrating Epics in Iran." *Traditional Storytelling Today: An International Sourcebook.* Ed. Margaret Read MacDonald. Chicago: Fitzroy Dearborn, 1999. 326–40.

Østrup, Johannes. *Studien über 1001 Nacht: Aus dem Dänischen (nebst einigen Zusätzen) übersetzt von O[skar] Rescher.* Stuttgart: W. Heppeler, 1925.

Pellat, Charles. "Alf-layla wa-layla." *Encyclopaedia Iranica.* Vol. 1. London: Routledge and Kegan Paul, 1985. 831–35.

Pertsch, Wilhelm. *Verzeichniss der persischen Handschriften der Königlichen Bibliothek zu Berlin.* Berlin, 1888.

Ramazâni, Mohammad, ed. *Hezâr va yek shab: Tarjome az Alf leile va-leile* (The [Persian] Thousand and One Nights. A Translation of the [Arabic] Thousand and One Nights). 6 vols. Tehran: Kolâle-ye khâvar, 1315–16/1936–37.

Ritter, Hellmut. *The Ocean of the Soul: Man, the World and God in the Stories of Farîd al-Dîn 'Attâr.* Trans. John O'Kane. Leiden: Brill, 2003.

Safi-nezhâd, Javâd. *"Hezâr-o yek shab va châp-e sangi"* ("The *Thousand and One Nights* and Lithographic Printing"). *Farhang-e mardom* 3.11–12 (1383/2005): 17–27.

Samini, Naghme. *Ketâb-e 'eshq va sha'bade: Pazhuheshi dar Hezâr va yek shab* (A Book of Love and Trickery: A Study of the Thousand and One Nights). Tehran: Nashr-e Markaz, 1379/2000.

Sattâri, Jalâl. *Afsun-e Shahrazâd: Pazhuheshi dar Hezâr Afsân* (The Magic of Shahrazâd: A Study of the Thousand Stories). Tehran: Tus, 1368/1989.

———. *Goft-o-gu-ye Shahrazâd va Shahriyâr* (The Conversation between Shahrazâd and Shahriyâr). Tehran: Daftar-e pazhuheshi-ye farhanghâ, 1382/2003.

Sims, Eleanor, with Boris I. Marshak and Ernst J. Grube. *Peerless Images: Persian Painting and Its Sources.* New Haven: Yale UP, 2002.

Sironval, Margaret. "Histoire des princes Amgiad et Assad." *Communications* 39 (1984): 125–40.

Tasuji, 'Abd al-Latif. *Hezâr va yek shab* (The Thousand and One Nights). Lithographed ed. Tehran, 1275/1858.

———. *Hezâr va yek shab* (The Thousand and One Nights). 6 vols. Tehran: Jâmi, 1379/2000.

———. *Hezâr va yek shab. Tarjome-ye Tasuji-ye Tabrizi* (The Thousand and One Nights. The Translation of Tasuji Tabrizi). Ed. Mitrâ Mehrâbâdi. Tehran: Afsun, 1380/2001.

Titley, Norah M. *Persian Miniature Painting and Its Influences on the Art of Turkey and India: The British Library Collections.* London: British Library, 1983.

Vakiliyân, Ahmad, ed. *Farhang-e mardom* 2.2–3 (1382/2003).

Van Gelder, Geert Jan. *Close Relationships: Incest and Inbreeding in Classical Arabic Literature.* London and New York: I. B. Tauris, 2005.

Waugh, Earle H. "Alexander in Islam: The Sacred Persona in Muslim Rulership *adab.*" *Subject and Ruler: The Cult of the Ruling Power in Classical Antiquity.* Ed. Alastair Small. Ann Arbor: Oxbow, 1996. 237–53.

Yamanaka, Yuriko. "From Evil Destroyer to Islamic Hero: The Transformation of Alexander the Great's Image in Iran." *Annals of [the] Japan Association for Middle Eastern Studies* 8 (1993): 55–87.

Zokâ', Yahyâ. *Zendegi va âsâr-e ostâd-e Sani' al-molk, 1229–1283 h.q./Life and Works of Sani' al-Molk, 1814–1866.* Ed. Cyrus Parham. Tehran: Markaz-e nashr-e dâneshgâhi/Sâzmân-e Mirâs-e farhangi-ye keshvar, 1382/2003.

14

The *Arabian Nights*, Visual Culture, and Early German Cinema

Donald Haase

Introduction

In this essay I focus on a specific moment in German cultural history. That "moment" spans several decades in the late nineteenth and early twentieth centuries, from approximately 1880 to 1935. Within that period I will be considering two significant cultural developments and how they intersect. One is the robust reception of the *Arabian Nights* in print. The other is the emergence of visual culture in the form of motion pictures.

German interest in the exotic tales of the *Arabian Nights* had been strong ever since the eighteenth century, of course; but the late nineteenth and early twentieth centuries witnessed especially lively publishing activity around the *Nights*. Between 1895 and 1928, three major translations appeared in Germany: Max Henning's popular translation published by Reclam (1895–99), Felix Paul Greve's German rendering (1907–8) based on Sir Richard Burton's English version, and Enno Littmann's important scholarly translation from the Arabic (1921–28). In addition, a steady stream of selections and adaptations for a juvenile audience appeared during this period (see Fähndrich 103). The collection of the Internationale Jugendbibliothek in Munich alone attests to over forty children's editions issued by German publishers between 1880 and 1920. Most of these are illustrated editions. Some are lavishly produced and offer impressive cover illustrations that catch the reader's eye and generate interest even before the book is opened.

Many of the illustrated volumes from this period use innovative technologies in the reproduction of images and colors. For example, an

1889 reprint of a popular edition of *Arabian Nights* tales adapted for children by Albert Ludwig Grimm boasts the inclusion of eight original watercolors reproduced by chromolithography (Grimm). This new technology, which reached its zenith in Europe during the 1880s and 1890s, enabled illustrators to have their exotic Oriental scenes reproduced in brightly and intensely colored book illustrations (Ries 289–90; Caracciolo 39–40). In 1880 the publisher of a selection of six stories from the *Arabian Nights* adapted and illustrated by Theodor von Pichler announced that the selection offers six *Transparent-Verwandlungs-Bilder* (Pichler). These illustrations—produced on a plate bearing a double impression—are transparent pictures that, when held to the light, reveal additional images that change the scene and thus make the story's action visible (see Ries 54, n. 3). For instance, viewed before a light source, the transparent image illustrating the story of "Aladdin and the Magic Lamp" shows Aladdin moving up a set of stairs toward the magic lamp (Pichler facing p. 12). By visually advancing the action and creating the illusion of movement, the image is a picture of motion, if not precisely a motion picture. Innovations like these in the visual presentation of the stories suggest the degree to which books in general and these editions of the *Arabian Nights* in particular contributed to the genesis of visual culture. These editions of the *Arabian Nights* were not simply to be read, but to be viewed as spectacles in their own right.

The transformation of readers into spectators takes place concurrently with the birth of cinema. The first motion pictures were taken by Étienne-Jules Marey in 1882, and over the next three decades technological advances in the form of the Kinetograph, the Kinetoscope, and the improved equipment made by Europeans such as the Lumière brothers facilitated the development of cinema both artistically and commercially. Germans began participating in the new visual culture as spectators in 1895, when the first public screening of films occurred in a commercial setting in Berlin. Although Germany did not have its own "native film production until about 1910" (Hansen 159), once German filmmakers became involved in production—especially during the Weimar Republic—they turned out pioneering works of visual art. Among these are several important films from the early 1920s that draw inspiration from the motifs, stories, settings, and narrative techniques of the *Arabian Nights*. I am referring specifically to Ernst Lubitsch's *Sumurun* (*One Arabian Night*) of 1920, Fritz Lang's *Der müde Tod* (*Destiny*) of 1921, and Paul Leni's *Das Wachsfigurenkabinett* (*Waxworks*) of 1924.

It is remarkable that a book revolving around the act of storytelling is adapted by important filmmakers at this turning point in Western culture. Just as writers and editors adapted folktales in the early nineteenth century to negotiate the shift from orality to literacy, so do the pioneers of visual culture seem to adapt the *Arabian Nights* in order to work through the transition from print to film. This intersection of the *Arabian Nights* with the visual turn in Western culture leads to the fundamental question I want to explore: How do the *Arabian Nights* come to be a focal point in the development of visual culture and in early German cinema? To understand why filmmakers such as Lubitsch, Lang, and Leni turned to the *Arabian Nights,* we first need to examine how literary editors and commentators during this era came to understand and portray the *Nights* as a visual experience.

Reading the Arabian Nights as Spectacle

In a 1935 book review of Enno Littmann's *Arabische Märchen,* Hermann Hesse laments the "decline and fall of the art of narration" ("Niedergang und Zerfall der Erzählungskunst"). Praising the *Arabian Nights* as a classical collection exhibiting "the Oriental style of narration at its pinnacle" ("den orientalischen Erzählungsstil auf seiner Höhe"), Hesse finds that these more recent tales told by a woman storyteller in Jerusalem at the turn of the twentieth century pale in contrast. Although they do not possess the classical style of the *Arabian Nights*—which display "the naive passion for narration in tandem with an extremely sophisticated literary and religious-intellectual background" ("die naive Erzählerlust im Bund mit einer überaus hohen literarischen und religiös-denkerischen Bildung")— Hesse maintains that the folktales collected by Littmann have nonetheless been able to preserve "the genuine tradition of Oriental storytelling" ("die echte Tradition des morgenländischen Erzählens"). As is typical of the discourse that mourns the decline of orality and storytelling, Hesse's critique implicates the destructive effects of modern media and modern cultural practices:

> That Orient of the fairy tale, of the pleasure taken in images, of contemplation has been destroyed more thoroughly by the books, newspapers, business practices, and work ethic of the West than by its armies and machine guns.
>
> Jenes Morgenland des Märchens, der Bilderfreude, der Kontemplation ist durch die Bücher, Zeitungen, Geschäftspraktiken und Arbeitsmoral des

Abendlandes noch gründlicher zerstört worden als durch seine Armeen und Maschinengewehre. (Hesse 12: 56)

It is only thanks to small communities of orality, Hesse concludes, that "[j]enes Morgenland des Märchens"—"[t]hat Orient of the fairy tale"—survives:

> And it lives on not simply in libraries but also here and there in a family, in a circle of friends of the Orient, wherever the old magical art, even though it is nearly displaced by cinema and newspaper, comes to life again in the mouth of a storyteller.

> Und doch lebt es nicht bloß in den Bibliotheken weiter, sondern da und dort auch noch in einer Familie, einem Freundeskreis des Orients, wo immer noch, obwohl von Kino und Zeitung fast verdrängt, je und je im Mund eines Erzählers die alte Zauberkunst wieder lebendig wird. (Hesse 12: 56–57)

Hesse's critique of modernity and its impact on storytelling seems at first predictable. After all, the demise of the folktale and the oral tradition had long been linked to the printing press and the rise of literacy. Since the eighteenth century cultural critics had been constructing a mythology that placed the spoken and the written word in opposition, a mythology in which the printed book became the nemesis of folk narrative. Hesse's critique, however, modifies the conventional myth of the folktale's decline on two points. One is his explicit acknowledgment that literary sophistication brought storytelling to its pinnacle in the *Arabian Nights*. The other is his reference to cinema—*Kino*—as a contemporary force threatening the existence of the narrative culture that he identifies with the "Orient of the fairy tale." Cinema assumes a special interest in this context because its inclusion by Hesse updates the romantic concern over storytelling's decline. By adding cinema to the list of threatening cultural products, Hesse—writing in 1935, just two years before the premiere of Walt Disney's *Snow White and the Seven Dwarfs*—expands the terms of the debate. No longer is it simply a question of literature's destructive effect on oral tradition, but of the threat posed to literary and oral narration by the visual (see Hesse 11: 247–75).

Yet despite his apparent mistrust of film, Hesse portrays the narrative art of the East and the *Arabian Nights* as predominantly visual experiences. In 1929 he described the *Arabian Nights* as "the richest picture book in the world" ("das reichste Bilderbuch der Welt") (Hesse 11: 346).

And in the very review where he mentions the threat posed by motion pictures, Hesse also stresses the visual dimension of Eastern narrative art when he invokes "[j]enes Morgenland der Märchen, der Bilderfreude, der Kontemplation"—"that Orient of the fairy tale, of the pleasure taken in images, of contemplation." We find joy in images when we view them, of course. And *Kontemplation*/contemplation—deriving from the Latin verb *contemplari*—is first and foremost the act of gazing upon an object (*Duden* 764; *Oxford English Dictionary* def. 1). So for Hesse the *Arabian Nights* and the world of Eastern narrative are characterized by the visual. The words Hesse chooses to characterize classical Eastern narrative— *Bilderfreude*/pleasure taken in images and *Kontemplation*—do not really describe the narrative itself but the experience and activity of the auditor or reader. In fact, his descriptions imply that we do not hear or read the *Arabian Nights*—the world's "richest picture book"—but that we gaze with pleasure upon it.

Since Hesse was also a painter, it is perhaps understandable that he would use visual metaphors to describe creations of the oral and literary tradition. However, this perception is not unique to Hesse, for late nineteenth- and early twentieth-century German commentators frequently conceived of the *Arabian Nights* in visual terms. In 1907 another German poet, Hugo von Hofmannsthal, published an introduction to Felix Paul Greve's German edition of the *Arabian Nights*, and in it he repeatedly uses visual references to describe the work and the interactions of readers with it. According to Hofmannsthal the *Arabian Nights* appeals to both the intellect and the senses—especially the senses:

> The boldest intellectuality and the most complete sensuousness are woven here into one. There is no sense in us that is not aroused, from the most superficial to the most profound; everything in us is brought to life and called to pleasure.

> [H]ier ist die kühnste Geistigkeit und die vollkommenste Sinnlichkeit in eins verwoben. Es ist kein Sinn in uns, der sich nicht regen müßte, vom obersten bis zum tiefsten; alles, was in uns ist, wird hier belebt und zum Genießen aufgerufen. (Hofmannsthal 102)

But of all the senses stimulated by this sensuous collection of stories, Hofmannsthal privileges sight. He not only refers repeatedly to the text's appearance before the reader's "eyes" (101, 104), he also compares the book itself to "a magic plate embedded with gems that, like glowing eyes, form wondrous and uncanny figures" ("einer magischen Tafel, worauf eingelegte Edelsteine, wie Augen glühend, wunderliche und unheimliche Figuren bilden") (101). He claims that "the most tremendous sensuousness" ("[d]ie ungeheuerste Sinnlichkeit") pervades the *Arabian Nights*, and he elaborates this claim with a telling comparison to painting: "In this poetic work [the sensuous] is what light is in the paintings of Rembrandt and color on the panels of Titian" ("[Die Sinnlichkeit] ist in diesem Gedicht, was das Licht in den Bildern von Rembrandt, was die Farbe auf den Tafeln Tizians ist") (103). The scholar Wolfgang Köhler is correct when he glosses this climactic passage with the observation that Hofmannsthal considered the essential characteristic of the *Arabian Nights* to be "the visually ascertainable" (66).

The spectacular nature of the *Arabian Nights* derives for Hofmannsthal from its color (102), its rich materials and weave (103–4), and the unfailing and unbounded concreteness of its description (103). These are the same visual characteristics ascribed to the work by Enno Littmann in a lecture of 1923, where he compares reading the *Arabian Nights* to the experience of viewing a remarkable weave of colors, whether artificial or natural:

> This jumbled tangle of fairy tales and legends, novels and novellas, sagas and fables, humorous tales and anecdotes creates an impression on the reader as on the viewer of a colorful Oriental rug or like an artfully decorated title page of an Arabic or Persian manuscript, or like an Oriental meadow covered with many types of flowers. One is often astonished at how many different colors are united there in a single image, which nonetheless remains unified precisely because, like the meadow, it has grown that way naturally, or, like the rug and the artful title page, is modeled on nature.

> Dies durcheinander gewürfelte Gewirr von Märchen und Legenden, Romanen und Novellen, Sagen und Fabeln, Schwänken und Anekdoten macht auf den Leser etwa den Eindruck wie auf den Beschauer ein bunter orientalischer Teppich oder wie ein kunstvoll verziertes Titelblatt einer arabischen oder persischen Handschrift, oder auch wie eine mit vielerlei Blumen übersäte Wiese im Morgenlande. Man staunt oft, wie viele verschiedene Farben dort zu einem Gesamtbilde vereinigt sind, das aber dennoch einheitlich bleibt, eben weil es, wie die Wiese, von Natur so gewachsen ist, oder, wie der Teppich und das kunstvolle Titelblatt, der Natur nachgebildet ist. (Littmann, *Tausendundeine Nacht* 5)

Commentators in late nineteenth- and early twentieth-century Germany could not find enough metaphors to describe the visual experience induced by reading the *Arabian Nights*. At the end of the popular Reclam edition, translator Max Henning—in an afterword dated 1897—portrays the collection of tales that has been paraded before the reader as a theatrical spectacle:

> We are at the end. The curtain has fallen over the scene that brought before our eyes a changing panorama of countless images that were magnificently colored, sometimes fantastic and grotesque, sometimes true-to-life, gentle and charming or crudely humorous.

> Wir sind am Ende. Der Vorhang ist über die Scene gefallen, die uns ein Wandelpanorama von zahllosen farbenprächtigen, bald phantastisch-grotesken, bald wieder lebenswahren, zartempfundenen und entzückenden oder derbhumoristischen Bildern vor die Augen führte. (Henning 8: 206)

Like Hofmannsthal and Littmann, Henning too locates the visual dimension of the *Arabian Nights* in their seemingly endless variety of subject matter and in their color, a visual concept that stands for the rich materials of narration and their equally rich description. Henning differs from Hofmannsthal and Littmann, however, in his description of the *Arabian Nights* as a theatrical event and a changing panorama, and in depicting the reader as a spectator in an audience. Whereas Hofmannsthal and Littmann compare the text to visual objects that are static—such as paintings, carpets, and illustrated title pages—Henning sees the *Arabian Nights* as a moving succession of countless images that pass before the spectators' eyes. He is talking about theater, of course, but he makes the comparison in 1897—the era of primitive film and the first commercial performances in the public sphere—so one might also think he is describing the *Arabian Nights* as a motion picture.

That is exactly the case in the introduction to another early twentieth-century edition of the *Arabian Nights*: Carl Theodor Ritter von Riba's translation titled *Die Liebesgeschichten des Orients aus den tausend Nächten und der einen Nacht* (Oriental Love Stories from the Thousand Nights and The One Night). In an introduction dated 1913 and titled "Einblick und Umblick"—which I translate as "Insight and Panorama"—von Riba explicitly compares the reader's experience of the *Arabian Nights* to the spectator's experience of cinematography. He aims primarily to draw attention to the historical, social, and cultural content of the *Arabian Nights*, but he begins by acknowledging that the collected tales from Arabic-Islamic tradition are considered simply fairy tales by those adults "who remember the books of our childhood and see fairies and nightmares surface before our mind's eye" ("die wir uns der Bücher unserer Kindheit erinnern und vor unserm Geist Feen and

Schreckgespenster auftauchen sehen") (Riba 5). Following a predictable litany of the strange and fabulous motifs that readers see paraded before them when reading the *Arabian Nights*, von Riba invokes cinematography to explain the psychological significance of this experience:

> If this were all, it would be hardly worth warming up childhood memories again, unless the adult yearns to escape the colorless cold of everyday life and return to the uncritical, carefree dream-time of youth, which takes pleasure precisely in the inexplicable, the unexpected, and surrenders completely to the magic of this magical world. That this psychological moment is a factor that should not be underestimated has been evident now for years in the success of the cinematograph, which to a certain extent reawakens the memories of our youth, the magical land of our childhood dreams: perhaps it is not the worst of us who, there in the darkened room, follow the improbable images and find more pleasure in them than in the sensational, nerve-racking "Kinodramas" or even in the instructive and edifying images of landscapes. Yes, these are in themselves still somewhat wondrous—distant lands come alive before us, the dead return to life, even speak to us (Kinetophon!), and we sit silently and need hardly stir in order to view all these surprises. Isn't it in part the poet-types who rejoice in the natural-unnatural? It would be truly worthwhile to write a psychology of the cinematograph.

> Wäre das alles, so verlohnte es sich nicht übermäßig, die Erinnerungen der Kindheit wieder aufzuwärmen, es sei denn, daß der Erwachsne sich aus der farblosen Kälte des Alltagslebens wieder zurücksehnt in die unkritische, sorgenlose Traumzeit der Jugend, die sich gerade am Unerklärlichen, überraschenden erfreut und sich rückhaltlos dem Zauber dieses Zauberdämmers hingibt. Daß dieser psychologische Moment ein nicht zu unterschätzender Faktor ist, beweist ja seit Jahren der Erfolg des Kinematographen, der bis zu einem gewissen Grad die Erinnerungen unserer Jugend, das Zauberland unserer Kinderträume wiedererweckt: es sind vielleicht nicht die schlechtesten unter uns, die dort im finstern Raume den unwahrscheinlichen Bildern folgen und daran mehr Freude finden als an sensationellen, nervenzerreißenden "Kinodramen" oder selbst an belehrsamen und erbaulichen Landschaftsbildern. Ja, diese selbst sind doch ein Stück Wunder—ferne Länder leben vor uns auf, Tote erwachen zum Leben, sprechen gar zu uns (Kinetophon!), und wir sitzen still und brauchten uns kaum zu rühren, um all diese Überraschungen zu schauen. Sind es nicht ein wenig Dichternaturen, die sich dort am Natürlich-Unnatürlichen erfreuen? Wahrlich, es lohne sich, eine Psychologie des Kinematographen zu schreiben. (Riba 6)

Although wishing that adults would attend more soberly to the sociocultural content of the *Arabian Nights*, von Riba posits that grown readers are affected by the tales in the same way that spectators are seduced by the images projected before them in the darkened cinema. There, in the darkness, adults longing to escape the stress and monotony of modern life—"the colorless cold of everyday life"—allow themselves to be transported psychologically back to childhood by viewing the seemingly magic succession of marvelous images, which evokes the magical consciousness of childhood and its pleasure in the succession of fairy-tale images appearing before the mind's eye. That it is the sequence of moving pictures in the cinema and the serial, episodic nature of the images and stories in the *Arabian Nights* that stimulate this psychological reaction becomes evident when von Riba compares the *Kinematograph* to the *Kinodrama* and landscape film, which are certainly capable of evoking wonder in their own right, but which lack a cinematically shaped narrative and its stream of diverse and "improbable images."

Von Riba's juxtaposition of the *Arabian Nights* with the early twentieth-century experience of cinema offers another remarkable example of how writers, translators, and editors conceived of this fairy-tale collection in visual terms at the turn of the century. It also focuses our attention directly on the intersection of the *Arabian Nights* and early German film.

The Arabian Nights and Early German Film

The visual aspects highlighted in the late nineteenth- and early twentieth-century literary reception of the *Arabian Nights* are reflected in the productions of Weimar-era filmmakers who drew on the *Arabian Nights*. Perceived in visual terms and described as a visual experience comparable to that of viewing a motion picture, the *Arabian Nights* apparently presented itself as a source and narrative model for filmmakers involved in the creation of the new visual culture. Fritz Lang, Ernst Lubitsch, and Paul Leni did, in fact, create films that are informed in diverse ways by the *Arabian Nights* and inspired by the idea of its visual features and spectacular nature.

The visual dimension of the *Arabian Nights* that most obviously appealed to filmmakers was its color, which each of the literary commentators surveyed above had foregrounded in their descriptions of the collection. "Color," of course, is used metaphorically to describe the subject matter and rich descriptions in the literary text. Color refers above all to exotic sights and settings, to the fantastic objects, characters, and events, to the abundant variety of these, and to the generic diversity of the tales throughout the *Nights*. Since the primitive period in filmmaking, films had exploited the sensational—the out of the ordinary and the exotic (see

Hansen 162)—and the colorful *Arabian Nights* certainly offered filmmakers a rich treasury of fantastic and foreign settings, characters, scenes, and props. Georges Méliès's film of 1905, *Le palais des Mille et une Nuits*, which Robert Irwin has identified and described as "an opulent . . . vision of the gorgeous East" (Irwin 291), exemplifies the fit between the *Arabian Nights* and the new medium's proclivity for exotic spectacles. Lotte Reiniger's later silhouette film *Die Abenteuer des Prinzen Achmed* (1926; The Adventures of Prince Achmed) also illustrates the close ties between the spectacular and the exotic. The visual spectacle Reiniger creates from paper, scissors, and light relies almost entirely on the "colorful" lines and shapes that signal the exotic landscapes, architecture, and costumes associated with the Orient.

Costume films produced in Germany during the early years of the Weimar era continued to showcase the unusual and the exotic and in notable cases to do this by evoking the *Arabian Nights*. Ernst Lubitsch's *Sumurun* (1920; released in America in 1921 as "One Arabian Night") and Fritz Lang's *Der müde Tod* (1921; known in English as "Destiny") are both important films that incorporate exotic settings inspired by the *Nights*. Lubitsch, in fact, chose to film *Sumurun* shortly after deciding to abandon shorts and make only feature films. "The challenge of evoking the Arabian Nights on the screen," Herman G. Weinberg has noted, "was irresistible" (Weinberg 35). In her classic study of early German cinema, Lotte Eisner has observed that the many German costume films appearing between 1919 and 1924 expressed "the escapism of a poverty-stricken, disappointed nation which, moreover, had always been fond of the glitter of parades" (75). In this context it is useful to recall von Riba's emphasis on those adults who use the *Arabian Nights* and the cinema "to escape the colorless cold of everyday life." According to this early view, the exotic *Nights* and nights at the cinema provide the "color"—the "glitter," as Eisner would later call it—that compensates for a "colorless" contemporary existence.

Von Riba's brief analysis of 1913 and Eisner's argument of 1953 may or may not accurately describe the actual experience of spectators between 1919 and 1924; but these parallel views do suggest that Weimar-era filmmakers would have considered the *Arabian Nights* a useful vehicle for thematizing questions about the filmmaker's role, the public's response, and the social function of film. This would have occurred logically from considering the *Arabian Nights* in visual terms. By characterizing the *Nights* as a visual experience and equating its serial narrative with the successive flow of images in cinema, commentators at the turn of the century essentially erase the distinction between storyteller and filmmaker. The narrative art of the *Arabian Nights,* in other words, becomes identical to filmmaking, turning the filmmaker into a storyteller. And once the reader of the *Arabian Nights* is transformed into a spectator—who either derives pleasure from contemplating the colorful images (as Hesse and Hofmannsthal posited) or compensates for an impoverished, colorless reality by surrendering to the flow of colorful images (as von Riba and Eisner argue)—the *Nights* are positioned to thematize contemporary debates about the effects of film on the audience and the new medium's social function.

Early German filmmakers clearly drew on the fundamental narrative strategy of the *Arabian Nights*—the frame story and succession of stories told within it, which Thomas Elsaesser has called "the most distinctive feature of narration in Weimar films" (Elsaesser 82). Certainly there are many films utilizing a frame that do not replicate the exotic settings and subject matter of the *Arabian Nights.* And certainly the *Nights* are not the only literary model for framing and nesting narratives (83). However, films like *Destiny* and *Waxworks,* which embed a series of exotic and unusual tales within a frame story, clearly involve the *Arabian Nights* as a significant intertext. And by invoking the narrative strategy of the *Nights,* these films thematize the filmmaker's role as storyteller.

In Fritz Lang's film *Destiny,* the central figure and ultimate storyteller is Death—*Der müde Tod*—who takes the life of a young man. When the young man's fiancée pleads with Death to return her lover to the world of the living, Death offers her the chance to rekindle his extinguished light by saving another human life. Death presents the young woman—and the audience—with three tales set in distant places, including an (unspecified) "city of the faithful," Renaissance Italy, and China. He seems not to tell the stories verbally, but to set them in motion visually by lighting a candle at the beginning of each tale. All three stories end tragically, with no life capable of being saved; and each tale ends when the candle that set it in motion is extinguished. That Death's exotic stories ensue visually from the illumination of candles that he himself lights suggests that this master of light and shadow is the filmmaker himself. As Thomas Elsaesser has quipped, "in the sombre and eery fairy tale *Der müde Tod,* . . . death plays magic lanternist to the hapless bride" (149). While the film's self-reflexivity may be obvious, the intertextual connection to the *Arabian Nights* operates more subtly. Like Shahrazâd, who tells her tales night after night to defer her own execution, the figure of Death projects a series of tales in the attempt to reverse—and thus delay—the young man's inevitable death. The difference is that Shahrazâd's serial storytelling enables her to deny death and define her destiny, whereas Death's sequence of visions—and by implication the filmmaker's own moving pictures—seem powerless to derail destiny.

In Paul Leni's *Waxworks*, the filmmaker's identification with a story-telling character is even more apparent. Responding to a classified ad placed by a showman, a writer arrives at a fair and is hired to compose imaginative stories about the wax figures in the showman's *Panopticum*. The menacing wax figures include Jack the Ripper, Ivan the Terrible, and Haroun al-Rashid, the caliph of Baghdad. The writer, inspired in part by his attraction to the showman's daughter, pens a series of tales revolving around each figure, tales that begin with his written narration and then quickly continue in visual form. Quite literally the imaginative words of the writer become images seen by the film's audience, creating a metacommentary on the narrative art of filmmaking. But if *Destiny* explores the filmmaker as a failed Shahrazâd, unable to defer death through the art of narration, *Waxworks* offers a different commentary on the function of film.

The tales of tyrants embedded in *Waxworks* succeed one another chronologically, moving from Haroun al-Rashid in historically distant Baghdad to Ivan the Terrible and finally to present-day Jack the Ripper. We view this last tale as the writer's dream, which takes place at the fair and in the *Panopticum* itself. Confusing the reality of the amusement fair with the writer's nightmare, the tale ends and the writer awakens when, unable to protect the showman's daughter, he dreams that he is stabbed by Jack the Ripper. While this final tale projected by the mind of the dreaming writer threatens to erase the line between illusion and reality, in the end the tyrants paraded before our eyes seem to be simply harmless amusements confined to the sensational world of the *Panopticum*, a mere entertainment in the escapist world of the fair. The series of tales visualized for spectators by the writer and showman in the *Panopticum*—whatever threat of tyranny they may imply—are not told to defer death, as in the literary *Arabian Nights* and in *Destiny*, but to amuse a paying public in search of escape from modern reality.

To suggest that Leni's vision of the *Panopticum* offers a self-reflection of the filmmaker is not to imply that he uncritically embraces film as escapist fare for the masses. Ernst Lubitsch's costume drama *Sumurun* has been called "escapist" (Weinberg 37), but Lubitsch very clearly uses this "One Arabian Night" to reflect critically on the filmmaker and his audience (Kracauer 50). *Sumurun* does not use a frame story, but like *Waxworks* it thematizes the vision of the film's director and the gaze of the audience for whom the director makes his films. Lubitsch himself plays a hunchback/clown who is part of a traveling troupe of entertainers. Unlike *Sumurun*'s voyeuristic crowds, who are captivated by the spectacle of the troupe's public performance, Lubitsch's hunchback is depicted in a series of scenes as a secret observer of less visible realities. He observes what is obscured from public view, what transpires behind walls among the powerful. His deeper vision (in the film's final scene he appears as the lone artist with his eyes closed) enables him ultimately to avenge the tyranny of evil. The exotic settings of *Sumurun* may appeal to the masses in search of entertaining spectacles, but it is evident that Lubitsch critiques their shortsighted expectations. As his film tells us—warns us, in fact—in its opening titles: "With such a tale as this did Sheherazade beguile her angry lord."

Shahrazâd's beguiling storytelling—which resists tyranny by entertaining it—is a model for each of these directors. By amusing King Shahriyâr, Shahrazâd protects her own life and enables the survival of many others. As she herself says, "I will begin to tell a story, and it will cause the king to stop his practice, save myself, and deliver the people" (Haddawy 16). Shahrazâd's storytelling is an entertainment for its listeners, but the thousand and one nights of entertainment are also a courageous survival strategy and a pragmatic political response to social trauma and tyranny.

Much of the scholarship about Weimar cinema has grappled with its relation to contemporary society, modernity, the trauma of World War I, and Germany's sociopolitical trajectory from Romanticism to the tyranny of National Socialism (see, e.g., Kracauer; Eisner; Elsaesser 18–60). This brief essay cannot do justice to that debate or adequately explore the complex nuances in the films I have cited. However, I do think further contemplation of the role of the *Arabian Nights* in the visual culture and films of this period can help illuminate these matters. Those late nineteenth- and early twentieth-century writers, translators, and editors who conceived of the *Arabian Nights* as spectacle implicated it in contemporary discourse about visual culture, and their commentaries help us understand the *Nights*' appeal to filmmakers. Beyond its exotic subject matter and its technique of nesting a series of stories in a narrative frame, however, filmmakers responded to something even more fundamental in Shahrazâd's model of storytelling. Shahrazâd's secret struggle with tyranny and trauma, her ironic balance of entertainment with sociopolitical purpose, and her conscious manipulation of an audience seduced by amusement, made the *Arabian Nights* a perfect intertext for filmmakers who were exploring the artistic and social potential of a new medium that offered itself as entertainment for a postwar audience who faced the political challenges and consumer culture of modernity.

Conclusion

In this essay I have shown how the *Arabian Nights* entered the discourse about visual culture at the turn of the twentieth century, and how the perception of the *Nights* as a visual experience was manifested in a select set of German films from the Weimar period. There are, of course, still other connections that need to be explored and questions that need to be asked about the reception of the *Arabian Nights* in visual culture and film. For example, the "colorful" qualities that preoccupied so many commentators in their descriptions of the *Nights* need to be further considered in the context of Orientalism and its manifestation in visual culture (see Fähndrich). Similarly, the pleasure of contemplating the *Arabian Nights*—as evident in Hesse's *Bilderfreude* and in Hofmannsthal's emphasis on the intense sensual stimulation provoked when the reader's eyes encounter the "glowing eyes" of the text—needs to be further scrutinized in light of theoretical work on the "gaze" and scopophilia (see Mulvey). The eroticism inherent in the visual pleasure ascribed to the *Nights*, and the fact that the commentators and filmmakers I have examined are all men, raises questions about the role that gender plays in the visual reception of the *Arabian Nights*. Just as male editors invoked archetypal female storytellers while appropriating traditional folktales for their own collections during the transition from oral to print culture, so did male filmmakers appropriate the literary tales and narrative techniques of Shahrazâd and cast themselves as the serial storyteller during the developing years of visual culture. We might well probe not only the implications of this phenomenon but also the reception of the *Arabian Nights* by women filmmakers, in particular Lotte Reiniger's remarkable silhouette film of 1926, *Die Abenteuer des Prinzen Achmed*. The numerous film and television adaptations of the *Arabian Nights* subsequent to the Weimar era also deserve closer inspection. To what degree do these visual texts inspired by Shahrazâd's stories still rely on the ideas about the *Nights* articulated during the formative years of modern visual culture?

Certainly the perception of the *Arabian Nights* as a visual experience has been strong and persistent. Consider, in conclusion, the 1996 paperback edition of *Die schönsten Märchen aus 1001 Nacht*, a collection of radio plays by Günter Eich. In his introduction to this edition, Karl Karst takes pains to emphasize the value of Eich's radio plays—these *Hörspiele*—by underlining the primacy of aural reception in storytelling. He invokes not only the archetypal circle of children listing to stories from the *Arabian Nights* but also the early twentieth-century introduction of radio as an antidote to the decline of creative memory brought on by the culture of print (Karst 9–10). Yet it is remarkable that Karst's defense of aurality depends on visual metaphors and visual descriptions of the *Arabian Nights*. His very first sentence portrays the *Nights* as a visual stimulus: "There they sat and listened: the mother read while the children's eyes were kept busy visualizing Shahrazâd's sparkling gems." ("Da saßen sie also und hörten zu: Die Mutter las, während die Kinder alle Augen voll zu tun hatten, sich die funkelnden Edelsteine Shehrezáds . . . auszumalen."). When he quotes Hesse's description of the *Nights* as "the richest picture book in the world," he quickly qualifies the analogy by asserting, "A picture book for the imagination, not for eye sight" ("Ein Bilderbuch der Imagination, keines der Augen-Sicht") (Karst 9). Karst's struggle to tame these metaphors reveals just how deeply ingrained the image of the *Arabian Nights* as a visual experience has become. We need only look at the seductive photograph decorating the front cover of this book of German radio plays, where a colorful and richly bejeweled young woman of the Orient, her hands modestly covering nearly all her face, meets our own gaze by staring out at us with a single open eye.

WORKS CITED

Caracciolo, Peter L. "Introduction: Such a Store House of Ingenious Fiction and of Splendid Imagery." *The Arabian Nights in English Literature: Studies in the Reception of The Thousand and One Nights into British Culture*. Ed. P. L. Caracciolo. London: Macmillan, 1988. 1–80.

Duden: Das große Fremdwörterbuch: Herkunft und Bedeutung der Fremdwörter. Mannheim: Dudenverlag, 1994.

Eisner, Lotte H. *The Haunted Screen: Expressionism in the German Cinema and the Influence of Max Reinhardt*. Trans. Roger Greaves. Berkeley: U of California P, 1969.

Elsaesser, Thomas. *Weimar Cinema and After: Germany's Historical Imaginary*. London: Routledge, 2000.

Fähndrich, Hartmut. "Viewing the Orient and Translating Its Literature in the Shadow of The Arabian Nights." *Yearbook of Comparative and General Literature* 48 (2000): 95–106.

Greve, Felix P., ed. *Die Erzählungen aus den tausendundein Nächten: Vollständige deutsche Ausgabe auf Grund der Burton'schen Ausgabe*. 12 vols. Leipzig: Insel, 1907–8.

Grimm, Albert Ludwig. *Märchen der Tausend und einen Nacht für die Jugend bearbeitet*. Neunte durchgesehene Auflage mit acht in Chromo-Lichtdruck ausgeführten Bildern nach Original-Aquarellen von F. Simm. Leipzig: Gebhardt, [1889].

Haddawy, Husain, trans. *The Arabian Nights.* New York: Norton, 1995.

Hansen, Miriam. "Early Silent Cinema: Whose Public Sphere?" *New German Critique* 29 (1983): 147–84.

Henning, Max. *Tausend und eine Nacht.* 8 vols. Leipzig: Reclam, 1895–99.

Hesse, Hermann. *Gesammelte Werke.* Ed. Volker Michels. 12 vols. Frankfurt: Suhrkamp, 1970.

Hofmannsthal, Hugo von. "Tausend und eine Nacht." *Gesammelte Werke.* Vol. 3. Berlin: S. Fischer, 1924. 101–6.

Irwin, Robert. *The Arabian Nights: A Companion.* London: Penguin, 1994.

Karst, Karl, ed. *Die schönsten Märchen aus 1001 Nacht von Günter Eich.* Frankfurt: Insel, 1996.

Köhler, Wolfgang. *Hugo von Hofmannsthal und Tausendundeine Nacht: Untersuchungen zur Rezeption des Orients im epischen und essayistischen Werk mit einem einleitenden Überblick über den Einfluß von Tausenduneine Nacht auf die deutsche Literatur.* Berne: Lang, 1972.

Kracauer, Siegfried. *From Caligari to Hitler: A Psychological History of the German Film.* Princeton: Princeton UP, 1974.

Lang, Fritz. *Destiny (Der müde Tod).* Screenplay by Thea von Harbou. Directed by Fritz Lang. 1921. DVD. Image Entertainment, 2000.

Leni, Paul. *Waxworks (Das Wachsfigurenkabinett).* Screenplay by Henrik Galeen. Directed by Paul Leni. 1924. DVD. Kino International, 2002.

Littmann, Enno, ed. *Die Erzählungen aus den Tausendundein Nächten: Vollständige deutsche Ausgabe zum ersten Mal nach dem arabischen Urtext der Calcuttaer Ausgabe vom Jahre 1839 übertragen.* 6 vols. Leipzig: Insel, 1921–28.

———. *Tausendundeine Nacht in der arabischen Literatur.* Tübingen: J. C. B. Mohr, 1923.

Lubitsch, Ernst. *One Arabian Night (Sumurun).* Screenplay by Hans Kraly. Directed by Ernst Lubitsch. 1920. VHS. Video Yesteryear, 1985.

Mulvey, Laura. "Visual Pleasure and Narrative Cinema." *Visual and Other Pleasures.* London: Macmillan, 1989. 14–26.

Oxford English Dictionary, The Compact Edition. Oxford: Oxford UP, 1971.

Pichler, Theodor von. *Sechs Märchen aus Tausend und eine Nacht für die Jugend bearbeitet mit 6 Transparent-Verwandlungsbildern.* Stuttgart: Weise, 1880.

Reiniger, Lotte. *The Adventures of Prince Achmed (Die Abenteuer des Prinzen Achmed).* Directed by Lotte Reiniger, 1926. VHS. Milestone, 2001.

Riba, Carl Theodor von, trans. *Die Liebesgeschichten des Orients aus den tausend Nächten und der einen Nacht.* Leipzig: Borngräber, [1913].

Ries, Hans. *Illustration und Illustratoren des Kinder-und Jugendbuchs im deutschsprachigen Raum 1871–1914.* Osnabrück: Wenner, 1992.

Weinberg, Herman G. *The Lubitsch Touch: A Critical Study.* New York: Dover, 1977.

15

Shahrazâd Is One of Us: Practical Narrative, Theoretical Discussion, and Feminist Discourse

Susanne Enderwitz

Setting out to investigate the frame story of the *Nights* and its impact on Eastern and Western literature, I was unaware of the wealth of studies that have been published. They range from strictly philological research to postmodern literary studies. The former often include considerable reservations about the latter and their seemingly inflated interpretations of details. For this reason, I have largely restricted myself to reconsidering previous theses and theories and will regroup different approaches as to content, form, or both while focusing on Shahrazâd's different roles as "heroine," "narrator," and "woman."

Introduction

"Your name's really Sherazade?" "Yes." "Really? It's . . . it's so . . . How can I put it? You know who Sheherazade was?" "Yes." "And that doesn't mean anything to you?" "No." "You think you can be called Sherazade, just like that? . . ." "No idea." He looked at her, standing the other side of the high, round counter at the fast-food, unable to believe his eyes. "And why not Aziyade?" "Who's that?" "A beautiful Turkish woman from Istanbul who Pierre Loti was in love with, a hundred years ago." "Pierre Loti I've heard of. Not Aziyade." ". . . Aziyade belonged to the harem of an old Turk. She was a young Circassian slave, converted to Islam." "Why you telling me about this woman? She's got nothing to do with me." "She had green eyes, like you." "That's no reason." Sherazade was drinking her Coke out of the can.

> She wasn't listening any more. Julien Desrosiers went back to reading the small ads in *Libération.*" (Sebbar 1–2)

Shahrazâd seems to be common property for Arabs and Europeans, natives and migrants, the educated and the uneducated alike. Beyond the diffusion of Shahrazâd's own story and the repertoire of her stories into many cultures, there is also evidence for their origins in many cultures. The collection known as *Thousand and One Nights* is the result of a "cultural and ethnic melting process" (Walther 12), in which Indian and Persian elements blend (not to mention Greek, Arab, and Turkish). Against this multinational backdrop, the principle of intertwined stories corresponds to Arab concepts of *adab* by underlining the power of the word and of brilliant speech. Shahrazâd herself is a cultural amalgam, for she speaks the Arabic language, bears a Persian name (meaning "of noble appearance and/or origin"), and employs an Indian narrative mode, the frame-story device. Moreover, it has repeatedly been pointed out that, long before Galland's French translation of the *Nights* started its triumphant march through the Western world, its forerunners had already stimulated European and Judeo-Christian culture. The *Sindbad* cycle has been compared to Homer's *Odyssey*, and Shahrazâd has been considered—and refuted—to be a sister of the biblical Esther (De Goeje; Cosquin), while the opening story of the two kings Shahriyâr and Shâhzamân has been believed a variation of paradise lost and regained (Ghazoul 18).

Whatever common grounds the *Nights* and the foundation myths of Judeo-Christian culture may have, there is no doubt that before they were even translated into French, English, and German, the *Nights* made their mark on European literature, in particular on the literature of Renaissance Italy (Walther 17; Littmann 359). In Europe and America as well as in the Near East, writers in the twentieth century (in fact more so than ever) still used the characters of Shahrazâd's tales and her narrative mode as models for their own writings. With this in mind, Fedwa Malti-Douglas states: "Were the Arabic Shahrazad to awaken, like some fairy tale princess, centuries after she first wove the stories in the *Thousand and One Nights*, she would undoubtedly be surprised by her numerous literary transformations" ("Shahrazad Feminist" 40). Robert Irwin states that it is probably easier to specify the few Western or non-Arab authors who were not affected by the *Nights* (Irwin 358; Pinault 65–66) than to present a comprehensive list of those who were—this list ranging from Johann Wolfgang von Goethe, Sir Walter Scott, and William Thackeray through Gustave

Flaubert, Stendhal, and Gérard de Nerval to H. P. Lovecraft, John Barth, and A. S. Byatt, Jorge Luis Borges, and Salman Rushdie. Similarly, many an Arab writer, if only in the second part of the twentieth century, has adapted the tradition of the *Nights* for his or her own literary work. To mention but a few: Tâhâ Husain, Tawfîq al-Hakîm and Naguib Mahfouz, Emil Habibi and Jabra Ibrahim Jabra, Idwâr al-Kharrât and Jamâl al-Ghitânî, Ilyas Khouri or Nawâl al-Sa'dâwî, as well as francophone North African writers like Tahar Ben Jelloun or Leila Sebbar. All of them have contributed to "making the medieval *Alf layla wa-layla* a vital and influential part of the Arab literary heritage today" (Pinault 76).

The Heroine

What is true for the whole corpus of the *Nights* is certainly true for the frame story, which, due to Shahrazâd's preeminent role, will be the main point of reference for my essay. "The frame story of the *Thousand and One Nights*—that is, the work's prologue and epilogue, as they are usually termed—is without doubt one of the most powerful narratives in world literature" (Malti-Douglas, *Woman's Body* 11), and it stands out by its special status. In the frame story, contrary to the *Nights* themselves, the voice of the narrator is not Shahrazâd's voice; instead, Shahrazâd is the heroine of the text, or of parts of it. At the same time the frame story is what Eva Sallis has called the "signature story" for all the stories of the *Nights*: "It is Sheherazade's life and narrative power which are remembered long after we become hazy about the myriad details of the contents" (*Looking Glass* 87).

But Shahrazâd in her role as a woman, a wife, a narrator, and, in the epilogue, a mother, is not only the first person one remembers when talking about the *Nights*, she is also the first character to appear in the earliest preserved information about the *Nights*. This information is given in various Arabic sources of the ninth and tenth centuries. The earliest is a ninth-century paper fragment of a text called "A Book Containing Tales of a Thousand Nights" (*kitâb fîhi hadîth alf layla*), representing the title page and an opening page to a storytelling session between Dînâzâd (Dunyâzâd) and, we assume, Shîrâzâd (Shahrazâd) (Abbott 152–53). Dating from the tenth century, an important reference is listed in the historical work *Murûj al-dhahab* (*Meadows of Gold*) by al-Mas'ûdî (d. 956), and a more detailed notice in the *Fihrist* (Catalogue) of Ibn al-Nadîm (written 987). There are only a few other records or references to the *Nights* that can be dated to before the first extant manuscripts (Sallis, *Looking Glass* 19). The full version of the prologue that became the basis for most of the printed versions—in spite of its comparatively recent date—still bears a logical resemblance to the early version mentioned above (Grotzfeld, *Erzählungen* 11–49; Walther 11–20).

The first part of the frame story, the prologue, runs as follows: Shahriyâr, the Sasanid king of the islands of India and China, longs to see his brother, Shahzamân, the king of Samarkand of the Persians whom he has not seen for many years. The latter, about to fulfill his brother's wish of a visit, surprises his wife enjoying herself with a black slave. Overwhelmed by pain, he kills both of them and proceeds to visit Shahriyâr. Once there, he discovers that his brother's wife also betrays her husband with a black slave. He eventually reveals this fact to his older brother, and the two set out on a journey, looking for someone even more unfortunate than themselves. On the voyage, both brothers are blackmailed into sexual intercourse by a young woman who has been locked up by a demon (*'ifrît*) who kidnapped her on her wedding night. From this interlude they deduce that no woman can be trusted. Shahriyâr returns to his kingdom, has his wife and her black lover killed, and begins his one-night stands with virgins whom he executes after the evening's entertainment. At this point, the highly educated Shahrazâd enters the scene as a vizier's daughter determined to offer herself as a new bride to the king. While her father tries in vain to discourage her, Shahrazâd replies that "either she would ransom the daughters of the people, or she would live" (Richard Burton, in his translation, observes that Shahrazâd is proposing to "Judith" the king). She joins the king, and when the night falls, she sends for her sister, Dunyazâd. With her sister's help, she recounts stories that conveniently stretch over the break of the day, and hence, keeps the king in suspense and herself alive (Malti-Douglas, "Shahrazad Feminist" 41–42; Sallis, "Sheherazade" 153–54).

The second part of the frame story, the epilogue or "closure" (Malti-Douglas, *Woman's Body* 25), is shorter and various versions exist. The version that made its way into the most widely spread editions contains the following: at the end of the storytelling cycle, the readers and/or listeners—together with the king—discover that Shahrazâd has given birth to three sons. The king spares her life, not only because she has given birth to his children who would otherwise lose their mother, but also because he has fallen in love with her for her purity, virtue, and piety. The city is lavishly decorated, marriage takes place, and they live happily together until they die. This version is basically identical with the account by Ibn al-Nadîm but differs from it with regard to an important detail. In Ibn al-Nadîm's summary, Shahrazâd tells her stories until she has given birth to one child only and is spared because of her motherhood. For Heinz and Sophia Grotzfeld, this conclusion, which offers a strong argument in favor of granting her pardon, seems to be closer to the unknown original text than other versions. In fact, the argument runs along the lines of motherhood itself, regardless of the additional number of children. Therefore, the Grotzfelds maintain that once the title *A Thousand and One Nights* was accepted, the links between the telling of stories and giving birth (as two parallel acts of procreation) were lost. Instead the *Nights* were just equated with the span of time it takes to give birth to three children successively, or vice versa. This is a rather more prosaic view of the issue, according to which the numbers 1,000 and 3 ruled out the inherent logic of the original story. At least one of the later compilers appears to have sensed a lack of motivation behind the number of nights and the number of children presented. In his version, perhaps with a parodistic undertone, the king is so bored at the end of the *Nights* by the sheer number of stories that he intends to have Shahrazâd executed, whereupon she presents her three sons and is saved. In another version, Shahrazâd's stories themselves, without the interference of motherhood, serve to heal the king from his hatred of women by confronting him with his own deeds. This helps him to gain the new insight that not all women are alike, as he had deduced from his experiences. After all, it depends on the version whether Shahrazâd's skillfulness as a storyteller or her biological faculties are highlighted or disregarded (Grotzfeld, *Erzählungen* 60–61; Grotzfeld, "Neglected Conclusions" 59–68).

Following the tremendous success of the *Nights* in Europe, the first author to rewrite the frame story with regard to its epilogue was Edgar Allan Poe in "The Thousand and Second Night" (1845). Malti-Douglas comments on the fact that in Poe's sardonic version Shahrazâd is killed at the end of the *Nights* by interpreting this as an act of male vengeance on female talent in storytelling: Shahrazâd's "power over words and her perceived ability to control discourse have provoked the envy of male writers from Edgar Allan Poe to John Barth" (*Woman's Body* 11). Leaving aside Malti-Douglas's polemical retaliation against misogynist adaptations, Poe's extension of the thousand and one nights by an additional night, which he pretends to have read in a forgotten manuscript of the ancient book "Isitsöornot," is a highly complex reflection of the role of women in literature and history. In this little piece Poe labeled a "grotesque," Shahrazâd the heroine loses within a single night all the favors Shahrazâd the narrator had gained from the king in a thousand and one nights, and she does so by virtue of her wit and self-assurance, not by her lack of them. Her wit and self-assurance place her ahead of all other women, in particular of the women of later, or more "advanced" ages. At the same time these qualities make the king suspicious of Shahrazâd's "female" qualities, that is, her power to divert his mind from his daily duties.

In her thousand and second night, Shahrazâd displays an enlightened attitude vis-à-vis the royal despot. This eventually leads to her execution since she transgresses the limits set for any woman. Referring to an old saying that reality in its miraculousness even surpasses invention, Shahrazâd as an enthusiast of modern technology narrates a whole range of miracles in her additional night that Poe's contemporary readers would easily identify as engines, telegraphs, or photomechanical devices. This not being enough, Shahrazâd, with her feminist awareness, turns upon her fellow women and satirically spreads out the follies of contemporary fashion, which she finds neither healthy nor aesthetically convincing. In the very last of her stories, a misguided spirit—as often before—turns up, this time, however, in the shape of:

> "A crotchet," said Scheherezade. "One of the evil genii who are perpetually upon the watch to inflict ill, has put it into the heads of these accomplished ladies that the thing which we describe as personal beauty, consists altogether in the protuberance of the region which lies not very far below the small of the back. Perfection of loveliness, they say, is in the direct ratio of the extent of this hump. Having been long possessed of this idea, and bolsters being cheap in that country, the days have long gone by since it was possible to distinguish a woman from a dromedary."

This very moment, when Shahrazâd steps out of her role as a fancy narrator and proves to be a rational being showing insight into the human nature and ridiculing female vanity, seals her fate as the heroine of the *Nights*. Shahriyâr is challenged in both his roles as a king and a man by Shahrazâd's performance, for it mirrors him as an unenlightened despot on the one hand and a thoughtless consumer on the other. Therefore the king, in order to save his face, finds himself immediately inclined to sacrifice Shahrazâd's life:

> "Stop!" said the king, "I can't stand that, and I won't. You have already given me a dreadful headache with your lies. The day, too, I perceive, is beginning

to break. How long have we been married?—my conscience is getting to be troublesome again. And then that dromedary touch—do you take me for a fool? Upon the whole you might as well get up and be throttled." (98–101)

Poe drops the prologue of the *Nights* completely and endows the epilogue with a likewise complete new meaning, as he focuses on Shahrazâd's orientation toward a man-made world. His heroine is the narrator of the *Nights*, only in this case she comes along with good news for mankind's inventive spirit instead of the encroachments of anachronistic evil spirits upon the world. However, the woman demanding her fair share in the process of progress is pushed even further back than ever before. Technological progress and the emancipation of mankind do not go well together. Even more than in former times, a woman of the modern world is defined by her role to amuse.

The Narrator

Poe equips Shahrazâd with a vision of the achievements of nineteenth-century technology and science, while the king remains medieval in his predilection for miracles. John Barth, for his part, endows Shahrazâd—whom he names "Sherry"—with a twentieth-century American touch, transforming her into "an undergraduate arts-and-sciences major at Banu Sasan University. Besides being Homecoming Queen, valedictorian-elect, and a four-letter varsity athlete, she had a private library of a thousand volumes and the highest average in the history of the campus" (13). In contrast to Poe, Barth simply reconstructs the story, fitting it into the circumstances of his own cultural setting, and therefore Shahrazâd ends up in her well-known destiny as a mother of three children and wife of Shahriyâr. Analogies with other writers are not found in the plot but elsewhere, especially in the structure of Barth's narrative. His multidimensional and polyphonous rewriting of the story comes close to more recent adaptations in Arabic, themselves more influenced by the form of Shahrazâd's narrative than by its content or her personality.

Searching for an indigenous Arabic narrative or for specific characteristics defining Arabic literature, a number of contemporary Arab authors are returning to their own cultural heritage in general and to the *Nights* in particular (Pflitsch 59). Whereas in 1934, 1936, and 1943 Tawfîq al-Hakîm and Tâhâ Husayn depicted Shahrazâd as a symbol for earthbound baseness, unbound creative fantasy, and a prudent advocate of humaneness (Walther 162–63), respectively, writers of the younger generations rather identify with Shahrazâd's narrative mode. Here, they find parallels to literary modernity and set out to revitalize it in a "postmodern" or "postmahfouzian" manner. Under the label of "radical constructivism" their compositions are characterized by an awareness not only of the constructedness of literature but of reality itself or, in short, of the double constructedness of reality (Pflitsch 62).

Even so, the connection between Shahrazâd the heroine and Shahrazâd the narrator, between the frame and the enframed stories, remains a controversial issue. While the predominance of the frame story over the ensuing narrative is often taken more or less for granted, this evaluation does not apply to the dependency of the stories on the frame. At the same time, even the frame story's unity is under discussion, as it seems to be made up "from bits and pieces" (Gerhardt 398). Based on Emmanuel Cosquin's research, the Grotzfelds distinguish three different parts of even the prologue: (a) the story of a husband who, being desperate about the infidelity of his wife, finds solace in the fact that a high-ranking person suffers the same fate; (b) the story of a superhuman being, whose wife or captive successively manages to seduce other men, even though he has imprisoned her; and (c) the story of a young woman who escapes from great danger threatening herself, her father, or both, by virtue of gaining time through only storytelling. To this tripartite introduction the epilogue as the fourth part of the frame may be added (Grotzfeld, *Erzählungen* 50–51). Other researchers detect four basically independent stories in the prologue (Ghazoul 18–19) or six in the whole frame (Malti-Douglas, *Woman's Body* 14).

As has been shown, the prologue displays two interrelated but at the same time independent focuses, Shahrazâd and Shahriyâr, turning it into an arabesque, "a play with symmetry emerging from the tension," so typical a form of the *Nights* in general (Karahasan 60). Therefore, not only the unity of the frame story but also its main protagonist is called into question. Peter Heath, for instance, vigorously claims that the readers' fascination with Shahrazâd should not blind them to the fact that by the standards of the romantic genre it is not she but King Shahriyâr who is the tale's main protagonist. In contrast to the traditional interpretation of the story, he maintains that the king is the one tested by Fate and who subsequently fails the test, degrades love, is unfaithful himself, acts inhumanely, courts death—"and this being romance, where unfaithful lovers meet fitting ends, he is in terrible danger" (18–19). In Heath's view, the issue at stake is indeed Shahrazâd's life, but also that of Shahriyâr. Besides, the central idea is now the restoration of the king's sound perception both of himself and of women. Implicitly, the most commonly accepted ending is also the *Nights'* main objective: a prosperous people, a happy couple, and healthy progeny.

With all these nuances in mind, most scholars ultimately agree about the cohesiveness of the frame story and Shahrazâd's central position in it. The Shahrazâd story "is all that a framing should be" (Gerhardt 398), as it functions as an "ever flexible border" (Naddaf 5) and has "endured from a time when the enframed stories are pure speculation" (Sallis, "Sheherazade" 154). It is a story capable of integrating other stories whatever their plot may be. At this point, however, a second fundamental objection against the unity of the *Nights* is raised. Some scholars discern a certain arbitrariness of the frame with regard to what follows. First, despite the basic structure of the *Nights* according to the old institution of *samar* (nightly entertainment), the manuscripts vary as to whether the compilers separate episodes into nights through to the end and whether the flow of stories is interrupted by the characters of the frame from time to time (Gerhardt 398–99). Second, the (psycho)logical unity of the frame and the stories is important. Mia Gerhardt denies this unity by arguing that the compilers did not strive to interrelate the two or to keep alive the reader's interest in the framing story itself. As she maintains, the readers, like the compilers, gradually forget Shahrazâd and her plight, and concentrate all their attention upon the stories she tells. Moreover, Gerhardt dismisses any possible interrelation, claiming that even the very first story ("The Merchant and the Jinni") introduces the theme of wicked wives, which renders it an unsuitable or, in the case of a wife having intercourse with a black slave, even tactless choice by a woman in such a dangerous situation as Shahrazâd's (399–400). This criticism, however, is contested by Muhsin Mahdi (131–34), Dzevad Karahasan (65–66), and Ferial Ghazoul, all of whom meticulously argue in favor of the aptness of exactly this story for the first night Shahrazâd and Shahriyâr spend together. Taking this story as a starting point, but without confining themselves to it, they detect a whole range of subtle messages beyond just the repetition of the king's experiences, which are not wasted upon him. As a matter of fact, Shahrazâd's successful survival night after night strongly supports this thesis as well as Malti-Douglas's remark that Shahrazâd is quite present as a narrator, appearing at least at the beginning and end of every night (*Woman's Body* 14).

The Woman

From a feminist point of view, Shahrazâd's inclination to include all kinds of stories should not be discarded at all as the indifferent attitude of the compilers; on the contrary, it should be appreciated as the integrative ability of a woman. "Shahrazad is characterized by nothing if not her fertility—both narrative and otherwise—and it is a tribute to her legacy of potentially infinite narrative generation that the text possesses an ability, indeed a willingness, to accommodate ultimately any tale between its ever-flexible borders, in the interest of maintaining narrative variety" (Naddaf 5). Other writers share this equation of biological and mental procreation, albeit with modifications. For Ghazoul, a master-slave dialectic seems at work, when Shahrazâd, embodying the very principle of female vulnerability, succeeds vis-à-vis her virile Oriental despot in turning women from objects of sex into objects of fantasy (23–24). For Paul Auster, in a rather sophisticated argument, Shahrazâd's procreative abilities appear to be justified mainly through the proof of her talent in telling stories of life and death. Shahrazâd "has borne the king three sons. Again, the lesson is made clear. A voice that speaks, a woman's voice that speaks, a voice that speaks stories of life and death, has the power to give life" (153). Still another author, Dzevad Karahasan, links being a female to fundamental creative powers, when he states: "It is my firm belief that this book has been told by a woman, maybe not a single one, but several, whose stories, over the years, have harmoniously blended." This is not due, in his view, to the meandering mode of Shahrazâd's narration or other techniques of a so-called feminine speech, like decentrism, avoidance of clear-cut definitions, paraphrases of the subject, and such, but to easily overlooked details of observation like the one "more visible than a banner and more beautiful than a red camel." Comparisons like these happen to enter literature, according to Karahasan, only by way of "accident"; they are spontaneous creations, having escaped "male" (self-)censorship that corresponds with the ruling canon (53).

We may wonder whether Karahasan is familiar with theories of oral transmission, but something else seems to be of greater importance here. Most scholars, indeed, attribute not only Shahrazâd's way of storytelling but also her outlook in general to intentions traditionally linked to female rather than male characters in literature. These intentions or, better perhaps, the raison d'être of Shahrazâd's storytelling, have been identified as belonging to the scheme of time-gaining, a therapeutic or didactic quest, and a complex web of "desire."[1] Shahrazâd's struggle to gain time and to instruct the king do not exclude each other. In consequence, Heath laconically writes: "[O]ne should remember that [Shahrazâd's] main purpose with this strategy [of daily storytelling] is not procrastination. This could not be so; even she would eventually run out of stories. On the contrary, Shahrazad is narrating tales primarily to instruct the king" (18; cf. Bettelheim 87). So we have a clear case of instruction by storytelling. It is again Karahasan who reminds us of the peculiar qualities of storytelling as opposed to other kinds of instruction: "A speech in a way of a theologian or philosopher would have been useless [for Shahriyâr]. . . . He was in need of a knowledge that is supplied only by experience and literature, a knowledge comprising human totality, body, soul, sentiment. . . . Therefore, Shahrazad instructs by way of narration." (64).

Malti-Douglas, in turn, dismisses both ways of understanding Shahrazâd's situation, as both the procrastination- and the healing-scheme identify Shahrazâd with speech. She argues that "[a]ll these views of Shahrazad and the frame have one overriding characteristic in common: they are prefeminist and pregender conscious, in the intellectual, not the chronological sense" (*Woman's Word* 13). Like others mentioned above, Malti-Douglas postulates a relation between femininity and discourse, stating that Shahrazâd shifts the problem of desire, the realm of Shahriyâr's trauma, to the seemingly more distant and more malleable world of the text. However, in picking up the catchword "desire," Malti-Douglas envisages not childbearing but sexuality.

> [Shahrazâd's] storytelling teaches a new type of desire, a desire that continues from night to night, a desire whose interest does not fall and which can, therefore, leap the intervening days. In sexual terms, this is a replacement of an immature male pattern of excitement, satisfaction, and termination with what can be called a more classically female pattern of extended and continuous desire and pleasure. Of course, it is this extension of desire through time that permits the forging of relationships, and with it the nonexploitive approach to sexuality. (*Woman's Body* 22)

While a reconciliation of the sexes is achieved, it runs along traditional lines. From the epilogue we learn that the king has fallen in love with Shahrazâd during the period of three years that has meanwhile elapsed; nevertheless, it is to her and our relief that she is able to reassure herself with her three sons, just in case the king still bears traces of his former character. In one of the epilogue's versions the king, as a proof of his utmost appreciation of Shahrazâd's tales, gives an order to have them writ-ten down. Desire may be one of the catchwords for psychoanalytically based studies; "literature" is the one for postmodern-oriented theorists. Shahrazâd has, indeed, narrated the stories, but Shahriyâr is the one to preserve them, as he has the male command over the authority and the permanence of the written word. "In the process, body has been trans-muted into word and back into body. Corporeality is the final word, as Shahrazad relinquishes her role of narrator for that of perfect woman: mother and lover" (Malti-Douglas, *Woman's Body* 28).

Here, in the epilogue, we have the starting point for a rewriting of Shahrazâd's story, Arab and other. In the early 1980s, Ethel Johnston Phelps published a new version of the story, her protagonists being a cruel old king and a versatile young Shahrazâd. Discontent with the traditional ending, she suggested another one. In her version, at the eventual death of the king (sultan), Shahrazâd was free to do "what any clever storyteller would do: Using her earlier education provided by the best tutors, she of course wrote down for posterity a more polished version of her one thou-sand and one tales" (173). But the American feminist Phelps was not alone in pointing out the fact that Shahrazâd stands for oral transmission, which is fugitive by definition, as the narrative is caught in space and time, de-pends on spontaneous performance, and lacks the authority of the written word. Led by the same discontent with the epilogue, Assia Djebar put for-ward a question, which has been picked up by many literary critics: "After all, had Shéhérezade not been narrating every night until dawn, but written, would she have killed the sultan?"

Djebar's modern Shahrazâd in *Ombre sultane* distinguishes herself more than any other from the original, including the protagonist of Leila Sebbar's *Sherazade*, a novel that confronts the reader with the identity search of a young woman from the "beurs"-milieu in Paris. Somewhat au-tobiographically, Djebar's heroine, Isma, comes from a privileged family and receives her education in France. There, she marries a fellow Algerian with whom she has a daughter. Seeking divorce, she comes into contact with her husband's second wife, Hajila, as she makes use of the traditional prerogative of the queen, that is, to choose her successor. Hajila, in con-trast to Isma, comes from a traditional background, in which female edu-cation is not regarded as a major issue. The (nameless) husband loses his impotence, which he has suffered from during the last years with Isma, and enjoys his conjugal rights in a way that may almost be regarded as rape. When Hajila sees Isma going around unveiled, she starts to secretly leave the house, but her husband beats her up and puts her under guard. Hajila, desperate because she is the victim of his violence, tries to kill herself but only loses her unborn child. The same day, Isma leaves the city to go live with her daughter in the place she has come from. For Djebar, reconciliation between the sexes is impossible to achieve, either with or without children. On the contrary, she pleads for solidarity among women in order to overcome male predominance. Isma "shadows" Hajila as she watches over her—but does not Hajila, too, "shadow" Isma by helping her to free herself from the "sultan"?

One cannot, however, speak about Djebar's novel without mentioning the second person who plays a key role in Shahrazâd's own story, in addition to the king's: Dunyâzâd, Shahrazâd's little sister. In the original plot, when alone with the king, Shahrazâd sends for Dunyâzâd in order to bid her farewell. From that moment on, Dunyâzâd serves as Shahrazâd's companion during the (roughly) three years of the *Nights*, but her real importance lies in her instigation of the storytelling. She is the one who raises the king's interest and keeps it alive by urging Shahrazâd to tell a story, by commenting upon it, and by interrupting it at the end of the night. The manuscripts of the *Nights* reflect her role in one of two ways, either by omitting her completely in the epilogue or by granting her an almost equal footing with Shahrazâd: in a long version of the epilogue she is married to Shahzamân, Shahriyâr's younger brother. Modern writers have felt that the character of Dunyâzâd contains a wealth of meanings and have made her a heroine in her own right. In Barth's *Dunyazadiad* (which turns her story into a "classical" one by the ending -iad, but at the same time Americanizes her name into "Doony," an equivalent to his "Sherry") she is the real narrator who tells her own and her sister's story to Shahzamân on their wedding night, whereas Shahrazâd has received all her stories from a jinni (who is none other than the author himself). In May Telmissany's *Dunyazad*, the heroine is a stillborn child of that name, whose only resemblance to her namesake is the fact that her death causes other people to tell their stories. But Djebar's novel is distinct. Shahrazâd is not a plagiarist, and Dunyâzâd does not serve merely as a catalyst. On the contrary, we learn that the privileged and emancipated Shahrazâd, who has been educated according to Western cultural standards, cannot free herself as long as the poor, uneducated, and veiled Dunyâzâd in her traditional setting remains in subjugation or, from a slightly different perspective, that the freedom of the former is at the expense of the latter. In aesthetical as well as in gender and political terms, Djebar's modern version of the two sisters' story is the most advanced and consequent: decentrist, feminist, and antieurocentrist.

NOTE

1. Desire as the main motive behind the actions taken by the characters in the *Nights* has been singled out, first of all, by writers like André Miquel, Edgar Weber, and Jamel Eddine Bencheikh, all of whom belong to the "French"—Lacan-inspired—school.

WORKS CITED

Abbott, Nabia. "A Ninth-Century Fragment of the 'Thousand Nights': New Light on the Early History of the Arabian Nights." *Journal of Near Eastern Studies* 8 (1949): 129–64.

Auster, Paul. *The Invention of Solitude.* London: Penguin, 1992.

Barth, John. "Dunyazadiad." *Chimera.* Boston: Houghton, 2001.

Bencheikh, Jamel Eddine. *Les Mille et une Nuits ou la parole prisonnière.* Paris: Gallimard, 1988.

Bettelheim, Bruno. *The Uses of Enchantment: The Meaning and Importance of Fairy Tales.* New York: Vintage, 1977.

Cosquin, Emmanuel. "Le prologue-cadre des Mille et une Nuits." *Revue Biblique* 6 (1909): 7–49. Also in *Études folkloriques.* Paris: Édouard Champion, 1922. 265–347.

De Goeje, Michael J. "De arabische nachtvertellingen." *De Gids* 50 (1886): 385–413.

Djebar, Assia. *Ombre sultane.* Paris: J. C. Lattès, 1987.

Gerhardt, Mia. *The Art of Story-Telling: A Literary Study of the Thousand and One Nights.* Leiden: Brill, 1963.

Ghazoul, Ferial. *Nocturnal Poetics: The Arabian Nights in Comparative Context.* Cairo: American UP, 1996.

Grotzfeld, Heinz. "Neglected Conclusions of the Arabian Nights: Gleanings in Forgotten and Overlooked Recensions." *Journal of Arabic Literature* 16 (1985): 73–87.

———, and Sophia Grotzfeld. *Die Erzählungen aus "Tausendundeiner Nacht."* Darmstadt: Wissenschaftliche Buchgesellschaft, 1984.

Heath, Peter. "Romance as Genre in 'The Thousand and One Nights.'" *Journal of Arabic Literature* 18 (1987): 1–21; 19 (1988): 1–26.

Irwin, Robert. *Die Welt von Tausendundeiner Nacht.* Frankfurt and Leipzig: Insel, 1997.

Karahasan, Dzevad. *Das Buch der Gärten: Grenzgänge zwischen Islam und Christentum.* Frankfurt and Leipzig: Insel, 2002.

Littmann, Enno. "Alf layla wa-layla." *The Encyclopaedia of Islam.* Vol. 1. Leiden: Brill, 1960. 358–64.

Mahdi, Muhsin. *The Thousand and One Nights (Alf Layla wa-Layla): From the Earliest Known Sources.* Vol. 3. Leiden: Brill, 1994.

Malti-Douglas, Fedwa. "Shahrazad Feminist." *The Thousand and One Nights in Arabic Literature and Society.* Ed. Richard G. Hovannisian and Georges Sabagh. Cambridge: Cambridge UP, 1997. 40–55.

———. *Woman's Body, Woman's Word: Gender and Discourse in Arabo-Islamic Writing.* Princeton: Princeton UP, 1992.

Miquel, André. *Sept contes des Mille et une Nuits, ou Il n'y a pas de contes innocents.* Paris: Sindbad, 1981.

Naddaf, Sandra. *Arabesque: Narrative Structure and the Aesthetics of Repetition in the 1001 Nights.* Evanston: Northwestern UP, 1991.

Pflitsch, Andreas. "Konstruierte Wirklichkeiten: Die zeitgenössische arabische Literatur, der radikale Konstruktivismus und die Erzählungen aus 1001 Nacht." *Understanding Near Eastern Literatures: A Spectrum of Interdisciplinary Approaches.* Ed. Verena Klemm and Beatrice Gruendler. Wiesbaden: Reichert, 2000. 59–71.

Phelps, Ethel Johnston. *The Maid of the North: Feminist Folk Tales from around the World.* New York: Holt, 1982.

Pinault, David. "Alf layla wa-layla." *Encyclopedia of Arabic Literature.* Ed. Julie S. Meisami and Paul Starkey. Vol. 1. London: Routledge, 1998. 69–77.

Poe, Edgar Allan. *Prose Tales.* Vol. 5. New York: Crowell, 1902. 80–101.

Sallis, Eva. "Sheherazade/Shahrazad: Rereading the Frame Tale of the 1001 Nights." *Arabic and Middle Eastern Literatures* 1 (1998): 153–67.

———. *Sheherazade through the Looking Glass: The Metamorphosis of the Thousand and One Nights.* Richmond: Curzon P, 1999.

Sebbar, Leila. *Sherazade.* London: Quartet, 2000.

Telmissany, May. *Dunyazad.* London: Saqi, 2000.

Walther, Wiebke. *Tausendundeine Nacht.* Munich and Zurich: Artemis, 1987.

Weber, Edgard, ed. *Le secret des Mille et une Nuits: L'inter-dit de Sheherazade.* Toulouse: Eché, 1987.

The *Arabian Nights* in
International Oral Tradition

16

In and Out of the *Arabian Nights*: Memories of Oriental Tales in Sicilian Folklore

Francesca Maria Corrao

When the Arabs conquered Sicily in the ninth century, they brought with them an extensive heritage of tales and stories. At the same time, they encountered a rich tradition of both Latin and Greek mythology on the island. While the narratives of the ancient Mediterranean civilizations can still be discerned in Sicilian folklore today, the important cultural and narrative elements contributed by the Arabs during their rule of the island are less evident. The author of the oldest collection of Sicilian folklore, Giuseppe Pitrè, however, was aware of traces of Arab influence in Sicilian tales (*Fiabe e leggende* 1; *Fiabe, novelle* 371). While talking about traces of the *Arabian Nights* in Sicilian folklore, one might start by locating one or more copies of Galland's adapted translation in private libraries.[1] At any rate, the spread of Oriental tales in Sicilian folklore is a rich field of research that enables us to discover further traces of Arabic heritage in Sicilian culture. In the following, I present a general survey of Oriental folktales contained, albeit not exclusively, in the *Arabian Nights* as they are encountered in the most famous collections of Sicilian folktales—those by Giuseppe Pitrè, Laura von Gonzenbach, and Sebastiano Lo Nigro.

Oriental tradition arrived in Sicily along two major channels: translation of the classic works of Oriental literature or oral tradition. A prominent example is the famous collection of fables known as *Kalîla and Dimna*, a Perso-Arabic adaptation of the Indian *Panchatantra*. In its voyage westward, this work never lost its original Indian identity. The fables included in *Kalîla and Dimna* had an enormous impact in the West through their moral yet playful approach to the more serious aspects of human relations. These stories may well have spread through Sicily during the Arab dominion. Under the rule of Roger the Second (1101–54), Admiral Eugene is said to have compared a Latin translation of the work's Arabic version with a previous Greek translation (Rizzitano 284; see also Jamison). The most famous motif contained in that collection is probably that of the moon in the well, of which numerous versions exist (Aarne and Thompson [henceforth AT] 1335 A). This story, together with that of the lion scared of his own image reflected in the water (AT 92), has been recorded in Sicily from both oral and written tradition (Pitrè, *Fiabe, novelle* 314f.).

Funny stories attributed to fools who occasionally proved wise are very common in Sicilian oral tradition. The protagonist of the best-known cycle of tales is Giufà, whose name indicates a possible relation with the Arabic character Juhâ (Corrao). Among these tales of fools is a version of a popular folktale that also appears in the *Arabian Nights* (Gabrieli 2: 400–402; Pitre, *Fiabe, novelle* 146–49). It is the story of the fool whose donkey is stolen by two thieves. While one of the thieves takes the donkey's place, his accomplice goes off to the market to sell the animal. The thief who had taken the donkey's place convinces the fool that his mother had turned him into a donkey because of his wrongdoings. The fool and the thief rejoice over his liberation and part. The fool then goes to the market to buy a donkey. When he recognizes the animal he previously owned, he whispers into its ear that he will not buy it as it has surely been misbehaving once again (AT 1529).

Between the twelfth and the fourteenth centuries, the schools of translation in Toledo and Palermo introduced the masterpieces of Islamic culture to Western tradition. Scientific works and philosophical treaties were translated along with narrative literature. The important role played by oral tradition in preserving gems of Arab heritage is quite evident in Sicily, where relatively few of the documents produced during the Arab dominion have been preserved. Moreover, the author of the *Novellino*, compiled toward the end of the thirteenth century, mentions that storytellers were welcomed by emperor Frederick II (1212–1250), who loved both old and new stories (Lo Nigro, *Novellino* 94). The editor of the *Novellino*, Sebastiano Lo Nigro, observes that the practice of introducing the tales with the expression "Qui conta d'uno favolatore" (Here he tells about a storyteller) is the

French adaptation of an expression used by Petrus Alfonsus (d. after 1121) in his *Disciplina Clericalis*, a prominent Latin collection of stories showing strong Arabic influence (Spies; Schwarzbaum).

Famous writers of the Middle Ages listened to those storytellers, and they also became acquainted with versions of narrative works translated from the Arabic. An interesting example is given by the good fortune of the *Libro di Kalila e Dimna* in the Spanish translation by John of Capua (1493). Copies of this translation circulated in Italy and met with considerable success. The book was then imitated by Agnolo Firenzuola in his *Discorsi degli animali ragionanti fra loro* (Discourses of the Animals Discussing Together), 1548, and by Anton Francesco Doni in his *Morale e filosofia* (Morality and Philosophy), 1570.

Of the Oriental tales circulating in Italy, the *Dyalogo di Salomone e Marcolpho* (Dialog between Solomon and Marcolph, 1502), a corpus of funny anecdotes attributed to these two characters, achieved particular popularity. Some of the tales contained in this collection still circulate in the Arab world today under the name of Juhâ. In Sicily, they are attributed to Giufà. The *Dyalogo* served as a model for Giulio Cesare Croce (d. 1609) who created the Italian trickster Bertoldo and his son Bertoldino and published their adventures in two booklets that have remained popular to the present day. Alessandro Banchieri (d. 1632) later added a booklet about Cacasenno, Bertoldino's son (Croce and Banchieri). In the version given by Pitrè, the story of Solomon is different from the *Dyalogo*. Here, the king has a cruel wife. Out of jealousy she convinces her husband to sentence his brother Marcolfo to death. Solomon is portrayed as a powerful man. He is said to have seven hundred concubines, adding further evidence to the fact that women—according to the narrator—have a strong hold over the King. At the outset, the story reminds one of the frame story of the originally Persian collection *Sindbâd-nâme*, known as *Sindbâd and the Seven Viziers* in the Western world and not to be confused with the tales of Sindbad the Sailor. A version of this collection is also included in the *Arabian Nights* (Gabrieli 3: 93–142). In the frame story, a jealous concubine wants the king to kill his son. In the Arabian tale, the seven wise men save the young man's life, whereas in the Sicilian story, the trick invented by Marcolfo to save his own life does not work and he dies (Pitrè, *Fiabe, novelle* 129–32).

Sicilian tradition also knows numerous tales containing magic events. "La storia del tignoso" (The Tale of the Stubborn Fellow) tells of a young man who acquires a magic horse that will help him find a cure for his blind father. He enters an enchanted garden where, on the advice of the horse, he gathers fruits that will help him overcome the obstacles lying in his way. He then goes to work for a gardener, and the king's youngest daughter falls in love with him. They get married against her father's will (Gabrieli 1: 262; Lo Nigro, *Racconti* 38–40; AT 314).

Another tale of magic is "La moglie perduta" (The Lost Wife). This tale tells of a young man who enters the service of a stranger who has promised to make him rich. The young man is sewn up in an animal's hide, and a raven carries him to the top of a mountain. On the mountain, he finds diamonds that he casts down to his master. When the stranger abandons him, the young man meets an ogre who instructs him to steal the magic garment of a bird-maiden bathing in a spring. Since deprived of her garment she cannot escape, and the maiden has no choice but to marry the young man and follow him to his house. Eventually, the young man's mother returns the garment to the maiden; she puts it on and promptly disappears. The young man then sets off in search of his lost wife and, with the help of some magic objects, eventually finds her (Lo Nigro, *Racconti* 52–54; Gabrieli 4: 131; AT 936* + AT 400). This tale is contained in the *Arabian Nights* under the heading of "Hasan of Basra" (Chauvin 7: 29–35, no. 212 A). The motif of recovering precious stones by being carried up to towering peaks in an animal hide that is carried by huge birds is also found in the stories of Sindbad the Sailor (Gabrieli 3: 18f.).

In "La moglie perduta," the jinnis of Arab tradition help the poor to become rich. In a similar vein, the final story of the *Arabian Nights* tells of a poor cobbler whose fortune is changed by the jinnis (Chauvin 6: 81f., no. 250). Sometimes devils play the same role. Probably the most famous story about jinnis is the tale of the jinni in the bottle (Lo Nigro, *Racconti* 49f.; AT 331) that corresponds to the story of the jinni and the fisherman in the *Arabian Nights* (Gabrieli 1: 27). It is the story of a poor fisherman who finds a bottle and opens it. A jinni emerges and explains that King Solomon has imprisoned him in the bottle. During the long time he waited to be freed from his prison, he has grown extremely angry and has vowed to kill whoever opened the bottle. He asks the fisherman to choose the way he prefers to die, but the fisherman feigns not to believe that the huge jinni could have lived inside the small bottle and tricks him into getting back inside. Now the jinni swears to make him rich if he will open the bottle again. With the jinni's magic help, the fisherman eventually catches a lot of precious fish that he takes to the king and receives a handsome reward.

The story of a boy who must bring a snuffbox to his owner without opening it, is another example of a jinni story (AT 1416). Out of curiosity, the boy opens the box. When the devils suddenly appear and ask him his wishes, he tells them to make one hundred water wells appear (Pitrè, *Fiabe e leggende* 331; Pitrè, *Fiabe, novelle* 374f.).

One of the most famous stories of the *Arabian Nights* is the tale of "Ali Baba and the Forty Thieves" (Pitrè, *Fiabe e leggende* 113f.; Gabrieli 3: 144f., 146f.; AT 676 + AT 954). In the Sicilian version, the hero is a young boy who is small like a "pea," and indeed his nickname is "Cicirrieddu" (Little Pea). Cicirrieddu is the only son of a poor family and a shepherd. One day he overhears the thieves entering the cave in which they have hidden their treasure, and on their departure he steals the treasure. At least two Sicilian variants of this tale exist, each capturing a different aspect of the celebrated story. The more elaborate version (Lo Nigro, *Racconti* 137f.) is about two brothers who live in misery. One brother sets out to seek his fortune and, surprised by a band of thieves, climbs a tree. From there he watches the thieves enter their cave after uttering the magic formula. The other brother wants to learn the source of his brother's unexpected wealth. He makes for the cave too but is caught and hewn to pieces by the thieves. The first brother succeeds in recovering the body and takes it to his wife, who has it sewn together by an artful cobbler. Seeking revenge, the thieves hide in oil jars that their leader delivers to the house. The serving woman discovers the trick and kills them. This variant more or less corresponds to the version of the *Arabian Nights*. The other variant is the tale of "The Twelve Thieves" (Lo Nigro, *Racconti* 223–25), which tells of a nun—a merchant's daughter—who sets out one evening for the house of the thieves. In the meantime, another nun has to keep watch over a lamp lit before the statue of a saint in the church. The lamp goes out, and when the nun goes to light it she finds the thieves in the house. The thieves had in fact hidden themselves in the oil jars purchased by the abbess of the monastery. They climb the walls of the building in which the two sisters live but are then killed.

In his collection of Sicilian folktales, Lo Nigro maintains that the two stories—together with the Sicilian version of the tale of "Aladdin and the Magic Lamp" (Lo Nigro, *Racconti* 114–16; AT 561)—were introduced to Sicily through an eighteenth-century English translation of Antoine Galland's *Mille et une Nuits* (1704–17). Italo Calvino, in his collection of Italian folktales, advances the conjecture, enforcing Pitrè's conviction, that French storytellers might have spread some stories from Galland's version of the *Arabian Nights* in northern Italy in the nineteenth century (Calvino 41). He writes that a few of the Italian stories he had collected for his compilation were in fact closer to the French version than to the translation of the Arabic text presented by Francesco Gabrieli. It is worth mentioning that Gabrieli's edition is based on the first Bulaq edition, published in 1835. The close relationship between oral or popular and written or literary tradition is responsible for the worldwide existence of numerous tales originating from the *Arabian Nights* in oral tradition. Some of the stories from the *Arabian Nights* present in Sicilian tradition are also found in a large collection of Spanish folk tales (Espinosa 3: 110; 2: 40) including, for example, the tales of "Cecino" and "Tignoso" (Lo Nigro, *Racconti* 139f., 38–40; Gabrieli 4: 262; Thompson, *Motif-Index* [hereafter Mot.] K 1818.2, B 184.1, B 401). Some other parallel tales are documented in Giambattista Basile's (1575–1632) famous collection *Lo cunto de li cunti, overo Lo Trattenemiento de' peccerille* (The Story of Stories, or the Pastime of the Little Ones), commonly known as the *Pentamerone* (literally: The Work of Five Days). It may be on these grounds that Lo Nigro was inclined to conjecture that the tales could more readily be traced back to a direct derivation from the Arabic. Recent research, however, has the tales of Aladdin and Ali Baba proven beyond any doubt to originate from the oral performance of the Syrian storyteller Hannâ, and they were certainly distributed in Europe and worldwide as a result of the popularity of the *Arabian Nights*.

A story in the *Arabian Nights* that might be quoted as evidence of the above argument is the tale "The Magic Ring," appearing both in the *Pentamerone* and in Sicilian tales (Gabrieli 4: 709; Basile 403–9; Lo Nigro, *Racconti* 113f.; AT 560). It tells of a father who, when dying, leaves all his possessions to his two elder sons, while the inheritance of the third son amounts to no more than a pan. When the young man sells the pan to a tinker, the pan is shaken and a magic ring falls out, thanks to which he is able to buy a palace facing the king's palace. Later, he marries the king's daughter. The jealous tinker disguises himself and sets off to acquire the ring from the princess. When he has succeeded, he makes the palace vanish and locks the princess up in a tower in the middle of the sea. In desperation, the young man ventures into the woods, comes across an old man, once again finds the ring, and frees his wife. In the *Arabian Nights*, this tale more or less corresponds to the second part of the tale of "Aladdin and the Magic Lamp." The existence of a European version of this tale prior to Galland's publication suggests two possibilities: either the tale was known in European, or at least Italian, tradition before Galland; or Galland profited from motifs prevalent in European tradition to embellish the version narrated by his informant, of which, notably, he only took down a condensed version in his diary.

Correspondences between Arab and Sicilian folklore are also to be found in stories about the trickery and unfaithfulness of women, some of which originate from the cycle of *Sindbâd and the Seven Viziers*. The Sindbâd cycle had been translated in Spain during the reign of the infant Fredrick in the thirteenth century under the title *Sendebar o Libro de los engaños e los asayamientos de las mujeres*. The cycle was later circulated in Europe as the *Libro de los siete sabios* or *Dolophatos* (Galmés de Fuentes 127). It was also integrated into versions of the *Arabian Nights*. The motif of the unfaithfulness of women is also found in two fables contained in the *Panchatantra*, one of which appears in the Sicilian tradition.

The typical pattern of this kind of story in the *Arabian Nights* is as follows. A wife betrays her husband as soon as he leaves the house. When all of a sudden he returns, she hides her lover inside a big box (AT 1419). In the Sicilian version (Pitrè, *Fiabe e leggende* 280–85) the husband hides inside the box on the advice of his friend, who wants to prove his wife's unfaithfulness. In a literary version contained in the *Piacevoli notti* (Pleasant Nights; 1: 5) by Giovanni Francesco Straparola (1480–1558), the lover hides inside the big box. A version closer to the Sicilian one is given in Basile's *Pentamerone* (2: 1); here it is the husband who hides in the big box. It is worth mentioning that the Sicilian version is closer to the *Panchatantra* version. In both versions, the husband has been told about his wife's unfaithfulness and pretends to leave the house only in order to discover the trick.

In another story, a woman invents a trick to hide herself when she betrays her husband. The Sicilian story is called "Lu cuturieri" (The Tailor). The Tailor's wife betrays him with the king. The poor husband has no chance to discover the secret because a wall of his house is next to the castle, so the woman can visit her lover simply by going through a hole in the wall. Even so, he is suspicious and keeps the front-door key to himself, but every time he gets back home, she is always there. One day he has to set off on his travels, and he wants her to stay close to the window in order to make sure she does not go out. The woman puts a pumpkin in her stead and covers it with a "saracinesca" shawl—a shawl of the Saracen style. The husband sees it from afar and believes that she is there. Once he has seen her at the window he tells her to draw back into the room, but the figure remains motionless. When he returns to make his wishes clear to her, he discovers the trick. In the Arabian tale, the king is a prince, and instead of the hole in the wall, his vizier takes the lover to the woman's house in a large box that he gives to the merchant as a present from the prince. When the husband wants to leave, he asks his wife to stand at the balcony to make sure she is not betraying him. Here again the woman puts the pumpkin in her stead; returning all of a sudden, the husband discovers her trick (Pitrè, *Fiabe e leggende* 308–13; Gabrieli 3: 123–27).

Basile played an important role in the spread of folktales in an elegant literary style in southern Italy, during a time when Sicily was part of the Kingdom of the Two Sicilies. Following the structure of Boccaccio's *Decamerone*, the author of the *Pentamerone* created a masterpiece in the Neapolitan dialect. In comparison to Boccaccio's vast fame, Basile's true value has long been underestimated. It was only in the nineteenth century that the literary critic Vittorio Imbriani cast new light on his masterpiece. According to Imbriani, Basile's tales do not primarily derive from popular origins, like those of Boccaccio, but are inspired by Greek and Latin mythology. Imbriani appreciated Basile's baroque style and pointed out the fact that the frame story of the *Pentamerone* was taken from an Indian cycle of tales (Basile 618, 636). Curiously enough, Imbriani missed several interesting details. Although he noticed that the frame story is of Oriental origin, it does not seem to have occurred to him that Basile might have taken it from *Orlando Furioso* by Ludovico Ariosto (1474–1533). Chapter 38 of *Orlando Furioso* has a frame story in terms of motifs overlapping that of the *Arabian Nights*: when the brothers Giocondo and Astolfo go hunting, one returns home unexpectedly and finds his wife betraying him. The same experience later befalls the other brother, and so they decide to set off and travel the world in search of a faithful woman.

As in the *Arabian Nights*, the antagonist in the *Pentamerone* belongs to an inferior class (a slave, as is also the case in Ariosto's story); it is a black woman in Basile's version and a man in Ariosto's. The antagonist represents the Other, the unknown danger of the wild world, and the theme thus treats the eternal struggle of civilization against barbarism. Other elements common to both collections are the tricks and cunning of women. This is also a prominent topic of numerous folktales. The women we encounter in folktales differ from those represented in classical Arabic poetry. In folktales their roles are apparently closer to the actual circumstances of social life. They use cunning as a strategy to get the better of the more powerful men. Telling these stories is meant to restore the violated order. The main infringement of the law indicated in the *Arabian Nights* is that of a king who is the serial killer of his wives; what is more, by doing so he refuses to give a future ruler to his country. Woman, as the one who gives life and restores the cycle of life, is represented in the *Arabian Nights* by the quintessential storyteller Shahrazâd; storytelling here is a therapy for the male who has lost the sense of life. In other stories there are different cases of infringement of the law. In general, the moral value lies in the fact that in the end there is a hero who restores justice. Bad women are punished, but the legitimate wives as well as the poor and the honest people get back what has been unjustly taken. In consequence, the dominant message received from the *Arabian Nights*, the Sicilian tales, and the *Pentamerone*, is not one of simple entertainment but one of justice. Even if it can be argued that not all the tales involved in the frame story have happy endings, the main story has a positive message: a human being can achieve justice through its own effort.

When Basile rewrote the stories taken from folk tradition he used both oral versions and written sources. By doing so he bore testimony to the fact that Italian literature has drawn upon Greek, Latin, and Arab traditions. Basile confirmed that Italian literature has learned from Oriental tales the ability to create equilibrium between didactic and sententious purpose on the one hand, and playful entertainment on the other. In oral Sicilian tradition, the storytellers, both grandparents and professionals, finished a serious narration by introducing a funny anecdote, most often related to Giufà, to lighten the atmosphere when a serious story could have produced a sad atmosphere (Sciascia in Corrao).

In many different civilizations, oral tradition is invoked for a variety of reasons. Writers might feel the need to recover a closer approach to real life, or to give a higher value to the small tragedies of daily life by virtue of using elegant prose. At times reference to folklore may have political significance, as in the case of Jâhiz, the famous Arabian man of letters of the eighth century, who collected a substantial quantity of oral traditions and tales to disseminate knowledge among the newly converted. In doing so he set out to oppose the detractors of Islamic culture, the heirs of other conquered civilizations. Centuries later in Egypt 'Abbâs Mahmûd al-'Aqqâd revived the popular hero Juhâ to enforce the claim for national independence during British rule. In a comparable manner, even today certain Sicilian writers consider the revival of the Arab heritage an important step to reaffirm the Mediterranean roots against a tide that threatens to wash away its historical memory.

NOTE

1. While there are no copies of Galland's *Mille et une Nuit[s]* in the Biblioteca Centrale della Regione Siciliana, there is a translation of the French edition published in Naples in 1867 and printed by F. Giannini, titled *Mille e una Notte: Novelle Arabe tradotte da Antonio Galland.* A copy is available at the Biblioteca Civica Centrale in Turin. It is possible that storytellers spread these stories throughout the Kingdom of the Two Sicilies. It is unlikely that the old women who told their narratives to both Pitrè and later von Gonzenbach could have simply heard these stories recounted by a storyteller, since they claim that the narratives passed on to them from generation to generation. I myself am a witness of Juhâ stories handed down to me from my grandmother, who in turn had heard them from her grandmother. As for the Galland edition published in Venice in 1722, there is not evidence that any copies reached Sicily.

WORKS CITED

Aarne, Antti, and Stith Thompson. *The Types of the Folktale: A Classification and Bibliography.* Helsinki: Academia Scientiarum Fennica, 1961.

Basile, Giambattista. *Il racconto dei racconti (ossia il Pentamerone).* Trans. Ruggero Guarini. Ed. Alessandra Burani and Ruggero Guarini. Milan: Adelphi, 1994.

Calvino, Italo. *Fiabe Italiane.* Turin: Einaudi, 1967.

Chauvin, Victor. *Bibliographie des ouvrages arabes ou relatifs aux arabes.* Vols. 4–8. Liège: Vaillant-Carmanne, and Leipzig: Harrassowitz, 1900–1903.

Corrao, Francesca M., ed. *Le storie di Giufà.* Palermo: Sellerio, 2001.

Croce, Giulio C., and Adriano Banchieri. *Bertoldo, Bertoldino e Cacasenno.* Milan: Mùrsia, 1973.

Espinosa, Aurelio M. *Cuentos populares españoles.* 3 vols. Stanford: Stanford UP, 1923–26.

Gabrieli, Francesco. *Le Mille e una Notte.* 4 vols. Turin: Einaudi, 1967.

Galmés de Fuentes, Alvaro. *La épica romanica y la tradición árabe.* Madrid: Gredos, 2002.

Gonzenbach, Laura. *The Robber with a Witch's Head: More Stories from the Great Treasury of Sicilian Folk and Fairy Tales Collected by Laura Gonzenbach.* Ed. Jack Zipes. London: Routledge, 2004.

Jamison, Evelyn. *Admiral Eugenius of Sicily.* London: Oxford UP, 1957.

Lo Nigro, Sebastiano. *Racconti popolari siciliani: Classificazione e bibliografia.* Florence: Olschki, 1956.

———. *Novellino e conti del duecento.* Turin: Utet, 1963.

Najjâr, Muhammad R. *Juhâ al-'arabî.* Kuwait: Dhât al-salâsil li-'l-nashr wa-'l-tibâ', 1989.

Pitrè, Giuseppe. *Fiabe e leggende popolari siciliane.* Ed. A. Rigoli. Palermo: Il Vespro, 1978.

———. *Fiabe, novelle e racconti popolari siciliani.* Ed. A. Rigoli. 4 vols. Palermo: Il Vespro, 1978.

Schwarzbaum, Haim. "International Folklore Motifs in Petrus Alphonsi's Disciplina Clericalis." *Jewish Folklore between East and West.* Ed. Eli Yassif. Beer-Sheva: Ben-Gurion U of the Negev P, 1989: 239–358.

Rizzitano, Umberto. *Storia e cultura della Sicilia saracena.* Palermo: S. Flaccovio, 1975.

Spies, Otto. "Arabische Stoffe in der Disciplina Clericalis." *Rheinisches Jahrbuch für Volkskunde* 21 (1973): 170–99.

Thompson, Stith. *Motif-Index of Folk-Literature.* 6 vols. Copenhagen: Rosenkilde and Bagger, 1955–58.

17

The *Arabian Nights* in Greece: A Comparative Survey of Greek Oral Tradition

Marilena Papachristophorou

Working on the repercussions of the *Arabian Nights* in Greek oral tradition is an exciting task, as the field proves to be, more or less, virgin. This, however, implies a number of difficulties.[1] First and foremost, a full translation of the *Arabian Nights* into Greek has never been published; and second, previous studies by Greek folklorists are rather modest. They comprise no more than a few general references and are mostly limited to stating the typological analogies between the two narrative corpora in scattered remarks about an "Oriental origin." Yet research concerned with the literary history of the *Arabian Nights* is much more developed. The shortcomings of previous research make the present approach all the more interesting. While existing studies indicate a certain silence about the relationship of Greek and Oriental narrative traditions, they also reveal the preference of Greek scholars for connecting modern Greece to its classical and Western history.

This essay is presented in two parts. The first part supplies a historical survey of Greek translations of the *Nights*, and the second part documents the tale-types common to both narrative corpora while discussing specific examples drawn from Greek oral tradition.

The Greek Translations

A detailed bibliographical documentation of the Greek translations of single stories from the *Arabian Nights* published in reviews and journals or as separate editions for children is lacking. Monograph translations of the collection have been described by Yorgos Kehayoglou. Early documents on the history of the *Arabian Nights* in Greece include texts of Byzantine and early Greek literature as well as the reports of travelers who had visited Greece during the Ottoman occupation. According to those documents, single elements of the collection might have been introduced to Greek tradition by way of oral transmission. The actual history of Greek translations of the *Nights*, however, begins only in the eighteenth century and was initiated from western Europe.

The first Greek translation of the *Arabian Nights* was published in two steps and under two different titles, 1757–62 in Venice and 1791–94 in Vienna, by the first important publisher in the history of modern Greece, Polyzois Labanitziotis from Yannina. Its full bibliographical data are as follows (see Legrand no. 500; Iliou nos. 183, 186, 198):

> *Aravikon Mythologikon*, periechon dhiigiseis kai symvevikota pleista perierga, kai oraia. Syntethen eis tin Aravikin Dhialekton para tou polymathous Dhervis Aboubekir. Nyn proton. Ek tis Italikis eis tin imeteran dhialekton metafrasthen, typois te ekdhothen. Kai meta pleistis epimeleias Dhiorthothen (*Arabian Mythology, containing narrations and happenings mostly peculiar and fascinating.* Composed in the Arabic dialect by the eminent Dervish Abu-Bakr. Now for the very first time translated from the Italian into our own tongue, and issued in print. And most assiduously corrected). Venice: Antonio Tzattas, vol. 1: 1757, vols. 2–3: 1762.

> *Nea Halima itoi Mythologikon Aravikon*, periechon dhiigiseis kai symvevikota lian perierga kai oraia, syntethen eis tin aravikin dhialekton para tou polymathous Dhervis Aboubekir. Nyn proton ek tis italikis dhialektou metafrasthen, kai typois ekdhothen para [tou] Pol[yzois] Lamp [anitziotis] (*New Halima, i.e., Arabian Mythology*, containing narrations and happenings very peculiar and fascinating, composed in the Arabic dialect by the eminent Dervish Abu-Bakr. Translated from the Italian and printed by Pol[yzois] Lab[anitziotis]). Vienna, vol. 1: 1791, vol. 2: 1792, vols. 3–4: 1794.

The *Aravikon Mythologikon* was a great publishing success. Until the end of the nineteenth century it experienced at least fifteen reprints in Venice and Athens (1777, 1783, 1792, 1803, 1804, etc.), and numerous reprints were published at the beginning of the twentieth century. Some of the reprints bear different titles, and some fragmentary editions of isolated stories appeared as chapbooks. There are no data available for reprints of *Nea Halima.*

The first Greek translation of the *Arabian Nights* contains a selected adaptation of tales following an Italian translation of Antoine Galland's *Mille et une Nuits*. In consequence, its text is quite distant from whatever Arabian original. This had, in fact, already been the case for its French or Italian mediator; moreover, the Greek translation is quite distant from its mediators. As for content, the *Aravikon Mythologikon* contains tales from the *Thousand and One Nights* only in its first volume, while the second and third volumes present texts from the *Thousand and One Days* by François Pétis de la Croix (1710–12). *Nea Halima*'s four volumes, on the contrary, draw exclusively from the *Nights*. Altogether, six of Galland's twenty-two main stories are missing along with six of the secondary tales and the end of the frame story. This means that some of the better-known groups of stories, such as "The Hunchback's Tale" (Chauvin, *Bibliographie* no. 105), "Ali Bin Bakkar and Shams al-Nahar" (no. 76), "Aladdin" (no. 19), and "Ali Baba" (no. 24) do not appear in that translation. As for the *Days*, two of the nineteen stories in the original collection are missing, as is the end of the frame story. Although Labanitziotis announced in 1794 that he would publish the remainder of Galland's text, he never did.

Besides the divergence in quantity, some important alterations in quality were also introduced: First, the composition of the original collection is here attributed to a certain "Dervish Abu-Bakr"—a purely fictional author.[2] Second, the text is presented without the division into nights. And third, the main characters appear under different names: Shahrazâd became Halima, Shahriyâr became Aidin, Dînâzâd became Medina, and Sindbad (the Sailor) became Sevah. Some of these new names have remained very popular in Greek tradition until today. "Halima's Tales" are probably more familiar to present-day Greeks than the *Thousand and One Nights*; in fact, the expression, "Halima's Tales" has become proverbial. As for Sindbad, the Arabian equivalent to Ulysses, he is still known as Sevah the Seaman (even if that implies an unconscious etymological pleonasm; see Trikoglidis 1: 14). The persistence of the new names is partly due to the collection's great popularity. Moreover, the Greek translation has served as the basis of translations into other Balkan languages in whose title "Halima" also figures. The new names were also retained in various other translations based on Galland and published in the nineteenth century (cf. Kehayoglou, "Hilies ke Mia Nythes" 52).

The second large Greek translation of the *Arabian Nights* was published by Vlassis Gavriilidis in 1890. It contained a more complete text and replaced the first one on the market:

> *Halima itoi Hiliai kai Mia Nyktes*, aravika dhiigimata. Metafrasis eis tin ellinikin ypo ****. Ekdhosis oikogeneiaki (*Halima, i.e., Thousand and One Nights*, Arabian novels. Translated into Greek by ****. Family edition). vols. 1–2, Athens: V. Gavriilidis, 1890.

This translation was first published in continuously paginated fascicles that were subsequently bound in volumes. One of the main characteristics of this edition is its rich decoration with woodcuts drawn from the French edition by Bourdin (1838–40). Moreover, the translation contains a vivid language—or, better even, a creative recasting. It was obviously prepared by a well-known writer of the period, probably Alexander Papadiamandis (1851–1911; see Kehayoglou, "Hilies ke Mia Nyhtes" 53). While the main source text used was Richard Burton's English version, the Greek text again provided only a selection of stories. The publication's title undoubtedly reflects the intention to be faithful toward the original, but the names of the main characters are retained from the first edition. Certain abbreviations and some variations in comparison to Burton's text indicate the use of additional sources, probably Turkish or European partial translations. While the edition of 1890 was reprinted in seven volumes in 1895, data for further reprints are not available.

The only Greek translation prepared directly from an Arabic text is the product of Greek Diaspora in Egypt. It was published in 1921–23 and 1925 by Kostas Trikoglidis. This translation still deserves a prominent place in Greek literature both for its precision and sumptuousness.

> *Agnostou Arava Syggrafea, Hilies kai Mia Nyhtes (Halima)*. Metafrasis Kosta Trikoglidhi apo to gnision Aravikon keimenon. Bibliothiki "Eklekta Erga," ar. 31–35 (*Thousand and One Nights [Halima]*. Translated from the original Arabic text by Kostas Trikoglidis. "Library of Select Works," nos. 31–35). Athens: G. I Vassiliou, vols. 1–2: 1921, vols. 3–5: 1923; plus: *Halima: Epilogi apo tis Hilies kai mia Nyhtes*. Metafrasis apo to aravikon keimenon K. Trikoglidhi (*Halima: A Selection from the Thousand and One Nights*. Translated from the Arabic text by Kostas Trikoglidis). vols. 1–2. Athens: Eleftheroudakis, 1925) (reprint in 7 vols. Athens: Iridanos Editions, 1978–79).

Trikoglidis was educated in Alexandria, where he spent twenty years of his life. According to his detailed afterword, he began his translation in 1902 with the assistance of an Egyptian scholar who was also his mentor. At first, he completed about five-eighths of the text according to the Bulaq (1835) edition. He then continued on his own, consulting an unspecified contemporary Cairo edition. By 1910 he had completed the whole translation in the formal, archaic form of the Greek language (*katharevousa*). Following this, he revised the text adapting it to contemporary spoken Greek. While taking that step he also referred to the European translations, in particular Burton's and Lane's. Trikoglidis's linguistic competence enabled him to reach a perfect balance between the collection's "Oriental" and "Occident" components. He widely annotated his translation borrowing from "Burton and Lane, from the Koran, the Talmud, the Holy Bible, the ancient Greek sources and from the notes [he] was using to comment on the social, religious, national, and family life of the Egyptian people" (Trikoglidis 7: 240–41.). The cultural kinship between Greece and the Orient probably supported the development of a style faithful to the original, as it allowed the exact rendering of integral expressions as well as of everyday habits and features (Preface by Voutieridis in Trikoglidis 1: 15).

Trikoglidis translated the whole of the *Nights* into Greek. Unfortunately, his translation has never been published in its entirety. The published part includes about half of the stories considered as canonical—that is, the beginning of the frame story and about sixty of the main stories (for a total of about one hundred stories). Trikoglidis also abandoned the division into nights. Some of the stories in his translation had never before been translated into Greek. Actually, the published part might contain more original plots than the sheer numbers indicate, since Trikoglidis must have selected at least one from each group of the stories that occur in more or less identical form within the collection. A representative of this phenomenon is the "Tale of the Portress" (Chauvin, *Bibliographie* no. 148), included in the "Three Ladies of Baghdad" (no. 33), and its male equivalents (Bencheikh et al. 98–99). "The Mock Caliph" (Chauvin, *Bibliographie* no. 174), "The Young Merchant from Baghdad and the Unknown Lady" (no. 175), "Story of the First Lunatic" (no. 176), "Manjab" (no. 177), and "The Supplier" (no. 305). From this group of six stories only two have been published in Greek.

Trikoglidis's translation is divided into seven volumes. The initial six volumes are organized into "books," or thematic units, that are subtitled with the name of the plot's main figure. The seventh volume contains three stories that were not part of the original Arabic corpus of the *Nights*: "Aladdin's Wonderful Lamp," "The Two Sisters Who Envied Their Cadette" (Chauvin, *Bibliographie* no. 375), and "Ali Baba and the Forty Thieves." In addition to those seven volumes, the independent volume *Syntipas* was published:

Syntipas i i panourgies kai i mihanorrafies ton gynaikon. Metafrasis Kosta Trikoglidhi apo tin araviki ekdhosi (*Sindibad, or Women's Trickeries and Intrigues.* Trans. Kostas Trikoglidis from the Arabic edition). Athens: Ganiaris [1923] (reprint Athens: Iridanos Editions, 1982).

Even though that collection and its embedded stories are included in the principal Oriental editions of the *Nights*, their history in the Greek language has been independent, as a Greek version of *Syntipas* already existed in the eleventh century. Trikoglidis added some stories omitted from the original collection's last vernacular edition (Venice 1815; see Chauvin, *Bibliographie* 8: 6) to his translation. With the addition of these stories, the total number of stories from the *Arabian Nights* translated into Greek is 130.

Trikoglidis's translation presented the Arabic original to Greek readers in a new manner. Contrasting with the previous translations, he introduced Shahrazâd's original name and also mentioned several of the other main characters by their original name. Only Sindbad remained Sevah, as his name was so well established in the Greek language that it was difficult to introduce a different name (Trikoglidis 1: 12–14). At the same time, the translator's sensibility and his academic accuracy enabled him to offer a Greek text that was both quite faithful to the original and bare of the prudishness ruling previous translations. In his afterword, Trikoglidis states that "after all, the *Thousand and One Nights* are not a chrestomathy. They do not intend scrupulously to teach and moralize with the common boring pedagogical means" (8: 215). Even so, he did not dare to faithfully translate the adventure of "Abu Nuwas with the Three Boys" (Chauvin, *Bibliographie* no. 297) and committed, as far as we know, his only major infidelity toward the original. The homosexual element was covered up and the story was presented as "The Story of Abu Nowas and the Three Girls."

A final and more recent Greek translation of the *Nights* to be mentioned is based on the French version by Joseph Charles Mardrus (1899–1904).

Hilies kai mia nyhtes. Metafrasi—Epilogi Stavrou A. Vlachou (epimeleia Aggelou S. Vlachou) (Thousand and One Nights. Translated and Selected by Stavros A. Vlahos [Edited by A. S. Vlahos]). Athens: Hermeias, 1977.

This translation also contains only a selection of 34 stories from the *Nights*, nine of which do not belong to the canon (Kehayoglou, "Hilies ke Mia Nyhtes" 54).

Most of the larger editions of the *Nights* in Greek rely mainly on either Galland's French translation, Burton's English translation, itself mainly based on the Calcutta II edition (1839–41), the Bulaq I edition (1835), or Mardrus's French translation, which is based on Bulaq. We can thus safely assume that any influence of written versions of the *Nights* in Greek oral tradition is due to the European translations, in particular those by Galland and Burton. The only Greek translation prepared directly from an Arabic text comes too late to interfere decisively with oral tradition.

The publication of isolated stories from the *Nights* in children's magazines in the late nineteenth and early twentieth centuries, as mentioned above, should also be considered as an independent source of influence for some special themes, such as the attribution of justice, the cleverness of thieves, or the tale of "The Three Golden Sons" (cf. Kaplanoglou 126–35).

However, the most important observation concerning the Greek translations is related to the fact that at least half of the main corpus of the *Nights* has never been published in Greek translation. According to Kehayoglou's ("Hilies ke Mia Nyhtes") estimate, the eighteenth-century editions presented only about one-sixth of the collection to the Greek public, whereas the edition by Gavriilidis in the nineteenth century presented about two-fifths and the translation by Trikoglidis at the beginning of the twentieth century published about half of them. Thus, the end of the frame story with the denouement of Shahrazâd's own adventure is missing in Greek, as are several other very well known stories, such as the voluminous romance of chivalry of "The King Omar Bin al-Nu'uman and His Sons" (Chauvin, *Bibliographie* nos. 277, 60, 71, 278), "The History of Gharib and His Brother Ajib" (no. 13), "The City of Brass" (no. 16), "Abdallah the Seaman and Abdallah the Land's Man" (no. 3), "Ali Shar and Zumurrud" (no. 28), and "Abu Qir and Abu Sir" (no. 10). This gap could probably be filled with the publication of the unpublished part of the Trikoglidis translation.

Written Literature and Orality

The exchange between Greek oral tradition and Oriental tradition neither begins nor ends with the Greek translations of the *Nights*. Well before European translations from Arabic, oral channels of transmission existed. These channels must be considered in a mutual perspective. On the one hand, traces of classical and Hellenistic Greek literature and culture have been detected in the corpus of the *Nights* (see Chauvin, "Homère;" Macdonald; Horovitz; Grunebaum ch. 9). On the other, Greek folklorists usually consider the long Ottoman occupation an influential phase in the exchange between Greece—and the Balkans in general—and the Orient. Turkish interest in the *Nights* together with an inclination toward folktales incumbent in Turkish culture supplied new vigor to Greek folktales. While, during this process, Turkish culture may to some extent have transmitted its own imagery through the Arabian tales, the effect of direct Arabic influence on Greek tradition is considerably lighter. Traces of the former kind concern characters such as the "Arab" (who is black, of a huge stature, and with large lips), the vizier, the bey, or the qadi (cf. Meraklis, "Annotations" 49–58). In this respect, prominent Greek folklore scholar Georgios A. Megas (1893–1976) suggests that, in terms of parallels, Greek folktales referred to Turkish folktales (see Eberhard and Boratav) more often than to the *Nights*. Eighteenth-century travelers in Greece already observed that kind of narrative kinship, which they largely attributed to an Oriental and Arabic heritage (de Guys 347; Imellos 224).

Nikolaos G. Politis (1852–1921), the founder of folklore studies in Greece, also referred to those analogies in one of his early studies in discussing a motif from the *Odyssey* (Politis 93). Politis avoided committing himself to any particular origin, instead preferring to explain the phenomenon by a model of three traditions communicating with one another: ancient Greece, the Orient, and modern Greece. Contrasting with Politis's pragmatic solution of this matter, nineteenth-century Greek scholars insisted on the "didactic" aspect of the *Nights*, especially concerning matters of etiquette, charity, justice, and morals (Dragoumis 71; Politis 94). Even though their emphasis is a misunderstanding, probably resulting from the unsatisfactory translations existing in that period, it certainly served the pedagogical spirit of the modern Greek Enlightenment and obviously affected the selection of the stories published in children's magazines.

In general, the distinct cultural background of each era affected the thematic loans as well as the style of narration ruling the various translations. During my first reading of the collection in Trikoglidis's translation, I was profoundly impressed by the numerous detailed descriptions of objects and situations that are, in contrast, usually presented in summary form in Greek folktales. As a case in point, explicit references to sexual intercourse are extremely rare in Greek oral tradition where meaningful standard expressions are preferred instead. Greek folktales would mention a general "they had a wild time" to summarize a whole night of feasting and lovemaking (cf. Papachristophorou 186), so common in the *Nights*. Similarly, Greek folktales rarely refer to the romantic passion of love, unless it is caused by a supernatural being. Another stylistic difference is the way a woman's beauty is described in the *Nights* by comparing it to radiant sunshine, or by simply naming her the "Beauty of the world." A similar abstract style of description (in Greek folktales) is applied to violent incidents in the *Nights* that receive a strictly narrative function, either to serve the plot or to apply justice in the end, excluding details such as in the torture of the princess in the "Second Kalandar's tale" (Chauvin, *Bibliographie* no. 116).

In terms of accounting for these differences, it has been said that the *Nights* had to present as literary a narrative form as possible in order to safeguard its corpus of tales by providing it with the "passport" of a literary work (Bencheikh et al. 55). In contrast, oral folktales such as the majority of the registered Greek tales, opt for an everyday type of speech avoiding complicated expressions. In a similar vein, Greek folktales would extend their length by adding episodes, whereas tales in the *Nights* turn to describing details or deviate into poetry (see Macdonald 370; El-Shamy 79–80). The distinction between Greek folktales and stories from the *Arabian Nights* relates to both narrative style and cultural specifics. At the same time it is in accordance with the mnemonic procedure of remembering and retelling folktales as well as the maintenance of an interior rhythm during the time of narration.

Another possible reason for the stylistic differences between the *Nights* and Greek folktales is the sociohistorical context of the two corpora. The registers of the Greek folktales referred to here originate from traditional agricultural communities of the late nineteenth and the twentieth centuries. This means that the narration was clearly posited in the framework of an acceptable social behavior according to the rules of those communities. Their rules would include a sense of economy, and the resulting modesty would permit a certain degree of diversion only for jocular narratives, even though there again detailed descriptions would not be tolerated. In other words, laughing about a jocular narrative is more due to the signified than to the signifier. In any case, Greek folktales follow the general rules of the European folktale as depicted by Max Lüthi. These stylistic arguments affect all of the tale-types discussed below.

Greek Oral Folktales and the *Arabian Nights*

The following discussion is primarily concerned with stories from the *Nights* referenced in Antti Aarne and Stith Thompson's international classification of the Indo-European folktale (henceforth AT), together with their oikotypes (even if not mentioned in AT). It also considers the so-called orphan stories (Gerhardt 12–14) that were introduced into the corpus of the *Nights* by Galland (Elisséeff 46–47; Marzolph 161–62), such as the stories of Aladdin, Ali Baba, the Ebony Horse, and Ahmad and Perî Banû. As for tales from the *Nights*, the comparative survey has profited considerably from previous documentation and research (especially AT; Thompson, *Motif-Index* [henceforth Mot.]; El-Shamy). The comparative data for Greek folktales rely on the published (Angelopoulou and Brouskou) as well as the unpublished parts of Megas's catalogue of the Greek folktale and the folktale database of the Hellenic Folklore Research Center in Athens which has not yet been completed. Therefore, the amount of registered Greek variants in the following table above all indicates the dissemination of a given tale-type in the Greek territory before 1976.

A first glance at the table clearly shows that about half of the discernible tale-types included in the *Nights* are not (or rarely) represented in the Greek corpus, and approximately one-third of those stories have been translated into Greek. Yet only a few of the tales belong to those popular in Greek tradition (with more than twenty registered variants) while not regularly corresponding to a translated story from the *Nights*. The quantitative evaluation suggests that the Greek translations of the *Nights* are not a main point of entrance into Greek oral tradition for those tales. At the same time, the so-called orphan stories enjoy a great success in Greek oral tradition (see AT 676: *Open Sesame* + AT 954: *The Forty Thieves*, AT 707: *The Three Golden Sons*, AT 653 A: *The Rarest Thing in the World*, AT 561: *Aladdin*). Their (additional) popularity with children is both connected to the fact that a considerable amount of the Greek variants was collected from children and that some of these tales were frequently published as children's literature (cf. Kaplanoglou 126–35).

Independent of a high or low dissemination of the Greek variants, some of the plots and themes have evolved in unexpected ways in Greek tradition. For instance, the story of "The Sultan of Yemen and His Three Sons" (Chauvin, *Bibliographie* no. 182; see list no. 11) has a common plot with the Greek variants of AT 550: *Search for the Golden Bird*. In the Greek variants, on the one hand, several elements are not represented, such as the lower maternal origin of the third son or his marriage with two or three princesses during his adventures. On the other hand, the Greek plot is filled with numerous other elements, such as the object of the quest (which is not necessarily a wonderful bird, but also some other magic object that guarantees the king's sovereignty), the help received by the grateful animal(s), and especially that the hero is eliminated by his brothers when he arrives.

Table 1

No.	AT Classification	No. in Chauvin	Translated into Greek	Registered Greek Variants
1	178 A	31 (vol. 8, 66)	✓	None
2	207 A	104 (vol. 5, 179)	✓	38
3	322*	117 (vol. 5, 202) 373 (vol. 7, 86, n. 1)	✓	None
4	331	195 (vol. 6, 25)	✓	13
5	402	286 (vol. 6, 133)	✓	49
6	449	371 (vol. 6, 198)	✓	None
7	471	168 (vol. 8, 160)		(2)
8	513 A	392 (vol. 7, 124)		28
9	514	11 (vol. 8, 43f.)		6
10	516	vol. 8, 57; vol. 7, 98		60
11	550, 551	182 (vol. 6, 6f.)		100 (AT 550) 12 (AT 551)
12	560	20 (vol. 5, 68)	✓	67
13	561	19, 20 (vol. 5, 55)	✓	34
14	575	130 (vol. 5, 221)		5
15	612	vol. 8, 119		6
16	653	286 (vol. 6, 133) 45 (vol. 8, 76)	✓	78
17	653 A	286 (vol. 6, 133)	✓	30
18	655	438 (vol. 7, 159) 439 (vol. 7, 162f.) 63 (vol. 8, 92)		16
19	670	104 (vol. 5, 179)	✓	100
20	676	24 (vol. 5, 79)		83
21	681	94 (vol. 6, 106)		None
22	706	67 (vol. 5, 138)		47
23	707	375 (vol. 7, 95)		263
24	712	323 (vol. 6, 159)		18
25	726	6 A (vol. 7, 61, n. 4)		1

No.	AT Classification	No. in Chauvin	Translated into Greek	Registered Greek Variants
26	726**	72 (vol. 5, 146)		None
27	736	202 (vol. 6, 32)	✓	1
28	736 A	10 (vol. 5, 17) 68 (vol. 5, 141) 202 (vol. 6, 32)	✓ ✓	1
29	745	137 (vol. 2, 129)	✓	None
30	745 A	137 (vol. 2, 129)	✓	7
31	757	51 (vol. 2, 161)	✓	None
32	766	376 (vol. 7, 102)		None
33	785	73 (vol. 8, 101)	✓	4
34	836*	72 (vol. 5, 146)		3 (*836)
35	838	95 (vol. 8, 113, n. 1)		None
36	851 A	113 (vol. 5, 191)		2
37	881	30 (vol. 5, 94)		47
38	883 A	323 (vol. 6, 159f.)		55
39	885 A	63 (vol. 5, 134)		None
40	890	245 (vol. 8, 200ff.)		8
41	893	vol. 9, 15f.		4
42	901	27 (vol. 2, 155)		34
43	910 A	367 (vol. 6, 195) 136 (vol. 8, 138)	✓	23
44	910 B	136 (vol. 8, 138) 116 (vol. 8, 138)	✓	105
45	910 C	139 (vol. 8, 140)		9
46	910 D	63 (vol. 5, 133) 65 (*vol. 8, 94)		4
47	920	26 (*vol. 5, 86, n. 1)	✓	13
48	921	205 (vol. 6, 35)		1
49	921 B	244 (*vol. 8, 199)		None
50	921 E	207 (vol. 6, 39)		None
51	922 A	207 (vol. 6, 38, n. 5)		1
52	930 B	80 (vol. 8, 104)	✓	32

No.	AT Classification	No. in Chauvin	Translated into Greek	Registered Greek Variants
53	934	150 (vol. 5, 253) 80 (vol. 8, 105)	✓	1
54	935**	202 (vol. 6, 31)		2
55	954	24 (vol. 5, 83, n. 3)	✓	73
56	960 A	425 (vol. 7, 146)		None
57	970	37 (vol. 5, 106)		None
58	973	no. 212 A (vol. 7, 30, n. 2)		None
59	976	110 (vol. 8, 123ff.)		None
60	981	244 (vol. 8, 199)		44
61	992 A	170 (vol. 8, 161)		None
62	1132	201 (vol. 6, 30)		None
63	1137	373 C (vol. 7, 15)	✓	2
64	1240	47 (vol. 2, 201)	✓	None
65	1250	47 (vol. 2, 201)	✓	None
66	1353	48 (vol. 2, 158), 20 (vol. 2, 195)	✓	5
67	1377	224 (vol. 8, 184)		1
68	1381 B	280 (vol. 6, 126)		None
69	1391	vol. 8, 88		None
70	1417	267 (vol. 6, 100)		1
71	1419 C	7, 8 (vol. 9, 20)		None
72	1419 D	7 (vol. 8, 39) 8 (vol. 9, 21)		1
73	1419 E	121 (vol. 5, 213) 67 (vol. 8, 96)	✓	38
74	1422	3 (vol. 8, 35f.)		None
75	1423	69 (vol. 8, 98) 34 (vol. 9, 39)		8
76	1430	3 (vol. 2, 100f., 118f.) 85 (vol. 5, 161ff., 296) 196 (vol. 8, 173)	✓	7

No.	AT Classification	No. in Chauvin	Translated into Greek	Registered Greek Variants
77	1430 A	209 (vol. 8, 178)	✓	None
78	1510	254 (vol. 8, 210)		None
79	1515	13 (vol. 8, 45)		None
80	1525 A	133 (vol. 8, 136)		44
81	1526 A	285 (vol. 6, 132)		12
82	1529	406 (vol. 7, 137)		None
83	1531	155 (*vol. 5, 274)	✓	None
84	1536 B	vol. 8, 72		9
85	1551	51 (vol. 2, 96) 430 (vol. 7, 150)	✓	None
86	1556	155 (*vol. 5, 274, n. 1)	✓	None
87	1562	187 (vol. 8, 170)		None
88	1563	342 (vol. 6, 180)		3
89	1591	28 (*vol. 8, 63)		3
90	1600	280 (vol. 6, 126)		19
91	1615	151 (vol. 5, 254, n. 2; vol. 7, 153)		1
92	1617	13 (*vol. 9, 24)		None
93	1620	32 (vol. 2, 156)		2
94	1641 A	81 (*vol. 8, 106)	✓	None
95	1642 A	280 (vol. 6, 126)		None
96	1645	258 (vol. 6, 94)	✓	None
97	1661	5 (vol. 9, 19)		None
98	1675	445 (vol. 7, 170)		3
99	1678	16 (vol. 3, 105)		3
100	1725	340 (vol. 6, 178)		25
101	1730	185 (vol. 6, 11) 186 (vol. 6, 13)		68
102	1737	147 (vol. 5, 247, n. 1)	✓	12
103	1741	341 (vol. 6, 179)		None
104	1889 H	73 (vol. 5, 151)	✓	None

Variants of the story of "The Bull and the Ass" (Chauvin, *Bibliographie* no. 104; see list no. 19) in Greek oral tradition also show a diverging plot while remaining close to the equivalent in the *Nights*. A major difference in the Greek variants of AT 670: *The Animal Languages* is the fact that the laborer has received the gift to understand the language of the animals from a grateful snake. This motif is also known from Greek mythology in the story of Melampous. A secondary difference—to be expected, however, in oral performance—refers to the variety of comic incidents that provoke the laborer's laughter. Instead of AT 207 A: *Ass Induces Overworked Bullock to Feign Sickness*, as in the *Nights*, these incidents may serve as an introduction to AT 670.

The Greek variants of AT 1730: *The Entrapped Suitors*, corresponding to three stories from the *Nights* (Chauvin, *Bibliographie* nos. 185, 186, and 187), show an interesting variation. In the Greek texts, faithfulness and faithlessness are described in the same contexts and become extremely confusing in very similar plots. Here, we recognize a process common in oral tradition, especially jokes and gossip, to consistently confuse truth and falsehood in order to veil deviant social behavior (Papachristophorou 222).

In several cases, adapted versions of entire episodes, themes, or motifs from the *Nights* circulate in Greek oral tradition and might at times affect the construction of Greek oikotypes. In the "Tale of the Ensorcelled Prince" (Chauvin, *Bibliographie* no. 222) the nocturnal adventures of the queen are quite similar to those of the ensorcelled princess in AT 306: *The Danced-Out Shoes* and precisely correspond to the tale-type's second episode. In some of the Greek variants the princess does not spend the nights in enchanted places but in the arms of a monstrous and insatiable "Arab" (i.e., black) lover, as in the version of the *Nights* (Papachristophorou 186; see also 180, 306). These impressive analogies suggest that the Greek variants of AT 306 combine the "Occidental" motif of the worn-out shoes with the "Oriental" motif of obsessive sexual love that is projected on a figure of Otherness, such as the Arab lover.

The motifs related to the clever peasant girl (Mot. J 1111.4 and H 561.1) dominating in tale-type AT 875: *The Clever Peasant Girl* and also encountered in the story of "King Kisra Anushirwan and the Village Damsel" (Chauvin, *Bibliographie* no. 198) are elaborated in completely different ways in the Greek corpus. Here the debate of the couple consists of a codified dialogue, quite different in each variant, or in the intelligent way the girl divides a roast chicken for the members of her family according to their status (such as in AT 1533: *The Wise Carving of the Fowl*). In that case we also have an interior circulation of the wise girl's theme in the collection itself, repeated in the tale of Tawaddud (Chauvin, *Bibliographie* no. 387; Miquel 41).

The story of "Khusrau and Shirin and the Fisherman" (Chauvin, *Bibliographie* no. 164) contains the motif of the king's image on the coin (Mot. J 1161.7) that dominates the plot of tale-type AT 922 B: *The King's Face on the Coin*. Apart from the clever argument, however, the two plots differ so much that they can hardly be considered as two variants of the same tale-type. While the protagonist of the Arabian story explains his cupidity as respect toward the king's image, the hero of the Greek folktale uses the argument to defend his incapacity to keep a secret.

Dissimulated inversions of certain themes are indicated by Greek variants of AT 898: *The Daughter of the Sun* that mirror the story of "Julnar the Sea-Born and Her Son King Badr Basim of Persia" (Chauvin, *Bibliographie* no. 73). In the Greek texts, the daughter of the sea refuses to speak to her human husband unless he tells her about her origins. Julnar in the *Nights*, on the contrary, breaks her self-imposed silence herself in order to tell her human husband about their forthcoming issue and explain her own origins.

The Motif of "Swan Maiden"

Analogies between the two narrative corpora under consideration are much more obvious in the case of a manifest exchange. The motif of the "Swan Maiden" (Mot. D 361.1) is very popular in both the *Arabian Nights* and in Greek imagery. It is a standard motif in the Greek variants of tale-type AT 400: *The Man on a Quest for His Lost Wife* and also appears in two stories of the *Nights*, "Hassan of Bassorah" (Chauvin, *Bibliographie* no. 212 A) and "Prince Ahmad and Perî Banû" (no. 286). Some of the Greek variants of this tale-type are introduced by tale-type AT 936*: *The Golden Mountain*, such as the story of "Hassan of Bassorah" in the *Nights* (see also Chauvin, *Bibliographie* no. 212 B, 153; Bencheikh et al. 163–92).

Through the motif of the supernatural wife, tale-type AT 400 is affiliated with types AT 402: *The Mouse (Cat, Frog, etc.) as Bride* and AT 465: *The Man Persecuted Because of His Beautiful Wife*. As Megas has shown (*Simeioseis* 148–63), these two types are fairly close to the story of "Prince Ahmad and Perî Banû," in fact the only one from the two stories mentioned above that has been translated into Greek. By further adding to the above-mentioned tales, tale-type AT 653: *The Four Skillful Brothers*, which is connected to the same story by the introduction of the three brothers who have fallen in love with the same woman, four tale-types from Greek oral tradition are in close connection with the tale from the corpus of the *Nights*.

The corpus of AT 402 in Greek oral tradition contains the main narrative elements typical for the story of "Prince Ahmad and Perî Banû"—the archery contest for the three brothers (in search of an unknown bride in the Greek corpus), the impossible tasks set by the king to his daughters-in-law in awarding the throne (presented in a different context), and their realization by way of the supernatural wife's interference. The main differences between the Arabian story and the Greek variants are the bride's animal form and the manifest question of the power going to the son who is allied with the fairy (this motif is much more dissimulated in the Greek corpus).

The archery contest serves as an alternative introduction for two more tale-types in the Greek corpus, AT 465 and AT 400. Tale-type AT 465 also preserves a considerable amount of points in common with the Arabian tale. The plot is enriched with the episode of the envious king (sometimes the hero's father) who desires the bride and sets the impossible tasks; the prince, following her instructions, manages to fulfill the tasks, culminating in the episode with the terrible little man who kills the king. Megas refers to a Greek variant registered in 1888 presenting an exact equivalent of the Arabian tale (*Simeioseis* 158). The animal form of the supernatural wife is also a dominant element in the Greek corpus of AT 465 A: *The Quest for the Unknown*, even in those variants that contain an alternative introduction. There, the hero is of low social condition, usually a fisherman, and the supernatural bride appears in the form of a turtle he has captured in his net. The couple's adventures start from the moment the fisherman destroys his wife's shell, thus exposing her to public view and arousing the king's envy. According to Megas (162f.), this form is a genuine Greek oikotype of a tale that arrived in Greece from the Orient. In Greece, it was adapted to the country's geographical conditions and to a social code not tolerating a father envious of his own son.

In AT 400 the husband, after breaking the taboo of destroying the skin of his supernatural wife, loses her and wears out iron shoes in the process of bringing her back. In spite of the introduction relating it to "Prince Ahmad and Perî Banû," this narrative form is closer to "Hassan of Bassorah." In addition, the tale-type is encountered in the Greek corpus with two other introductions, while the motifs of supernatural wife, her loss due to the hero's negligence, and the search for her have been preserved. The second group of variants adopts the "Swan Maiden" motif to express the animal form of the bride who transforms herself into a dove as in the *Nights*. Those variants are introduced by AT 936* with the further plot of abandonment on the golden mountain where the hero meets the Swan Maidens, such as in the tales of "Hassan of Bassorah," "Mazem," and "Djanshah." This form of the tale-type is so popular in the Greek corpus (thirty-two out of eighty) and so similar to the three stories from the *Nights* that it can be considered their Greek equivalent. The Greek variants do not mention the wife's animal form but attribute the fairy's supernatural qualities to a gossamer veil or dress.

These variants are close to the Greek legends about fairies with the only difference being that the quest for the lost wife is successful. The alliance with a fairy always brings the hero to a position of power and wealth, a development that is in accordance with the legendary benefactor effect of the alliance between fairies and human beings. Another persistent narrative element in those stories is the attachment of fairies to their children that is typical for fairy legends in general. Loans from legends appear to be quite common in the stories and tales we have examined on this occasion, revealing a more complex level of affiliation with this genre of orality, a suggestion enhanced by the kinship of the fairies of Greek oral tradition with the Nymphs and the *Moirai* (Fates) of Greek mythology (Papachristophorou 157–61, 170–72), connecting them with a more active disposal of human beings toward their destiny in many aspects of Greek imagery. The Greek fairies are thus close to the three Fates who always predict an irrevocable destiny for humans on the third day of their life. Moreover, they are close to the figure of Fortune that, while being unique for each human being, can be changed. This contradictory perception of destiny has probably affected the dissemination of several tale-types related to stories from the *Nights* elaborating the theme of destiny.

Conclusion

While Greek oral tradition offered a fertile soil for the creative adaptation of various tales included in the corpus of the *Arabian Nights*, it did not do so for all of them. At the same time, the similarities discussed above are neither always explicit nor do they always concern entire tale-types. Even so, they suggest a considerable exchange between the narratives of the *Nights* and Greek oral tradition. Most likely, the introduction of specific narratives into Greek oral tradition was not, however, due to the literary tradition of the *Nights* in Greek translation (or other European translations).

At the same time, this kind of transportation and mutation is decisively affected by the social beliefs of the receiving community (see Dégh 49; Holbek 408–9). Since the peoples of the eastern Mediterranean area share a secular history of cohabitation through both invasions and commercial exchange, the reception ground was even more fertile, an evaluation that applies particularly to the Balkan regions. The period of four or five centuries of Ottoman occupation had profoundly familiarized the peoples of the Balkan with Oriental mentality. That historical impact affected the approach of modern Greek scholars, who, starting with the middle of the eighteenth century, debated the argument of an uninterrupted historical continuity whose origins were posited in ancient Greece, and instead argued for a cultural kinship with the Occident toward which the newly born Greek nation was bound to turn (see Dimaras 121–44). Against that backdrop, the *Arabian Nights* at the historical moment of their introduction into scholarly consciousness in Greece could not offer an attractive field for comparative research. Nevertheless, the field for studying the similarities of narrative constituents and the sociocultural elements that facilitated their reception is vast, while divergence and variety bespeak the mechanisms of oral tradition.

NOTES

1. I would like to thank Ulrich Marzolph, Ioannis Guialopoulos, and Nikos Grekos for providing bibliographical documentation not found in Greek libraries.
2. The attribution to a fictional character was probably inspired by Pétis de la Croix, who attributed his *Mille et un Jours* to a fictional dervish "Moclès" (see Pétis de la Croix; Marzolph, *Arabia ridens* 1: 4).

WORKS CITED

Aarne, Antti, and Stith Thompson. *The Types of the Folktale: A Classification and Bibliography.* 2nd rev. ed. Helsinki: Academia Scientiarum Fennica, 1961.

Angelopoulou, Anna, and A. Brouskou, eds. *Georgiou A. Mega: Katalogos ellinikon paramythion* (George A. Megas: Catalogue of Greek Folktales). Vol. 2: AT 700–49; Vol. 3: AT 300–499. Athens: Hellenic Research Foundation, 1999.

Bencheikh, Jamel Eddine, Claude Bremond, and André Miquel. *Mille et un contes de la nuit.* Paris: Gallimard, 1991.

Chauvin, Victor. *Bibliographie des ouvrages arabes ou relatifs aux Arabes publiés dans l'Europe chrétienne de 1810 à 1885.* Vols. 4–7. Liège: Vaillant-Carmanne, 1900–1905.

———. "Homère et les Mille et une Nuits." *Le Musée Belge* 3 (1899): 6–9.

Dégh, Linda. *Folktales and Society: Story-Telling in a Hungarian Peasant Community.* Trans. Emily M. Schossberger. Bloomington: Indiana UP, 1969.

Dimaras, Konstantinos Th. *Neoellinikos Diafotismos* (Modern Greek Enlightenment). Athens: Ermis, 2002.

Dragoumis, Nicolaos. "Oi kata tin Anatolin Mythologoi" (Mythologists in the Orient). *Pandora* 1.3 (1850): 69–71.

Eberhard, Wolfram, and Pertev Naili Boratav. *Typen türkischer Volksmärchen.* Wiesbaden: Steiner, 1953.

Elisséeff, Nikita. *Thèmes et motifs des Mille et une Nuits: Essai de classification.* Beirut: Institut Français de Damas, 1949.

El-Shamy, Hasan: "Oral Traditional Tales and the Thousand Nights and a Night: The Demographic Factor." *The Telling of Stories: Approaches to a Traditional Craft.* Ed. Morten Nøjgaard et al. Odense: Odense UP, 1990. 63–117.

Gerhardt, Mia I. *The Art of Story-Telling: A Literary Study of the Thousand and One Nights.* Leiden: Brill, 1963.

Grunebaum, Gustave E. von. *L'Islam médiéval: Histoire et civilisation.* Paris: Payot, 1962.

Guys, Pierre Auguste de. *Voyage littéraire de la Grèce, ou lettres sur les Grecs, anciens et modernes, avec un parallèle de leur mœurs.* 4 vols. Paris: Veuve Duchesne, 1783.

Holbek, Bengt. *Interpretation of Fairy Tales: Danish Folklore in a European Perspective.* Helsinki: Academia Scientiarum Fennica, 1987.

Horovitz, Josef. "The Origins of the Arabian Nights." *Islamic Culture* 1 (1927): 36–57.

Iliou, Philippos: *Prosthikes stin elliniki vivliografia: A. Ta vivliografika kataloipa tou E. Legrand kai tou H. Pernot, 1515–1799* (Additions to the Greek Bibliography. A. Legrand's and Pernot's Bibliographical Remains, 1515–1799). Athens: Diogenis, 1973.

Imellos, St. D. "Laografikai eidhisis peri to Gallo periigiti P. Aug. De Guys" (Folkloristic Report on the French Traveler P. Aug. De Guys). *Epetiris tou Laografikou Arheiou* 13–14 (1960–61): 204–51.

Kaplanoglou, Marianthi. *Elliniki Laiki Paradosi: Ta paramythia sta periodika gia paidia kai gia neous* (Greek Folk Tradition: The Folktales in Children's and Youth's Magazines). Athens: Ellinika Grammata, 1998.

Kehayoglou, Yorgos. "Hilies ke Mia Nyhtes: Stathmoi stis tyhes tou ergou kai i metafrasi tou Kosta Trikoglidhi" (Thousand and One Nights: Milestones in the Fortunes of the Work and Kostas Trikoglidis's Greek Translation). *Diavazo* 33 (1980): 42–59.

———. "I defteri kai oi trites ekdoseis tou Aravikou Mythologikou" (Aravikon Mythologikon's Second and Third Editions). *Ellinika* 29 (1976): 358–62.

———, ed. *Ta Paramythia tis Halimas* (Halima's Tales). 4 vols. Athens: Hestia Bookstore, 1994/98.

Legrand, Émile. *Bibliographie Hellénique ou description raisonnée des ouvrages publiés en Grec par des Grecs au dix-huitième siècle.* Vol. 1. Paris: Garnier, 1918.

Lüthi, Max. *The European Folktale: Form and Nature.* Trans. John D. Niles. Bloomington: Indiana UP, 1982.

Macdonald, Duncan B. "The Earlier History of the Arabian Nights." *Journal of the Royal Asiatic Society* (1924): 353–97.

Marzolph, Ulrich. *Arabia ridens: Die humoristische Kurzprosa der frühen adab-Literatur im internationalen Traditionsgeflecht*. 2 vols. Frankfurt: Klostermann, 1992.

———. "Re-Locating the Arabian Nights." *Orientalia Lovanensia Analecta* 87 (1998): 155–63.

Megas, Georgios A. "Simeioseis eis ta tsakonika paramythia" (Notes on the Tsakonian Tales). *Laographia* 17 (1957): 124–78.

———. *To elliniko paramythi. Mythoi Zoon* (The Greek Folktale—Animal Tales). Athens: Academy of Athens, Publications of the Hellenic Folklore Research Center, 1978.

Meraklis, Michael G. Annotations in *Paramythia tou Livissiou kai tis Makris* (Folktales of Livisi and Makri). Ed. K. Moussaiou-Bouyoukou. Athens: K. M. S., 1976.

———. *Ta paramythia mas* (Our Folktales). Athens: Endos, 2001.

Miquel, André. *Sept contes des Mille et une Nuits*. Paris: Sindbad, 1981.

Papachristophorou, Marilena. *Sommeils et veilles dans le conte merveilleux grec*. Helsinki: Academia Scientiarum Fennica, 2002.

Pétis de la Croix, François. *Les Mille et un Jours: Contes persans*. Ed. Paul Sebag. Paris: Christian Bourgois, 1980.

Politis, Nicolaos. "Peri paramython para tois neoterois Ellisi" (On the Folktales of Modern Greeks). *Pandora* 18 (1867): 93–95.

Thompson, Stith. *The Folktale*. New York: Dryden P, 1946.

———. *Motif-Index of Folk-Literature*. 6 vols. Copenhagen: Rosenkilde and Bagger, 1955–58.

Trikoglidis, Kostas, trans. *Hilies kai Mia Nyhtes* (Thousand and One Nights). 7 vols. Athens: Iridanos, 1978–79.

18

Alf layla fârsi in Performance: Afghanistan, 1975

Margaret A. Mills

Considerable scholarly effort has been invested in tracing the probable lineage of the Arabic *Thousand and One Nights*—most commonly known as the *Arabian Nights*—back to Persia and India (Cejpek 663–66), and the presence in Persian folktales of motifs and plotlines familiar to readers of the *1001 Nights* has been noted. Yet little research has been done on the particular life of the story-collection as it was returned to modern Persian, as through the mid-nineteenth-century Persian translation of the work. The published translation itself was little discussed until recently, and with dubious accuracy. According to Mohammad Ramazâni, the editor of the 1935 Tehran edition, 'Abd al-Latif al-Tasuji, who translated the work under the patronage of Prince Bahman Mirzâ, governor of Azerbaijan, began the project in the reign of the Qajar king Mohammad Shâh, completing it in 1261/1845, and the book was first published in 1280/1863, in the reign of Nâseroddin Shâh. Recent research on the history of Qajar illustrated books offers other, more accurate dates: the translation would have been completed by Tasuji and the poet Mirzâ Sorush, who supplied Persian verses in place of some of the original Arabic poetry, in 1259/1843, with the first publication of a lithographed, two-volume edition in 1259/1843 and 1261/1845. Nâseroddin Shâh commissioned a lavishly illustrated, calligraphed manuscript of the book (in 2280 folio pages) for himself in the 1850s, finished in 1859 and now in the Golestân Library. This manuscript has been called "the last outstanding specimen of the traditional art of the book in Qajar Iran" (Marzolph, "Alf leile va leile"). Royal enthusiasm notwithstanding, Dehkhodâ's *Loghat-nâmeh* does not mention Tasuji or the work, perhaps deeming it beneath serious literary notice. On a more popular level, the introduction added to the lithographed Lahore edition under discussion here (Tasuji 1915) enthusiastically recommends the book as a rare and beautiful work, valued by tellers and readers of stories, and describes the Persian translation as intended to make the work accessible to readers of Persian, not just to scholars of Arabic. Interest in the book as a resource for live performance was thus both expected and promoted by its publishers.[1]

It was as a resource for one teller and reader of stories that the Lahore edition of *Alf layla fârsi*, as it is called on its title page, came into my possession in Herat in 1975. This was the result of a conversation about stories and literary sources with Gholâm Nabi "Binawâ" ("The Helpless," as he called himself in his poetic *takhallos* or nom de plume), one of my most productive and informative story contributors. He was a native of Navin village, near Herat, a devotee of the small Sufi shrine there, an improvisational poet, and a well-known local storyteller especially renowned for his performance of the locally famous oral romance of *Moghol Dokhtar-o Arab Bachcheh*, which by 1975 had found its way onto an audio cassette sold in the bazaar of Herat City. By profession he was the owner and driver of a famously decrepit horse taxi (*gâdi*) in and around Herat. I met him not long after I arrived in Herat, in the winter of 1974–75, at the Sufi shrine of Navin Bâlâ, introduced by the then Khalifa of the shrine, the grandson of its founding saint. A gentle and generous man, Gholâm Nabi befriended me and later introduced me to his family. I was able to record stories from him on several other occasions, at his house in Herat City as well as at my residence there. Our conversation about *Alf layla* and his performance of two stories from it, together with some other stories, occurred on August 15, 1975, at his house in Herat City, with his wife and six children, four of them his own, listening in. He told me that his wife also knew and told stories, and by their comments, it appears that they shared some oral performance connections. She remarked that her husband had learned stories from her paternal uncle, and Gholâm Nabi replied, "No, he learned stories from me," illustrating the possibility of two-directional transmission.

Our discussion of written sources for tales, which prompted his telling of the two *Alf layla* stories, was a topic I initiated. One of my major interests while tape recording live narrative performances in Herat and Kabul in 1974–76 was to trace any visible relationships between oral narrative traditions and literary ones, popular or more formal. My concern was to try to understand how, in a predominantly nonliterate population, the resources of a long-standing written tradition were or were not accessible to the general population, how individuals maintained narratives mnemonically in an oral repertoire, and how the existence of written versions might influence their oral transmission and performances. I thus asked storytellers about the source or sources of each story they told. While most of the more than 750 narrative performances I was able to record, from many different men and women and a few children, were thoroughly oral in style, performed in Herat or Kabul dialect, attributed by the tellers to oral sources and not considered by them to exist in writing, I found that performers generally could accurately identify certain stories as *ketâbî* ("from a book" or "literary"), especially those multi-episodic, prose adventure tales called in Iranian (but not in Afghan) Persian, *dâstân*. So in general, whether people were literate or not, they had a fairly clear idea of the literary or nonliterary existence of the stories they told, at least as to whether they were to be found in the chapbook literature, which, until then, was still available in bazaar bookshops. I was very excited to find that Gholâm Nabi included items from the *Thousand and One Nights* in his repertoire because it was not a book to which many storytellers attributed stories. The *Tuti-nâmeh* ("Book of the Parrot"), the *Sendbâd-nameh*, also known as *Ketâb-e Haft Vazir* ("Book of the Seven Viziers") and Hosein Vâ'ez Kâshefi's *Anvâr-e Sohayli* ("The Lights of Canopus") were story collections more likely to be mentioned.

Not long after this recording session, Gholâm Nabi and I visited a bazaar bookshop, where he definitively identified a copy of the 1915 Lahore *Alf layla fârsi* as the identical edition from which he had learned his stories. He was the only one among my prose storytelling sources who so clearly identified or could furnish a specific edition of the book he had learned from, though a few other men attributed tales to specific books they had read in years gone by but no longer possessed (cf. Mills, *Rhetorics* 229–54). In his case, too, the book had belonged to a friend named 'Omar from the nearby provincial district of Pashtun Zarghun, who had read stories to him from it. A day or two after identifying it, he went back and purchased the book for me at my request, as we had planned to record a sample of his "book-reading" style. I had told him I was interested in the art of reading aloud, as well as storytelling, and he volunteered that he could read as much as I liked. I had no reason to doubt this, but unfortunately we never got around to recording his reading style as planned. (To my knowledge, the art of story-reading still remains unstudied.) Thus the comparison offered here is between the identified source text of a story and a performance given years after the storyteller had heard and learned the tale, not a comparison of proximal performances of reading aloud versus oral improvisation of the same story. He also described himself as having heard the stories he knew, read by the book-owner, which makes it possible that his oral performance is not one but two oral transmission steps away from his identified written source text. This distance is itself a point of interest, allowing us to observe how the story was adjusted and maintained in his oral repertoire in the years after his direct contact with the written source (whether read aloud to him or orally paraphrased) ended. In the following, I discuss these points while focusing on the Persian articulations of the tale of "Judar and His Brothers."

Alf layla fârsi and Its Arabic Sources

A few words are in order about the qualities of the Persian source text itself, since Tasuji was creating a text in some sense responsive to Persian sensibilities, not just a "trot" for Persian students of Arabic. Tasuji's stated intention was to write a Persian version of *Alf layla* in a language that was attractive but also accessible to general readers of Persian (estimated to be well under 25 percent of the male population in the mid-nineteenth century and low single digits for women when he undertook the project, with similar figures prevailing in Afghanistan down to the late twentieth century). Syntactically, Tasuji's text employs straightforward, simple and compound sentence structures, with little embellishment in the way of parallel constructions or word play, and no attempt to mimic passages of Arabic rhymed prose. Arabic poetry in the original was replaced with Persian verses composed for the purpose by Mirzâ Mohammad 'Ali "Sorush" (1228–85/1813–68/69). Compared to either Herat or Kabul dialect, however, the text still contains a relatively large number of Arabic loanwords, including some that would be unfamiliar or sound "literary" to unlettered Afghan Persian speakers, and some obviously deployed for Arabic "local color," as when the characters in the story greet each other with "Marhabâ!"—a standard Arabic welcome not used in colloquial Persian. As for content, Tasuji's translation in most details corresponds exactly to the Arabic texts used by Lane and Burton. Although Judar has become Judaz, and the city of Fâs becomes Fârs, other personal and most place names remain as in the Arabic. Tasuji omits details at the level of the specifically named gate of Cairo through which Judaz returns from the Maghreb. He also identifies the captain who kidnaps Judaz only as a sea captain, not specifically the naval officer supervising shipping in the Suez, whose responsibility would include press-ganging or purchasing galley slaves.

Conversational exchanges seem for the most part plucked verbatim from the Arabic, with only a few exceptions, for example, a somewhat reduced frequency of pious statements, prayers by Judaz's mother, and allusions to fate by the hero. Tasuji also reduces some of the exuberant descriptive detail of the original, such as the very Cairene list of elaborate dishes produced by the magic saddlebag to the astonishment of the hero, and the detailed description of the book of magic (a compendium key to mysteries and unlocking of treasures) which the Maghrebi brothers are in competition to claim from their father's estate. Tasuji also shortens slightly the description of the four magical objects to be retrieved from the Treasure of Shamardal. At first mention of the treasure, there is also what seems to be a content error, describing the third object not as a kohl bottle but as "a volume" (*yak jild*).[2] This is corrected in subsequent descriptions of the treasure. (There is a similarly minor lapse in the later scene when the Amir 'Osmân is routed by Judâz's *'ifrît* servant, who at first is said to strike 'Osmân with the flat of his own sword, rather than with his own mace.) There are a few minor scribal errors in the Lahore edition, including what appear to be omissions of a few words and repetitions of a phrase or sentence here and there.

Generally, the structural repetitions of narrative detail in Arabic, starting with directions given, followed by action scenes and subsequent recapitulations (e.g., Judaz reporting to the Maghrebi on his action in the treasure house) are only occasionally shortened by Tasuji.[3] Such stylistic repetitions are of interest because, as a mainstay of oral text structure, they are "slots" for optional elaboration where the performer can lengthen or shorten according to his or her own taste and perception of the audience's understanding and interest.

Occasionally, Tasuji shows a more explicit visual or dramatic imagination than Burton or Lane, as when he implies that the "Great Names" that must be spoken to command the *'ifrît* servant in the magic saddlebag are inscriptions woven into the bag's design, making the bag itself a sort of woven talisman. When Sâlem and Salim, the evil brothers, come to tell their mother of Judaz's disappearance after they have had him kidnapped, Tasuji elaborates a more psychologically subtle exchange in which the brothers pretend to think that Judaz is just sleeping late, leaving their mother to infer that he has voluntarily departed with the guests of the night before. In general, Tasuji leaves the dramatic role of Judaz's mother well elaborated, slightly reducing her dialogue lines in some places (e.g., in chastising her evil sons) but enlarging them a bit in others. The forty beautiful white slave girls attached to Judaz's magic palace become a thousand in the Lahore edition, while the other slave cohorts of forty each remain the same. Tasuji has Judaz sit in state "like a king" with his slaves arrayed on both sides of him when the king of Mesr comes calling. Prior to that, when the stupid and vain Amir 'Osmân is sent to summon Judaz and his brothers to the king, in Tasuji's version 'Osmân abuses the insolent eunuch guarding the gate (actually the *'ifrît* Ra'd al-Qâsif) for "lounging like some pregnant woman," while Burton/Lane use the more generic "like a gallows bird" (Burton) or "like those who have no shame" (Lane).

In general, Tasuji reduces somewhat the colorful detail of courtly and political dealings, as when he omits the observation made in Lane/Burton by the Egyptian king's wise vizier, that the king need not fear Judar's taking over his kingdom, since Judar already enjoys a condition superior to the king's and it would be beneath his dignity to do so. The congregational mosque that Judar builds over the grave of his eventual father-in-law, the king of Egypt, becomes a mausoleum, as for a shrine, in Persian. Tasuji also makes other minor changes in descriptive detail in keeping with differences between Cairene and Persian customary dress or house furnishings. Because Tasuji preserves verbatim the overwhelming majority of exchanges between characters and descriptive detail, it is tempting to try to infer some stylistic or conceptual intentions when he does not do so, but perhaps the main interest in such subtle patterns of emendation is to see that some of them are more radically carried out, perhaps for other reasons, in Gholâm Nabi's oral performance. In general, Tasuji preserves the novella- (or *dâstân-*)like specificity of the Arabic text, with its details of Cairene and Maghrebi geography, its occasionally pungent and psychologically resonant dialogue, the elaborate background story of the Maghrebi brothers' competition for the unique book in their father's estate, and the exotic, novel quality of its descriptions of unusual and enigmatic magical objects and persons.

From Written Text to Oral Performance

Admirers of the particular, rich atmosphere of the Cairene story of Judar and his brothers may feel disappointed at the general direction and pervasiveness of its simplification and alteration in Gholâm Nabi's oral performance. I would argue, though, that an assumption of devolutionary processes ("forgetting," narrative incompetence, or inarticulateness) from written to oral literature is not a sufficient basis for understanding such changes because it does not situate the observer to understand conditions of effective oral performance that influence the performer's choices, whether those choices be conscious or below awareness. Hence the observations offered here will be a sampling of comparisons organized around certain issues pertaining to oral genres and performance style, rather than a comprehensive description of this performance. Gholâm Nabi's rapidly enunciated oral text, at twenty-five minutes long, is unfortunately too long to include verbatim or analyze comprehensively in this discussion, though it is of medium length for an oral story according to my recording experience, perhaps even a little on the short and succinct side for an adept male narrator used to holding the stage, such as Gholâm Nabi was. At a few points early in his performance, he used the phrase, *kutâhî sokhan*, "speaking briefly," indicating that he was consciously shortening or summarizing the story in certain ways.

With regard to speech register, Gholâm Nabi alternated in this story between use of standard Persian formations (verb endings, formations of pronouns, and the object marker), which were regarded as *ketâbî* ("book-style") by Heratis, and a more purely colloquial Herat dialect style affecting these formations as well as certain forms of metathesis. The alternation is so fine-grained as to vary even within sentences, for example, a colloquial subject pronoun or object marker combined with a book-style verb ending, or alternations of register within one reported speech segment by the same person, suggesting overall that he was not deploying the literary/colloquial register alternation intentionally to demarcate different kinds of speakers or speech situations, but was lapsing in and out of *ketâbî* style as something appropriate to mark a story drawn from literature, but not fully demanded by our particularly informal, domestic performance situation. (*Ketâbî* style was in my limited observation constantly employed for reading aloud in performance, thus used in varying degree by oral storytellers to mark a tale as literary.) In his use of cadence, pitch, and pause, Gholâm Nabi fell readily into a rapid, somewhat loud, clearly enunciated, rhythmic and also rather emphatically tonal declamatory speech style, which he was able to sustain for long periods of monologue, projecting his words amply and clearly. His rapid pace allowed little room for interruption by audience commentary or questions. All in all, his narrative speaking style was well designed to take and hold the conversational floor, even in a larger setting where extraneous noise might be a problem. This declamatory style was, to that extent, also a male style, since women's narrative performance settings were exclusively private and domestic.

Another stylistic choice marking Gholâm Nabi's categorization of this tale as *ketâbî* was his use of tale-opening formulas commonly attached only to stories regarded as literary, being derived from the opening formulas used in *dâstân* or chapbook romances to refer their authority to oral tradition: *ammâ râbiyân-e akhwâl o nâqelân-e âsâr, mohaddesân-e shirin sokhan goftâr chandin rewâyat mikonan[d] keh dar ayyâm-e qadim . . .* (Now, the repeaters of sayings/news and the narrators of [literary] remains, the reciters of tradition, sweet of speech, so relate that in ancient days . . .).[4]

A number of the simplifications of content most striking in Gholâm Nabi's performance invoke generic or formulaic expectations for the Persian magical folktale (*afsâne*), some of which are present but strikingly subverted in the Arabic and Persian literary tale of Judar/Judaz. One might usefully approach the *Judar* story as an inversion and/or subversion of folktale patterns that are well known to this performer, and to see his approach to the story partly in that light. Judar as the youngest, virtuous brother in a set of three partakes of a standard motif in *afsâne* and in international folktale tradition. If there are three siblings, male or female, two will be incompetent and/or wicked and the third and youngest ("youngest last and best") will triumph heroically. The three Maghrebi adventurers repeat this structure, two brothers who fail the test and one who succeeds, extragenerically adding yet a fourth brother who partakes of the Proppian role of a test-setting or donor figure.[5]

Most strikingly, *afsâne*, like European Märchen in almost all cases, end happily with the apotheosis of the hero or heroine, in a royal wedding and happy afterlife: Judar/Judaz gets his apotheosis, with a triumphant return home and royal wedding followed by ascent to the throne, only to be murdered finally and unheroically by his wicked brothers, who in the standard *afsâne* version of this plotline would have already been exposed and neutralized, often killed, as part of the hero's apotheosis. Instead, the hero has rescued them from deserved incarceration (punishment for their last betrayal of him) and installed them as his viziers. Burton observed that most of the tales in the *1001 Nights* do preserve poetic justice. He sees the unjust outcome of Judar's story as perhaps its main point: "Judar in all his goodness proved himself an arrant softy and was no match for two obvious villains. And there may be overmuch of forgiveness as of every other category" (Burton 6: 255, n. 1).

The configuration of bad and good brothers in its generic folktale form was demonstrably ready to mind for Gholâm Nabi. During the same storytelling session, immediately before telling his version of a single voyage from the Sindbad series in the *Nights*, which he told just prior to *Judaz*, he had told a story he titled *Soltân Sekandar*, in which the hero is betrayed by his two brothers, who repeatedly try to get him killed as they pursue various quests. Although they maim him, cutting off his hands, and leave him for dead, Sekandar eventually defeats them and they are disposed of, as is not uncommon for Afghan folktale villains, by being burned alive in dog manure.[6] Prior to that, however, he also is rescued and joined by two other men, a hunter and a blind man, who become his foster brothers and, when he gains the throne, his viziers. Thus, like the *Judaz* story, this tale told in the same session also contained a contrastive foil (loyal foster brothers of Sekandar, noncombatively competitive Maghrebi brothers) to the main configuration of three brothers, two of whom are murderers.

It was my asking whether this first romancelike story, named after Sekandar, was *ketâbî* or not that led to our discussion of the *Thousand and One Nights* and Gholam Nabi's performances of the single Sindbad episode[7] and *Judaz*, the two stories he identified in his own active repertoire as being from the *1001 Nights*. Whether or not the preceding three brothers motif cued his memory of the Judaz story in particular, it is striking that in his version of *Judaz* he did not use the sibling rivalry concept as elaborated in the *1001 Nights*, the three brothers from the same mother, two of them perversely abusive toward their own mother (while Judaz is an ideal son just as he is an endlessly, even mindlessly, loyal brother). Rather, Gholâm Nabi deployed the form of this motif that is ubiquitous in polygynous Afghanistan (and also used elsewhere in the Arabic *1001 Nights*; see El-Shamy): Judaz, the youngest son, is from a different mother than his brothers. In Afghan folktale logic this is sufficient to explain their murderous jealousy, because the junior wife is presumed to be preferred over the senior wife, together with her offspring. Afghan oral tradition includes some very negative portrayals of polygyny, articulated differently by men and women no doubt, but the impossibility of treating two wives equally well, mentioned in the Koran, is also a basic assumption underlying sibling rivalry themes in Afghan tales. Gholâm Nabi has only to state that they are three sons from two mothers, and no more needs to be explained about the two elders' hostility. This is, of course, also the relationship of Yusof (the biblical Joseph) and his elder brothers, a story universally known both from the Koran and from many literary and oral renditions and references. (The mother of Salim and Sâlem is not introduced into the plot by Gholam Nâbi—presumably she is dead.) Thus rather than retain the more fluctuating, nuanced, novelistic portrayal of the two elder brothers' manipulative relationship with their own mother, which intensifies their villainy beyond simple sibling rivalry, Gholâm Nabi simplifies by falling back on a generic folktale motif, half-siblinghood (the psychological equivalent of step-relations in European tales), that requires little or no character development to drive the plot.

Furthermore, Gholâm Nabi describes the process of litigation between the brothers over the legacy of their father in terms most familiar to rural farmers, not urban Heratis. The witnesses to the father's division of his property before his death are not his relations and the representatives of the *qâzi* (religious judge), as in the literary versions, but the *arbâb* (village head) and *rish-safidân* (elders, "white-beards"), the normal witnesses to such transactions in villages. The brothers do not demand their father's portion (which was left to the mother who now resides with Judaz), but instead, they demand that their three shares be reconsolidated and redivided after their father's death, because he has divided unfairly. Specifically, they allege that he has given Judaz the land lying at the upper end of the irrigation channel (*milk-e sar*) and given them the land lying at the lower end (*milk-e pây*), which is less productive because it tends to get less water, or none at all in times of drought. This would be reasonable grounds for complaint in a village environment, if true, but Judaz refuses to redivide, whereupon they lodge complaints with the government (this being a desperate strategy for those denied by local village elders, bound to involve corruption and bribes; see Mills, "The Lion and the Leopard"; Mills, *Rhetorics* 203–4) and impoverish themselves in litigation.

One striking structural reduction running through the whole story is Gholâm Nabi's omission of any mention of the magical objects that are the means and goal of the Maghrebi brothers' competitive questing, nor indeed any mention of the complicated background story of their rivalry over their father's legacy, specifically their father's book, as arbitrated by their father's teacher (in both the literary versions). The three are still called brothers, but Gholâm Nabi calls them not "Maghrebi" but simply *mollâ,* in the sense not of clergymen but of learned, literate folk. They are not competing to see who can possess their father's best book of magic, but simply to win a treasure. No backstory is ever told about their friendly but potentially fatal (and greedy) rivalry over their father's legacy, which in the literary versions could be a mirror to Judar/Judaz's dangerously unstable relationship with his own evil brothers. In Gholâm Nabi's telling, the treasure does not contain magical objects, but only an endless amount of wealth (the same valuables that Judar/Judaz is instructed to ignore in the literary tales), and is not presided over by the magically undecayed body of the mysterious, ancient sorcerer Shamardal (who is not mentioned), but becomes instead one of innumerable treasures sealed away by the magic-wielding Solomon the Prophet, whose magical arrangements more or less litter the imaginary landscape of Afghan oral tradition.

Even the magical saddlebag, which so rivets the attention of the hungry and impoverished Judar when he first travels with the Maghrebi, is not introduced by Gholâm Nabi until Judaz is told to name his reward after he has enabled the *mollâ* to retrieve the treasure. Then Gholam Nabi simply mentions that the *mollâ* had this object and that Judaz saw it as a better remedy for his perpetual poverty than a supply of treasure that would eventually run out. Instead of saying, as in the literary versions, "You should have chosen something better, with greater power, this only supplies food," Gholâm Nabi's *mollâ* says, "I had in mind just this thing for you," and also gives him a share of treasure and a riding horse to take home.

Just as there are no magical objects in the treasure, there are no supernatural *'ifrît* helpers accompanying the treasure hunter or Judaz, except later, when the treasure-hunting *mollâ* again meets the kidnapped and impoverished Judaz in Mecca, where he buys him out of a servant relationship and sends him home with a gift, not the seal ring of Shamardal with the impressive Ra'd the *'ifrît* at its command, as in the literary versions, but two *pari* (female fairies), called Nurjân and Hurjân. They transport him home in an instant and summon their pari friends and relations to build him a palace overnight, *yak khesht-e talâ o yak khesht-e noghreh* ("one brick of gold and one brick of silver"), the usual *afsâne* shorthand for such *pari* constructions (in contrast to the more elaborate discussion of the building, decoration, and furnishing of the palace by Ra'd, the "Servant of the Ring" and his cohort of *'ifrît* helpers in the literary versions of the tale). Taking a second motif right out of *afsâne* vocabulary, Gholâm Nabi has the king and his vizier notice this remarkable new structure at dawn, when they see a light breaking in the west rather than the east, shining off the resplendent building.

This simple and formulaically familiar mode of detection of magical palaces replaces a much more intricately plotted process of revelation. In both literary versions, Judar/Judaz first learns from his old benefactor, the Maghrebi diviner, while in Mecca, of his brothers' incarceration after his kidnapping and the king's confiscation of the magical saddlebag and his other possessions, which his brothers were quarreling over. Angry at the plight of his imprisoned brothers (but evidently not blaming them for having him kidnapped), he goes home directly to confront the king. He has Ra'd, the *'ifrît* servant of his newly acquired magic seal-ring, free his brothers from prison immediately and magically empty the king's entire treasury as well as build the magical palace and staff it with beautiful, grandly dressed slaves overnight. The king, in fury, is consulting with his advisors about who could have looted the treasury without breaking any locks or digging any holes, when the policeman who first overheard the quarreling brothers and got them arrested remarks that he has watched the building of an immense palace overnight, and learned that the returned Judaz is occupying it with his brothers, who have been mysteriously released from prison. Only because of the miraculous emptying of his treasury does the king notice all of Judaz's other doings. In Gholâm Nabi's telling, Judaz does not seek to learn the whereabouts of his brothers or his former possessions at all, until after he has married the king's daughter, succeeded to the throne on the king's death, and undertaken an inventory-tour of the treasury and the prison. There he finds his possessions and frees his brothers, immediately making them his viziers (as he also does in the literary versions). This simplification following a stripped-down sequence in which the king in short order invites Judaz to court with a quick letter of invitation and contrives for him to fall in love with his daughter, rather than gradually developing a trusting friendship with him, substantially mutes the theme of the king's injudiciousness, justice, and injustice (mostly the latter), developed in the literary tales.

Gholâm Nabi retains the major repetitive structures of folktale quests presented in the literary tale (three brothers, the last one successful; the hero making two attempts to fulfill his quest, the first being unsuccessful because he failed to follow an injunction). Three Maghrebi brothers are cast into the sea, only the last survives. Judaz must attempt the treasure twice, a year apart, because he succumbed to the pleadings of the illusory figure of his mother, not to make her strip naked, in the first try. Furthermore, his brothers make three attempts to destroy Judaz, the first through litigation, the second through kidnapping, and the third, successful one, through poison.

Much else is compressed, however, as illustrated by the above examples. Geographically, also, Gholâm Nabi eliminates much rich detail but maintains narrative coherency in all but a few details. Arab local color is virtually eliminated: He does not name the Maghreb and other Arab-land destinations, except for Mecca, nor the various places around Cairo. Both the three *mollâs* being cast into the water and the opening of the treasure occur at the same point by the sea where Judaz has been fishing (called the *daryâ*, designating either a sea or a wide, large river in Herâti, not otherwise named).

Judaz helps the Maghrebi catch one fish, not obviously magical, simply described as a very big fish, not the two small, red fish–'*ifrît* brothers, sons of the Red King that the literary Maghrebi must master in order to approach the treasure. That fish is not mentioned again. Then the surviving *mollâ* loads Judaz on his horse and takes him to his own home in preparation for opening the treasure, but the home is not said to be any distance from the seaside scene of the quest. Nor is there any extended waiting, feasting, and otherwise enjoying the *mollâ*'s hospitality and hearing his mysterious history, before the astrological moment when Judaz can make his first attempt. When he fails, the *mollâ* simply sends him back to his own home with money to keep him (and presumably his mother) until the following year, when he meets the mollâ again by appointment (carefully kept by Judaz) at the waterside. Once he succeeds at the second attempt on the treasure, Judaz is sent home on horseback with his rewards, but no magical travel on '*ifrît* mules is required. Gholâm Nabi retains the emotional scene in which Judaz finds his mother begging by the side of the road, throws himself down to embrace her, sets her on his horse, leads her home tenderly, and feeds the starving woman from the magic saddlebag, but the emotion and logic of this reunion are somewhat marred by the fact that he apparently has not been away from home very long in this altered scenario. (Also she is offered a simple choice of the three commonest, most generic Afghan major meal types: "Do you want roast chicken, or rice, or meat soup [*shorwâ*], or what?" and regaled with a roast chicken and a large platter of rice, not the multiple delicacies more extensively and tantalizingly described in the literary versions.)

Character roles are also somewhat compressed: besides the reduction of the cast of supernatural characters, the generic sea captain who kidnaps Judaz at the invitation of his brothers befriends him when he sees what a willing and honest worker he is, instead of dying in a shipwreck from which Judaz barely escapes, as in both literary versions. Thus this same sea captain is the one who later takes him as a paid servant to Mecca, not a subsequent rescuer as in the literary tales. This sort of contraction is certainly of Gholâm Nabi's own devising (if not that of his friend, 'Omar the book-reader), and not governed by any generic character pattern in folktale nor simply an omission, but a simplification of roles, which nonetheless remains both psychologically plausible and serviceable in support of the general plot structure. This compression also provides a more vivid illustration of Judaz's essential goodness, which converts one of his would-be oppressors to an ally (as the king of Mesr is later and more elaborately converted in the literary versions of the story).

Interestingly, Gholâm Nabi also changed entirely the story the brothers told the sea captain to persuade him to kidnap Judaz, not necessarily for the sake of simplicity, but perhaps toward a tighter plot logic. Instead of having the eldest brother (the instigator and planner of attacks on Judaz) tell the sea captain the true story of the conflict between them, only lyingly reversing the roles to make Judar/Judaz the instigator, as in the literary tale, Gholâm Nabi has the elder brother explain that Judaz is a servant, and a good one, but one whom they must remove from their household against his will for reasons unstated (such unstated reasons might include an attachment to a woman of the house, not something to be mentioned to outsiders). Then when Judaz, at his brothers' treacherous request, receives the sea captain in his own home and serves him and his brothers with his own hands as if he were their servant (a normal behavior for a male Afghan host without a lot of household servants, but not what one would expect from a man so vicious to his brothers as the literary brothers have described him to be), it is easy for the brothers to represent Judaz to the sea captain as the servant they want to sell, or even give away, due to some unspoken family need. If anything, Gholâm Nabi's revision of this scene achieves a tighter surface narrative logic than the literary versions, but loses the savage irony and deep psychology of blaming the victim, contained in the villainous Sâlem's precisely describing and condemning his own self-destructive rapacity against his brother, but attributing his own actions to his saintly sibling.

Where the literary tale has sevens, Gholâm Nabi has contracted to patterns of three: Judaz goes fishless for three days before he meets the first *mollâ*. The treasure only confronts him with three tests, not seven: he must withstand only two attacks, a blow from a dagger aimed at his head (which turns on the attacker and kills him) and another aimed at his breast (turned likewise), rather than the sequence of five violent attacks with different weapons (sword, lance, bow and arrow, lion, dragons), interspersed with a password exercise linking the fifth and sixth doors. In all versions, the real test for Judar/Judaz is to be violently and sexually aggressive toward the simulacrum of his mother, forcing him to override his impeccable devotion to her in the real world. Gholâm Nabi's treatment of this scene is vivid in its evocation of Herati lived experience, as was his treatment of the original quarrel between the brothers. The illusory mother greets Judaz with affectionate Herat-dialect baby talk and cites not just his generic debt for her milk but her intimate services to him in highly local color: "I gave you chewed meat" (*gosht-e nâzeh*), a reference to Herati mothers' practice of masticating meat to place in the mouth of a teething child, and "When the smallpox came I sat up with you through the nights," a vivid reminder of the frequency and seriousness of smallpox in Afghan family experience prior to the latter half of the twentieth century when vaccination drives eradicated it.

While Judar/Judaz's reciprocated devotion to his mother is the touchstone of his virtue in all these stories, she slips from view before the end, disappearing into the magical palace in the literary versions when he ceremoniously invites her to take up residence in it (along with his brothers), after which she does not again appear. Instead, as his new female companion, he falls in love with and marries the princess who proves also to be his posthumous ally. She is more of a doer than the mother, acting to avenge his death (and avoid his double-fratricide brother's lustful demands that she marry him) by a feigned invitation to her chambers followed by a quick dose of poison for Sâlem in a glass of water. This is perfect reciprocity for his poisoning his all-too-trusting brother at the dinner to which he invited him. In both literary versions, but not in Gholam Nabi's telling, she then restores order by destroying the ring and the saddlebag, the magic objects the men have coveted, so that they will never again be the cause of quarrels, and in highly proper deference to male and religious authority, she sends word to the Sheikh ol-islâm to arrange for the selection of a new king.

In Gholâm Nabi's telling, Judaz's mother disappears earlier, not reappearing after Judaz's return from Mecca, when he so quickly converts himself to a royal son-in-law. Gholâm Nabi makes the princess bride more martially heroic and less proper than her literary counterpart. Instead of resorting to poison, this girl sharpens and hangs a dagger behind her door, ushers the evil brother into her chamber deferentially (punk that he is, he pushes ahead of her, not to let her take a seat first), and seizing the dagger slices off his head from behind "like a carrot." She says defiantly (and highly colloquially) to his corpse, *"Dutar keh to koshti, yeki raun be meh mireseh keh man bakoshom"* ("Now that you've killed two, my turn's come to kill one"). Then she dons a black mask (*niqâb*) to set aside her social role as a female,[8] takes the throne, and rules for herself, "all topsy turvy" (*chappeh chappeh hokm mikard*). With this newly configured scene, Gholâm Nabi thus ends this injustice- and blood-stained antifolktale on a slightly comical note, emphasizing yet undercutting the girl's heroic action in the absence of appropriate male authority, and leaving the polity in a condition of ludicrous imbalance (from an Afghan point of view) with a woman in charge of the state.

He ends with a brief improvisation on an oral-style *afsâne*-closing formula (normally some statement of separation from the story world, paraphrasing "And they stayed there, and we came here to tell about it"): *wo i dar bâdeshâhi bud, mâ âmadim dar radd-foqrâwi-e khod* ("And she was on the throne, [and] we came along in pursuit of our poverty"). On this final note, it is well to remember the storyteller's devotion to Sufism, in which "poverty" or "beggars' ways" (*foqrâwi*) can be glossed as spiritual poverty, a highly desired position of humility vis-à-vis God and the materialistic world. This seemingly comical, self-denigrating or even begging ending was thus only superficially or deceptively so for this speaker, who had taken as his poet's name (*takhallos*) "Binawâ," or "helpless," which also refers to spiritual abjection and submission to God.

In sum, Gholâm Nabi's narrative abandons most of the rich circumstantial detail of the literary Judar/Judaz story, in favor of elements drawn directly from the discourse of Afghan Persian oral folktale (*afsâne*) and locally familiar cultural arrangements. Yet this is not a problem of erosion or default to a well-known genre, but a systematic editing process, certainly conscious in some aspects and perhaps not so conscious in others. While he (and/or his source, 'Omar the book-owner) changes large and small aspects of the plot, setting, and characters, the story remains coherent. "Local color" elements and voices are shifted and added to appeal to his local audience, but, most interestingly, he preserved the ironic or genre-subversive trajectory of the plot, as a subverted or inverted fairy tale. It would be simple enough for him, as a fluent narrator, to "fix" the ending of this story that Judaz's brothers are punished and he lives on happily with a wife and a kingdom as a folktale hero should. All that would have to happen is that Gholâm Nabi have Judaz, like any normally canny folktale hero, simply take the precaution of surreptitiously rotating that platter of rice when it is presented to him laced with poison on his side, so that the poisoner, eating in feigned friendliness from the other side, would be undone by his own poison. It happens often enough in folktales.

Clearly, though, if our storyteller was thoroughly familiar with folktale motifs, our hero was not, or else was, as before, temporarily deprived by his brotherly affection of the folktale hero's quick-witted sense of self-preservation, because he was not ultimately resident in that world of poetic justice. Nor are we. As jarring as this tale was to me, heard in a sequence of happy-ending tales (even Sindbad's that went before it), and by its tripartite structure and contents right up to the end evoking the logical world of folktale in which everything somehow comes out right in the end, the great wrongness of this tale's conclusion invokes that world of folktale and causes us to reflect on the question of justice as we wish it were, and as it may not be. Gholâm Nabi, for and even because of all his fluent reliance on the idiom of folktale, preserved the dark heart of this story in a relocated social, stylistic, and performance setting that if anything intensifies its challenge to any audience attuned to its folktale idioms.

NOTES

I am indebted to the United States Fulbright-Hayes Fellowship program and the Sheldon Fellowships program of Harvard University for the original financial support for this research. Kazem Alami helped with corrections of the transcription and glosses for Herat dialect expressions. Dick Davis and Ulrich Marzolph are to be thanked for information and encouragement. Most of all, I am indebted to the late Gholâm Nabi "Binawâ" for his artistry, generosity, and graciously good-humored friendship. All errors of interpretation remain my own achievement.

1. That this popular edition was more intended for hearing than for looking is perhaps indicated by its economy of illustration. There are a total of thirty-two workmanlike lithographed illustrations, about half of them courtly audience scenes, in the two volumes.
2. The word, which also means "skin" or "cover," may possibly have suggested to some Persian folktale listeners a changeling's coat or cover, though that motif in Persian is almost exclusively limited to the *jeld-e kabutar,* or dove skin, that *pari* (fairy) women may put on to fly around the human world, thus giving their human male admirers something to steal, so as to capture them when they are caught bathing. This association does not fit the overall motif pattern of the treasure trove though.
3. Lacking Arabic myself, I am dependent on Lane's and Burton's translations for comparison; Lane himself seems to omit or reduce some repetitions that Burton leaves in, which are also present in Persian, so I take Burton as the better indicator of the degree of repetition in Arabic.
4. Transcribed to reflect Herat dialect vocalization. Even in this explicit evocation of written sources the narrator includes characteristically Herati colloquial forms: *akhwâl* for *aqwâl,* "speeches, sayings, words," equally possible to be understood under dialect metathesis rules as *akhbâr,* ("news, information"), and *mikonam* for *mikonan(d).* For nonliterary stories, there is a separate body of opening formulas using comical, rhymed nonsense mininarratives to frame the story that follows as fanciful or fictitious. See Mills, *Rhetorics* 201–3 and Marzolph, *Typologie* 22f.
5. Vladimir Propp argues that the fairytale genre deploys a set list of only seven formulaic character roles, one of which is the "donor," a figure who may test the hero or heroine's character but then supplies him or her with information or equipment necessary to success in a quest. If the fourth Maghrebi acts as a sort of referee for his brothers and a sort of donor for Judar/Judaz, the surviving Maghrebi treasure hunter becomes clearly the donor to Judar/Judaz as hero, Judar/Judaz's treasure retrieval on behalf of the Maghrebi being readable as a

particularly elaborate form of the donor's test, after which the hero is rewarded with magical objects to help solve his own problems.

6. A devastatingly polluting death. Burning is considered to presage their treatment in Hell. Dog manure is the impurest of the impure. Note also the reversible punishment of bad siblings through transformations into female dogs in the *1001 Nights*, discussed by El-Shamy. Another level of irony in such transformations, explicit in other stories including dogs, from Afghan sources, is the implication of the loyal nature of dogs vis-à-vis humans despite their abject impurity.

7. Gholâm Nabi calls him Sonnad-e Hammâl and does not name the other porter who listens to his story. Unfortunately there is no room here to analyze this performance as well.

8. Donning a *niqâb* is one of the acts of a woman assuming a masculine role in folktales.

WORKS CITED

Burton, Richard F. *The Book of the Thousand Nights and a Night.* 17 vols. Privately printed: The Burton Club, 1885.

Cejpek, Jiří. "The Iranian Element in the *Book of a Thousand and One Nights* and Similar Collections." Jan Rypka. *History of Iranian Literature.* Ed. Karl Jahn. Dordrecht: D. Reidel, 1968. 663–69.

El-Shamy, Hasan. "Siblings in Alf laylah wa-laylah." *Marvels & Tales* 18.2 (2004): 170–86.

Lane, Edward W. *The Arabian Nights' Entertainment, or the Thousand and One Nights.* 4 vols. New York: Tudor, 1927.

Marzolph, Ulrich. "Alf leile va leile (Hezâr-o yek shab)." *The Beginning of Printing in the Near and Middle East: Jews, Christians and Muslims.* Ed. Lehrstuhl für Türkische Sprache, Geschichte und Kultur, Universität Bamberg, Staatsbibliothek Bamberg. Wiesbaden: Harrassowitz, 2001. 88.

———. *Typologie des persischen Volksmärchens.* Beirut and Wiesbaden: Franz Steiner, 1984.

Mills, Margaret. "The Lion and the Leopard: The Composition of a New Fable in Traditional Style Articulates a Family Dispute." *Arv* (1981): 53–60.

———. *Oral Narrative in Afghanistan: The Individual in Tradition.* New York: Garland, 1990.

———. *Rhetorics and Politics in Afghan Traditional Storytelling.* Philadelphia: U of Pennsylvania P, 1991.

Propp, Vladimir. *Morphology of the Folktale.* Trans. Laurence Scott. Austin: U of Texas P, 1968.

Tasuji, 'Abd al-Latif al-. *Alf layla fârsi.* 2 vols. (bound as one). Lahore: Islamieh P, 1332–33/1915.

———. *Alf layla wa-layla.* Ed. Mohammad Ramazâni. Tehran: Tâbesh Printing House, 1315/1935.

19

The Tale of "Aladdin and the Magic Lamp" in Balochi Oral Tradition

Sabir Badalkhan

During my field work in Pakistani Balochistan,[1] I have on three different occasions recorded oral performances of the tale of "Aladdin and the Magic Lamp," commonly known from its inclusion in the *Arabian Nights*. In September 1996, I recorded the tale in Gwâdar from Swâlî, an illiterate blind man in his late eighties. The narrator was originally from a village near Ball Nigwar in the Dasht valley and had now settled in Gwâdar. He had worked as a cameleer (*sârbân*) all his active life and had learned most of his tales in the course of his travels. I recorded the same tale twice from Jangyân, a man in his mid-forties. The first variant (Jangyân-1) was recorded on October 5, 1997, in his native village of Shâpuk (east of Turbat), the second one (Jangyân-2) on September 5, 2003, at the same location. Jangyân works as a daily laborer. Being illiterate, he had learned his tales from oral sources but did not remember any details about the process. While the tale of "Aladdin's Lamp" is also listed in Amanullâh Ghâzî's collection of Balochi folktales from Panjgûr, it is not contained in the book.

In the following, I discuss the Balochi versions of the tale of Aladdin and the relation of their themes and motifs to the version of the *Arabian Nights*.

The Origin of the Tale of "Aladdin and the Magic Lamp"

The tale of Aladdin is one of the most popular tales in the *Arabian Nights*. It is basically a magic tale with the magic lamp as the main motif (Thompson,

Motif-Index [henceforth Mot.] D 845: *Magic object found in underground room;* D 1162.1: *Magic lamp;* D 1662.2: *Magic lamp works by being stroked;* D 1470.1.16: *Magic wishing lamp;* D 1421.1.5: *Magic lamp summons genie,* etc.). The tale does not occur in any of the known Arabic texts of the *Nights* prior to the translation by Antoine Galland, who got hold of it by a stroke of luck. When Galland was finishing the seventh volume of his translation of the *Nights* and had exhausted the manuscript material available to him, he was introduced "to a Maronite from Aleppo, named Hanna, brought to France by the traveller Paul Lucas. Hanna related to him in Arabic some of the stories which fill his last four volumes and gave him copies of some of them in writing" (Macdonald 157; Elisséeff 73–74). In 1888, Hermann Zotenberg published an Arabic manuscript of the tale preserved in the Bibliothèque Nationale in Paris, France. However, doubts were raised about the authenticity of the tales later added to the original manuscript, and some scholars even thought that they had been invented by Galland (Clouston 345). The tale's Arabic text as published by Zotenberg, originally believed to be copied from a lost manuscript written in Baghdad in 1703, has meanwhile been proven to constitute a deliberate forgery produced by the Lebanese scholar Michel Sabbagh (Mahdi 61–72). In subsequent popular tradition, the tale of Aladdin has become one of the most widely known tales of the *Arabian Nights.*[2]

The Balochi Variants

The introduction of tales from the *Nights* to the Baloch people probably did not take place in a direct manner. Balochi is basically a nonwritten language, and the media of instruction are Urdu in Pakistani Balochistan, Persian in Iranian Balochistan, and Dari or Pushto in Afghani Balochistan. I have not heard of any translation of tales from the *Nights* into Balochi. Even if those translations existed, literacy is so low among the Baloch that very few people would be able to access them. Yet it is known for sure that the *Nights* was translated into Urdu long ago. Several translations have appeared in Urdu beginning from the second quarter of the nineteenth century (Chauvin 19–21; Azim 447; Jayn 405–7), and cheap Urdu editions of selected tales are easily available in Pakistan today. Some of the famous tales, such as "Sindbad and His Voyages," "Ali Baba and the Forty Thieves," and "Aladdin and His Magic Lamp" are also available in chapbook format in all major cities in Pakistan. Even so, I have not seen any of these chapbooks in interior Balochistan. Their absence is probably due to the low rate of literacy or the lack of a tradition of reading folktales.

While Swâlî did not provide a title to his performance of the tale, Jangyân called it "Alladin's Lamp" (*Alladînî chirâg*). Jangyân's 1997 performance was solely organized to record the tale, so the audience was selective, comprising my hosts, their children, and a few neighbors. We were all male. As on other occasions, I recorded the tale during the night—which is the only time when wonder tales can be narrated. On this occasion, Jangyân seemed not to embellish his tales very much. The 2003 recording took place in his home when a lot of people were present. The narrator was very lively and presented a good picture of traditional storytelling. In this kind of performance, narrators used to embellish their tales with nonsense formulas (called *kissa-ey châbuk*, "whip of the tale," or *kissa-ey tâm*, "flavour of the tale"; Badalkhan 171), lengthy descriptions, funny statements, and/or melancholic gestures.

The Hero's Birth

In all versions of the *Nights* considered here, the narrator begins by mentioning that Aladdin was born to a tailor. The tailor is poor in all versions but Swâlî, where he is the royal tailor. No details about the birth are given except for Jangyân-2 where the couple does not have a child and begs a *faqîr* (dervish) to pray for them so that God may give them a child. The *faqîr* reads some magic spells (*dam*) above some water and gives it to the tailor's wife, telling them that if a son is born they should name him Alladin ("Given by God").[3] Exactly after nine months, a son is born to the couple. In comparison to the other versions, motifs Mot. T 548.1: *Child born in answer to prayers*, and Mot. T 527: *Magic impregnation by use of charm (amulet)* have been added. In contrast to Jangyân, and closer to the version of the *Nights*, Swâlî pronounced the protagonist's name Aladdîn or 'Alâ'uddîn ("Glory of Religion").

In versions of the *Nights* mentioning the name of Aladdin's father, it is given as Mustafâ. Among the Balochi variants, Swâlî does not give a father's name. Jangyân calls him Hasan Darzî, or Hasan, the tailor.

The Arrival of the Magician

In the *Nights*, the story takes place in China while the magician is from inner Morocco. In the Balochi variants no place is mentioned. Swâlî mentions that the *gûrû* (a Hindu religious guide or learned person, but also a witch in Balochi) came from Pilpilistân (literally "country of spices," probably a "wonderland"). Jangyân calls the magician a *jâtû* or *jâdûgir* (sorcerer, witch, magician). Even though he does not mention the magician's original homeland, one gets the impression that he came from Baghdad, as he asks the ogre to transfer the palace to Baghdad when he has obtained the lamp.

In the *Nights*, the magician finds the boy Aladdin playing with other boys, and he realizes that this is the person he has been looking for. In the Balochi variants, the magician turns to geomancy and discovers that only a boy can get the lamp. So he starts from his country and comes to Aladdin's city where he claims that he is Aladdin's uncle who has been away for many years. In Jangyân, the magician through magic disguises himself so that people believe him to be Hasan Darzî's lost brother and, hence, Alladin's uncle. In all Balochi variants, as in the *Nights*, the magician spends generously on the boy and his parent(s) and thus gains their confidence.

The Magician Takes Aladdin for an Outing

In the *Nights*, the magician takes Aladdin on a walk to the gardens. In Swâlî he also promises him a trip out to the woods, while in Jangyân he takes him to his home country to give him money.

In the Balochi variants the magician treats him with kindness as long as they are inside the town, but as soon as they are out of town, he starts treating him with a strong hand. In Swâlî, he first has him ride a horse but later asks him to dismount and mounts himself. In both versions of Jangyân they walk on foot. When, after a long walk, the boy tires and cannot walk any farther, the magician warns him that he is "not his uncle, but his death" and threatens to kill him if he does not obey his orders. At first, Alladin does not take the warning seriously. When he stops walking, the "uncle" gives him such a hard slap on his ear that his face is turned to the other side.

In the *Nights*, the magician and the boy go around the gardens until they reach a high hill. Aladdin, who has never been out of the city, is so tired that he has no power to walk any farther. The magician soothes him with kind words until they reach the entrance of the cave. The magician asks Aladdin to collect small woodchips and dry sticks, which he does. Then the magician brings out "a casket which he opened, and drew from it . . . incense; then he fumigated . . . muttering words none might understand" (Burton 657). When Aladdin intends to run away, the magician stops him by "giving him a violent blow" (Lane 518; Burton 658).

The Cavern and the Lamp

In all variants, the lamp is kept inside a cavern. Both in the *Nights* and in the Balochi variants, only Aladdin can lift the slab. However, the *Nights* has it that the magician asks him not to cease pronouncing his own name and the names of his father and mother. In Jangyân, nobody needs to touch the slab, as the cave opens as soon as the magician reads a spell and blows upon the earth.

Swâlî mentions that when Aladdin lifts the big flat stone he sees the opening of a well. Then the false uncle orders him to go down the well. Aladdin goes down and finds a garden illuminated with lights. There is a fortress inside the garden and a palace inside the fortress. He passes through the palace and sees a lamp, whose light turns yellow, red, and white. He takes the lamp and returns. Jangyân-1 does not supply details about the bottom of the well. Jangyân-2 mentions three ogres (*balâ*) on the way guarding the lamp. Alladin jumps over them and reaches the lamp.

In the *Nights*, there are four halls and the magician explains to Aladdin: "when you go to the first hall, take up your robe and bind it closely round you. Then be sure you go on to the second one without stopping, and from thence in the same manner to the third" (Lane 520).

In all variants, the return way is full of troubles. In Swâlî, Aladdin climbs up the well until he reaches the opening. When he calls upon his "uncle" to take him out, he is told to first hand him the lamp. Aladdin returns to the bottom of the well where he collects three fruits from trees laden with fruits of gems and emeralds. Because of his young age, he has no idea about their value, so he takes them just out of curiosity. He finally is able to leave the well and finds that his false uncle has left. In the *Nights*, the cave contains a garden with trees laden with fruits that are gems—emeralds and diamonds. Aladdin, although unaware of their value, collects many of them (Lane 521–22).

In Jangyân's variants, Alladin collects the lamp and returns to the opening of the well, calling the magician to throw the rope. The magician asks him to first tie the lamp to the rope. Now Alladin realizes that the "uncle" has sent him through all these troubles just for that lamp, so there must be something important about it. As he refuses to send the lamp, the "uncle" gets angry, reads some incantations, and the stone covers the well's opening. Entrapped inside, Alladin finds himself lost. He becomes angry at the lamp for whose sake he has gone through all these troubles and, out of anger, hits it with a stone. Immediately, an ogre appears telling him that he is the lamp's slave (*battî-ey gulâm*) and will do whatever is asked of him. Alladin asks him to deliver him instantaneously to his mother's house. In the blink of an eye, the ogre takes him there, carrying him on the palm of his hand.

Magic Objects

In all variants, the main object is the magic lamp that is supplied with a powerful demon who obeys any commands voiced by the lamp's owner. In the *Nights* the slave of the lamp is a jinni, in Jangyân a *balâ* (ogre), in Swâlî a serpent. Swâlî explains that the serpent is the "power" (*barkat*) of the lamp.

The second important object in the *Nights* is a magic ring the magician gives to Aladdin just before he enters the cave. The ring is absent in Swâlî. In both versions by Jangyân it appears only after the magician has got hold of the lamp and has transferred the palace to Baghdad. When the king gives Alladin some time to recover the princess, Alladin sets out with no particular destination. One day, when he is exhausted, he sits down to rest. Here, in both recordings, the narrator recites some nonsense formulas, inserted at scene shifts, to flavor the tale. He explains that "it is not me who is saying so, it is the narrator of the tale (*kissa wâlâ*) who says that from the day of his birth he had a ring on his finger." Alladin notices the ring on his finger and out of boredom starts rubbing it against a stone. As soon as he does so, a *balâ* appears and tells him that he is the slave of the ring and will fulfill any command made by the ring's owner.

Aladdin and the Princess

In most variants, the hero falls in love with the princess after he has acquired the lamp and discovered its miraculous qualities. As the princess is first married to a vizier's son, Aladdin commands the jinni to abduct her and place her in his bed. While they sleep, Aladdin puts an unsheathed saber between himself and the princess. When this is repeated for three consecutive nights, the vizier's son divorces the princess. Only then is the princess married to Aladdin.

In Jangyân, Alladin falls in love with the princess right at the tale's beginning, and the magician arrives as the princess is being married to the vizier's son. Alladin insists on separating the princess from her bridegroom by any means, otherwise he will kill himself. Seeing Alladin's determination, the magician does not want him to put his life in danger and assures him he will find a way to separate the princess from the vizier's son. For three nights the magician orders the jinnis under his command to take the bridegroom from the nuptial bed, dip him into a gutter full of human excrement, and then place him next to the princess. The first two times the groom begs the princess not to mention his mischief to anybody. When the same thing happens a third time, the princess beats him until he runs away from the wedding chamber. The princess then informs her father about what happened to her husband during the nights. After the king has confirmed the news, he asks the bridegroom to divorce the princess. It is only after the divorce that Alladin agrees to accompany his false uncle who promises him money and other riches so that he can ask the princess to marry.

As in other variants, in Jangyân the wedding takes place after Alladin has obtained the lamp and discovered its qualities. He sends his mother—without any gifts—to the king to ask for the hand of the princess. She goes for two consecutive days, but has no courage to talk to the king. Then Alladin warns her that if she returns a third time without having spoken to the king, he will kill himself. Desperately, the mother leaves the house and attends the king's assembly. Seeing her poor family background against the king's elevated status, she again does not dare to speak to the king. When the assembly breaks up in the afternoon and everybody starts going home, the king notices the old woman who has been coming to the assembly for three consecutive days without saying a single word. He asks an attendant to stop her and bring her to him. Only then does Alladin's mother, with great fear and hesitation, tell the king why Alladin has sent her. The king assures her that her demand is perfectly normal, and the narrator adds him saying that "the house of the parents of a young unmarried daughter is like the shop of a Hindu merchant where everybody gives his bid, and it is up to the father whether to give the hand of the daughter or not." The king has no objections to the match but demands, for bridal gifts, that they should build a palace of the finest glass, fill three wells with pure silver and gold, and dig an underground tunnel linking his palace to that of his daughter so that when she intends to visit her parents she should not go out in the open.[4] He grants Alladin three months respite (see also Burton 684) and warns his mother that if he fails to meet his demands, Alladin will be executed so that people of humble origin will stop having high dreams about the future.

Weeping, the mother goes to her son knowing that Alladin will never be able to fulfill the king's demands, and that the death of her only son is certain. Alladin, however, rubs the lamp and orders the ogre to fulfill all the demands in a single night. When the king wakes up in the morning he finds that all his demands have been met in a single night and feels sorry for having lost his daughter to Alladin, the son of a hag and orphan of a poor tailor. Even so, he gives the princess in marriage to Alladin. They live in great comfort and happiness until the magician through geomancy finds out about Alladin's fate. The magician comes again, obtains the lamp through tricks, and causes new troubles for Alladin and his family.

In Swâlî, Aladdin falls in love with the princess after he has obtained the lamp. When he sends his mother to the king with jewels, for two consecutive days she returns without having mentioned a single word. When, on the third day, the king stops her, she tells him about her request and presents him with ten large gems as a bridal gift. Thrilled about the gem's tremendous value, the king immediately accepts the request. But, as the vizier is also expecting the hand of the princess for his son, he warns the king not to accept the son of a poor hag as his son-in-law. The vizier then goes to the bazaar, finds the old woman, and tells her that the king will only accept her demand in return for forty additional baskets full of gems, carried by forty slave-girls. With the help of the serpent demon of the lamp, Aladdin arranges all this and is taken to the king. The king is surprised and tells Aladdin's mother that the previous presents were more than enough and that he had not asked for more. She tells him that the vizier had told her that the king had demanded more jewels as the bridal gift. The king rebukes the vizier for having lied in his name and assures Aladdin's mother that the engagement is confirmed. The vizier, however, does not give up and at last manages to have his son married to the princess. Here also, for three consecutive nights, on Aladdin's command, the serpent takes the bridegroom out of the bridal chamber, gets seven loads of animal dung, puts him inside, and burns the dung so that he is blinded. On the third night, he decides to divorce the princess whose marriage has caused him such troubles. Soon after that, Aladdin is married to the princess and they live in great comfort and happiness until the arrival of another magician who succeeds in getting the lamp and causing new trouble for Aladdin.

The Return of the Magician

In the *Nights*, a number of years pass before the magician finds out that Aladdin has come out of the cavern alive together with the lamp, and "that he was living in the greatest splendour, immensely rich, highly respected and honoured, and that he had married a princess" (Lane 594). He soon starts his journey to China on a Barbary horse. After having reached China, the African magician goes to a shop and buys a dozen well-polished silver lamps. He puts them inside a basket and goes around shouting, "New lamps for old ones." One of the maidservants suggests to the princess to exchange their master's old lamp for a new one. Once the magician obtains the lamp, he stops his business and leaves the town. At night he rubs the lamp and orders the jinni to transport himself and the palace together with its interior to the utmost confines of Africa, and the jinni does so.

In Swâlî, the first *gûrû* is not mentioned again. Instead, in the country of Pilpilistân, another *gûrû* sees through magic that Aladdin has acquired great wealth and resolves to steal the magic lamp. At times flying, running, or walking, the magician reaches Aladdin's city while Aladdin has gone out to hunt. The magician buys several new lamps and goes around the city offering "new lamps for old ones" and succeeds in acquiring the magic lamp. He leaves the city, rubs the lamp and orders the serpent demon to transport the palace, with all the people inside, to his country Pilpilistân. On the way, he throws Aladdin's mother out of the palace. Aladdin, on his way in search of the palace, finds her dead and gives her a proper burial.

This episode is quite similar in Jangyân's narration, but with the addition that the magician gives one or two rupees as commission for each exchange of lamps. In Jangyân-2 he gives a hundred rupees to the maidservant who brings him the magic lamp. In Jangyân, Alladin's mother is left behind and is not taken with the palace when the magician orders it to shift.

Aladdin Recovers the Lamp

In the *Nights*, the king at first wants to execute Aladdin. When he realizes that the people love Aladdin and might revolt against his orders, he releases him. Once escaped from the gallows, Aladdin spends three days in the city in complete misery. Seeing his wretched condition, he decides to abandon the city. He goes to a river where he inadvertently rubs his magic ring with a stone while doing his ablutions (Burton 723). The ring's demon appears and Aladdin asks him to return the palace to its original position. As this request is beyond the jinni's powers, Aladdin asks to be taken to where the palace is. In the morning, a maidservant notices him and informs the princess, who calls him up to the palace.

Aladdin now plots to poison the magician. He buys some drugs and instructs the princess in how to poison the magician. The princess dines with the magician and drinks wine with him. After a while, the princess, as a token of friendship, offers to exchange cups with the magician, offering him her cup that contains the poison. The magician empties the cup and drops dead. Aladdin arrives, takes the lamp, rubs it, and orders the jinni to return the palace to China. When the king witnesses their return, he announces ten days of public rejoicing and festivities. Aladdin orders the magician's dead body to be thrown as prey to the beasts and birds.

Soon after, the magician's younger brother finds out through geomancy that Aladdin has killed his brother, and he plots to avenge his brother. After having killed Fâtima, the town's holy woman, he disguises himself in her clothes and visits Aladdin's palace. Knowing that the demon of the lamp will kill anybody asking for the egg of a roc-bird, he makes the princess desire that egg. When Aladdin commands the jinni to procure the egg, instead of killing him the demon informs him that this request has originated from the magician's wicked brother who is staying in the palace disguised as Fâtima. While the magician in disguise attempts in vain to stab Aladdin, Aladdin kills him. Only then do Aladdin and the princess live happily ever after.

In the Balochi variants, it is also the maidservant who finds Aladdin roaming about the palace. She then informs the princess who calls him in. In Swâlî, after being fed, Aladdin is hidden in one of the rooms. Together with the princess they plot to make the magician believe that she has decided to marry him. Spending the evening together, the princess gets the magician drunk, takes the lamp, and brings it to Aladdin. The next morning, when all the *gûrû*'s people arrive to congratulate him on his wedding, Aladdin rubs the lamp and asks the serpent to return the palace to their country. During their airborne journey, the serpent drops all the *gûrû*'s people. The palace is returned to its original place, and Aladdin and the princess live in peace and prosperity ever after.

Jangyân elaborates the recovering of the lamp. After Alladin succeeds in convincing the king that his execution will not secure the return of the princess, he is given three months respite to go look for her.[5] As he has no idea where the palace might have been taken, he roams around aimlessly. One day, when he has tired, he decides to sit down and rest for a while. While he is resting he notices that he has a ring on his finger. As he scratches the ring against a stone out of boredom, the ogre appears, and Alladin asks to be transported to the princess. The ogre informs Alladin that the magician is very powerful in black magic and will have him destroyed if he enters his area. However, the ogre agrees to take him to the neighborhood of the palace. The magician finds out through geomancy that Alladin has arrived in the neighborhood. Three times, he sends his jinnis to kill Alladin. First, they throw him from the top of a steep hill, but, as he falls on the ground, the ring touches a stone and the slave of the ring appears to pick him up and take him back. Again the magician consults his geomancy and finds him alive. This time he sends his jinnis to throw him from up in the air. As Alladin falls down between the trees, the ring touches a twig and the slave of the ring appears, picks him up, and takes him back. When the magician consults geomancy again, once more he sees that Alladin is safely back. The third time he tells his jinnis to throw Alladin into the open sea. Again, Alladin is miraculously saved as he falls onto a shark. As soon as the ring is rubbed against one of the shark's fins, the slave appears, picks him up, and safely takes him back.

This time, the magician believes Alladin to be dead for sure and decides to go hunting. Alladin manages to come to the palace where a maidservant sees him and informs the princess who calls him up. After having fed him and changed his ragged clothes with clothes of fine selection, she asks a maidservant to take him to a nearby shrine and leave him there. The reason for this is that she knows the magician cannot see him inside the shrine, since his geomancy has no access there.

When the magician returns in the evening, he finds the princess completely changed, welcoming him with a smiling face and presenting herself prepared like a bride. The magician gets suspicious thinking that Alladin might have survived this time again. He consults geomancy but cannot see Alladin anywhere, so he believes that this time Alladin is dead for sure. The princess tells him that a long time has passed since she has been separated from her husband, and that now she has made up her mind that it is of no use to continue waiting for him. When she has succeeded in convincing the magician of her sincerity, she tells him that she has prepared some juice with great love and wants him to drink a glass with her. The princess asks a maidservant to put the glass with poison in front of her and the one with pure juice in front of the magician. When they sit on the sofa, and the magician sees that the princess is demonstrating an unprecedented love for him all of a sudden, he suspects that she is plotting to poison him. In order to outdo her ruse, he takes the glass in front of the princess and places his glass in front of her. Now that the glass with pure juice is placed in front of the princess she drinks it immediately to the last drop. The magician, seeing that she has drunk the juice without any hesitation, also empties his glass in one gulp. Soon after, he starts shouting from severe pains in the stomach and falls to the ground rolling on the floor. At this point, the princess calls for Alladin who comes and attempts to kill the magician with his sword. The princess advises him: "Use his own sword, and you have only a single chance. If you strike him a second time, he will come to life again."[6] Alladin takes the magician's sword and, with a single blow, chops off his head. He opens the window and throws the body outside. Then he rubs the lamp and commands the genie to transport the palace back to its original place. The ogre does so instantly, and when the king wakes up the following morning he is almost blinded by the reflection of the sunshine from Alladin's palace. Then Alladin visits him and tells him that he has returned the palace and all the people safely. As a final gesture, the king orders the grand vizier and his assistants to be tied to horses and dragged around until they are torn to pieces, for, if he had acted according to their advice and executed Alladin, he would have never seen his daughter again.

Jangyân finished his tale with a common formula, used for announcing the end of a tale in Balochi: "Sir, my tale ends here. I received a quarter rupee. I bought a wooden bowl (*kâsag*) with that money. I took it in my hands. On the way (back home) I stumbled and fell down. My bowl broke into pieces. I stood and watched it. They became wife and husband, father-in-law and mother-in-law, and I returned with empty hands."

The Number Three in Balochi Tradition

In Indo-European tradition, the number "three" holds a specific meaning (of perfection) and is particularly frequent in folklore and folktales (Dundes 134–59; Lüthi). So also in the Balochi variants, as the following sample documents:

• The light of the magic lamp has *three* different colors, yellow, red, and white (Swâlî).

- Aladdin collects *three* pieces of precious stones from the gardens at the bottom of the well (Swâlî).
- There are *three* ogres in the cavern guarding the lamp (Jangyân).
- Aladdin's mother visits the king with *three* pieces of precious stones for *three* consecutive days to ask for the hand of the princess for her son (Swâlî; Jangyân has only *three* days with no presents).
- Of the *three* things the king asks from Alladin's mother as bridal gifts, one is to fill *three* wells with pure silver and gold (Jangyân).
- The king gives Alladin's mother *three* months respite to meet his demands (Jangyân).
- Despite the king's promise to Aladdin, the princess is first married to the vizier's son. The slave of the lamp takes the bridegroom out of the nuptial bed for *three* consecutive nights before the vizier's son decides to divorce the princess. In the *Nights*, the bride is abducted from the bridal chamber and put next to Aladdin for *three* consecutive nights before the vizier's son divorces her.
- Jangyân explains that according to the tradition in the king's country a newlywed couple does not leave the bridal chamber for the first *three* days, nor do people visit them during that period. Only on the *third* day do people go to visit the couple and offer their congratulations.
- When the magician comes to China to get hold of the lamp, he finds that Aladdin has gone on an eight-day hunting excursion of which *three* days have passed (*Nights*).
- When the magician transfers the princess and the palace, the king gives Alladin *three* months respite to bring the princess back (Jangyân).
- Alladin, in his desperate wanderings in search of the palace, spends *three* days in ignorance before he realizes that he has a magic ring on his finger (Jangyân).
- The magician learns through geomancy that Alladin has reached the neighborhood of Baghdad. He tries to get him killed *three* times through his jinnis: by getting him thrown down a steep hill, by getting him dropped from the sky into the woods, and by getting him dropped into the open sea (Jangyân).
- When Aladdin finds that the magician has taken away his palace, he mounts his horse and rides up to the sea. From there, he is transported by *three* fishes onto the other side: first by a dolphin, then by a kind of

a shark, and finally by another kind of shark who drops him on the beach next to the palace (Swâlî).

- Aladdin escapes death *three* times: first, in the cavern when the magician has the opening closed while leaving him inside; second, when the king orders to execute him after the palace and the princess have been transported by the magician; and third, when the magician's younger brother enters the palace in disguise and plots to stab him with his dagger (*Nights*).

- The magician and the princess drink *three* glasses of wine before she asks a maidservant to bring the goblet with the powder (*Nights*).

Conclusion

The Balochi variants evidently derive from the text included in the *Arabian Nights*. As they constitute orally learned and transmitted versions, the narrators do not intend to produce verbatim renderings of their source text but have both added and omitted details. It is hard to tell how the Balochi narrators learned their tales, as both of them are illiterate and have little or no knowledge of Urdu, the most probable linguistic medium through which a written version of the tale might have reached them. The narrators themselves did not remember from whom, where, and when they had first learned their tales. At the same time, their performances show how a tale with a written origin leaves its course of transmission through the medium of written literature and becomes an oral tale.

Above all, the Balochi variants document the narrators' creativity through numerous variations, such as those concerning the name, profession, and status of Aladdin's father, the magic ring, and the magician. As the bridal gifts differ in all these variants, so do the means with which Aladdin gets to where the magician has transported the palace; the respective country is Africa in the *Nights*, Baghdad in Jangyân, and "across the sea" in Swâlî.

Comparing the themes, motifs, and minor details of the Balochi variants with one another, and of the Balochi variants with the version of the *Nights*, it is difficult to establish the amount of common details with any certainty. Even though the oral versions retain the basic plot as to form and structure, in terms of detail they diverge extremely from the written source text. In her research about the cultural position of the marketplace in Morocco, Deborah Kapchan has analyzed a similar phenomenon. According to Kapchan, "the stories told in the Moroccan marketplace today may well come from an Arabic translation of Galland's *Mille et une nuits* . . . which the Moroccan narrator then elaborates or reduces to create a second order oral text . . . which itself may enter the written tradition when collected and documented" (23). In a similar manner, the Balochi oral performers develop their source text independently by creatively drawing upon a wealth of motifs and embellishments rooted in local narrative tradition.

NOTES

1. This paper is based on field data collected in Pakistani Balochistan in 1996, 1997, and 2003. Trips to Balochistan were partially funded by MIUR under *Ethnolinguistics of Iranian Area and Subject-Index of Iranian Folktales* projects, directed by Professor Adriano Rossi, University of Naples "L'Orientale," Italy. Thanks are due to him for his kind help. I am also grateful to Professor Margaret Mills and Professor Patrick Mullen, Ohio State University, Columbus, for their help and encouragement.

2. For a folklorist assessment of the tale see Ranke.

3. The meaning "Given by God" was mentioned by the storyteller, probably in order to emphasize that the boy was born resulting from a divine intervention following the incantation. The Sindhi name Alla Dinna and the Punjabi name Alla Ditta both mean "Gift of God" or "Given by God." Both names are common male names in those ethnic groups. In Urdu, *dena* means "to give." Alladin (Allah Din) is also a common male name in Balochistan where the meaning is taken to be the same as in Sindhi or Punjabi, although "din" in Balochi (as in Arabic and Persian) in most cases means "religion."

   In the following, the spelling Alladin is used to indicate the version Jangyân-2. The spelling Aladdin refers to the other versions as well as to the tale in general.

4. In the *Nights*, Aladdin causes the jinni to lay down a fine velvet carpet so that the princess walks upon it when she leaves her father's palace (Lane 581).

5. In Jangyân-1 he is given forty days respite.

6. It is interesting to observe here that, as in the case of Polyphemus in Homer's *Odyssey*, the hero can only be destroyed with a weapon coming from his own possession (see also Mills 128). In this passage, the magician is imagined as a *ghûl*. In Arabic popular belief and legends, a *ghûl* is considered a demonic being inhabiting burial grounds and deserted places, and possessing the ability to assume different shapes. Arabs believed that "men could kill it, but only by giving it one single blow, for a second restored it to life" (Macdonald and Pellat 1078; Mot. E 11.1; Marzolph no. 107).

WORKS CITED

Azim, Waqâr. *Hamârî dâstânen* (Our Narratives). Lahore: Urdu Markar, (1964?).

Badalkhan, Sabir. "An Introduction to the Performance of Verbal Art in Balochistan." *Annali dell'Istituto Universitario Orientale* 60–61 (2000–2001): 161–96.

Burton, Richard F. *The Arabian Nights' Entertainments, or, The Book of a Thousand Nights and a Night.* A Selection of the Most Famous and Representative of these Tales from the Plain and Literal Translations by Richard F. Burton. New York: Modern Library, 1959.

Chauvin, Victor. *Bibliographie des ouvrages arabes ou relatifs aux arabes.* Vol. 4. Liège: Vaillant-Carmanne, and Leipzig: Harrassowitz, 1900.

Clouston, William A. "Aladdin's Wonderful Lamp: A Second Chapter on the Thankful Beasts." *Popular Tales and Fictions: Their Migrations and Transformations.* Vol. 1. London: William Blackwood, 1887. 314–46.

Dundes, Alan. *Interpreting Folklore.* Bloomington: Indiana UP, 1980.

Elisséeff, Nikita. *Thèmes et motifs des Mille et une Nuits: Essai de classification.* Beirut: Institut Français de Damas, 1949.

Ghâzî, Amanullâh. *Gîdî qissa* (Folk Tales). Quetta: Baluchi Academy, 1971.

Jayn, Gayanchand. *Urdû kî nasrî dâstânen* (Prose Narratives in Urdu). Karachi: Anjuman-e Taraqqi-e Urdu, 1969.

Kapchan, Deborah. *Gender on the Market: Moroccan Women and the Revoicing of Tradition.* Philadelphia: U of Pennsylvania P, 1996.

Lane, Edward W. *The Arabian Nights: A Selection, for the Most Part from Lane's Translation.* London: Oxford UP, 1915.

Lüthi, Max. "Drei, Dreizahl." *Enzyklopädie des Märchens.* Vol. 3. Berlin: Walter de Gruyter, 1981. 851–68.

Macdonald, Duncan B. "Thousand and One Nights." *Encyclopaedia Britannica.* 28th ed. Vol. 22. Chicago, London, and Toronto, 1960. 157–60.

———, and Charles Pellat. "Ghûl." *The Encyclopaedia of Islam.* New ed. Vol. 2. Leiden: Brill, 1965. 1078–79.

Mahdi, Muhsin. *The Thousand and One Nights (Alf Layla wa-Layla): From the Earliest Known Sources.* Vol. 3. Introduction and Indexes. Leiden: Brill, 1994.

Marzolph, Ulrich. *Arabia ridens: Die humoristische Kurzprosa der frühen adab-Literatur im internationalen Traditionsgeflecht.* Vol. 2. Frankfurt: Klostermann, 1992.

Mills, Margaret A. *Rhetorics and Politics in Afghan Traditional Storytelling.* Philadelphia: U of Pennsylvania P, 1991.

Pellat, Charles. "Alf layla wa-layla." *Encyclopaedia Iranica.* Vol. 1. Costa Mesa: Mazda, 1985. 831–35.

Pinault, David. *Story-Telling Techniques in the Arabian Nights.* Leiden: Brill, 1992.

Ranke, Kurt. "Alad(d)in." *Enzyklopädie des Märchens* Vol. 1. Berlin: Walter de Gruyter 1977. 240–47.

Thompson, Stith. *Motif-Index of Folk-Literature.* 6 vols. Copenhagen: Rosenkilde and Bagger, 1955–58.

Zotenberg, Hermann. *Histoire d'Alâ al-Dîn, ou La lampe merveilleuse: Texte arabe avec une notice sur quelques manuscrits des Mille et une Nuits.* Paris: Imprimerie Nationale, 1888.

Contributors

NOELANI ARISTA is a doctoral student in American history at Brandeis University and holds an MA in Hawaiian religion from the University of Hawai'i at Mānoa. She is interested in the intersections between Hawaiian and Euro-American cultural forms and epistemologies and in their impact upon Hawaiian identity. She received a grant from the International Center for Writing and Translation (University of California, Irvine, 2003) for translating *kanikau*, grief chants from nineteenth-century Hawaiian-language newspapers. She is also the translation editor for *'Oiwi*, a Native Hawaiian journal.

CRISTINA BACCHILEGA, professor of English at the University of Hawai'i at Mānoa, is the author of *Postmodern Fairy Tales: Gender and Narrative Strategies* (1997) and the coeditor of *Angela Carter and the Literary Fairy Tale* (2001). Her interests focus on folk and literary narrative, and on the fairy tale. Her current work includes a study of "legendary Hawai'i" and the politics of place. She is the review editor of *Marvels & Tales: Journal of Fairy-Tale Studies* and advisory editor of *Fabula: Journal of Folktale Studies.*

SABIR BADALKHAN holds a PhD in folklore and teaches at the Istituto Orientale, University of Naples, Italy. He has also taught folklore classes at Ohio State University, Columbus. His research interests include folklore and folk life in Balochistan, both in the Pakistani and the Iranian areas, and the Luri itinerant musicians, singers, and storytellers in Southwest Asia. He has published widely in international journals and conference proceedings on topics related to Balochi folklore and oral tradition.

HANDE A. BIRKALAN-GEDIK is an assistant professor in the Department of Anthropology, Yeditepe University, Istanbul, Turkey. She specializes in folklore theories and methods, Turkish folklore, folk art, narrative, and gender issues in Turkey. She has contributed articles to the *Encyclopedia of Women and Islamic Cultures,* to *Archetypes and Motifs in Folklore and Literature,* the *Enzyklopädie des Märchens,* and *Folklor/Edebiyat.* She is a member of the editorial committee of the journals *Cultural Analysis* and *Septet* and a member of the History Foundation of Turkey Boratav Archive.

ABOUBAKR CHRAÏBI is Maître de Conférences in Medieval Arabic Literature at the Institut National des Langues et Civilisations Orientales (INALCO) in Paris, France. He works on the *Thousand and One Nights* and on medieval Arabic narrative literature. He has published a monograph *Contes nouveaux des Mille et une Nuits* (1996), an essay "Les à-côtés du récit ou l'enchâssement à l'orientale" (in *Poétique,* 1999), and a Web site on the *Nights* at http://www.univ-tours.fr/arabe; in 2004 he organized a symposium on the Nights and published the proceedings (*Les Mille et une Nuits en partage,* 2004).

FRANCESCA MARIA CORRAO is a professor of Arabic language and literature at the Istituto Orientale, University of Naples, Italy, and a member of the editorial committee of *Africa e Orienti.* Besides her studies on Arabic literature, she also deals with the narrative tradition of the Near East, with particular emphasis on Arab folk narrative and popular literature. Her publications include *Poeti Arabi di Sicilia* (1987), *Le Storie di Giufà* (1989), *Il Riso il Comico e la Festa al Cairo nel XIII sec.* (1996), *Adonis: Nella pietra e nel vento* (1999), and *Ibn Daniyal: Il Fantasma della Fantasia* (2001).

HASAN EL-SHAMY is professor of folklore, Near Eastern languages and cultures, and African studies at Indiana University, Bloomington. He specializes in psychosocial processes in folklore. His publications include: *Brother and Sister, Type 872*: A Cognitive Behavioristic Text Analysis of a Middle Eastern Oikotype* (1979), *Folktales of Egypt* (1980), *Folk Traditions of the Arab World: A Guide to Motif Classification* (1995), *Tales Arab Women Tell* (1999), and *Types of the Folktale in the Arab World* (2004). He has also edited Maspero's *Popular Stories of Ancient Egypt* (2002).

SUSANNE ENDERWITZ is a professor of Islamic and Arabic studies at the Ruprecht-Karls University in Heidelberg, Germany. Her research covers Arabic literature both in its classical (religious literature, *adab,* poetry) and modern (novel, autobiography) genres. Her publications include

Liebe als Beruf: Al-'Abbâs b. al-Ahnaf (gest. um 807) und das Gazal (1995), *Shaitan/Iblis: Der Teufel als Figur der islamischen Kulturgeschichte* (2001), *Unsere Situation schuf unsere Erinnerungen: Palästinensische Autobiographien zwischen 1967 und 2000* (2002), *Palestinian Autobiographies: A Source for Women's History?* (2002), and *Essen, Kultur und Identität: Eine arabische Perspektive* (2003).

THOMAS GEIDER is a scholar in African studies specializing in oral and written literature. He has conducted fieldwork in Kenya and Nigeria and has written his PhD thesis on the ogre character of the Pokomo (1990). His Habilitation focuses on motif research in Kanuri folktales (2003). He has also published on Swahili literature and is the coeditor of the annual *Swahili Forum*. Teaching at the University of Frankfurt-Main, Germany, he currently lives in Cologne and also works as a freelance editor.

GEERT JAN VAN GELDER is Laudian Professor of Arabic at the University of Oxford, England. He has published numerous studies on classical Arabic literature, including *Beyond the Line* (1982, on medieval Arabic poetics), *The Bad and the Ugly* (1988, on Arabic invective poetry), *Of Dishes and Discourse* (2000, on the theme of food in Arabic literature), and *Close Relationships: Incest and Inbreeding in Classical Arabic Literature* (2005). He is executive editor of *Middle Eastern Literatures.*

HEINZ GROTZFELD is professor emeritus of Semitic philology and Islamic studies at the Westfälische Wilhelms University in Münster, Germany. He has published, together with his wife, Sophia Grotzfeld, *Die Erzählungen aus Tausendundeiner Nacht* (1984), a survey of research into the *Nights*. His research in connection with the *Arabian Nights*, published in numerous articles between 1985 and 2003, focuses on the history of the Arabic text(s) of the *Nights* prior to the Bulaq I and Calcutta II editions.

DONALD HAASE is a professor of German and chair of the Department of German and Slavic Studies at Wayne State University, Detroit. He is editor of *The Reception of Grimms' Fairy Tales: Responses, Reactions, Revisions* (1993), *English Fairy Tales and More English Fairy Tales* (2002), and *Fairy Tales and Feminism: New Approaches* (2004). He is also editor of *Marvels & Tales: Journal of Fairy-Tale Studies* and general editor of the Series in Fairy-Tale Studies, both published by Wayne State University Press.

LEE HARING is professor emeritus of folklore and literary theory at Brooklyn College of the City University of New York. He conducts research on the oral literatures of the islands of the Southwest Indian Ocean and is President of the Fellows of the American Folklore Society. He has written *Malagasy Tale Index* (1982) and *Verbal Arts in Madagascar* (1992) and translated *Ibonia, Epic of Madagascar* (1994) and *Indian Ocean Folktales* (2003).

ROBERT IRWIN is a novelist; a senior research associate of the University School of Oriental Studies in London, England; Middle East editor of *The Times Literary Supplement*; and a Fellow of the Royal Society of Literature. His nonfiction includes the *Arabian Nights: A Companion* (1994, reissued 2003), *Night and Horses and the Desert: An Anthology of Classical Literature* (1999), and *The Alhambra* (2004).

SYLVETTE LARZUL specializes in Arabic studies. She is a graduate of the Institut National des Langues et Civilisations Orientales (INALCO) in Paris, France, and holds a PhD from the Université de Paris III. Her thesis, published in 1996, treats the French translations of the *Mille et une Nuits*. She is currently affiliated with the Centre d'Histoire Sociale de l'Islam Méditerranéen (EHESS) and is particularly interested in the history of French Orientalism.

ULRICH MARZOLPH is a professor of Islamic studies at the Georg-August University in Göttingen, Germany, and a senior member of the editorial committee of the *Enzyklopädie des Märchens*. He specializes in the narrative culture of the Near East, with particular emphasis on Arab and Persian folk narrative and popular literature. Recent publications include *Narrative Illustration in Persian Lithographed Books* (2001), *The Arabian Nights Encyclopedia* (2004, with Richard van Leeuwen), the volume of collected essays *Ex Oriente Fabula* (2005), and *The Arabian Nights Reader* (2006). He is the review editor of *Fabula: Journal of Folktale Studies* and advisory editor of *Marvels & Tales: Journal of Fairy-Tale Studies*.

MARGARET A. MILLS is professor of folklore and Persian studies at the Ohio State University Department of Near Eastern Studies, Columbus, Ohio. She is the author of *Oral Narrative in Afghanistan: The Individual in Tradition* (1990), and *Rhetorics and Politics in Afghan Traditional Storytelling* (1991), coeditor, with Arjun Appadurai and Frank Korom, of *Gen-*

der, Genre, and Power in South Asian Expressive Traditions (1991), coauthor with Ravshan Rahmoni of *Conversations with Davlat Khalav: Oral Narratives from Tajikistan* (2000), and coeditor with Peter Claus and Sarah Diamond of *South Asian Folklore: An Encyclopedia* (2003).

SADHANA NAITHANI is assistant professor at the Centre of German Studies, Jawaharlal Nehru University, New Delhi, India. She specializes in German literature and folklore, and her recent research has been in the areas of colonialism and folklore theory. Her articles have been published in *Journal of Folklore Research* and *Folklore*, among others. She has recently edited and introduced *Folktales from Northern India* (2002) and *In Quest of Indian Folktales* (2006).

MARILENA PAPACHRISTOPHOROU is a researcher at the Hellenic Folklore Research Center of the Academy of Athens, Greece. She specializes in the narrative tradition of Greece, with particular emphasis on oral folktales and storytelling in modern society. Her publications include *Sommeils et veilles dans le conte merveilleux grec* (2002), and, together with Despina Damianou and Maria Mirasyezi, a volume titled *Laiki Philologia* (2002).

JOSEPH SADAN is professor of Arabic literature and Muslim civilization at Tel Aviv University, Israel, where he holds the Irene Halmos Chair of Arabic Literature. He has published widely on medieval Middle Eastern civilization and material culture (furniture, wine, writing tools) as well as on classical and postclassical Arabic literature (Adab, poetry, and the *Arabian Nights*), most recently a volume of tales from postclassical Arabic literature (2004).

Index

Note: All stories and tales are indexed under the main heading "tales."

Index

Index

Matâli' (al-Ghuzûlî), 74
Mauritius storytellers, 137–38
Mazungumzo ya Alfu-Lela-Ulela, au Siku Elfu na Moja (Brenn and Johnson), 192–93
Mchumba na ndugu watatu (Velten), 189
Megas, Georgios A., 298
Mehrâbâdi, Mitrâ, 235–38
Méliès, Georges, 254
Mille et une Nuits, Les (Galland): Breslau edition and, 62n9; didactic aim of, 23; Hannâ's tales in, 18–20, 23–30; inclusion of "Ali Baba" in, 4; influence of French classical aesthetics on, 24; Italian translation of, 293; moral scope of tales in, 22; Oriental atmosphere in, 23–24; repertoire of, 58–59; Shahrazâd narrations, length of, 54; transition formula in, 56; travel experiences of Galland and, 20–21; written source material for, 17–18
Mille et un Jours (de la Croix), 19
Mille et un Quarts d'heure, Les (Gueullette), 35
mirror-for-princes literary genre, 103, 108–9
Mirzâ 'Ali-Qoli Kho'i, 233
Mirzâ Hasan, 233
Mirzâ Rezâ Tabrizi, 233
Mirzâ Sorush of Esfahan, 231
Mirzâ Zein al-'âbedin Khân Neishâburi, 230–31
Moghol Dokhtar-o Arab Bachcheh, 314
Mohammad Hosein Tehrâni, 231
Mollâ 'Abd al-Latif Tasuji, 231
mo'olelo (history/story), 159–60, 164–65
moral values, in *Arabian Nights,* 22, 105–8, 287
motifs: *afsâne* standard, in Gholâm Nabi's performance of "Judar and His Brothers," 327–28; jinni of the tree, 8; in *Kalîla wa-Dimna,* 280; in *Mille et une Nuits,* 21; serpent king, 206; of sibling rivalry in Afghan tales, 321–22; of Sindbad the Sailor in Sicil-

ian folktale, 282; slave-girl lost and regained, 65–70, 73, 75–76; of supernatural wife, 306–7; of the "Swan Maiden," 306–8; in tale of Ali Baba, 6–7, 9, 12–13; of unfaithfulness of women, 285–86
Mount Qâf (Mount Kaf), 204
Muhabbar (Ibn Habîb), 66, 71
Munjîk of Tirmidh, 224
Muntazam (Ibn al-Jawzî), 76–77
Murad, Sultan, 207
Mustajâd (al-Tanûkhî), 73
Mustatraf (al-Ibshîhî), 71

narrative elements, in slave-girl lost and regained stories, 67
narrative pattern inconsistencies, among manuscripts, 53
narrative traditions. *See* oral traditions
Nâser al-Din Shâh, 231–32, 313–14
Nasîhat al-mulûk, 103
Nazif, Ahmet, 207–8
Nea Halima, 292–93
nesting technique, 135. *See also* framing
Nguvu za uganga (Velten), 189
night breaks and night formulas, 54–57
Nishwâr (al-Tanûkhî), 73–74, 76–77
Nizâm al-Molk, 108–9
Nogelmeier, Puakea, 163
Novellino (Lo Nigro), 280
Nûr al-qabas (al-Marzubânî), 72
Nuzhat al-Zamân, 105–6

Odyssey (Homer), 345n6
Onaran, Alim Şerif, 208, 213
oppositional fables, 110
oral narratives, textualization of, 120
oral performers: and framing formulas, 135–36, 138–42, 144–45; Gholâm Nabi "Binawâ," 319–29; Jangyân, 331; Malagasy, 137
oral traditions: reasons for invocation of, 287; relationship of literary tradition to, 314–15; *Rig Veda* and,

225–26; "Jewish Judge and His Pious Wife," 89; "Judar and His Brothers," 87–89, 316–29; of Judaz (*See* tales: "Judar and His Brothers"); "Julnar the Sea-Born and Her Son King Badr Basim of Persia," 306; "Khalifa and Khalifa" (Clermont-Ganneau), 208; "Khusrau and Shirin and the Fisherman," 306; "King Jali'âd of Hind and His Vizier Shimas," 106–7; "King Kisra Anushirwan and the Village Damsel," 305; "King 'Umar (bin) al-Nu'mân and His Two Sons Sharkân and Daw' al-Makân," 55, 91–93, 105-6; "Lazy Hamîda," 37, 41–44; "Man Who Learned the Animal Language" (Velten), 190; "Mazem," 308; "Merchant and the Jinni," 269; "Mohammed the Languid" (Steere), 186; "Moolelo no Samesala Naeha," 168–70; "Night Adventure of Sultan Mohammed of Cairo," 112–13; "No Ke Kanaka Lawaia!" 160–61, 171–75; "Nu'ma and Nu'm," 100; "Nûr al-Dîn 'Alî and His Son Badr al-dîn Hasan," 54; "Nûr al-Dîn and Maryam al-Zunnâriyya," 79; "Old Man with Two Black Dogs," 85–86; "Polyphemus," 205; "Porter and the Three Ladies of Baghdad," 58, 233–34; "Qamar al-zamân," 228; "Rhampsinitus," 12–13; "Righteousness of King Anurshirwan," 107; "Shahriyâr and his Brother Shâhzamân," 85, 161; "Sindbâd and the Seven Viziers," 281, 285; "Sindbad the Sailor," 59, 112, 195, 205, 282; "Siren-Girl," 144–46; of Solomon, 281; "Soltân Sekandar," 321; "Stubborn Fellow," 281–82; "Sûl and Shumûl," in Tübingen manuscript, 56; "Sultan of Yemen and His Three Sons," 300; "Swan Maiden," 306–8; of Tawaddud, 68; "The Magic Ring," 284; "Third Qalandar's Tale," 233–34; "Third Royal Mendicant," 189; "Told

by the Jewish Physician (The Murderous Sister)," 98–99; "Trader and the Jinni," 54; "Truth and Falsehood," 12–13; "Twelve Thieves," 283; "Two Kings and the Vizier's Daughter," 106; "Vizier Nûr al-Dîn with Badr al-Dîn, His Brother," 86–87; "War of the Camel" (anon.), 187; "Water Spirits," 147; "Zubaydah," 97–98

Tales from Shakespeare (Lamb), 187
tale types. *See* AT (Aarne and Thompson)
tale types (El-Shamy), 85–86, 91–93, 95, 97–98
Taluy, Nihat Yalaza, 211
al-Tanûkhî, 66–67, 71, 73–77, 109
Tanzanian *Ujamaa* politics, 195
taqiyya, Islamic practice of, 228
Tasuji, 'Abd al-Latif al-, 233, 235–37, 239n4, 313–18.
Tazyîn (al-Antâkî), 74
teaching stories, 105, 132–33
Tekin, Şinasi, 202, 206, 213–15
Telmisany, May, 273
Tepegöz, in tales of Sindbad, 205
Tevfik, Riza, 209–10
textualization of oral narratives, 120
Thamarât (Ibn Hijja), 73
Thompson, Stith, 299–306
Thousand and One Days (de la Croix), 293
Thousand and Second Night (Poe), 265–67
Tolayan, Hovannes, 208
translations of *Arabian Nights*: British colonial influence on, 230; for children's literature, 211, 246, 300; illustrations in, 194–95, 231–33, 245–46; interjections of translators in, 175. *See also languages of translation*
Trikoglidis, Kostas, 294–96
Tübingen manuscript, 54–56, 62n5
Tunisian manuscript, 60
Turkish culture: folktales, 204, 209–10; influence of *Arabian Nights* on